Fundamentals of Risk Management

Seventh Edition

Fundamentals of Risk Management

Understanding, evaluating and implementing effective enterprise risk management

Kate Boothroyd

with Clive Thompson

First published in Great Britain and the United States in 2010 by Kogan Page Limited
Seventh edition 2025

2nd Floor, 45 Gee Street
London
EC1V 3RS
United Kingdom

8 W 38th Street, Suite 902
New York, NY 10018
USA

www.koganpage.com

Kogan Page books are printed on paper from sustainable forests.

ISBNs

Hardback   978 1 3986 1868 8
Paperback 978 1 3986 1865 7
Ebook   978 1 3986 1867 1

British Library Cataloguing-in-Publication Data

A CIP record for this book is available from the British Library.

Library of Congress Cataloging-in-Publication Data

2024043960

Typeset by Integra Software Services, Pondicherry
Print production managed by Jellyfish
Printed and bound by CPI Group (UK) Ltd, Croydon, CR0 4YY

To a safe, secure and sustainable future

CONTENTS

PART ONE Introduction to risk management

PART TWO Enterprise risk management

PART SEVEN Organizational environment, resilience
and sustainability

LIST OF FIGURES AND TABLES

Figures

Tables

FOREWORD: NAVIGATING THE NEW ERA OF RISK

In today's rapidly evolving landscape, the complexity and scale of risks confronting organizations are unprecedented. Geopolitical uncertainties continue to reshape global dynamics, presenting fresh challenges to enterprises everywhere. Meanwhile, the rise of artificial intelligence offers both extraordinary opportunities and substantial threats, demanding a nuanced approach to risk management. At the same time, the intensifying urgency to address climate change compels organizations to adopt sustainable practices and policies as part of their core strategies.

In this intricate and shifting environment, organizations face the dual challenge of managing these diverse risks while meeting ever-higher stakeholder expectations. Strong corporate governance, ethical conduct, and social responsibility are no longer optional—they are the foundation on which modern enterprises must build their resilience and reputation. To navigate this terrain successfully, the demand for educated and expert risk professionals has never been greater.

The seventh edition of *Fundamentals of Risk Management* has been comprehensively updated to reflect the latest trends, standards, and best practices in the field. Aligned with the Institute of Risk Management's (IRM) Certificate in Risk Management, this edition equips readers with the most relevant and practical insights to manage risk in an increasingly digital, interconnected world. It offers an invaluable resource for both aspiring students and experienced practitioners, distilling the essential knowledge needed to address the challenges of today's risk landscape.

As the global risk environment continues to evolve, this book provides more than just foundational theory – it is a roadmap to help navigate the complexities and uncertainties of the future. Whether you are new to the field or seeking to deepen your expertise, the insights contained within these pages will empower you to excel in the critical task of risk management.

The world of risk is transforming, but with the right tools and understanding, we can turn these challenges into opportunities. I invite you to embrace the learnings in this edition and use them as a guide to thrive in this new era of risk.

Stephen Sidebottom
Chair, Institute of Risk Management

ACKNOWLEDGEMENTS

The continuous changes in the external and internal context of all organizations in every sector, industry and region, regardless of their size and complexity, bring risks, both opportunities and threats, that need to be recognized and managed accordingly.

This has kept the focus on risk management and the need for experienced and competent risk practitioners to support organizations in achieving their objectives. It has also resulted in more changes in the risk management sphere, from governance regulations to risk management standards and the fluctuating world of sustainability.

As such, it is time to develop this seventh edition of *Fundamentals of Risk Management*. Although the text has been built on many of the basic principles developed by Paul Hopkin, there has been a need for a reorganization and update of the book to align it with the recent revision to the IRM's international qualification on enterprise risk management. This means that although Paul's name is no longer on the front cover of the book, his contribution is still very much acknowledged as the original author of this core book for the IRM.

Clive Thompson is still on the cover of the book, thankfully. As the key reviewer of this body of work and based on the insight he brought to the sixth edition, Clive's expertise and knowledge of risk management is still the base of and reflected in the updates to this text. In addition to this, Clive has been a key adviser and supporter and has encouraged me throughout this journey. I'm not sure he recognizes how much I appreciate it.

In addition, I have had considerable support from a cohort of risk practitioners who I work with often for the IRM, as trainers, tutors and updaters of the enterprise risk management international certificate, and who I am also lucky to work with professionally. Sarah Gordon from Satarla and John Crawley and Emer McAneny from Expert Partners have long been my 'partners in crime', and the work we have done, expertise we have developed and learnings in the risk management field that we have obtained can be evidenced in this text through case studies, tools, techniques and their direct input to six of the later chapters.

I would also like to thank Jane Walde for providing her insight, and for letting me talk incessantly about the book when having fun facilitating workshops together. Charlie Lynn from Kogan Page has challenged me throughout and has also been very patient with some fine timelines that I created. As any author should state, any mistakes, of course, remain my own.

Finally, I could not have undertaken this task without the support of my family. My husband, Jim and son, Matthew, have encouraged me all the way and put up with the stupidly early hours I have crept into the office to write. My daughter,

Eleanor, has been my biggest supporter, shouting from the sidelines (or from the car travelling to and from her work) and cheering me on at every step, even though she hasn't been overly interested in the topic itself.

Experience in, and lessons learnt from implementing risk management have again been integrated throughout the text of the seventh edition. As noted in the COSO (2017) definition of enterprise risk management, it is as much about the 'culture, capabilities and practices' as it is the processes and procedures that enable risk management to create, maintain and protect value for an organization. I hope the readers of this book and students who use it in their studies find the information held within it useful, not just from an academic but also from a practical perspective.

I could not write the last paragraph of this section any better than Clive Thompson did in the sixth edition:

> Developments in risk management will continue apace. Technology will have a greater role to play in helping risk managers not only to control risk, but also to exploit opportunities. The scope of risk management will expand as it contributes to the modifications necessary to cope with climate change. In that respect, some of the processes described in this text will age but, as it says in original title, the fundamentals of risk management will remain. There are some exciting developments ahead, and the future for the new entrants to risk management will be bright if they equip themselves with these fundamentals.

Boost your career with the IRM

IRM is the leading professional body for Enterprise Risk Management (ERM). We drive excellence in managing risk to ensure organisations are risk ready for the opportunities and threats of the future.

We provide globally recognised qualifications and training, publish Thought Leadership and run insightful events open to both our members and the wider public, all of which are underpinned by our professional standards, defining the requirements risk managers need to meet.

What IRM offers Risk Professionals

TRAINING COURSES
Our risk management training gives you the knowledge, tools and techniques you need to protect your organistation.

FREE WEBINARS
You can access free webinars that cover a wide range of presentations, helpful for professionals at every level.

BLENDED LEARNING
Increase your chances of exam success and learn directly from module coaches in our face-to-face Blended Learning workshops.

QUALIFICATIONS
Our risk management qualifications give you the broad knowledge and the practical skills you need to manage risks.

BUILDING A COMMUNITY
We help people connect with our sector-specific Special Interest Groups, Regional Groups and social media platforms.

"IRM qualifications provide a practical framework and a structured way of thinking. This is vital to success in a risk role."

Find out more at www.theirm.org >>

irm

Introduction

This book is intended for all who want a comprehensive introduction to the theory and application of risk management. It sets out an integrated introduction to the management of risk for all organizations. Studying this book will provide insight into the world of risk management and may also help readers decide whether risk management is a suitable career option for them.

Many readers will wish to use this book in order to gain a better understanding of risk and risk management and thereby fulfil the primary responsibilities of their jobs with an enhanced understanding of risk. This book is designed to deliver the syllabus of the International Certificate in Enterprise Risk Management qualification of the Institute of Risk Management. However, it also acts as an introduction to the discipline of risk management for those interested in the subject but not (yet) undertaking a course of study.

Risk management

We all face risks in our everyday lives. Risks arise from personal activities and include those associated with health, personal financial decisions and domestic and relationship issues, but these are outside the scope of this discussion. This book is primarily concerned with risks that arise through organizational activities in the private, public or charity/third sectors.

Recent events have brought risk into higher profile. The extreme weather events, geopolitical upheavals, cyber-attacks, tensions in banking markets and other global shocks mean that the world seems to be in a constant state of instability and insecurity – or a permacrisis. These extreme risks exist in addition to the daily, somewhat more mundane, risks organizations face.

Understanding the range of risks organizations face and the real controls needed to manage them effectively is fundamental for the successful achievement of objectives. This is also at the heart of the decision making, accountability and risk management within an organization.

Organizations face a very wide range of risks, both threats and opportunities, that can impact the outcome of their operations. Risk management needs to offer an integrated approach to the assessment, control and monitoring of these risks, related to the context within which an organization exists and the objectives it is trying to achieve.

Realizing benefits from risk management depends, initially, on what 'good' risk management looks like for an organization and the value that is expected from it. It also requires the design and successful embedding of a suitable and sufficient risk management framework, which will enable the carefully planned implementation of the risk management process in an organization. By setting out an integrated approach to risk management, this book provides a description of the fundamental components of successful management of organizational risks. It describes a wealth of risk management tools and techniques and provides information on the successful delivery of an integrated and enterprise-wide approach to risk management.

The principles for risk management and what it should achieve will vary depending on what it is expected to deliver. For most organizations, this will depend on the level of risk management maturity, but it should support the creation, maintenance and protection of value for an organization, rather than be a box-ticking exercise.

These principles are supported by a risk management framework within an organization, which is presented and described in different ways in the range of standards, guides and other publications that are available. In all cases, the key components of a successful risk management framework are the governance, communications and reporting structure (architecture), the overall purpose of risk strategy for an organization (strategy) and the set of guidelines and procedures (protocols) that have been established. The importance of the risk architecture, strategy and protocols (RASP) is discussed in detail in this book.

The risk management process is a well-established concept, although, once again, it is presented in a number of different ways, often using differing terminologies. A simplified description of risk management that sets out the four key steps in the process has been developed. This supports an organization in defining the context and objectives, assessing risks, managing risks and monitoring, reviewing and reporting on those risks.

The combination of principles for effective risk management, the description of the framework, and the process for implementation, constitutes a risk management standard. There are several risk management standards in existence, including the International Standard, ISO 31000, the American COSO enterprise risk management framework and the UK Government's 'Orange Book' guidance, which are explored in this book as benchmarks of best practice.

Risk management terminology

Most risk management publications refer to the benefits of having a common language of risk within an organization. Many organizations manage to achieve this common language and common understanding of risk management processes and protocols at least internally. However, it is usually the case that within an industry or sector, and sometimes even within individual organizations, the development of a common risk language can be very challenging.

Abbreviations and acronyms are used throughout the book as an aid to learning and understanding. A list of all abbreviations and acronyms is included in Appendix A.

Reference and supporting materials use a great range of terminologies. The different approaches to risk management, the different risk management standards that exist and the wide range of guidance material that is available often use different terms for the same feature or concept. This is regrettable and can be very confusing, but it is inescapable.

To assist with the difficult area of terminology, Appendix B sets out the basic risk management terms and definitions that are used in this book. It also provides cross-reference between the different terms in use to describe the same concept. Where appropriate and necessary, a table setting out a range of definitions for the same concept is included within the relevant chapter of the book, and these tables are cross-referenced in Appendix B.

Book structure

The book is presented in nine parts, together with two appendices. An introduction to risk and risk management is provided in Part One. Part Two examines the application of these concepts across an enterprise as a whole. Parts Three and Four describe the implementation of risk management through four simple steps, being: 1) defining the context and objectives; 2) assessing risks; 3) managing risks; and 4) monitoring, reviewing and reporting on risks. The people and decision-making aspect of risk management is considered in Part Five through the concepts of risk culture and risk appetite and tolerance. Part Six describes risk governance and how to obtain assurance on risk management and the management of risk.

These first six parts provide an understanding of the breadth of risk management. Parts Seven and Eight consider risk management in more depth. Part Seven explores risk management in the organizational environment, including its relationship to strategy, resilience and sustainability. Part Eight considers risk management through different lenses or approaches, including insurance, banking, operational, projects, health and safety, legal, the supply chain and IT.

Part Nine takes a step back to close the loop in considering the value and benefit that risk management and the risk practitioner can bring to organizations. This includes understanding the maturity and competency levels within organizations, and how they can be continually improved.

As noted earlier, Appendix A provides a list of the main acronyms and abbreviations used in the book. Appendix B provides a glossary of terms and cross-references the different terminologies used by risk management practitioners.

In order to bring the subject of risk management to life and provide context to the ideas and concepts that are described, boxes are included within the text. These boxes either provide practical examples of the application of the theory being discussed, or they provide opinions and commentary on real situations that have arisen.

Changes for the seventh edition

Risk management continues to be a dynamic and developing discipline and the changes that were necessary in this seventh edition reflect that fact. Certain types of risk have increased dramatically, and the need for a robust ERM initiative to be adopted by organizations has never been greater.

One of the important considerations in producing this edition was for it to remain closely aligned to the updated structure of the Institute of Risk Management (IRM) International Certificate in Enterprise Risk Management. The book has been based on and maintains some of the key concepts from the sixth edition, although a reorganization of the chapters to align with the updated Certificate was required. Another change relates to updated risk management standards and guidance, such as the Orange Book (2023) and the UK Corporate Governance Code (2024). A third key change has been the inclusion of further detail on the relationship between risk management and strategy setting, resilience and sustainability. Finally, the book now ends with a focus on the value that risk management and the risk practitioner can and should bring to an organization.

PART ONE
Introduction to risk management

LEARNING OUTCOMES

Having studied this section readers will be able to:

- Distinguish between risk and risk management using a range of different recognized approaches.
- Explain the importance of risk management.
- Produce and articulate a range of established definitions of risk and risk management and describe the efficacy of these definitions.
- Summarize the origins and development of the discipline of risk management.
- Distinguish between and state the key features of the best-established risk management standards, including ISO 31000, the COSO ERM framework and the Orange Book.

What risk is and why it is important

While some might consider risk management originating from the insurance or finance sector, risk affects all organizations and whatever we think of as 'risk', it is changing in the digital age. Organizations of all types – government, local and health authorities, manufacturers and service providers, financiers and criminals – now use computers and are digitally processing immense amounts of data. Almost half of all households worldwide have a computer at home, and while it is estimated that number is a third of households in developing countries, the impact on everyday lives and activity cannot be underestimated.[1]

As our everyday activity is changing, so should our attitude to risk. Mark Zuckerberg famously said that 'in a world that is changing really quickly, the only strategy that is guaranteed to fail is not taking risks'. In this book the processes to manage risk that have been developed over the last century will be outlined with particular consideration to the changes and disruption brought about by our increased reliance on computing and data analytics.

Definitions of risk

Risk is often perceived as being undesirable: the *Oxford English Dictionary* defines risk in terms of hazard, danger, loss or adverse consequence. If we go back in time to discover the origin of the word 'hazard' this probably comes from the Arabic for a dice (al-zahr) and became common in 12th-century Europe when referring to a game of chance, or the throw of a dice. Risk in this sense means the opportunity for gain as well as a threat.

There has been extensive academic discussion as to the concepts of risk and uncertainty. In 1985 Perry and Hayes[2] differentiated the two concepts through measurement where 'risk is a measurable uncertainty, while uncertainty is an unmeasurable risk'. Another way of looking at it was provided by Flanagan and Norman[3] in 1993, who stated that 'Uncertainty is a situation where no historical data exists or previous history related to the situation under scrutiny'. This is a particularly important concept to bear in mind when seen from the perspective of the 2020s. Our digital age has seen the generation of, and enabled unrestricted access to, almost unlimited amounts of data when compared to the 1980s.

These different perspectives on the term risk, and even the definitions that follow have not always been helpful in guiding organizations in those risks that need to be managed to successfully achieve objectives.

Hillson[4] simplifies the definition of risk, noting that all risks are uncertainties, but not all uncertainties are risks. He goes further to explain that the key determinants of risk are that they need to be uncertain, and that they need to matter to the objectives an organization is trying to achieve. As such, risks are 'uncertainties that matter'. Organizations can be aware of many uncertainties that don't affect their objectives, so they are not risks to them, but may be risks to others.

Definitions of risk can be found from many sources, and some key definitions are set out in Table 1.1. The international guide to risk-related definitions, ISO 31073, and the UK Government's Orange Book[5] define risk as the 'effect of uncertainty on objectives'. This is neither negative nor positive and offers a more nuanced view than that of the 'popular' or dictionary definition. Both go further to explain that an effect may be positive, negative or a deviation from the expected; these outcomes show risks are opportunities, threats or both. They also note that risk is often described by a potential event, a change in circumstances, a consequence, or a combination of these, and how they may affect the achievement of objectives.

Different disciplines define the term risk in very different ways. When looking to manage risk it is important that the definition chosen is the most appropriate for an organization. The definition can be as narrow or as comprehensive as necessary.

Risk in an organizational context is usually defined as anything that can impact the fulfilment of the organization's objectives, which means it is fundamental that the organization's objectives are understood, even if they are not always fully established and agreed.

It is generally accepted that risk is best defined by concentrating on events. This is the route taken in many standards and associations in Table 1.1.

Table 1.1   Definitions of risk

Organization	Definition
ISO 31073:2022	Effect of uncertainty on objectives. Note that an effect is a deviation from the expected. It can be positive, negative or both, and can address, create or result in opportunities and threats.
COSO:2017	The possibility that an event will occur and affect the achievement of strategy and business objectives – negative and positive outcomes.

(continued)

Table 1.1 (Continued)

Organization	Definition
Institute of Risk Management	Risk is the combination of the probability of an event and its consequence. Consequences can range from positive to negative.
Institute of Internal Auditors	The uncertainty of an event occurring that could have an impact on the achievement of the objectives. Risk is measured in terms of consequences and likelihood.
HM Government: The Orange Book: 2023	The effect of uncertainty on objectives. Risk is usually expressed in terms of causes, potential events and their consequences.

Types of risks

As noted above, risk may have positive or negative outcomes, being opportunities or threats. In previous editions of this book, it was considered useful to divide risks into four categories, rather than two:

- compliance (or mandatory) risks;
- hazard (or pure) risks;
- control (or uncertainty) risks;
- opportunity (or speculative) risks.

It is important to note that there is no 'right' or 'wrong' subdivision of risks. Readers will encounter other subdivisions in other texts, and these may be equally appropriate. Within this book, for ease of reference, risks will be described using opportunity and threat, as appropriate, in line with ISO 31000. Consideration has been given to readers of earlier versions of the book, who may prefer to use the four categories of risks as noted above, and that categorization and references to it has been retained in Table 1.2. However, in order to provide consistency around threat and opportunity, all references to compliance, hazard and control risks will be termed threats, with their sub-categorization provided as a side note, where appropriate, from this point forward.

Whatever the theoretical discussions, the most important issue is that an organization adopts a risk classification system that is most suitable for its own circumstances.

Table 1.2   Types of risk

Risk type		Key feature
Threats	Compliance risks	The importance of compliance risks should not be underestimated. They are associated with adherence to the law of the country and the regulations that apply to the sector in which you operate. Compliance risk captures the legal and financial penalties for failing to act or acting inappropriately and is especially significant for those business sectors that are heavily regulated. Compliance with mandatory requirements represents a 'licence to operate' and failure to achieve the level of compliance required by the relevant regulator will impact routine business activities. Penalties may be financial but increasingly they are personal to the management involved, such as the Senior Managers and Certification Regime imposed after the global financial crisis by the Financial Conduct Authority in the UK.
	Hazard risks	In the true sense of the term, hazards are things that can cause harm, with the risk being the chance that those hazards will actually cause harm. The term hazard risk has been used here, defined as the most common risks associated with operational risk management, including occupational health and safety programmes. A good example of a hazard risk faced by many organizations is that of slips, trips or falls. Organizations usually accept some hazard risks, but they need to be managed within tolerable levels.
	Control risks	These are associated with unknown and unexpected events. They are sometimes referred to as uncertainty risks and they can be extremely difficult to quantify. Control risks are frequently associated with new projects where it is known that events will occur, but the precise consequences of those events are difficult to predict and control. Therefore, the approach is based on managing the uncertainties around the timing, eventual cost or delivery of the project.
Opportunities	Opportunity risks	Opportunities are the positive outcomes from the occurrence of risks. Some organizations consider opportunities only exist at a strategic level – where changes to the strategic direction of an organization are considered. Although opportunities are taken with the intention of obtaining a positive outcome, this is not guaranteed. In the rapidly changing environment caused by such things as the global pandemic, geopolitical confrontation, financial crises and so on, organizations have deliberately taken risks in order to survive. Some organizations have altered their business models, for example a farm shop providing new services such as 'click and collect' or delivery services. The purpose has been to take action that involves risk to achieve positive gains or, in extreme cases, survival. Opportunities also exist through enhancements and advancements at tactical and operational levels. These are not just part of any continuous improvement process, but as deliberate decisions to explore and research new approaches to the way things are done within organizations.

STARTING UP A COMPANY SUPPLYING TECHNOLOGY TO THE FINANCIAL SECTOR

For those readers who intend to apply the four different types of risk, the example of a 'start-up' in the financial sector may be helpful to understand the distinction between compliance, hazard, control and opportunity risks. The company will need to be authorized by the relevant authorities, which in the UK is the Financial Conduct Authority, and the company will need to nominate senior managers to be responsible for its compliance risks. Theft or fraud caused by an employee is an operational or hazard risk. When they design their new software package, control risks will be associated with this project. When released, the software may have the potential to be used by clients in a sector they had not specifically targeted, thereby creating an opportunity risk; the intention is to achieve results by attracting customers, but it is possible that the project will fail to deliver the functionality that was intended. In fact, the failure of the functionality of the new software system may critically undermine the operations of an organization.

Why understanding risk is important

Following the Covid-19 pandemic, geopolitical confrontations, economic crises, focus on sustainability and climate change and other recent global events, many organizations have taken a greater interest and a proactive approach to risk and risk management. It is increasingly understood that the explicit and structured management of risks brings benefits. Organizations that manage risks will be able to achieve improvement across their breadth and depth, simplified into the following four areas, which are abbreviated as STOC throughout this book:

- **Strategy:** Because the risks associated with different strategic options will be fully analysed, better strategic decisions will be reached.
- **Tactics:** Because consideration will have been given to selection of the tactics and the associated risks involved, available alternatives can be evaluated. It is worth noting that projects and programmes of work usually represent the tactics by which strategy is implemented.
- **Operations:** Because events that can cause disruption will be identified in advance and actions taken to reduce their likelihood of occurring, the damage caused by these events will be limited and the costs contained, with the opposite being true of opportunities.
- **Compliance:** This will be enhanced because the risks associated with failure to achieve compliance with statutory and customer obligations will be addressed.

It is undesirable for organizations to find themselves in a position whereby unexpected events cause disruption to normal operations. Stakeholders expect that organizations be resilient and take full account of the risks that may cause operational, project or strategic issues.

Risk and reward

Building on the opening to this chapter, risk can be desirable and deliver benefits or rewards. A business will launch a new product or service because it sees opportunities from the successful marketing of that product or service. In undertaking the launch, an organization will allocate resources which may be wasted if the launch is not successful. These resources represent the value at risk and need to be within the risk appetite of an organization.

When an organization puts value at risk in this way, it should do so with the full knowledge of the risk to which an organization is becoming exposed. Even more importantly, it should ensure that it has sufficient resources to cover the exposure. In other words, the exposure should be quantified, the appetite to take that level of risk should be confirmed, and the capacity of an organization to withstand any foreseeable adverse consequences should be clearly established (in other words, an organization should consider effective resilience).

A relevant example is how the digital age has disrupted the traditional lifecycle of product or service launches. There is now a continuous need to innovate and develop new products and services from the new opportunities presented by the digital age of data and enhanced processing power. This trend explains, in part, the enhanced need for risk management as the rewards from exploiting digital powers are many multiples of 'analogue' solutions. This means that the traditional lifecycle of a product or service may be faster than before digital disruption, but it is useful to analyse the cycles that products or services undergo.

The simple maturity cycle described in Figure 1.1, illustrates the lifecycle of a product or service, in relation to the potential reward versus the level of risk being undertaken. Appropriate risk management techniques are needed when considering the opportunities that will arise from new products. The nature of these risk responses and the nature of their impact are considered in Part Four of this book.

Risk management effort should produce rewards. In the case of threats, that reward will be fewer disruptive events in future. In the case of project risks, the reward for increased risk management effort will be that the project is more likely to be delivered on time, within budget and to specification/quality.

For opportunities, risk management should result in a higher rate of successful new product or service launches or (at worst) a lower level of loss for all new activities or new products. In all cases, profit or enhanced level of service is the reward for taking risk.

Figure 1.1   Risk and reward

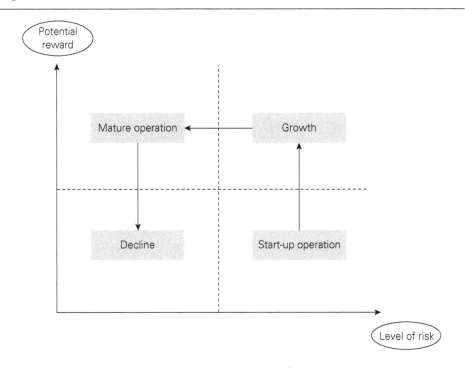

Attitudes to risk

Different organizations will have different attitudes to risk. ISO 31073[6] defines risk attitude as an 'organization's approach to assess, and eventually pursue, retain, take or turn away from risk'. The IRM's paper[7] on risk culture defines risk attitude as 'the chosen position adopted by an individual or group towards risk, influenced by risk perception and pre-disposition'. In consideration of these definitions, some organizations may be considered to be risk averse, while others will be risk aggressive. The attitude of an organization to risk will depend on the attitude of the board, the nature of the sector and the marketplace within which it operates.

Risks need to be considered inside the context that gave rise to them. An organization may appear to be risk aggressive about an opportunity the board has decided should not be missed. That particular opportunity needs to have been fully considered for an organization to evaluate that risk correctly.

One of the major contributions from successful risk management is to ensure that strategic decisions that appear to be high risk are taken on an informed basis. Improvement in the robustness of decision-making activities is one of the key benefits of risk management. Attitude to risk is a complex subject and is closely related to the risk appetite of an organization, but they are not the same. Risk *attitude* indicates the way an organization perceives and approaches risk. Risk *appetite* indicates the amount of risk an organization is willing to seek or accept in pursuit of its long-term objectives. Risk attitude is explored further in Chapters 23 and 24. Risk appetite is considered in more detail in Chapters 25 and 26.

Taking calculated risks

Risk management is about helping leaders to learn to take more risk and to accept failure. To perform better than its competitors an organization must take more risk, but it should be calculated risk. The risk that is taken should be known and understood; it is not acceptable to take risks unwittingly. This applies across different sectors. For example, the Orange Book states:

> Public sector organizations cannot be risk averse and be successful... Effective and meaningful risk management in government remains as important as ever in taking a balanced view to managing opportunity and risk. It must be an integral part of informed decision making.

Note here that although the Orange Book considers that the consequence of a risk occurring could be positive or negative, it still used the term 'opportunity and risk'. As noted earlier, organizations can choose any definition for risk that is appropriate, but they should be consistent in its use.

Definitions of risk management

Providing a suitable definition of risk management is as difficult as providing a suitable and universally accepted definition of risk. Because it is commonly accepted that risk management should be concerned with both threats and opportunities, a description and definition is required that reflects the broad scope of risk management activities, as shown in Table 1.3.

Table 1.3   Definitions of risk management

Organization	Definition
ISO 31073:2022	Co-ordinated activities to direct and control an organization with regard to risk.
COSO:2017	The culture, capabilities and practices, integrated with strategy-setting and its execution, that organizations rely on to manage risk in creating, preserving and realizing value.

(continued)

Table 1.3   (Continued)

Organization	Definition
Institute of Risk Management	Process which aims to help organizations understand, evaluate and take action on all their risks with a view to increasing the probability of success and reducing the likelihood of failure.
Institute of Internal Auditors	Selection of those risks a business should take and those that should be avoided or mitigated, followed by action to avoid or reduce risk.
HM Government: The Orange Book: 2023	The co-ordinated activities designed and operated to manage risk and exercise internal control within an organization.

The importance of risk management

Further to the risk concepts explored in this chapter, such as risk and reward and taking calculated risk, the effective management of risk is important for any organization. The list in Table 1.4 demonstrates the ways in which risk management supports organizations in creating, maintaining and protecting value. The list also shows that the application of risk management has moved a long way from its origins in the insurance world and from opinions that it is only relevant to the management of threats.

THE IMPORTANCE OF RISK MANAGEMENT

Calisen is a British smart energy technology company, who procure, install, service, finance and track smart energy infrastructure assets. With its focus on sustainability, the company recognizes the importance of risk management in not only managing its current and emerging risks effectively, but also in supporting an organization in being sustainable and resilient.

In the 2022 annual report[8] an organization states:

Risk and internal control management is an important process as it not only provides assurance to the Board, but also demonstrates that Calisen understands and is managing its current and emerging risks. This isn't just as a reflection of the current environment, social and governance requirements, but also taking account of risk in terms of our own plans, sustainability and resilience.

In addition, the report states that risk management supports an organization in meeting its objectives and in gaining future competitive advantage. This clearly demonstrates that risk management is being undertaken because the company recognizes that it adds and protects value across an organization.

Table 1.4   Importance of risk management

Managing an organization	• Variable cost or availability of raw materials
	• Cost of retirement/pension/social benefits
	• Desire to deliver greater shareholder value
	• Greater transparency required from organizations
	• Pace of change in business ever increases
	• Impact of e-commerce on all aspects of business life
	• Increased reliance on information technology systems
	• Increasing importance of intellectual property
	• Greater supply chain complexity/dependency
	• Reputation becomes more and more important
	• Contributing to carbon reduction and supporting climate change initiatives
	• Regulatory pressures continue to increase
	• Changes/variation in national legislative requirements
	• Joint ventures becoming more common
Changes in the marketplace	• Digital approaches disrupting the commercial and marketplace environment
	• Globalization of customers, suppliers and products
	• Greater customer expectations, often led by competitors
	• Need to respond more rapidly to stakeholder expectations
	• Constant need to make bold strategic decisions
	• Short-term success required, without long-term detriment
	• Product innovation and continuous improvements
	• Rapid changes in (consumer) product technology
	• Threats to world/national economy
	• Threat of more pandemics in future caused by zoonotic diseases
	• Increasing occurrences of civil unrest/political risks
	• Extreme weather events resulting in population shift

The importance of risk management and its evolution from more specialized and traditional approaches to enterprise risk management are explored further in Chapters 2 and 4 and later in Chapter 40.

Notes

1 Statista (2021) Share of households with a computer at home worldwide from 2005 to 2019, www.statista.com/statistics/748551/worldwide-households-with-computer (archived at https://perma.cc/R4HE-UM2J)

2 Perry, JG and Hayes, RW (1985) Risk and its management in construction projects, *Proceedings of the Institution of Civil Engineers*, 78 (3), pp 499–521.

3 Flanagan, R and Norman, G (1993) *Risk Management and Construction*, Wiley-Blackwell, Oxford.

4 Hillson, D (Ed) (2023) *The Risk Management Handbook*, Kogan Page, London.

5 HM Government (2020) *The Orange Book: Management of risk – principles and concepts*, https://assets.publishing.service.gov.uk/government/uploads/system/uploads/attachment_data/file/866117/6.6266_HMT_Orange_Book_Update_v6_WEB.PDF (archived at https://perma.cc/ATK7-D5B5)

6 ISO (2022) *ISO 31073 Risk Management – Vocabulary*, https://www.iso.org/obp/ui/en/#iso:std:iso:31073:ed-1:v1:en (archived at https://perma.cc/QAJ7-7DFL)

7 IRM (2012) *Risk Culture: Under the Microscope Guidance for Boards*, https://www.theirm.org/media/4703/risk_culture_a5_web15_oct_2012.pdf (archived at https://perma.cc/5MF5-XEAX)

8 Calisen (2023) *Annual Report and Accounts*, https://admin.calisen.com//media/zfci0ing/calisen_ar22_231108.pdf (archived at https://perma.cc/USJ2-AUPQ)

The evolution of 02
risk management

Origins of risk management

Risk management has evolved from a variety of origins. It can therefore mean different things to different areas of practice. While each area of practice has developed its
own terminology, tools and expectations, there are similarities across each. Lessons
can be and are being learnt by understanding how risk management is used in different practices and the history of how each form of risk management has evolved.

Different practices

Key areas of practice that have developed forms of risk management include everything from health and safety to insurance and finance to project management.

In respect of compliance, UK governments have regulated working conditions
since the earliest Factory Acts in the 19th century, but the introduction of the Health
and Safety at Work Act in 1974 gave regulators more authority to apply the principles of a risk-based approach in relation to improving working conditions.

As far as pure risks (or threats) are concerned, from the early 19th century insurance firms increasingly imposed risk mitigation and control standards if they were
required to underwrite the risk. For example, insurers provided their own fire bri-
gades and provided their clients with marks to identify which houses should be
saved in the event of a fire. Similarly, marine insurers championed the use of the
'Plimsoll line' to indicate the level of cargo that a ship could safely transport without
being dangerously overloaded.

A brief timeline has been produced by Felix Kloman[1] and refers to the development of the practice from insurance purchasing, with Massey Ferguson introducing
the concept of 'cost of risk' as being more than just buying insurance in the 1960s.
In the US the insurance function of organizations includes healthcare provision for
employees, and as a result that function was well resourced and received considerable attention from management on costs. Their approach was based on earlier
studies which argued the teams that managed insurance purchases would be better
engaged if they refocused efforts on managing risk. Kloman's analysis follows the
development of the practice through a risk financing lens and demonstrates how

financial concerns were at the root of changes in emphasis in the earliest days of the study and practice of risk management.

The linkage of insurance, or risk financing, with risk control was developed in Europe during the 1970s, building on the concept of total cost of risk championed by Massey Ferguson. This concept is explained further in Chapter 26. As this approach became established, it also became obvious that there were many risks facing organizations that were not insurable. The tools and techniques of risk management were then applied to other disciplines, as discussed later in this chapter.

Education, formal training and standards

As risk management became more mature, education programmes emerged to support the development of risk management as a profession, which in turn led to the development of risk management qualifications in the 1980s. Risk management regulations associated with corporate governance were introduced and regulators became increasingly concerned with threats in relation to particular business sectors, for example in financial institutions.

The development of education and qualifications in risk management, as well as the more structured approach of regulators, led to the emergence of risk management standards. Risk management standard AS/NZS 4360:1995 was one of the early examples of a comprehensive approach to the management of risk. As well as the generic risk management standards applicable to all industries, specific risk management approaches also emerged in particular sectors, including the finance sector. The emergence of regulated capital requirements for banks and insurance companies indicated the increased level of risk management maturity required of financial institutions.

Of course, the IRM was formed in 1986, offering risk management education to its professional members, covering a wider syllabus than just insurance or financial services and providing access to a variety of different perspectives on the subject. In the absence of an international standard, they issued their Risk Management Standard in 2002, which provided guidance for practitioners for many years.

Widening the scope of risk

The corporate risk management role started to extend beyond insurance purchase and into contingency planning, which became more important to organizations. There was increased emphasis on loss prevention and safety management, which developed from the 1960s when commercial organizations started to form their own (or captive) insurance companies to obtain more competitive insurance rates. During the 1970s and 1980s this trend expanded globally and places like Bermuda, the

Cayman Islands, Guernsey and the Isle of Man developed legislation to attract the formation of such entities.

At the same time, during the 1960s and 1970s there were considerable developments in the risk management approach adopted by occupational health and safety practitioners. During the 1980s the application of risk management techniques to project management developed substantially. Financial institutions continued to develop the application of risk management tools and techniques to market risk and credit risk. During the 1990s, the financial institutions further broadened their risk management initiatives to include structured consideration of operational risks.

Also, during the 1980s, treasury departments began to develop the financial approach to risk management. There was recognition by finance directors that insurance risk management and financial risk management policies should be better co-ordinated. During the 1990s, risk financing products emerged that combined insurance with derivatives. At the same time, corporate governance and listing requirements encouraged directors to place greater emphasis on enterprise risk management (ERM), and the first appointment of a chief risk officer (CRO) occurred at that time.

Additionally, education for other specialist areas in risk management began to gain traction. For example, the Association of Project Management in the UK produced their first guidance, Project Risk Analysis and Management (PRAM guide) in 1997, with the Institute of Civil Engineers issuing their first Risk Analysis and Management for Projects (RAMP) guide in 1998.

Uniting into a single function

During the 2000s, financial services firms were encouraged to develop internal risk management systems and capital models. There has been a rapid growth of CRO positions in companies from many different industries and sectors, from energy to banks and insurance companies. Boards started to invest more time in ERM due to the Sarbanes-Oxley Act in 2022 in the US. More detailed risk reporting and other corporate governance requirements have also been introduced.

Despite these trends, the financial crisis of 2008 called into question the contribution that risk management can make to corporate success, especially in financial institutions. There is no doubt that risk management failed to prevent the global financial crisis. This failure was, however, due to the inability of organizations to correctly apply effective risk management processes and procedures, rather than inherent defects in risk management as a discipline, as can be seen by the HBOS case study.

HBOS FAILURE TO ACT ON RISK MANAGEMENT ADVICE

It is a matter of public record that the risk manager of HBOS, Paul Moore, warned senior management, including the chair and chief executive officer (CEO), of the dangers of misalignment of rewards to management and the over-emphasis on meeting aggressive sales targets. James Crosby, then the CEO, dismissed Mr Moore in 2004, disregarding his clear warnings, and replaced him with a sales manager who was unqualified in risk management. In 2008 HBOS required £21 billion of UK taxpayers' money to remain afloat, and in 2012, in anticipation of the parliamentary inquiry, Mr Crosby resigned as the Deputy Chair of the Financial Services Authority (a position he had subsequently been awarded) and surrendered the knighthood he had received in 2006.

The financial crisis resulted in changes to regulations, such as the update to the COSO ERM framework in 2017 and ISO 31000 in 2018. In addition, the failure of a global facilities management organization, Carillion, based in the UK, and other company failures, led to the introduction of the Wates Principles, requiring large private organizations in the UK to follow corporate governance guidance.

Increasing globalization and the increasing interconnectivity of organizations across the world, coupled with Covid-19, the many large and smaller-scale interstate conflicts, and requirements regarding, and impacts of, climate change have led to a change in focus. There is increasing attention on organizations to ensure effective risk management and internal controls, to improve decision making and challenge regarding both and to take appropriate accountability. This has been seen in the update of the Institute of Internal Auditors (IIA) Three Lines Model for assurance (2020), in the update to the Orange Book (2023) that now includes a section on risk controls, and the update to the UK Corporate Governance Code (2024) including the requirement for Boards to establish and maintain a risk management and internal control framework and to disclose information on material controls.

The maturity of the risk management discipline is now such that the links with insurance are much weaker. Insurance is only one of the risk control techniques, only applicable to a portion of threats and is irrelevant to the majority of risks facing an enterprise. The range of different approaches to risk management is illustrated by the definitions of risk management, as seen in Chapter 1.

Effective and efficient core processes

Insurable risks can have an immediate impact on operations. Therefore, the initial application of risk management was to ensure continuation of normal efficient operations.

As risk management has developed, emphasis has been placed on providing enhancements to core business processes. These processes must be effective in that they deliver the results that are required, as well as being efficient. For example, there is limited value in having a software program that is efficient if it does not deliver the range of functions that are required.

Strategic decisions are arguably the most important that an organization has to make. Risk management delivers improved information so that strategic decisions can be made with greater confidence. The strategy that is decided by an organization must be capable of delivering the results that are required. There are many examples of organizations that selected an incorrect strategy or failed to successfully implement their selected strategy. Many of these organizations suffered corporate failure. As noted in Chapter 1, the COSO definition of risk management focuses on both setting and applying strategy in an organization.

Strategy should be designed to take advantage of opportunities. For example, in terms of growing revenues, sports teams may identify the possibility of selling more products to their existing fan base. Some clubs will establish a travel agency for fans of the club who travel overseas, together with the provision of associated travel insurance. Also, there is the possibility of creating a club credit card that will be managed by a new finance subsidiary.

Having identified these possibilities, clubs will need to look at the uncertainties associated with these investments and devise suitable projects to implement the selected strategies. Ensuring that adequate account is taken of risk during all of these activities will increase the chances of selecting the correct strategy. It is worth noting that projects and programmes of work represent the tactics by which strategy is implemented.

Organizations that have effective and efficient tactics, operations and compliance but an incorrect overall strategy will fail. This will be the case however good the risk management activities are at operational and project level. Incorrect strategy has resulted in more corporate failures than ineffective or inefficient operations and tactics. Nevertheless, the importance of compliance activities cannot be over-emphasized as failure to comply could result in the complete shutdown of operations. More information on effective and efficient core processes is included in Chapter 5.

THE IMPORTANCE OF COMPLIANCE

HSBC had been dogged by stories of money laundering across its global operations and faced legal actions in the US and Switzerland throughout the 2010s. In 2015 it paid £28 million to the Swiss financial authorities, a record at the time, for the 'organizational deficiencies' which allowed HSBC to bank the illegal proceeds of its clients, including political corruption and arms trafficking – essentially a failure of its compliance team.

This was followed in 2021 with a fine of nearly £64 million from the UK's Financial Conduct Authority[2] after weaknesses were found in HSBC's transaction monitoring systems over a period of eight years, most notably in relation to anti-money laundering.

Specialist areas of risk management

Risk management is a constantly developing and evolving discipline. As noted in the 'different practices' section of this chapter, as well as having its origins in the insurance industry and in other branches of managing threats, risk management has strong connections with credit and treasury functions. Many functions within large organizations will have a significant risk management component to their activities, such as tax, treasury, human resources, procurement and logistics. However, it is unlikely that specialists in those areas will consider their activities as simply a branch of the risk management discipline.

Perhaps one of the best-known and specialist areas of risk management is that of health and safety at work. Another specialist area is that of business continuity management, which includes disaster recovery planning and business continuity planning. Also, there is no doubt that quality management is a very well-developed branch of risk management, given the high profile attached to quality management systems such as ISO 9000.

Further information on different approaches to risk management and how these can be aligned through enterprise risk management can be found in Chapters 36 and 37.

Notes

1 F Kloman (2009) A short history of risk management, *Risk Journal*, https://riskjournal.blogspot.com/2009/02/short-history-of-risk-management.html (archived at https://perma.cc/HYN2-L7PU)
2 FCA (2021) The FCA has fined HSBC Bank plc (HSBC) £63, 946,800 for failings in its anti-money laundering processes, https://www.fca.org.uk/news/press-releases/fca-fines-hsbc-bank-plc-deficient-transaction-monitoring-controls (archived at https://perma.cc/5ES7-8WG4)

Risk management 03
standards

Risk management standards set out the overall approach to the successful management of risk, including a description of the risk management process, together with the suggested framework that supports that process. There are a number of established risk management standards and frameworks issued by various global bodies such as the International Organization for Standardization (ISO) based in Switzerland, which is an overarching and co-ordinating body for various national standards bodies, including the British Standards Institute and Standards Australia.

The Committee of Sponsoring Organizations of the Treadway Commission (COSO) is also considered, which is largely US based and which has issued comprehensive standards on risk management. As well as the established standards and frameworks, a considerable amount of guidance on risk management has been published by various government departments. In addition, an insight to the application of risk management in a governmental/public sector context is provided through the UK HM Treasury's highly respected suite of papers, which also provide a wider understanding of such things as risk appetite and risk reporting.

In this chapter, consideration is principally given to the International Standard ISO 31000 in its 2018 version, the COSO framework of both 2004 and 2017 and the UK HM Treasury's guidance of 2023, from which definitions of risk and risk management were given in Chapter 1. These four approaches are considered in this chapter, with relevant details of each being discussed in later chapters.

ISO 31000 is an internationally recognized and highly influential risk management standard. COSO have applied standards to two concepts, and it is important to be clear which one is used and for which purpose. COSO provides a standard against which to measure internal control frameworks and has become most widely used in the US. The COSO internal control framework will be considered further in Chapter 28. The COSO Enterprise Risk Management (ERM) Framework was first released in 2004 as the ERM 'cube' and then updated as the 'rainbow double helix' in 2017. Given the spread and influence of US companies, the standard has been adopted and/or adapted by numerous countries and businesses around the world. The UK HM Treasury's guidance, called the Orange Book, is based on best practice from ISO 31000.

Although some standards are better recognized than others, organizations should select the approach that is most relevant to their particular circumstances. The standards considered in this chapter are designed for use primarily by specialist risk management practitioners, although each or all of them are often used by organizations as a benchmark in establishing and reviewing their risk management practices as examples of best practice.

The standards are reviewed and updated at regular intervals, and this book explores the changes in the most recent versions. This provides a good indication of the 'direction of travel' for risk management.

Before going any further, it is important to distinguish between a risk management standard and a risk management framework. In simple terms, a risk management standard is the combination of a description of the risk management process, together with the recommended framework. The key features of a risk management framework are described later in this chapter.

Use of risk management standards for listed companies

As noted above, risk management standards are widely used as a way of measuring how an organization is managing their risk, particularly for listed companies that are publicly traded. For organizations listed on the New York Stock Exchange, the COSO ERM framework is the preferred risk management standard, along with the COSO internal control framework (considered further in Chapter 28), which is a requirement of the Sarbanes–Oxley Act of 2002 (SOX). SOX also applies to subsidiaries of US-listed companies around the world. Therefore, the COSO approach is internationally recognized, and in many circumstances is mandated.

For many stock exchanges, the greater emphasis in the listing requirements and associated corporate governance code has been on internal control, rather than risk management. The focus in the updated UK Corporate Governance Code requires a risk management and internal control framework to be established and maintained, putting an emphasis on the important relationship between risk management and internal control. This relationship is considered further in Chapter 28.

Apart from the ISO and COSO frameworks, a number of others are also well regarded and in widespread use. The Corporate Governance Code Guidance from the UK's Financial Reporting Council was updated in 2024. The updated risk guidance can be found as a free download from the website of the Financial Reporting Council (www.frc.org.uk). In a similar way, corporate governance requirements in other countries include risk management and internal controls, such as King IV in South

Africa (2016), the French Corporate Governance Code (2022) and the G20/ Organization for Economic Co-operations and Development (OECD) Principles of Corporate Governance (2023). Corporate governance is explored in Chapter 27.

Some of the available standards were developed by risk management professionals, while others were developed by accountants or auditors. There are two distinct approaches followed in the various standards:

- 'risk management', followed by ISO 31000 and the COSO ERM frameworks;
- 'internal control', developed by COSO internal control framework and by corporate governance requirements, such as the FRC guidance.

As noted earlier, due to the update to the UK Corporate Governance Code requiring organizations to have a risk management and internal control framework, some organizations are now establishing a more formal link between the two, providing 'risk management and internal control'. Links between the two will be explored in relevant chapters in the book, and in detail in Chapter 28.

The standards in more detail

ISO 31000

ISO 31000:2018[1] provides a statement of risk management principles (what good risk management looks like), a description of the risk management framework (what is needed to support effective risk management) and guidance on the process (how to implement risk management) all based around the central purpose of creating and protecting value. The diagram used to illustrate the risk management process in ISO 31000 is reproduced in Figure 3.1.

A summary of these eight principles is set out below and can be seen to be closely aligned to the PACED model set out in Chapter 5:

- Framework and processes should be customized and proportionate.
- Appropriate and timely involvement of stakeholders is necessary.
- A structured and comprehensive approach is required.
- Risk management is an integral part of all organizational activities.
- Risk management anticipates, detects, acknowledges and responds to changes.
- Risk management explicitly considers any limitations of available information.
- Human and cultural factors influence all aspects of risk management.
- Risk management is continually improved through learning and experience.

The risk management framework is presented as a continuous improvement model similar to the PIML model discussed in Chapter 9. The detailed information in the

Figure 3.1 ISO 31000 risk management principles, framework and process

Risk management principles   Risk management process

Risk management framework

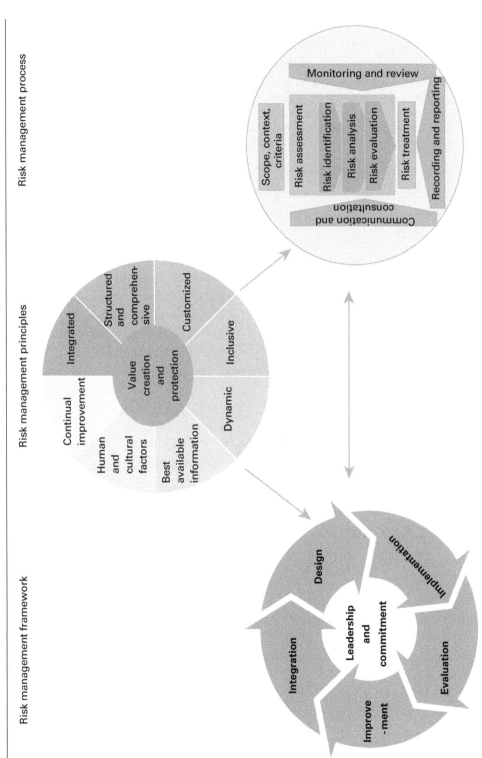

SOURCE Permission to reproduce extracts from ISO 31000 is granted by BSI

standard describes the necessary features of the risk management framework that are required to achieve continuous improvement and implement risk management effectively. This book reorganizes these necessary features into the RASP (Risk architecture, strategy and protocols) framework for risk management, which is set out in Chapter 6 and covers:

- how risk management integrates with the structure of an organization; the risk architecture;
- the tone from the top; the risk strategy, and
- the documentation, tools, methodologies and techniques to support the successful implementation of risk management; the risk protocols.

The risk management process included in this standard consists of six steps, which are condensed in this book, but are usually considered to start with 'scope, context and criteria', followed by 'risk assessment', comprising risk identification (what are the risks?), risk analysis (how big or small are they?) and risk evaluation (so what? – do we need to do anything further?). At this point, the risk treatment step considers what controls can be put in place to modify the risks, and the implementation of these controls. Surrounding these core steps there is communication and consultation (actually considered to be the first step in the standard), monitoring and review, and recording and reporting. These are all important steps in checking, informing and giving assurance that the risks to an organization are being managed effectively, to support decision making at all levels of an organization.

ISO clearly recognizes the interlinkage of the component parts, similar to the COSO ERM cube, by stating the following: 'Although the risk management process is often presented as sequential, in practice it is iterative.'

COSO ERM cube

The COSO ERM (2004) framework is commonly referred to as the COSO ERM cube. It is a very influential risk management framework that was first produced in 2004, and although superseded in 2017, is still used by some organizations, mainly due to its relationship to the COSO internal control framework (the ICF cube).

A diagram of the COSO ERM cube is reproduced here as Figure 3.2 and a brief description of the risk management process within the ERM cube is set out in Table 3.1.

The approach adopted by COSO suggests that enterprise risk management is a multidirectional, iterative process in which almost any component can and does influence all other components. In simple terms, this standard suggests that in order to achieve a successful ERM initiative an organization needs to implement all eight components shown on the front of the cube in relation to each of the four categories of objectives indicated across the top, in all parts of an organization, as indicated on the side of the cube.

Figure 3.2   COSO ERM cube

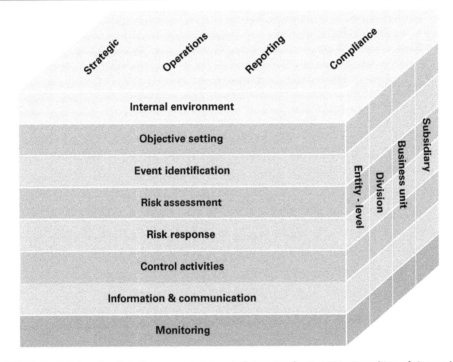

Table 3.1   COSO ERM cube risk management process

Internal environment – The internal environment encompasses the tone of an organization and sets the basis for how risk is viewed and addressed.

Objective setting – Objectives must exist before management can identify potential events affecting their achievement.

Event identification – Internal and external events affecting achievement of objectives must be identified, distinguishing between risks and opportunities.

Risk assessment – Risks are analysed, considering likelihood and impact, as a basis for determining how they should be managed.

Risk response – Management selects risk responses: avoiding, accepting, reducing or sharing risk.

Control activities – Policies and procedures are established and implemented to help ensure the risk responses are effectively carried out.

Information and communication – Relevant information is identified, captured and communicated so that people can fulfil their responsibilities.

Monitoring – The entirety of enterprise risk management is monitored and modifications made as necessary.

COSO ERM rainbow double helix

In 2017 COSO[2] published additional guidance on ERM and how it can be integrated with strategy and performance. The update brings greater focus to the positive contribution to performance that can be made by enterprise risk management.

The basis of the 2017 COSO guidance is that ERM should be embedded into the activities of an organization, beginning with the mission, vision and core values. In developing strategy, business and performance objectives, an organization should consider the implications of the selected strategy, the risks to strategy and performance, and the possibility of the strategy not aligning with core values.

As previously stated, it is instructive to consider the changes or trends that were considered in the design and reissue of this approach. The revision emphasizes that organizations need to become more adaptive to change. In that sense, it reflects the approach to risk stated at the outset in Chapter 1 and its evolution in Chapter 2 where risk management is required because of the fast-paced nature of change for all organizations. The revision declares that leaders need to adopt better thinking on how to manage the increasing volatility, complexity and uncertainty in the marketplace. The updated ERM framework is designed to meet the needs of executive management and the board with a principles-based approach that integrates risk with strategy and performance.

Figure 3.3   COSO ERM rainbow double helix

RECOGNITION OF CULTURE, CAPABILITY AND PRACTICES

The COSO ERM framework also highlights that policies and procedures do not guarantee that risks are being managed. An organization's 'culture, capability and practices' are important aspects in ensuring that the risk management process creates, maintains and protects value, and that risks are managed effectively.

Lessons learned through the financial crisis of 2008 show that the culture, capability and practices were not being considered appropriately, especially by banks and financial institutions. There are many papers and articles on this subject, most noting that there was a perceived culture of financial organizations taking reckless and uncontrolled risks. Blame was also pointed at regulators and consultants, and their monitoring and auditing of consequences of this reckless risk-taking.

More details on risk culture will be provided in Chapter 23.

This updated COSO ERM framework (2017) adopts a components and principles structure. It differentiates between ERM and internal control, noting that both have distinct and different focuses, although they do connect, and enhances the references to risk appetite and risk tolerance.

The framework outlines principles that can be applied from strategic decision making through to performance. These principles are organized into five interrelated components:

1 Governance and culture: Governance sets the tone for an organization and establishes oversight responsibilities for ERM. Culture relates to ethical values, desired behaviours and understanding of risk.

2 Strategy and objective setting: ERM, strategy and objective setting work together in the strategic planning process. Risk appetite should be aligned with strategy and business objectives to successfully implement strategy.

3 Performance: Risks that can impact achievement of strategy and business objectives need to be identified, assessed and prioritized by severity in the context of risk appetite, so that risk responses can be selected. (Note the term 'severity' used here, while the framework itself says that it considers risk as having both positive and negative aspects.)

4 Review and revision: By reviewing entity performance, an organization can consider how well the ERM components are functioning over time and following substantial changes, and what revisions are necessary.

5 Information, communication and reporting: ERM requires a continual process of obtaining and sharing necessary information, from both internal and external sources, which flows up, down and across an organization.

UK HM Treasury Orange Book

The UK Government issued its updated Orange Book: Management of Risk – Principles and Concepts[3] in 2023, providing insight into both risk management and risk control from a public sector perspective. It is intended for use 'by everyone involved in the design, operation and delivery of efficient, trusted public services'.

The Orange Book is based on five risk management principles and its risk control framework:

Part I: Risk Management Principles

A. Governance and Leadership

B. Integration

C. Collaboration and Best Information

D. Risk Management Processes

E. Continual Improvement

Part II: The Risk Control Framework

A. Structure of the Risk Control Framework

B. Assurance

The Guidance is based on best practice from ISO 31000, corporate governance and assurance, combining and relating the practice of risk management and internal control, much as COSO has attempted to do with its enterprise risk management and internal control frameworks.

Updating of risk management terminology

There is considerable benefit in adopting a risk management standard, but it is undoubtedly the case that organizations will need to change and adapt the detailed requirements of that standard to their specific circumstances and/or external, internal and risk management contexts. Greater acceptance of a risk management approach within an organization will be achieved when the approach has been customized by an organization specifically for an organization itself.

An important part of customizing the approach to risk management is to establish the risk terminology to be used throughout an organization. There is considerable variation in the terminology used in different branches of the risk management profession and Appendix B includes alternative definitions for many terms. ISO itself has published two separate guides to risk-related vocabulary: ISO 31073: 2022 Risk Management – Vocabulary and ISO/IEC Guide 51: 2014 Safety aspects – Guidelines for their inclusion in standards.

Figure 3.4 HM Government Orange Book (2023)

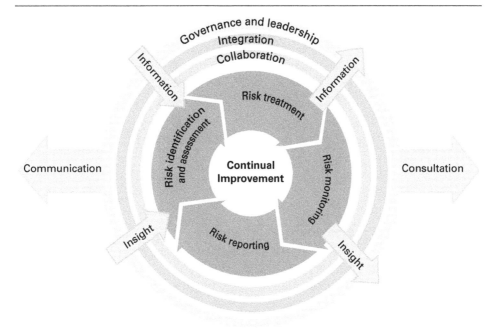

SOURCE HM Government (2023) *The Orange Book: Management of Risk – Principles and Concepts*, p 9, https://assets.publishing.service.gov.uk/government/uploads/system/uploads/attachment_data/file/866117/6.6266_HMT_Orange_Book_Update_v6_WEB.PDF

As various organizations update their terms and definitions, there is a clear shift towards ensuring that any definition of risk includes a consideration of opportunities or the upside of risk. This is reflected in King IV (2016),[4] which states that 'risk thus balances the traditional, negative view of risk with one that recognizes the potential opportunities inherent in some risks'. The COSO 2017 guidance states that organizations need to identify the best framework for optimizing strategy and performance in order to integrate ERM throughout an organization to achieve benefits, including (inter alia) identifying new opportunities.

In addition to risk management standards, there are also a number of internal control standards in existence. These internal control frameworks have a different emphasis and are outside the scope of this book, with the exception of the COSO Internal Control Framework (2013). Both approaches are considered in more detail in Chapters 28 and 29.

As well as developing ISO 31000, work has also been completed on other risk management-related standards and guides within the ISO 31000 'suite'. The guide to risk assessment techniques, IEC 31010:2019: Risk management – Risk assessment techniques is a very comprehensive publication, which reflects current good practice in the selection and utilization of risk assessment techniques. In addition, ISO 31022 (2022) provides guidelines for management of legal risks, ISO/TS 31050 (2023) provides guidelines for managing emerging risks to enhance resilience, and there are other separate standards relating to travel and managing school trips.

Standards institutions around the world have a requirement for routine review of standards, typically every four years. Therefore, the existing standards, as well as those additional standards that are being developed, will be subject to review on a regular basis. This will ensure that the advice and guidance given in the various standards will remain up to date and in line with current practice.

Notes

1 ISO (2018) *ISO 31000: Risk Management – Guidelines*, https://www.iso.org/obp/ui/#iso:std:iso:31000:ed-2:v1:en (archived at https://perma.cc/7KEH-Y5HE)

2 COSO (2017) *Enterprise Risk Management: Integrating with Strategy and Performance*, www.coso.org/documents/2017-coso-erm-integrating-with-strategy-and-performance-executive-summary.pdf (archived at https://perma.cc/4KFC-9BYN)

3 HM Treasury (2023) *The Orange Book: Management of Risk – Principles and Concepts*, https://assets.publishing.service.gov.uk/media/6453acadc33b460012f5e6b8/HMT_Orange_Book_May_2023.pdf (archived at https://perma.cc/38D4-9ENK)

4 Institute of Directors South Africa (2016) *King IV Report*®, https://www.iodsa.co.za/page/king-iv-report (archived at https://perma.cc/E2XX-3SHF)

PART TWO
Enterprise risk management

LEARNING OUTCOMES

Having studied this section readers will be able to:

- Explain the features and importance of the enterprise risk management (ERM) approach.

- Explain the characteristics and benefits of ERM.

- Summarize the principles (proportionate, aligned, comprehensive, embedded and dynamic) and aims of risk management and its importance to strategy, tactics, operations and compliance.

- Describe the key outputs of risk management in terms of mandatory obligations, assurance, decision making and effective and efficient core processes.

- Explain the key components of the risk architecture, strategy and protocols (RASP) for an organization and how these fit together.

- List the main sections of a typical risk management manual, describe the importance of each section and summarize the range of risk documentation and records.

- Explain the importance of the allocation of risk management responsibilities, including the governance responsibilities of non-executive directors.

- Describe the key stages in the risk management process.
- Outline the steps required in order to achieve successful implementation of an enterprise risk management initiative.
- Explain the features of a risk competency framework and the relationship to plan, implement, measure and learn (PIML).
- Outline the need to set risk management performance objectives.

Enterprise risk management

04

Enterprise-wide approach

As explored in Chapter 2, risk management has developed over the course of the last 50 years and has been practised and improved in specialist areas such as portfolios, programmes, projects, energy, finance, health and safety and supply chain risk management. This has delivered benefits in these distinct areas, but it does not benefit an organization as a whole if some areas of risks are well managed within a 'silo' at the expense of the organization as a whole.

There are many examples of organizations that have well-developed and, in some cases, leading-edge risk management practices in, for instance, health and safety risk management areas, but ultimately have failed due to the absence of financial or strategic risk management. For this reason, organizations have embraced the desire to take a broader approach to the practice of risk management.

Various terms have been used to describe this broader approach, including holistic, integrated, strategic, 'risk intelligent'[1] and enterprise-wide risk management. It is the term enterprise or enterprise-wide risk management (ERM) that is now the most widely used and generally accepted terminology for this broader approach.

ERM takes a unifying and more integrated approach. The ERM approach means that an organization looks at the uncertainties that it faces across all operations that it undertakes. ERM is concerned with the opportunities and threats that can impact the objectives, key dependencies, core processes or stakeholder expectations of an organization.

The ERM approach addresses the fact that many risks are interrelated. Even in the smallest or simplest organizations, risks and their controls will be interconnected, where a risk for one person could be another's cause or consequence, and one control could be managing the same or different risks across an organization. Specialist areas of risk management often fail to address the relationship between risks in their field and other internal, or external, risks. The integration and interconnectedness of risks through ERM will be explored further in Chapters 8 and 38.

With the ERM approach, the relationship between risks and their controls can be better recognized and understood, improving engagement and buy-in to the process. This understanding can reduce gaps and overlaps in the management of risks and risk management process, thereby improving efficiency and reducing effort. Many disasters have arisen in the past because of the failure to address the interconnectivity of risks, an example of which is provided in the box below.

FAILING TO RECOGNIZE THE INTERCONNECTEDNESS OF RISKS

bp's 2010 investigation into the causes of the Gulf of Mexico tragedy at the Macondo Well highlights how risks are related:

- The cement and shoe track barriers at the bottom of the well failed to contain hydrocarbons within the reservoir.

- The results of negative pressure tests were incorrectly accepted by bp and Transocean.

- The Transocean rig crew failed to recognize the influx of hydrocarbons.

- The well-flow was routed to a mud-gas separator, venting gas directly onto the rig, rather than overboard.

- The gas flowed into the engine rooms, which was not prevented by the fire and gas system on the rig.

- The rig's blow-out preventer on the seabed failed to automatically seal the well after the explosion.

SOURCE Extract from bp report on causes of Gulf of Mexico tragedy, https://www.bp.com/en/global/corporate/news-and-insights/press-releases/bp-releases-report-on-causes-of-gulf-of-mexico-tragedy.html

---

Organizations practise risk management in a number of different ways. However, there are many common features to most of these approaches. Table 4.1 gives an overview of the features of enterprise risk management as a comparison to the silo-based approach whereby risk management tools and techniques are applied to different types of risks independently. ERM allows an organization to gain an overview of all the risks it faces so that it can take co-ordinated actions to manage these risks. Nevertheless, the specialist risk management functions, such as health and safety and business continuity, continue to make a valuable contribution.

This more integrated or holistic approach can be considered to be a unifying philosophy that draws together management of all types of risks, rather than a new or different approach.

When an organization considers all the risks that it faces and how these risks could impact its strategy, projects and operations, it is embarking on an ERM approach. The US risk management association, the Risk and Insurance Managers Society (RIMS),[2] defines enterprise risk management as:

> A strategic business discipline that supports the achievement of an organization's objectives by addressing the full spectrum of its risks and managing the combined impact of those risks as an interrelated risk portfolio.

An enterprise-wide approach has considerable advantages, because it analyses the potential for disruption to overall stakeholder expectations. Health and safety, for example, is then viewed as a component in ensuring that staff are always available so that the overall operational core process will not be disrupted, rather than (or perhaps as well as) a separate hazard management issue.

An example of the ERM approach is to consider a sports team where the key objective is to maximize attendance at games. This process is made up of several activities, including marketing, advertising, allocation and sale of tickets as well as logistical arrangements to ensure that the experience at the game is as good as possible. Part of maximizing attendance at games will be to ensure there are adequate parking and transport arrangements, together with suitable catering and other welfare arrangements in the ground.

Table 4.1   Features of an enterprise-wide approach

1	Encompasses all areas of organizational exposure to risk (financial, operational, reporting, compliance, governance, strategic, reputational, etc.).
2	Prioritizes and manages those exposures as an interrelated risk portfolio rather than as individual 'silos' of risk.
3	Evaluates the risk portfolio in the context of all significant internal and external contexts, systems, circumstances and stakeholders.
4	Recognizes that individual risks across an organization are interrelated and can create a combined exposure that differs from the sum of the individual risks.
5	Provides a structured process for the management of all risks, whether those risks are primarily quantitative or qualitative in nature.
6	Seeks to embed risk management as a component in all critical decisions throughout an organization.
7	Provides a means for an organization to identify the risks that it is willing to take in order to achieve strategic objectives.
8	Constructs a means of communicating on risks, so that there is a common understanding of those faced by an organization, and their importance.
9	Supports the activities of internal audit by providing a structure for the provision of assurance to the board and audit committee.
10	Views the effective management of risk as a competitive advantage that contributes to the achievement of business and strategic objectives.

By identifying the key activities that deliver the selected core process, the team is able to identify the risks that could impact both these activities and the core process. Targets can then be set for increased attendance at future games, and responsibility for the success of this core process has been allocated to the commercial director of the club. A consideration of the opportunities for increasing attendance at games can also be included in this broader approach.

Risk management and business continuity management

There is an important relationship between enterprise risk management (ERM) and business continuity management. The risk assessment required as part of the enterprise risk management process and the business impact analysis that is the basis of business continuity management (BCM) are closely related. The concept of BCM additionally feeds into the idea of 'resilience', which is a concept that is further discussed in Chapter 31.

The ERM approach to risk management is to evaluate objectives and identify the individual risks that could impact these objectives. The output from a business impact analysis is the identification of the critical activities that must be maintained for an organization to continue to function.

As such, the ERM and the BCM approaches are very similar, with both requiring the identification of functions that must be in place for the continuity and success of the business. This linkage between risk management and business continuity tools is also highlighted in Chapter 10 when considering the first step of risk management and the context in which organizations operate.

Where ERM and BCM differ is in timing and structural elements. ERM is concerned with the management of risks that could impact core processes and looks across an organization in an integrated fashion. Business continuity management is concerned with actions that should be taken to maintain the continuity of individual activities. The BCM approach has the very specific function of identifying responses that should be taken after the risk has materialized in order to minimize its impact. BCM relates to resuming operations with as minimal an impact on an organization as possible, for example cost containment and customer retention, as described in Chapter 31.

Over the longer term, ERM will enhance enterprise resilience – the ability to anticipate and respond to change. It helps organizations identify factors that represent not just risk, but change, and how that change could impact performance and necessitate a shift in strategy. All organizations need to set strategy and periodically adjust it, always staying aware of both ever-changing opportunities for creating value and the challenges that will occur in pursuit of that value.

Integrating strategy and performance

The COSO internal control model and its ERM frameworks of 2004 and 2017 were discussed in Chapter 3. The COSO 2017 framework was a response to the recognition that there needed to be stronger links between strategy, risk and performance. The later ERM framework clearly connects ERM stakeholder expectations, positions risk in the context of an organization's performance, and enables organizations to better anticipate risk.

It puts forward the argument that integrating ERM practices throughout an organization will help to accelerate growth and enhance performance. The advice is to build on the current level of risk management that already exists in the normal course of business.

The intention of the revised framework is to elevate discussion of strategy, enhance the alignment between performance and ERM, and more explicitly link ERM into decision making. The framework outlines principles that can be applied from strategic decision making through to performance. There is greater emphasis on the relationship between risk and value. Also, the benefits of the integration of ERM are emphasized. Finally, the revised framework underlines the role of culture in the achievement of successful enterprise risk management.

In addition, changes to the UK Corporate Governance Code[3] in January 2024 place more emphasis on the implementation of risk management in both the setting and the execution of an organization's strategy. More information on corporate governance will be provided in Chapter 27.

Organizations need to identify the best framework for optimizing strategy and performance in order to integrate ERM throughout an organization to achieve benefits, including:

- Increase the range of opportunities: Identify new opportunities and unique challenges associated with current opportunities.
- Identify and manage risk entity-wide: To sustain and improve performance.
- Increase positive outcomes and reduce negative surprises: Identify responses, reduce surprises and related costs or losses, while profiting from advantageous developments.
- Reduce performance variability: Anticipate the risks that would affect performance and put in place the actions needed to minimize disruption and maximize opportunity.

- Improve resource deployment: Assess overall resource needs, prioritize resource deployment and enhance resource allocation.

- Enhance enterprise resilience: Anticipate and respond to change, not only to survive but also to evolve and thrive.

ERM in practice

By taking a comprehensive approach to enterprise risk management, a wide range of benefits can be delivered, and these are set out in Table 4.2 and considered in detail in Chapter 40. It is for each organization to decide how the ERM initiative will be structured and how these benefits will be achieved. The benefits have been collated here using the FIRM risk scorecard (Financial, Infrastructure, Reputational, Marketplace), which is used elsewhere in the book as a useful categorization tool.

The key feature of ERM is that the full range of significant risks facing an organization is evaluated. The interrelationship between risks should be identified, so that the total risk exposure of an organization may be compiled. Having measured the total risk exposure of an organization, that level of risk exposure can then be compared with the risk appetite of the board and the risk capacity of an organization itself.

Table 4.2   Benefits of enterprise risk management

FIRM risk scorecard	Benefits
Financial	Reduced cost of funding and capital Better control of Capex approvals Increased profitability for organization Accurate financial risk reporting Enhanced corporate governance
Infrastructure	Efficiency and competitive advantage Resilience Improved supplier and staff morale Targeted risk and cost reduction Reduced operating costs
Reputational	Regulators satisfied Improved utilization of company brand Enhanced shareholder value Good reputation and publicity Improved perception of organization
Marketplace	Commercial opportunities maximized Better marketplace presence Increased customer spend (and satisfaction) Higher ratio of business successes Lower ratio of business disasters

Notes

1   Deloitte Risk Advisory (2015) Enterprise Risk Management: A risk intelligent approach, www.deloitte.com/uk/en/pages/risk/articles/enterprise-risk-management.html (archived at https://perma.cc/TL36-5VF9)

2   RIMS – the Risk Management Society (2021) About strategic and enterprise risk management (SERM), www.rims.org/resources/strategic-enterprise-risk-center/about-serm (archived at https://perma.cc/5WJ4-TQGN)

3   FRC (2024), UK Corporate Governance Code, https://media.frc.org.uk/documents/ UK_Corporate_Governance_Code_2024_ofM100g.pdf (archived at https://perma.cc/ NTK3-BKD2)

Risk management aims and principles 05

The aims of risk management

The importance of risk management has been explored in Chapter 1, and the benefits of adopting an enterprise approach are considered in Chapter 4. However, the real purpose or aims of implementing risk management should be bespoke for each organization.

The aims usually reflect an organization's risk management maturity. At the lower levels of maturity, the aims may be solely to be compliant – ticking boxes to indicate that a risk register exists or that the board talk about principal risks once a year, perhaps. In more mature organizations, risk management will be implemented to ensure it benefits an organization in two ways: tangibly, in terms of visible resource reductions, protection of reputation, or increase in share price, for example; and intangibly, in relation to improved risk attitudes, behaviour and culture. As such, it is being used to create, maintain and protect value. Risk management maturity is considered further in Chapter 39.

As part of setting the aims for risk management, organizations should consider what 'good' risk management should look like for them. One way to do this is to understand the principles of risk management.

Principles and attributes of risk management

The main purpose of risk management is that it delivers value to an organization by applying practices designed to achieve the best possible outcome, reducing volatility or uncertainty. This is achieved through the application of a broader set of aims and principles. There have been several attempts to define these principles.

As noted in Chapter 3, risk management standards and frameworks often contain principles, such as the twenty which support the five components of the COSO ERM Framework (2017),[1] or the five that are the basis for the UK Government's Orange

Table 5.1 Attributes of risk management (PACED)

Attribute	Description
Proportionate	Risk management activities must be proportionate to the level of risk faced by an organization.
Aligned	Risk management activities need to be aligned with the other activities in an organization.
Comprehensive	In order to be fully effective, the risk management approach must consider the full profile of risk to an organization, from both the internal and external context, and to look across an organization, rather than in silos.
Embedded	Risk management activities need to be embedded within an organization, taking account of the risk attitudes, behaviours and culture that currently exist and that may need to be improved.
Dynamic	Risk management activities must be dynamic and responsive to emerging and changing contexts, risks and controls.

SOURCE Adapted from Institute of Risk Management (2018) *Standard Deviations: A risk practitioner's guide to ISO 31000*, www.theirm.org/media/6907/irm-report-iso-31000-2018-v2.pdf

Book (2023).[2] The principles for these two approaches contain information on the 'how to' rather than just the 'why' implement risk management. Some lists of principles also include information on what risk management should do or deliver.

ISO 31000[3] includes a detailed list of the suggested principles of risk management, which outline the characteristics of effective and efficient risk management, highlighting the value that it can provide and its intention and purpose, which were considered in Chapter 3.

In Table 5.1 the acronym 'PACED' combines the eight principles of ISO 31000 to provide five attributes of effective risk management, which are the foundations of a successful approach to risk management within any organization.

Objectives of risk management

The five objectives for risk management being mandatory, assurance, decision making, and effective and efficient core processes, provide the acronym MADE2, with detail on each objective in Table 5.2. This denotes less disruption to normal operations, improved decisions in relation to evaluation and selection of alternative strategies and proactive management of risks in relation to tactics. In other words, a key part of risk management is improved organizational decision making.

The resources available for managing risk are finite, so risks should be evaluated and actions prioritized accordingly. The appropriate range of responses will depend on the nature, size and complexity of an organization and the risks it faces.

Table 5.2   Risk management objectives (MADE2)

Objective	Description
Mandatory	The basic objective for any risk management initiative is to ensure conformity with applicable rules, regulations and mandatory obligations.
Assurance	The board and audit committee of an organization will require assurance that risk management and internal control activities comply with PACED.
Decision making	Risk management activities should ensure that appropriate risk-based information is available to support decision making.
Effective and efficient core processes	Risk management considerations will assist with achieving effective and efficient strategy, tactics, operations and compliance to ensure the best outcome with reduced volatility of results.

As well as assisting with better decision making and improved efficiency, risk management also contributes to the provision of greater assurance to stakeholders through a formal process to identify risk and the consistent application of responses. This in turn allows for better reporting of information by organizations, including risk information. For example, the Sarbanes–Oxley Act of 2002 (SOX)[4] in the US has accuracy of financial reporting as its main requirement. It brings the issue of the accurate reporting of results to a higher priority (section 404), while also requiring full and accurate disclosure of all information about an organization (section 302).

Although SOX is a specific piece of legislation that only applies in certain circumstances, the principles it contains are vitally important to all risk management practitioners. Accordingly, Chapters 27 to 29 of this book consider governance, risk assurance and accurate reporting as integral components of the overall risk management process.

When deciding the importance of risk management in an organization, the design of the risk management initiative and the risk management framework should reflect the reasons why risk management is being undertaken in an organization, in terms of MADE2. These decisions will need to be taken with due regard to the risk management drivers for the particular organization. The drivers may be related to a particular consideration within MADE2, such as the effectiveness and efficiency of operational core processes.

For example, some organizations have appointed a loss control manager with specific responsibility for reducing the frequency and cost of accidents to people and of damage to plant and equipment. Sometimes, the initiative will be based on the desire to improve the reputation of an organization by enhanced compliance with applicable rules and regulations, or the ability to demonstrate more ethical behaviour – including in the supply chain.

Achieving benefits

This chapter has considered the aims and principles of risk management, what risk management should be and what it should deliver. Although organizations may realize that there are benefits from implementing risk management, its successful implementation has to be undertaken as a programme. Chapter 9 sets out the stages involved in the successful implementation of enterprise-wide risk management.

A critical success factor in this is the support of senior management and the sponsorship of the board. Also, as part of the programme to implement risk management the concerns of employees and other stakeholders need to be considered. This is normally included within the communication element of the programme. Although risk management is vital to the success of an organization, it is equally vital to communicate the benefits of the approach in order to persuade managers to engage with and implement the approach.

It is important to note that not all activities and functions undertaken by managers should be claimed by the risk manager as being done in the name of risk management. Not all activities in an organization will be driven by risk management, even if all decisions, processes, procedures and activities have risks embedded within them.

Notes

1 COSO (2017) *Enterprise Risk Management: Integrating with strategy and performance*, www.coso.org/documents/2017-coso-erm-integrating-with-strategy-and-performance-executive-summary.pdf (archived at https://perma.cc/4KFC-9BYN)

2 HM Treasury (2023) *The Orange Book: Management of Risk – Principles and Concepts*, https://assets.publishing.service.gov.uk/media/6453acadc33b460012f5e6b8/HMT_Orange_Book_May_2023.pdf (archived at https://perma.cc/6S99-856F)

3 ISO (2018) *ISO 31000: Risk Management – Guidelines*, https://www.iso.org/obp/ui/#iso:std:iso:31000:ed-2:v1:en (archived at https://perma.cc/6ALZ-CA45)

4 Sarbanes Oxley 101 (2024) *Sarbanes Oxley (2002) 101*, https://sarbanes-oxley-101.com/ (archived at https://perma.cc/W9V3-4JRR)

Risk management framework – risk architecture, strategy and protocols 06

Risk management framework

In many risk management standards, it is stated that risk management activities should take place within the context of the business environment, an organization and the risks faced by an organization. In order for the risk management to be implemented effectively and embedded, it must fit into that context of how an organization operates.

All of the established risk management standards refer to the risk management framework, although this is represented in different ways. In order to provide a simple explanation of the scope of the risk management framework, the acronym risk architecture, strategy and protocols (RASP) has been developed. Figure 6.1 illustrates the key features of a risk management framework that is built around and supports the risk management process. The RASP approach is entirely consistent with the risk management framework described in ISO 31000, and other standards.

The risk management framework has two separate considerations. Firstly, it must be supportive of the risk management process, and secondly it must ensure that the outputs from the process are communicated to an organization and achieve the anticipated benefits for an organization.

The framework should then include the structure, responsibilities, administration, reporting and communication components of risk management to ensure that it is customized to the needs of an organization, and is integrated with other functions and activities. All these components would then be recorded in a 'manual' for risk management, which is considered further in Chapter 7.

Figure 6.1 Risk management framework (RASP)

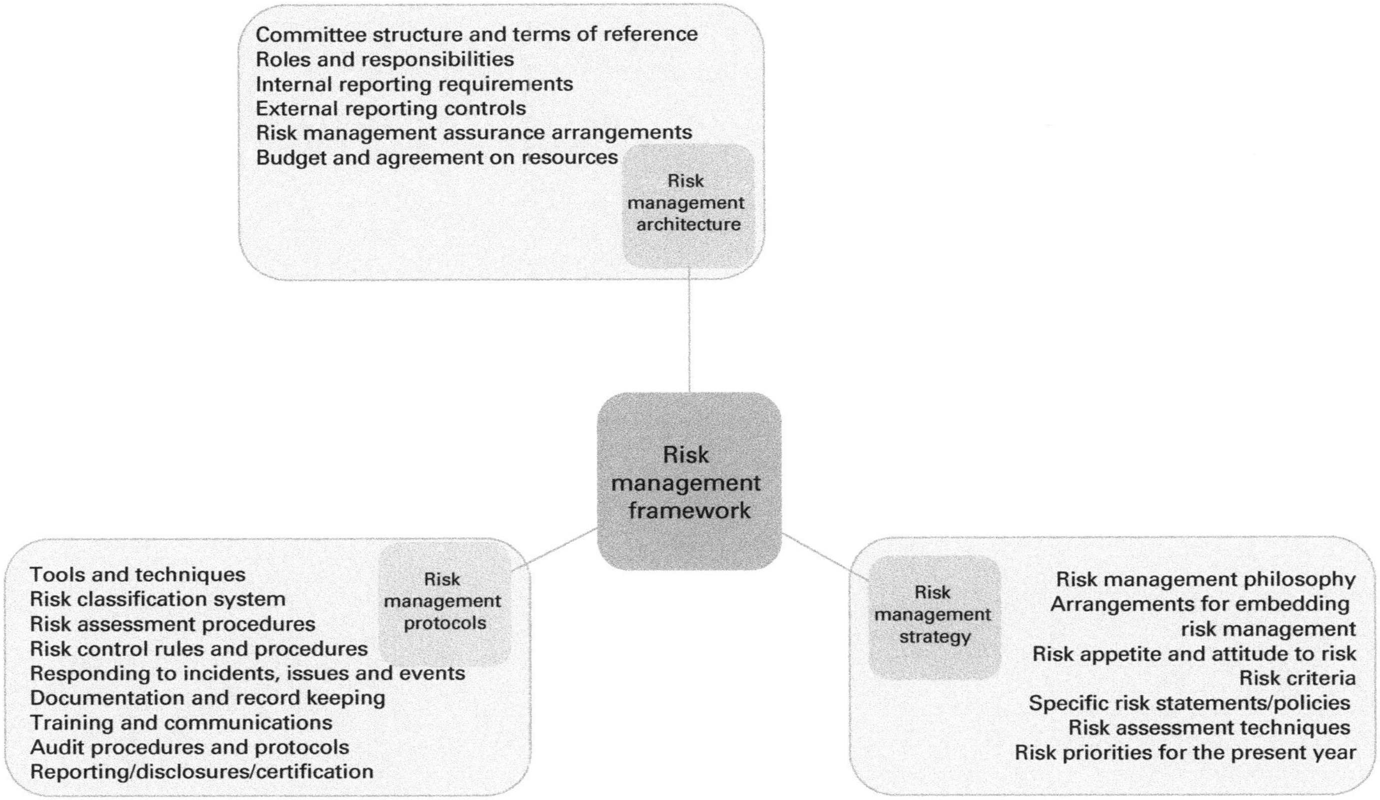

Risk management framework

Risk management architecture

Committee structure and terms of reference
Roles and responsibilities
Internal reporting requirements
External reporting controls
Risk management assurance arrangements
Budget and agreement on resources

Risk management strategy

Risk management philosophy
Arrangements for embedding risk management
Risk appetite and attitude to risk
Risk criteria
Specific risk statements/policies
Risk assessment techniques
Risk priorities for the present year

Risk management protocols

Tools and techniques
Risk classification system
Risk assessment procedures
Risk control rules and procedures
Responding to incidents, issues and events
Documentation and record keeping
Training and communications
Audit procedures and protocols
Reporting/disclosures/certification

It is these elements that define the framework within which the risk management process takes place. These three components of risk architecture, strategy and protocols are required for successful risk management activities. There needs to be a thorough understanding of the risk management process, followed by a clear definition of the framework that supports the process.

Architecture, strategy and protocols

The risk architecture, strategy and protocols consider how risk management can be embedded into the operation of an organization. Implementing risk management without understanding how things are done and decisions made, would lead to the process being 'bolted on' rather than 'built in'.

The architecture considers the structure of an organization and how decisions are made. It also defines how information on risk is communicated throughout an organization. The risk strategy provides the 'tone from the top', defining the overall objectives that an organization is trying to achieve with respect to risk management. Finally, the protocols provide the supporting material allowing people to implement risk management, basically the systems, standards and procedures that are put in place in order to fulfil the defined risk strategy. The risk management framework, in turn, is part of the overall risk governance arrangements within an organization.

Risk architecture

The risk management arrangements for an organization can be described as the risk architecture. The risk architecture sets out lines of communication for reporting on risk management issues and events and allocating ownership of particular risks within an organization. It also defines the governance arrangements in relation to risk management.

In order that risk management can be fully embedded into the core processes and operations of an organization, a clear statement of risk management responsibilities is required. Risk management responsibilities need to be clearly allocated to the following aspects of managing that risk:

- development of risk strategy and standards;
- implementation of the agreed standards and procedures;
- auditing compliance with the agreed standards.

The risk architecture can be represented diagrammatically as a means of identifying the committees with risk management responsibilities and the relationships between those committees. The risk architecture will include the terms of reference of the various committees, including details of the membership and responsibilities of those committees.

In addition, risk management roles and responsibilities at other levels within an organization should form part of the risk architecture, as well as guidance on how risk information is communicated between the various committees and across an organization. An important aspect of the risk architecture is to ensure that risk escalation procedures are embedded within an organization, including appropriate whistle-blowing arrangements.

The working relationship between risk management and internal control is critically important. The risk architecture should set out the details of how this close cooperation will be achieved in practice. As discussed further in Chapter 28, corporate governance requirements in many countries mandate both risk management and internal control frameworks. Risk management expertise rests in the assessment of risk and the identification of existing and additional controls. Internal control expertise usually rests with compliance and audit in the evaluation of controls and the testing of their efficiency and effectiveness.

More details on the different risk-related roles and responsibilities are provided in Chapter 7.

Risk architecture in practice

Figure 6.2 shows the risk architecture for a typical large corporate entity that is subject to the requirements of the Sarbanes–Oxley Act in the US. This risk architecture should be set out in the risk management manual for an organization. Terms of reference of the various committees and a schedule of the activities should also be established, either in the risk management manual or in a calendar of risk management activities. This schedule of activities should be aligned with the other corporate activities in an organization.

For a large organization with non-executive directors, the audit committee should also be shown in the risk architecture. The role of the audit committee and the role of the head of internal audit are important in fulfilling the risk management strategy of an organization.

For organizations subject to the requirements of the Sarbanes–Oxley Act, there will also be a requirement to ensure that all information disclosed by the company is accurate. In many large organizations, this requirement has resulted in the establishment of a disclosures committee. The role of the disclosures committee is to check the source and correctness of all information that is disclosed by an organization. Sarbanes–Oxley requires that financial information is evaluated to a higher level of scrutiny.

The risk architecture of an organization sets out the hierarchy of committees and responsibilities related to risk management and internal control. In the structure shown in Figure 6.2, the corporate risk management committee focuses on executive risk management activities.

Risk management responsibilities for activities at divisional or unit level should be allocated to divisional management. Divisional management is responsible for coordinating the identification of significant risks at divisional level, compiling the risk register for the division and ensuring that adequate controls are identified and implemented.

Figure 6.2   Risk architecture for a large corporation

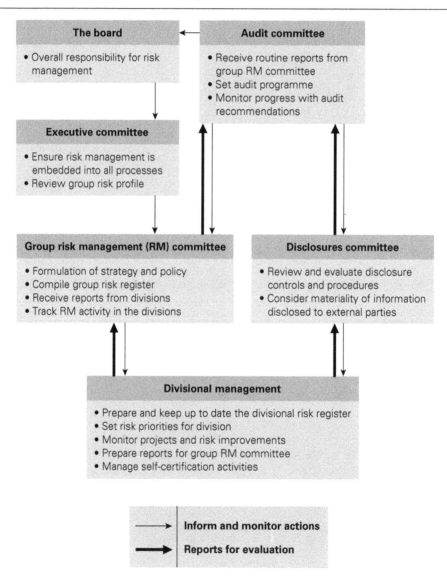

For a public sector or charity organization, the risk architecture will be somewhat different. Figure 6.3 sets out a typical risk architecture for a charity. In this case, risk management activities are focused on the governance and risk committee. The flow of information and the control of risk management activities are illustrated by the arrows in Figure 6.3.

Figure 6.3   Risk architecture for a charity

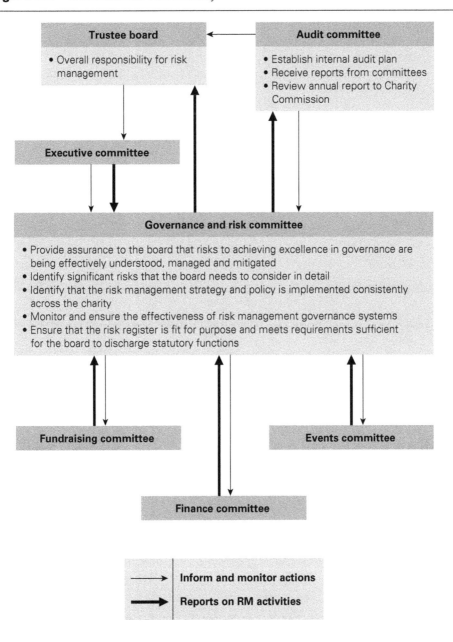

It is clear from Figure 6.3 that risk governance for charities is often a much higher-profile issue than in many other organizations. This implies that trustees of charities may consider that governance is more important than raising money for the charity that they support. This could be an example of concerns about risk management becoming so great that they deform the nature of an organization.

There are many ways for risk management reporting lines to be established. The reporting structure should be proportionate to the level of risk and the complexity of an organization. For high-risk organizations, such as those in the finance sector, the risk committee is likely to be a direct sub-committee of the board. In these circumstances, it is likely that the risk committee will be chaired by a senior director along with other senior representation from the board.

For organizations that are not operating in such a high-risk environment, it may not be necessary for the risk committee to directly report to the main board. In these circumstances, the risk committee may be a sub-committee of the executive committee or the operations committee.

However, there are no specified correct structures for the risk architecture of an organization. Provided that the risk committee delivers the required outputs, the membership and terms of reference will be for an organization to decide. Nevertheless, the general point remains that management of risk is an executive function, whereas audit activities should be led by non-executive directors.

More information on risk committees can be found in Chapter 7, and on committees of the board, in Chapter 27.

Risk strategy

It is important for an organization to have a clearly established strategy in relation to risk management and its purpose. The risk management strategy for an organization will be set out in the risk management policy statement. The strategy needs to be based on the overall approach of an organization to risk and risk management. An important component of that risk strategy will be the requirement that there is risk management input into strategy, tactics, operations and compliance (STOC).

Decisions will also have to be made in relation to the risk processes that will be adopted by an organization, as well as about the design and implementation of the risk management initiative that will be planned and implemented in order to fulfil the requirements of the risk strategy.

The risk management strategy will state what an organization is seeking to achieve. The strategy may set out what level of risk maturity is desired, together with the information on the level of contribution that is expected from risk management. In effect, the risk management strategy will establish the way in which risk management activities are aligned with the other activities in an organization and the contribution that is expected from risk management activities.

In order to establish the risk management strategy, important decisions will also need to be made about the risk appetite of an organization, ensuring that it is within the total risk capacity of an organization. Decisions will need to be taken on how the risk capacity will be calculated and how the total risk exposure of an organization will be captured and used in decision-making processes. More details on risk appetite statements can be found later in this chapter and in Chapter 26.

Risk management policy

The risk strategy component will normally be set out as a high-level or one-page statement of what an organization is seeking to achieve with respect to risk management. ISO 31073[1] refers to this one-page statement as the risk management policy and defines it as the 'statement of overall intentions and direction of an organization related to risk management'.

In the updated UK Corporate Governance Code from the FRC,[2] Boards are required to monitor an organization's risk management and internal control framework and, at least annually, carry out a review of its effectiveness. The FRC guidance suggests that this is undertaken through an organization's oversight procedures, although the board may wish to define how it wants to operate the monitoring of the framework in its policy. The guidance also suggests that the board may wish to include in the review whether the frameworks and procedures are in line with current market standard or practices.

Some organizations have a separate policy document, and others may have it as the opening statement in a risk management manual. It is common to find the risk management policy is kept as a separate short document. It is also usually the outward face of risk management for organizations; the document that is shared with third parties on request or hosted on an organization's website stating why they are doing risk management.

Although the risk management framework contains the architecture, strategy and protocols, the board is not required to approve all documents related to the framework. Typically, boards approve policies, but do not approve documents such as the risk management manual. Although boards should be engaged in the effectiveness of the framework, they are more involved in the strategic direction of an organization through the policy (the why), rather than the detail of how an organization gets there in the manual (the how to). More detail on the risk management manual is covered in Chapter 7.

The next box features a statement from the constitution of the Royal Borough of Kensington and Chelsea. This is the council that owned and outsourced management of the Grenfell Tower block, which caught fire in 2019 in the worst civil disaster in the UK since the Second World War. As can be seen in this policy, there is clear commitment to effective implementation of risk management, including explicit responsibilities for the board and executive team, which is required for a risk management statement/policy to be of any practical use.

A RISK MANAGEMENT POLICY FOR A COUNCIL

The Constitution of the Royal Borough of Kensington and Chelsea

Part 8: Procedures; Section 3: Financial procedure rules; Sub-section 5: Risk management and control of resources

Risk Management and Internal Control covers risk management and insurance, internal control, audit requirements, preventing fraud and corruption, assets, treasury management, investments and borrowing, trust funds and funds held for third parties, banking, imprest accounts and staffing costs.

1.12 The Audit and Transparency Committee is responsible for agreeing the authority's risk management policy statement and strategy and for reviewing the effectiveness of risk management within the Council.

1.13 The Executive Director Resources & Assets is responsible for developing, maintaining and advising upon robust systems for risk management and the control of resources. This will be monitored through an effective internal audit function.

1.14 Executive Directors are responsible for establishing and operating sound arrangements within these systems to manage and mitigate risk and for notifying the Executive Director Resources & Assets of any suspected non-compliance.

Part 5: Committees and non-executive functions; Section 2: Terms of reference of council committees; Sub-section 5: Audit and Transparency Committee

5.1 The purpose of the Audit and Transparency Committee is:

i. to provide independent assurance on corporate governance arrangements; the adequacy of the risk management framework and the associated control environment; independent scrutiny of the authority's financial and non-financial performance to the extent that it affects the authority's exposure to risk and weakens the control environment; and oversight of the financial reporting process;

ii. to oversee Council transparency; and

iii. to consider any complaints against Councillors referred to it following an investigation.

5.10 Terms of Reference, item (xvi) To monitor the effective development and operation of risk management in the Council.

SOURCE Royal Borough of Kensington and Chelsea (2021) The constitution, www.rbkc.gov.uk/council-councillors-and-democracy/how-council-works/constitution

Although many organizations include information on their risk appetite in the organization's risk management policy, it is common to find that a separate risk appetite statement document is produced.

Risk appetite statement

Risk appetite provides direction in relation to the amount of risk an organization is willing to take or accept in pursuit of its strategic objectives. Risk appetite should be approved by the board, aligned with strategy and embedded at the appropriate levels of decision making within an organization.

A risk appetite statement is a management tool that provides guidance from leadership to staff and puts decisions regarding the amount of risk that is acceptable (or not) in writing, tying them to an organization's objectives. It is a living document and critical to risk management since it helps to establish parameters and priorities for policies, procedures and internal controls.

Risk appetite statements will exist at the strategic, tactical and operational levels of an organization, from the external statements made through regulatory reporting through to detailed delegated levels of authority.

Further detail on risk appetite statements is given in Chapter 26.

Risk protocols

Most large organizations will document their risk protocols as a set of risk management guidelines. The range of guidelines that are required will vary according to the size, nature and complexity of an organization. The types of documentation that are usually kept include:

- risk management administration records;
- risk response and improvement plans;
- event reports and recommendations;
- risk performance and monitoring reports.

When considering the range of documentation that needs to be produced, organizations should distinguish between the risk protocols that are captured as part of the risk management manual and those documents or reports that are intended to track and monitor changes and improvements. The risk management manual is more of a static record of processes and procedures, whereas the other documentation, for example the risk register, should be a dynamic record of actions that are planned or are in progress.

Procedures and protocols for undertaking the assessment of risks to strategy, tactics (projects) and operations will need to be established in writing. An organization will also need to produce guidance on the frequency and nature of risk reports and who is responsible for compiling the information.

Risk management protocols are usually reviewed on a regular basis, so that they are kept up to date and an organization is taking advantage of any new technology that may have become available.

In large organizations, there is typically a quarterly review of the dynamic risk register, with a longer review cycle for the more 'static' policy, manual and associated documents. For organizations in the UK, the updated Corporate Governance Code requires an annual review of the risk management framework. More information on the review of risks and risk management is provided in Chapter 21.

A range of risk management protocols will need to be produced, and a typical set of protocols is listed in Table 6.1, indicating the extent of risk management guidelines or protocols that may need to be produced by an organization. This should not be seen as an exhaustive list and other types of protocols, guidelines or procedures may be necessary, depending on the exact nature of an organization and the risk strategy that it is following.

Table 6.1   Risk management protocols

1	**Risk assessment procedures**	Governance procedures
		Risk appetite requirements
		Response to significant risks
		Projects and Capex approvals
		Procedures for strategy and budgets
2	**Risk control objectives**	Brand management guidelines
		Health and safety at work
		Environmental protection
		Contract risk management
3	**Risk resourcing arrangements**	Project resource allocation
		Insurance programme
		Captive insurance company
4	**Reaction planning requirements**	Loss and claims management
		Disaster and recovery planning
		Cost containment procedures
		Risk management record-keeping
5	**Risk assurance systems**	Maintenance of risk register
		Corporate RM committee
		Terms of reference for audit committee
		Control self-certification arrangements

The risk management protocols can be seen as the standing instructions relating to risk management. They will often require the keeping of records, for example the risk register. The risk protocols should also describe the extent of record-keeping that is required. The detailed risk management protocols or guidelines will set out:

- risk assessment procedures;
- risk control objectives;
- risk resourcing arrangements;
- reaction planning requirements;
- risk assurance systems.

More information on documentation, in particular the risk management manual and risk registers, can be found in Chapter 7.

Notes

1 ISO (2022) *ISO 31073: Risk management – vocabulary*, https://www.iso.org/obp/ui/en/# iso:std:iso:31073:ed-1:v1:en (archived at https://perma.cc/FJK5-VWBA)
2 FRC (2024) *UK Corporate Governance Code*, https://media.frc.org.uk/documents/UK_ Corporate_Governance_Code_2024_ofM100g.pdf (archived at https://perma.cc/AWL6- H8DW)

Roles, responsibilities and documentation

07

Roles and responsibilities

Everybody working for an organization will need to be made aware of their risk management responsibilities, as will contractors and suppliers. There are many professional people in large organizations who have an understanding of risk and a substantial contribution to make to the successful management of the priority significant risks. Unfortunately, there is not always a common view of risk management or the issues that are important to an organization.

Ownership of core processes, key dependencies and risks is key, because it enables the risk management and audit committees (see Part Six) to monitor actions and responsibilities. This ownership is important for all risks, although the audit committee will only monitor the priority significant risks.

Any confusion of responsibilities and reporting structure must be eliminated. There should be clear statements of responsibilities for the following aspects of the management of each priority significant risk:

- setting required risk standards;
- implementing risk standards;
- monitoring risk performance.

A detailed set of responsibilities will ensure that the roles of risk owners, process owners, internal audit, risk management functions, members of staff, contractors and outsourced operations as well as all others are clearly defined and understood. The allocation of responsibilities to committees, as part of the risk architecture, is also an important consideration. The membership, responsibilities and reporting structure will normally be described in the terms of reference of each committee.

As stated at the start of this chapter, everyone in an organization has responsibility for risk management. Although specialist risk management roles will exist in most organizations, and there is overall accountability for risk at different levels of management leadership, there is still a responsibility on anyone in an organization to say something about activities, practices or behaviour that deviate from the expected.

Information on ownership of each risk should be included in the risk register. It is important that the activities of the risk manager, risk management committee, audit committee, internal auditors and others do not reduce local ownership of significant risks. Managers must see ownership of risks as integral to the management of core processes and business activities, not as a separate issue that is the responsibility of specialist professional risk management and/or internal audit practitioners.

Range of responsibilities

Table 7.1 sets out examples of the range of risk management responsibilities of line management, the main functional departments and individual employees involved in risk management. The risk management professionals involved may also include the following individuals, depending on the size of an organization:

- insurance risk manager;
- corporate treasurer;
- finance director;
- internal auditor;
- compliance manager;
- health, safety and environment manager;
- business continuity manager.

The structure of Table 7.1 is also important. Items 1, 2 and 3 allocate responsibilities to the management of an organization. Item 1 is concerned with the allocation of responsibilities to top management, being the executive. Item 2 is concerned with the allocation of responsibilities to heads of department or middle management. Item 3 is concerned with the allocation of risk management responsibilities to staff. Together, these three layers of management represent the first line of assurance in ensuring that adequate attention is paid to risk management and internal control.

Item 4 of Table 7.1 describes the responsibilities of the risk manager for an organization. Item 5 sets out the responsibilities of specialist risk management functions, such as health and safety or business continuity. In providing specialist support to management, these functions may be considered to be the second line of assurance in achieving satisfactory risk management and internal control. Item 6 of Table 7.1 sets out the responsibilities of the internal audit manager. Internal audit activities may be considered to be the third line of assurance in ensuring adequate standards of risk management and internal control. These lines of assurance will be considered further in Chapter 29.

Table 7.1   Risk management responsibilities

Key roles	Key responsibilities
1. The CEO	Determine strategic approach to risk Establish the structure for risk management Understand the most significant risks Consider the risk implications of poor decisions Manage an organization in a crisis
2. The location manager	Build risk-aware culture within the location Agree risk management performance targets for the location Evaluate reports from employees on risk management matters Ensure implementation of risk improvement recommendations Identify and report changed circumstances/risks
3. Individual employees	Understand, accept and implement RM processes Report inefficient, unnecessary or unworkable controls Report loss events and near-miss incidents Cooperate with management on incident investigations Ensure that visitors and contractors comply with procedures
4. The risk manager	Develop the risk management policy and keep it up to date Facilitate a risk-aware culture within an organization Establish internal risk policies and structures Co-ordinate the risk management activities Compile risk information and prepare reports for the board
5. Specialist risk management functions	Assist the company in establishing specialist risk policies Develop specialist contingency and recovery plans Keep up to date with developments in the specialist area Support investigations of incidents and near misses Prepare detailed reports on specialist risks
6. Internal audit manager	Develop a risk-based internal audit programme Audit the risk processes across an organization Provide assurance on the management of risk Support and help to develop the risk management processes Report on the efficiency and effectiveness of internal controls

Externally, insurance brokers, insurance companies, accountancy firms and external auditors also have a contribution to make to the improved management of risk in their client organizations. It is important that risk management professionals work together. However, it is also important that the benefits of risk management are embedded into the core processes of an organization.

RESPONSIBILITIES FOR PROVIDING ASSURANCE

An objective of operational risk management is not to remove operational risk altogether, but to manage the risk to an acceptable level, taking into account the cost of managing the risk as against the resultant modification in exposure.

To ensure appropriate responsibility is allocated for the management, reporting and escalation of operational risk, an organization may operate a 'three lines of assurance' model that outlines principles for the roles, responsibilities and accountabilities for operational risk management.

The three lines model and the policy standards may apply throughout an organization and be implemented taking into account the nature and scale of the underlying business. The standards provide the direction for delivering effective operational risk management. They comprise principles and processes that enable the consistent identification, assessment, management, monitoring and reporting of operational risk across the group. The objectives of the standards are to protect an organization from financial loss or damage to its reputation, its customers or staff and to ensure that it meets all necessary regulatory and legal requirements.

The three lines model will be explored further in Chapter 29.

There is a need to ensure that management of risks receives a sufficiently high profile. It will normally be a board member who sponsors risk management awareness at the board and presents risk management reports to the board. Typically, the risk manager will report to that board member, and have responsibility for the risk architecture, strategy and protocols (RASP).

One of the most important responsibilities to be allocated is that of 'risk owner'. ISO 31073[1] defines a risk owner as a 'person or entity with the accountability and authority to manage risk'.

Statutory responsibilities of management

There has been a developing trend in many countries towards ensuring greater clarity in regard to the obligations of company directors. The general duties of directors have developed in the common law over many years in most countries. For example, the Companies Act 2006 in the UK has consolidated the common law duties of directors and codified the general duties, as follows:

- act in accordance with allocated responsibilities;
- act in accordance with the constitution of the company;
- promote the success of the company;

- exercise independent judgement;
- exercise reasonable care, skill and diligence;
- avoid/declare conflicts of interest;
- not accept benefits from third parties.

The responsibilities of directors are important in relation to risk management, and adequate management of risk will assist in the successful fulfilment of these obligations. Risk management is particularly important in promoting the success of an organization and exercising reasonable care, skill and diligence. Directors of organizations need a good understanding of risk management so that they will be in a better position to fulfil their statutory and other duties.

Usually, board directors will be either executive or non-executive directors of an organization. In certain organizations, such as charities and most government departments, executive directors will meet separately as an 'executive committee' and the non-executive directors will form a 'board of governors'. Typically, executive directors will be full-time employees of an organization with a specific area of responsibility.

Non-executive directors have an important role to play in risk management within an organization. However, this role will normally be restricted to audit, assurance and compliance activities. It may be inappropriate for non-executive directors to become involved in the management of the individual risks, because of the conflict with non-executive audit responsibilities and because executive directors are in a better position to understand and deal with the risks that an organization faces. However, through corporate governance requirements, boards are required to establish and maintain risk management and internal control frameworks to ensure the effective management of an organization's risks.

The next box provides an example of the responsibilities and expectations of non-executive directors.

KEY RESPONSIBILITIES OF NON-EXECUTIVE DIRECTORS

The role of the non-executive director has the following specific key elements, according to the Institute of Directors:[2]

- Strategy: Provide a creative and informed contribution and to act as a constructive critic in looking at the objectives and plans devised by the chief executive and the executive team.

- Performance: Monitor the performance of executive management, especially with regard to the progress made towards achieving the determined company strategy and objectives.

- Remuneration: Determine appropriate levels of remuneration of executive directors.
- Communication: Help connect the business and board with networks of potentially useful people and organizations.
- Risk: Satisfy themselves on the integrity of financial information and that financial controls and systems of risk management are robust and defensible.
- Audit: Ensure that the company accounts properly to its shareholders by presenting a true and fair reflection of its actions and financial performance and that the necessary internal control systems are put into place and monitored regularly and rigorously.
- Expectations: Bring to an organization independence, impartiality, wide experience, special knowledge and personal qualities.

Role of the risk manager

There is no single established reporting position in the structure of an organization for the risk manager. Risk managers may report to the CEO, the finance director or treasury, the company secretary or group legal department or even to human resources or procurement.

A risk manager in most large organizations will be needed to enable an organization to apply risk management tools and techniques to a wide range of issues. The risk manager should be responsible for the corporate learning that has to take place so that an organization can understand the benefits of risk management. As the person having responsibility for the risk architecture, strategy and protocols (RASP), the risk manager will be necessary for developing the strategy, systems and procedures by which the required risk management outcomes for an organization are achieved.

The role of a risk manager now requires a greater involvement in project management and strategy formulation and delivery. The broad range of responsibilities enables the risk manager to obtain a better level of understanding and involvement than most other roles or functions achieve. The developing importance of organizational resilience may offer an opportunity for the risk manager to develop into the 'risk and resilience manager' and fulfil a much broader role that is designed to be more aligned with the success of an organization.

Many organizations in the finance sector have identified the benefits of bringing the management of credit, market and operational risks together. It has been the case for some time in the finance sector that risk management has been separate from the purchase of insurance. The development of the role of chief risk officer (CRO) in the finance sector reporting directly to the CEO reflects this fact.

Given that one of the key principles of risk management is that the approach to risk should be proportionate to the level of risk faced by an organization, it is unlikely that the majority of organizations will need to appoint someone of the seniority of a CRO. Nevertheless, organizations should, when reviewing their risk architecture, decide the appropriate range of responsibilities and level of seniority of the risk manager.

The introduction of the job title 'chief risk officer' is not universal, but it is becoming common outside of the finance sector. The next box provides an overview of the developing role of the chief risk officer. For organizations where it is proportionate for a CRO to be appointed, the contribution that can be made by that individual will be substantial.

ROLE OF THE CHIEF RISK OFFICER

As champion of the ERM process, the CRO plays a key part in bringing together disparate risk management processes to ensure that limited company resources are applied effectively. The COSO ERM cube defines the role of the CRO as working with other managers to establish effective risk management, monitoring progress, and assisting other managers in reporting relevant risk information up, down and across an organization.

The IRM's paper 'How to hire a great CRO',[3] sets out some core competencies of the chief risk officer, which include:

- Insights and context – using knowledge of internal and external influences to ensure robust risk management in responsive and agile organizations.

- Strategy and performance – developing a risk management strategy to meet organizational needs.

- Risk management process – managing the risk management process.

- Organizational capability – developing and managing a skilled, agile and responsive risk organization.

Internal auditors should work with the CRO as part of their risk management duties. In this role, internal auditors are responsible for evaluating the accuracy of ERM reporting and providing independent and value-added recommendations to management about its ERM approach. The Institute of Internal Auditors' International Standards specify that the scope of internal auditing should include evaluating the reliability of reporting effectiveness, efficiency of operations and compliance with laws and regulations. The responsibilities of the CRO are considered further in Chapter 41.

Table 7.2   Responsibilities of the RM committee

1   To advise the board on risk management and to foster a culture that emphasizes and demonstrates the benefits of a risk-based approach to risk management.
2   To make appropriate recommendations to the board on all significant matters relating to the risk strategy and policies of the company.
3   To monitor the performance of the risk management systems and review reports prepared by relevant parties.
4   To keep under review the effectiveness of the risk management infrastructure of the company, including: • assessment of risk management procedures in accordance with changes in the operating environment; • consideration of risk audit reports on the key business areas to assess the level of business risk exposure; • consideration of any major findings of risk management reviews and the response of management; • assessment of the risks of new ventures and other strategic, project and operational initiatives.
5   To review the risk exposure of the company in relation to the risk appetite of the board and the risk capacity of the company.
6   To consider the development of risk management and make appropriate recommendations to the board.
7   To consider whether disclosure of information regarding risk management policies and key risk exposures is in accordance with financial reporting standards.

Risk committees

Table 7.2 sets out typical responsibilities for a risk management committee (RMC). Most large organizations will already have an audit committee, chaired by a senior non-executive director. An option considered by many organizations is to extend the role of the audit committee to include all aspects of risk management or to establish a separate risk management group chaired by an executive director.

There is a strong argument for the RMC to be an executive group, rather than part of any existing non-executive audit committee. This is necessary because risks need to be managed in a proactive manner as an executive responsibility. The audit committee may treat the management of risk as a reactive auditing of compliance. Separation of executive responsibility for the management of risk from non-executive responsibility for auditing and review of compliance will also be consistent with good corporate governance principles.

Some organizations have established the RMC as a sub-committee of the audit committee. If this is the case, actions need to be taken to ensure that risk is managed as an executive responsibility, rather than audited as a compliance/assurance issue. In fact, establishing the RMC as a sub-committee of the audit committee could impair the work of the RMC because of increased bureaucracy and an unhelpful emphasis on auditing and compliance, rather than proactive management of risks.

Membership of the RMC is another question that needs to be addressed. The fundamental decision to be taken in large organizations is whether the committee should be a small senior executive group setting strategy and policy or whether it should be a knowledge-sharing group with representation from each of the units or departments within an organization. The answer will depend on the structure of an organization and the intended role of the committee.

The terms of reference and the position of the risk committee within the risk architecture of an organization have been the subject of much discussion. For some business sectors, the level of risk that an organization should take is a fundamental business strategy decision. This is certainly true in banks and other financial institutions. In these circumstances, deciding on a risk appetite and the monitoring of actual risk exposure becomes a high-profile board responsibility. Therefore, the risk committee will need to be a committee of the board with executive and non-executive membership.

There is no single answer that is appropriate for all organizations. The overall aim is to achieve a prioritized, validated and audited improvement in risk management standards in an organization. The risk management committee and the audit committee should, therefore, operate in a way that provides mutual support. However, combining the two committees into a single group, or placing one committee as superior to the other will not be the best way forward for most organizations. The major concern when combining risk and audit committees is that an organization will then be operating a two lines of assurance model, rather than the three lines of assurance model that will provide greater protection.

Further risk management roles and responsibilities around corporate governance are considered in Chapter 27.

Risk management documentation

Chapter 6 included a list of risk management protocols that could be included in an organization's risk management framework. The range of risk management documentation that may be necessary is extensive and Table 7.3 provides an overview of the types of documents that may be appropriate. The risk management documentation provides more information on how the risk protocols should be interpreted and how they should be delivered.

The documentation that is produced should be proportionate to the level of risk faced by an organization, in accordance with the principles that apply to risk management.

Table 7.3 Types of RM documentation

Activity	RM documentation
Risk governance	Risk management policy (and priorities)
	Specific risk statements (health and safety policy)
	Risk appetite statement
	Terms of reference of the risk/audit committees
	Risk protocols/procedures
	Risk management manual
	Risk awareness training records
Context and objectives	Extended enterprise
	Objectives
Risk assessment	Risk workshop report
	Risk matrix
	Risk register
Risk management	Risk control standards
	Risk improvement recommendations
	Risk assurance reports
Monitor and review	Risk and control self-assessment returns
	Audit procedures and protocols
	Internal audit reports
	Unit risk management reports
	External disclosure reports
	Business performance reports/key performance indicators
Report	Risk dashboard
	Loss/claim reports and recommendations
	Legal and litigation reports
	Enforcement action/customer complaints
	Incident and near-miss investigations
	Business continuity plans/disaster recovery plans

Whatever is produced will need to be structured in a way that suits an organization and is aligned with the other activities that take place within an organization.

The three core risk management documents are the risk management policy, risk management manual and risk appetite statement, noted previously in Chapter 6. The preparation of these provides a good opportunity for an organization to establish detailed procedures on a range of risk management topics, as well as setting out the risk management priorities for the following year. For example, some organizations produce an annual health and safety and/or environmental policy and procedures, and this should be an integral part of the risk management documentation.

Other organizations face significant risks that need routine or even constant management attention. This is particularly true in the case of threats, where, for example, the health and safety policy and procedures, business continuity plans and disaster recovery plans need to be routinely updated.

For many organizations, the risk documentation will be established in writing. Other organizations will operate a more informal means of embedding risk management into management activities. The example structure described in Table 7.3 reinforces the importance of the activities involved in the risk management process and each of these activities produces several outputs.

THE IMPORTANCE OF RECORDS

There are many benefits to be gained from maintaining good records. It is a key driver in increasing organizational efficiency and offers significant business benefits. Records management:

- reduces the time spent by staff looking for information;
- facilitates the effective sharing of information;
- reduces the unnecessary duplication of information;
- identifies how long records need to be kept;
- optimizes the legal admissibility of records to defend malicious litigation;
- supports risk management and business continuity planning.

In short, records management improves control over information assets, frees up staff time and other resources, and helps protect individuals and an organization from various risks. Records management means that too much reliance is not placed on the memories of a few individuals. Great care should be taken to ensure that information stored in this way is compliant with regulation surrounding privacy and data protection, such as General Data Protection Regulations (GDPR) in Europe.

Breaches of data protection have led to large fines for many organizations across Europe. At the time of going to press, the maximum fine for breaching GDPR was €20 million (about £18 million) or 4% of annual global turnover, whichever is the greater. In 2023, Meta Platforms Ireland Ltd, the parent company of Facebook and Instagram, was fined €1.2 billion for transferring EU user data to the US without adequate safeguards and processing children's data without valid parental consent. This followed a €390 million penalty earlier in the year relating to data practices surrounding personalized adverts on Meta's platforms.

However, it is not just large, private organizations or the way in which an organization collects data that the regulations relate to. The Dutch Tax and Customs Administration was fined €3.7 million in 2022 for wrongly inputting data into their Fraud Signalling Facility. In 2020, a Swedish hospital, Capio St. Göran AB, was fined €2.9 million after an audit found that too many employees had access to sensitive personal data and in 2019, Bulgaria's National Revenue agency had a data breach exposing people's names, contact details and tax information leading to a €2.6 million fine.

Risk management manual

The risk management manual, as the main 'how to' resource for an organization, will contain the details of all of the responsibilities, procedures, practices and guidelines regarding the risk management process and risk management governance for an organization. ISO 31073 uses the term risk management plan rather than manual, as the scheme within the risk management framework specifying the approach, management components and resources to be applied to the management of risk. It is noted that the components typically include procedures, practices, assignment of responsibilities, and sequence and timing of activities.

An illustration of potential contents for a risk management manual is set out in Table 7.4. Some of the contents should be part of the main body of the manual, whereas other, more detailed information could be included in appendices, such as definitions, responsibilities and prioritization approaches. This ensures the manual is a more usable and practical document for the reader.

The manual should confirm the process for undertaking the activities, supported by risk guidelines for an organization. Often, detailed risk guidelines are produced as a separate set of documents, or factsheets, that form the risk 'toolbox' for an organization. These guidelines can then be more easily updated, amended and added to as the risk management practice for an organization matures.

The risk management manual will also set out details of the systems and procedures that will be put in place to monitor performance, as well as the means for reporting and communicating on risk management. It will, in effect, define that context within which risk management activities take place.

Table 7.4   Risk management manual

A risk management manual should include the following sections:
- Risk management and internal control objectives
- Statement of the attitude of an organization to risk (risk strategy)
- Description of the control environment
- Level and nature of risk that is acceptable
- Risk management organization and arrangements (risk architecture)
- Arrangements for communicating risk information
- Standard procedures for risk recognition and rating
- List of documentation for analysing and reporting risk
- Risk management requirements and control mechanisms
- Allocation of risk management roles and responsibilities
- Criteria for monitoring and benchmarking risks
- Allocation of appropriate resources
- Risk priorities and performance targets
- Risk management calendar for the coming year

As can be seen from the list above, the framework that has been set up to achieve adequate and effective management of risks is usually presented in the risk management manual. It will then be for the individual companies within an organization to operate within the established framework and arrange their own additional procedures and protocols as necessary.

As noted in Chapter 6, many organizations find that it is necessary to update the risk management manual each year, even if the overall risk management strategy remains unchanged. This is undertaken for a number of reasons, including the desire to ensure that risk management activities and the overall risk management approach are in line with current best practice. Regularly updating the risk management manual also gives an organization the opportunity to identify the risk priorities for the coming year.

The risk management policy does not usually need to be amended on a yearly basis, although the formal issuing of the risk management policy every year signifies a board's engagement and commitment to risk management. It also ensures the board has paid appropriate attention to risk management and that an organization understands that it is a dynamic activity that requires constant management attention. In the UK, the updated Corporate Governance Code requires organizations to review the effectiveness of the framework on an annual basis, but does not require yearly amendments, unless they are necessary.

Risk management toolbox

The risk guidelines/factsheets that support the manual should define the means by which embedded risk management is to be achieved in an organization. The format for the risk guidelines will depend on an organization and the nature of the risks that it faces. These guidelines could contain information on such topics as the following:

- financial and authorization procedures;
- insurance arrangements;
- project risk management;
- incident reporting and investigation;
- risk articulation requirements;
- guidance on risk assessment tools and methodologies;
- controls and control effectiveness requirements (which may also form part of the internal control framework);
- event and reaction planning.

The risk documentation for a diverse group of companies may require each unit, division or department to set its own standards for internal control, including health and safety, fire safety, physical security, information security and environmental protection. This may be appropriate because of the diverse nature of the different units within an organization. ISO 31073 notes that the risk management manual (plan) can be applied to a particular product, process or project, and to part or the whole of an organization.

Embedded risk management will be achieved when the cycle of risk management activities is fully aligned with the planning cycle of an organization. A primary purpose of risk guidelines is to help managers understand the risk management framework of an organization. This understanding will ensure that managers pay appropriate attention to risk implications when making decisions.

Risk registers

The key reason for undertaking a risk assessment is so that risks can be understood, current controls can be validated and the need for any further actions to improve control of risk can be identified. The risk register is the means of recording information on risks, their current controls and details of intended additional controls. It is important that the risk register should not become a static document. It should be treated as a dynamic element and considered to be the risk action plan for a unit or an organization as a whole, if not actually linked to any business-as-usual action planning system or process.

Designing a risk register

Documentation can be as simple as a spreadsheet or table of risk, but it is more likely to involve some form of technology that enables manipulation of the data in various ways. Its form will depend upon the maturity of an organization, the resources available to the risk management function, who is to use it and what it will be used for. The register of these documented risks will be the repository for risk management knowledge for an organization.

Typically, the risk register will identify all risks and contain sufficient information to support prioritization and allow the significant risks to be highlighted from this repository of identified risk. For example, it will record the results of the risk assessment related to the process, operation, location, business unit or project under consideration.

Although there is no fixed format for this document (and in practice much of this will be driven by the software used) the detail should include such information as the objective at risk, category, cause/source, risk, consequence, inherent/current/target ratings, existing controls, new controls, risk owner, control owner, new control review date, and similar detail in as much granularity as is appropriate for an organization.

The purpose of the risk register is to form an agreed record of the risks that have been identified, and the control activities that are currently undertaken. It is also a record of the additional actions that are proposed to improve the control of the particular risk. The risk register has three functions:

- Collecting the risk information requires engagement from an organization and will establish the risk function credentials. Input will vary and can include workshops, incidents, other datasets, etc.

- To maintain the data in a form that enables manipulation to establish trends or relationships. It should be possible to identify possible actions (and unintended consequences) if the data allows building a network of risk for an organization. Documenting the components using appropriate software can establish complex linkages between various relationships.

- To provide the source material to establish actions, and communicate risk information to stakeholders, including escalating risks when appropriate.

These three functions are illustrated in Figure 7.1.

Figure 7.1   Components of a risk register

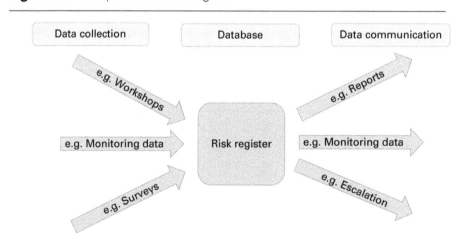

SOURCE   Components of a risk register (SATARLA). Used with permission

Using a risk register

A well-constructed and dynamic risk register is at the heart of a successful risk management initiative. For example, output from the risk register may form the centrepiece of discussion in a risk committee and be the subject of detailed discussion and challenge, requiring supporting information as backup. The risk register itself should not form a risk report directly but does provide information for effective reporting.

The output will need to be tailored to the function or person receiving the report and whether the reports require an action, control or escalation so that the message, purpose and reasoning are clear. The communication from the risk function is likely to be judged by the operation, and a well-constructed report will enable better engagement with the function so that the value of risk management becomes more compelling.

In some organizations, the risk register is given the status of a controlled document to be used by internal auditors as one of the key reference documents for undertaking risk-based auditing. Risk control activities should be described in sufficient detail for the controls to be auditable. This is especially important when the risk register relates to the routine operations undertaken by an organization. It should, for example, provide a record of the critical controls that are in place, together with the details of any additional controls that need to be introduced. This detail can form a risk action plan and clearly establish the responsibility for undertaking the actions identified.

A risk register could include both the risks of undertaking the strategy and an analysis of the risks associated with not undertaking the proposed strategy. Certainly, the output should be attached to a business plan as a record of the risks that could impact the achievement of that plan.

It is a common criticism of risk registers that they are reviewed once or twice a year and represent a static snapshot of the risks facing an organization. In order to be effective and make a significant contribution, risk management needs to be a dynamic activity that produces outputs that have an impact on an organization. If this is going to happen, then the risk register needs to become a document that drives changes and improvements. There are systems and applications available that can address this using technology.

Finally, the board will probably wish to see a risk report generated by the register on at least a quarterly basis, and more frequently if significant changes occur. This will ensure that the risk register remains a dynamic document and is kept more fully up to date. It will also ensure the necessary actions are taken and reported to the board.

The future for risk registers

It should be clear from the discussion previously that technology has a large part to play in the future of risk registers. The increased ability to collect data and analyse streams of information in real time will develop into bringing these registers into a more dynamic environment.

At the time of writing, it is recognized that there are disadvantages associated with the use of risk registers; the information needs to be correct, updated and to the right level of detail. Manually operated risk registers can become unwieldy if they contain too much detail, and open to criticism if they contain too little. Senior management may consider they have fulfilled their obligation to risk management by attending a risk workshop and producing a risk register, without the need for further engagement in the risk management process.

Without the benefit of technology to manipulate and analyse the complex array of information, the maintenance of risk registers can be such a key focus of activity that it becomes the process rather than a tool to achieve improvements. More importantly, unless supported by technology, it is difficult for a risk register to be a collaborative tool that exists in real time.

There are many different types of software solutions in use and being designed. It is likely that new technology will allow greater integration of different datasets and live streams of information from, for instance, remote operating monitors. These new forms of register will provide near instant analysis.

The enhanced technology will embrace machine learning (or other forms of artificial intelligence) at all levels of digital information. This may include taking those risk registers that are currently less well-structured in a digital fashion and transforming them into datasets which can become more meaningfully analysed. In other words, risk registers need to be ready to become more digitally enabled as technology advances.

Notes

1 ISO (2022) *ISO 31073: Risk management – vocabulary*, https://www.iso.org/obp/ui/en/#iso:std:iso:31073:ed-1:v1:en (archived at https://perma.cc/XYQ9-6VR9)

2 IoD (2018) *What is the role of the non-executive director?* https://www.iod.com/resources/factsheets/company-structure/what-is-the-role-of-the-non-executive-director/ (archived at https://perma.cc/FWF2-ZHC4)

3 IRM (2020) *How to hire a great CRO*, https://www.theirm.org/media/8461/how-to-hire-a-great-cro.pdf (archived at https://perma.cc/35PT-XS3C)

Risk management 08
process

Four core risk management standards/frameworks have been considered in Chapter 3. Each of those includes key steps to the successful identification and management of risks to achieve an organization's objectives.

All established risk management standards have similar processes. Many of the standards distinguish between the risk management process and the framework that implements and supports the process.

Although there are many ways of representing the risk management process itself, the basic steps are all similar. Table 8.1 lists the steps in the process from the perspective of the different standards.

Whatever approach or variation on an approach an organization decides to adopt, it is important that the steps are defined clearly and used consistently.

Bringing it all together in four simple steps

As noted in Chapters 1 and 3, risk management terminology is slightly different, whether looking at the standards shown above, or considering wider sources of risk management approaches, such as the Office for Governance, Ethics and Compliance (OCEG) GRC Capability Model (the Red Book), or health and safety risk assessments.

The risk management standards described in Table 8.1 also illustrate that slightly different terminology and stages in the process, but they all cover the same important steps. These four simple steps are shown in Figure 8.1.

Step 1 – Define context and objectives

It is important for organizations to understand both the external and internal context in which an organization operates, to better understand what the risk drivers and vulnerabilities are. The internal context describes activities that are undertaken by teams and functions, as well by an organization as a whole. The external context describes what is happening outside of the team or function, or outside of an organization.

Table 8.1 Risk management process step similarities

Standard / simple steps	ISO	COSO Cube	COSO Rainbow double helix	Orange Book
Define context and objectives	Scope, context, criteria	• Internal environment • Objective setting	• Governance and culture • Strategy and objective setting	• *Implicit in risk identification and assessment*

Assess risks	Risk assessment
	  • Risk identification
	  • Risk analysis
	  • Risk evaluation
		• Event identification
		• Risk assessment
			• Performance
			  o Identify risk
			  o Assess severity
			  o Prioritize risks
				• Risk identification and assessment

Manage risks	Risk treatment	• Risk response
		• Control activities
			• Performance
			  o Implement risk responses
			  o Develop portfolio view
				• Risk treatment

Monitor, review, report	• Monitoring and reviewing • Recording and reporting • Communication and consultation	• Information and communication	• Review and revision • Information, communication and reporting	• Risk monitoring • Risk reporting

Figure 8.1   Simple four-step ERM process

SOURCE Simple four-step ERM process (SATARLA). Used with permission

Basically, it provides an understanding of what is happening in the environment in which an organization is operating to help it understand why and how risks might occur.

Using the ISO 31000[1] definition of risk as the 'effect of uncertainty on objectives' it is also important to state what an organization, team, function, department or project are trying to achieve so that objectives are clear, and the understanding of what matters is consistent.

The internal and external context change on a constant basis, especially considering the global networks and relationships that organizations operate within. As such, the context and objectives are not static, and must be updated regularly and especially with key changes. Defining the context and objectives is considered further in Chapters 10, 11 and 12.

Step 2 – Assess risks

When assessing risks, there are three key stages: risk identification, risk analysis and risk evaluation.

Risk identification involves identifying, recognizing and acknowledging risks in relation to the context and objectives. Identified risks include both opportunities and threats, from many different sources or causes, which can be recognized using many different tools and techniques.

Risk analysis uses an iterative process to understand and prioritize the identified risks to highlight those which require the most management attention.

Risk evaluation involves considering the result of the risk analysis exercise and determining whether the risk is acceptable, or whether further action is required to bring the risk to an acceptable level, as part of effective decision making. Assessing risks is considered further in Chapters 13 to 17.

Step 3 – Manage risks

This is arguably a more important step than the risk assessment, which would be futile without taking the steps outlined below to manage them.

The management of risks requires the selection and implementation of controls and actions that take charge of and change or maintain and modify the risks to bring them to an acceptable level, whether that is minimizing threats or capitalizing on opportunities. This involves ensuring effective existing controls are in place or the development of new controls that address the causes of the risk and/or its effects should it occur.

ISO 31000 defines controls as 'measures that maintain and/or modify risk' and that they can include, but are not limited to any process, policy, device, practice or other conditions or actions. Managing risks is considered further in Chapters 18, 19 and 20.

Step 4 – Monitor, review and report

In this final step, monitoring considers changes in the risks, controls and context and whether new and emerging risks are considered appropriately. It requires that organizations understand the context and its objectives and ensure that any important changes prompt the risk management cycle to start again, embedding dynamic risk management.

Reviewing focuses on the effectiveness of existing and new controls to ensure risks are being managed to an acceptable level. The need to ensure existing controls are in place and new controls are developed, with both operating effectively, provides a clear link to compliance, internal audit and internal controls. As noted previously, the requirement to ensure there is a risk management and internal control framework within many organizations substantiates the need for that linkage, to ensure there are no overlaps or gaps in the management of an organization and of its risks.

Reporting allows the escalation of risks to relevant decision makers where appropriate. It involves the capturing of critical risk information and sharing it to relevant levels within an organization as part of effective decision making. It gives both insight and oversight of risk management, holding managers to account for actions taken and decisions made around risk and risk management.

The final arrow in this risk management process closes the loop, and allows the most important question to be asked, which is: 'Given the context in which an organization is working, the risks that are faced, and the extent to which they are managed, is it possible to achieve the objectives previously set?'

If the answer is 'YES' then an organization is operating and the risks are being managed effectively, and no more action is needed.

If the answer is 'NO' there are two core options:

1 The first is to apply more time, effort and resources to managing the risks. Where that option is not applicable/possible or desired, then

2 The second is to change the 'goalposts'. This would require a change to the organization's objectives, or perhaps even to change something in the organization's context.

There is also a third option where the other two are not viable and that is to accept and take accountability for the risk, on the understanding that it will impact on an organization should it occur. In this case, an organization is knowingly accepting the risk as opposed to naively running it. The monitoring, reviewing and reporting on risks is considered further in Chapters 21 and 22.

A key benefit of viewing risk management using the four simple steps is that it encourages the iterative nature of the process as noted earlier regarding the COSO ERM framework. Additionally, it focuses on decision making and accountability regarding the management and acceptance of risks.

This simple four-step approach is followed throughout the book, as the basis for considering the effective implementation and integration of risk management for any organization, in any geography, industry or sector.

Note

1 ISO (2018) *ISO 31000: Risk management – Guidelines*, https://www.iso.org/obp/ui/#iso:std:iso:31000:ed-2:v1:en (archived at https://perma.cc/MG9U-HLPA)

Implementing enterprise risk management 09

When implementing a new enterprise risk management approach, the change is likely to require senior management or board sponsorship. This is helpful if there are specialists already operating to manage a particular type of risk or control such as internal control specialists or the more traditional insurance risk management.

However, there are many barriers to the implementation of effective risk management. Hillson and Simon (2020)[1] attribute this to different factors, including the time and money to implement, the feeling that risk management is just common sense, the reality that people are too busy managing other issues, or the sentiment that no one can prove it works. These barriers are specifically related to the project management environment but can easily be translated into the business world in general, whether in the private, public or third sector.

As noted in Chapter 4, there is also no single style of specialist risk management that offers all the answers. Clearly, the various styles that are adopted should operate as complementary approaches within an organization. Enterprise risk management acts as the translation tool and escalation channel to inform decision making and decision taking at the appropriate level to ensure risks are managed or accepted effectively. As such, the integrated or enterprise-wide approach to risk management accepts that an organization must tolerate certain threats and must have an appropriate appetite for investment in opportunities.

Equally, as noted in previous chapters, there are many enablers for the implementation of risk management. The most important point to make is that the support of senior management and (ideally) the sponsorship of the board are essential.

Although organizations may realize that there are benefits from implementing risk management, its successful implementation should be undertaken as a project. As part of the project the concerns of employees and other stakeholders need to be considered. This is normally included within the communication element of the project. Although risk management is vital to the success of an organization, it is equally vital to communicate the benefits of the approach in order to persuade managers to implement the approach.

On the other hand, it is important the risk manager does not claim that all activities and functions in an organization are being undertaken in the name of risk management. Not all activities in an organization will be driven by risk management, even if all decisions, processes, procedures and activities have risks embedded within them.

Risk management drives and enables activities

Risk management enables operations, tactics and strategy in the same way the three pedals in a car enable it to drive at speed. Risk management acts as an accelerator to help the car go faster by helping an organization embrace strategic opportunities and seek rewards. It operates as a clutch to change gears by enabling the successful management of tactical change and the reduction of the associated uncertainty. Finally, it will act as a brake by managing operational risks and controlling those deviations from the expected, thereby enhancing operational efficiency.

Risk management input into strategy focuses on assessment of the various strategic options available to an organization and assists in making optimal decisions. Organizations undertaking strategic risk management will complete a careful review of viable new business prospects and undertake detailed risk assessment before making strategic decisions.

This book is concerned with taking an enterprise-wide approach to risk management and this chapter will take a high-level view of the implementation of the ERM approach in practice. While much of this book considers specific individual risks or approaches to risk management, this is done in order to provide the foundation for the wider ERM philosophy that consolidates the management of individual risks into a unified and consistent approach to risk across the whole enterprise.

The high-level approach taken in this chapter is intended to provide an overview from which the reader can develop their own investigations but with the context of the overall process clearly in mind. To that extent, what follows should be seen as a roadmap for the remainder of the book, as a pointer to further topics, as well as a high-level plan for the implementation of ERM.

Investment in change

Before considering the actions required to implement an ERM approach, it will be necessary to gain senior management approval and support. The full nature of the changes required to implement an ERM approach will depend upon how an organization is currently structured. Moving to a fully mature ERM approach from a risk management style that was, perhaps, more siloed will need cultural as well as organizational change, requiring investment of time and, probably, investment in technology to upgrade recording and analytical processes.

The largest investment to be made is likely to be that of employing a Chief Risk Officer, a risk manager or a risk management function that will design, facilitate and drive the implementation and running of an ERM framework.

A fully functioning ERM programme will have an impact across an entire organization and, depending on the sector, size, complexity and geographies in which an organization operates, it will take time to be accepted by those actors involved in running an organization. The commitment from the board and extent of active engagement by the leadership of an organization will determine the speed of that acceptance. A period of between three and ten years has been suggested as a reasonable timeframe in which to implement ERM fully. Given the speed of change brought on by technology and shifts in ways of working, it is unlikely that an organization that takes ten years to implement such change will be in existence at the end of that time.

Along with the leadership's commitment, the extent of the investment required to implement the ERM approach should be governed by a sense of proportionality. In Chapter 5, the PACED principle was discussed; the ERM approach will need to be proportionate, aligned, comprehensive, embedded and dynamic.

A worthwhile change

Implementing an ERM approach will affect the culture of an organization and will seek to monitor and address aspects of the culture that may require behavioural modification. This can be seen from the lessons learned in the financial crisis, illustrated by the HBOS case study in Chapter 2.

The extent of the impact and changes sought will depend upon the start point, but in order for ERM to be fully embedded and its benefits fully realized an organization will require process and behavioural change from everyone involved.

Integrating processes, reviewing and improving

Successful implementation of ERM that brings about cultural change within an organization will, as we have seen, take time to implement. It is likely to be an ongoing process that involves applying an initial methodology and through iterations continuously improving the process, to enable as mature and embedded an approach as possible within an organization.

While ERM is an embedded process in some organizations, and being adopted by others, there is no single, combined or overwhelmingly accepted methodology that forms ERM. It will vary between organizations, based in part on the context of the risks to be managed and in part on the culture and existing processes into which ERM is to be applied.

BUILT IN, NOT BOLT ON

'This isn't about adding new processes; it is about ensuring that effective risk management is integrated in the way we lead, direct, manage and operate. As an integrated part of our management systems, and through the normal flow of information, an organization's risk management framework harnesses the activities that identify and manage the uncertainties faced and systematically anticipate and prepare successful responses.'

SOURCE HM Government (2023), *The Orange Book: Management of Risk – Principles and Concepts*, p 3, https://assets.publishing.service.gov.uk/media/6453acadc33b460012f5e6b8/HMT_Orange_Book_May_2023.pdf

---

Academics have found it difficult to agree a consistent method of application for ERM since the ERM approach has been implemented to overlay against many of the existing processes that an organization undertakes. In other words, its application has been moulded to the existing organization, and not imposed in a predetermined fashion. This is in accordance with the PACED principle that 'proportionality' is important.

Regulators will rarely impose a precise form in which ERM must be implemented. They will advise which areas they expect to be managed and will judge the appropriateness of that management, but it will remain up to an organization itself how to implement ERM.

The variation in practical application of the methodology contributes to what has been termed an 'ERM mix'[2] and makes it difficult to characterize the imperatives that must be used. What this book explains in more detail is that successfully implementing ERM requires the interlinking of two components: the technical aspects of risk management and the practical understanding of an organization into which ERM is to be embedded. The true skill of the ERM implementer is to be able to blend technical knowledge with organizational knowledge.

Plan, implement, measure and learn (PIML)

In Chapter 3 the concept of applying a consistent methodology to change, the PIML approach, was mentioned. The PIML structure is very similar to plan–do–check–act

(PDCA). The PDCA construct emanates from the 'quality' management process and can be traced to the 1920s. It is sometimes called the 'Deming' cycle and has had some additions in the intervening years, including 'Observation' as an initial step and 'Study' as an interim step. Regardless of whether it is OPDCA (for observation) or PDSA (with S for study), the main idea is that it is a consistent way of analysing an issue and, through taking planned steps, making an improvement to a process which can be reviewed and then, after further planning, itself be improved upon.

The PIML acronym is preferred in risk management for two reasons. Firstly, it implies a structured and proactive approach that places specific emphasis on measuring and learning, and secondly it distinguishes risk management from quality management.

The key steps to implementing a risk management process are shown in Figure 9.1, which outlines each stage of the process. The centre arrows indicate that the process is continuous, in that once the process has been completed, from planning through to learning, the final phase leads into a further round of planning improvements after an appropriate time, and regular review is required.

This regular review is more necessary than ever in fast-moving times, given external pressures on an organization, whether brought about through technology improvements, demographic changes, changes to working patterns, the Covid-19 pandemic, the geopolitical landscape or other external changes. For example, a risk management framework that was designed and implemented in the last few years may require revision and update in light of the need to build the risks of climate change into the ERM system. A look at the top ten risks from the World Economic Forum's Global Risk Report, issued in January each year, shows how risks are changing. In the discussion of each stage in the cycle that follows, illustrations of how this might apply to this climate change example have been provided.

Planning

In the initial part of the process, it is important to identify and assess the benefits that will arise as a result of the change to be made, either in implementing a new risk management process or by iterations seeking an improvement to the existing process. These benefits can be identified in numerous ways within the context of an organization but suggestions can be made through reviewing the business model, taking into account the interests of all stakeholders (see Chapter 11), which will include external pressures or benefits that may be identified in terms of the value added by the ERM approach (see Chapter 40).

Figure 9.1   Implementing risk management by PIML

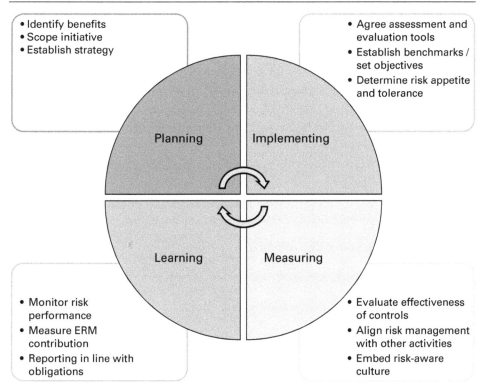

It is important to identify and have a clear view of the benefits in order to gain acceptance and sponsorship from the board or controlling powers in an organization. Once benefits are established, the planning phase will lead to more detailed scoping of the ERM initiative itself. This may require the development of a common taxonomy or defining improvements within the existing and well-understood language of an organization itself. Using existing phraseology often enables greater traction for the exercise through easier acceptance of the change required.

Simply controlling or eliminating risk from an organization is not taking an enterprise-wide (ERM) approach but may be more commonly found in a health and safety or compliance regime. A key difference of an ERM approach is that it seeks to exploit the advantages of taking risk, where the ambition is not to just maintain value, but also to create and add value to an organization.

The final element of this phase will be to establish the risk management framework, which was discussed in Chapters 6 and 7. This will include the role and responsibilities of those involved, perhaps an outline of relevant documentation such as the risk management manual, and the establishment of new procedures that need to be accepted. This documentation, along with other risk management tools, will be used in the next phase of the process.

PLANNING FOR ERM

For example, if improving an embedded risk management system to cater for climate change, issues that may have emerged may require an agreed taxonomy of risk. In this situation, two key risk categories have been identified: physical and transition risk. These will need to be defined specifically for an organization itself.

Gaining acceptance and sponsorship from the board may require providing evidence from other sectors, for example the finance sector, of the drive to encourage decarbonization.

Lastly, identifying the benefits of incorporating climate change into the ERM process might focus on being a more attractive proposition for the investment community and as a result reducing the costs of capital. This benefit might arise if an organization was the first in the sector to provide meaningful measures that institutional investors could assess, and by doing so create a higher demand to invest in their stock, reducing the requirement to deliver higher returns.

Implementing

This is the main phase of the project to bring risk management into an organization or the adaption and adoption of some of the key technical features of ERM discussed in more detail in later chapters. For example, the production of risk management guidelines and risk protocols (see Chapter 6), risk classification systems (see Chapter 14), and using different methodologies such as FIRM, PESTLE or SWOT (see Chapters 10 and 13).

This phase may also involve undertaking exercises within an organization to gain information or initiate the process of gaining acceptance to the initiatives that are being implemented. This may involve risk assessment workshops, producing and agreeing risk registers, or designing or improving risk management information systems (RMIS) (see Chapter 7).

The final element will involve designing or setting some measurements, such as determining and agreeing an organization's risk appetite and risk tolerance levels or evaluating the existing controls.

IMPLEMENTING ERM

In the example of developing a risk management protocol to cater for climate change issues, this may involve amending the risk management guidelines to include principles around activities requiring environmental assurance or carbon reduction procedures.

It could also, for example, involve running risk assessment workshops with managers, informed by details of recent or upcoming legal challenges expected from activists in other sectors to assess the likelihood such challenges might transfer across sectors.

Lastly, it is likely that the board will need to consider and agree a statement of its attitude to climate change and the activities it will undertake to become carbon neutral by a certain date. The risk function will need to build these statements into an action plan that can be monitored and reviewed.

Measuring

The emphasis on measurement is perhaps a main feature of risk management and goes beyond the 'check' phase of PDCA in the sense that it will overlap with internal audit in terms of measuring the effectiveness of existing controls and introducing improvements.

To become embedded in an organization's activities, the processes should have been designed to be aligned as far as possible with the existing processes taking place within an organization. This phase may involve monitoring in more detail the risk improvement plans or reaction planning such as business interruption analysis (see Chapter 32).

Within this phase, if ERM activities are aligned with others in an organization then a risk-aware culture will start to be embedded within an organization and it will become 'second nature' in terms of resource allocation and wider communications within an organization.

MEASURING ERM

For example, measurement of the risk management protocols that have been altered to cater for climate change issues will require analysis of the carbon footprint and performing risk impact analyses on activities that may reduce the footprint.

It may involve measuring how an organization's activities will be changed as a result of different scenarios of temperature increase. An example can be seen in the UK National Trust's analysis[3] of the threat to their estate at a 'worst-case scenario', in which gas emissions continue their current trajectory unchecked, captured in their Climate Hazards Map. They use the analysis to establish actions that can be taken to mitigate the physical risk they have identified.

Learning

The final phase before restarting the process involves learning from the measurement activity. This will take the form of monitoring and reviewing risk performance indicators to measure ERM contribution. It may involve work with an internal audit team to contribute to the audit plan or reviewing a learning from any self-assessment (such as risk and control self-assessment or RCSA) that has been completed (see Chapter 29).

Included within this phase will be reporting of risk performance internally to the board. External stakeholders such as listing bodies like the London Stock Exchange or the New York Stock Exchange will require reports on the ERM processes to be published. Additionally, many rating agencies will specifically consider the ERM processes of an organization before assigning a credit score. In the climate change example, this might involve producing reports for external stakeholders on the risks that have been identified or alerting investors to the processes that are in place in respect of climate change activities.

The ERM process might also take the measures of output from the activities and identify ways in which an organization might benefit from further modification of the ERM process, for example by investing in technology to enable more granular assessment of outputs to establish defences to possible future legal challenges.

Further information on the maturity of the risk management framework and its continual improvement is considered in Chapter 39.

Notes

1 Hillson, D and Simon, P (2020) *Practical Project Risk Management*. Berrett-Koehler Publishers Inc, Oakland, CA

2 Mikes. A and Kaplan, R (2014) *Towards a Contingency Theory of Enterprise Risk Management Working Paper 13-063*, https://www.hbs.edu/ris/Publication%20Files/13-063_5e67dffe-aa5e-4fac-a746-7b3c07902520.pdf (archived at https://perma.cc/JR7A-WUNF)

3 UK National Trust (2024) *National Trust Climate Hazard*, https://experience.arcgis.com/experience/0295557a52b5446595fc4ba6a97161bb/page/Page (archived at https://perma.cc/58DE-USTT)

PART THREE
Defining context and objectives and assessing risk

LEARNING OUTCOMES

Having studied this section readers will be able to:

- Describe the scope and importance of establishing the context as the first stage in the risk management process.
- Explain the importance of the relationship between the external context, internal context and the risk management context.
- Explain the importance of objectives, whether strategic, tactical, operational or compliance.
- Describe the importance of risk assessment as a critically important stage in the risk management process, comprising risk identification, risk analysis and risk evaluation.
- Explain the effective articulation of risk, and importance of acknowledging risks.
- Summarize some of the common risk identification techniques, plus the advantages and disadvantages of each technique.
- Explain emerging risks and their importance in making organizations more agile and resilient.

- Describe the importance of risk classification systems and describe the features of the established systems, including FIRM, PESTLE, the Orange Book and the World Economic Forum.

- Summarize the options for the attachment of risks to various characteristics of an organization.

- Explain the prioritization of risk in terms of likelihood and impact by means of a risk matrix.

- Illustrate, by using a risk matrix, the inherent, current and target risk rating.

- Describe other lenses through which to prioritize risk.

- Explain risk evaluation and its relationship to the management of risks.

Understanding the context

10

Scope, context and criteria

Most organizations consider that the first stage in the risk management process is to establish the scope, context and criteria, which is shown in Figure 3.1. Actually, according to the ISO 31000 this is the second stage in the process, with 'communication and consultation' being the first, signifying that communication and consultation are part of each step in risk management. Communication and consultation are considered later in Chapter 22 as part of reporting on risks and risk management.

Establishing the scope, context and criteria is a fundamentally important aspect of successful risk management, and it is also identified by other international standards as an essential early stage in implementing the process. ISO 31000 states that the purpose of the scope, context and criteria stage of the process is to:

> Customize the risk management process, enabling effective risk assessment and appropriate risk treatment. Scope, context and criteria involve defining the scope of the process, and understanding the external and internal context.

Scope

The nature and extent of the risk management process itself is a major consideration when establishing the context for risk management. The key question is what the risk management process is expected to achieve, or to answer the question of why an organization has risk management activities in place. It also takes into account the objectives and decisions to be made. The objectives will be explored in more detail in Chapter 12. The scope also includes consideration of who will be responsible and identifies the resources that will be required in order to fulfil risk management activities.

In addition, the time frame of the activities that risk management is being applied to should be taken into account. For strategic risks, this may be over the next three or five years depending on the organization's business lifecycle. For projects this could be one or two years, for example in construction. For major defence projects this could be 30 years and for nuclear decommissioning, the time frame could extend to 100 years or more.

Context

ISO 31000 refers to an organization's internal and external context. Other standards have referred to context as having three components: the external context, internal context and risk management context. The relationship between the three contexts is illustrated in Figure 10.1.

Figure 10.1   Three components of context

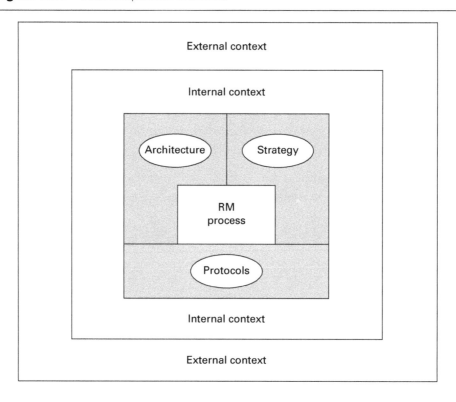

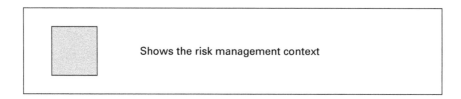

The three components of context may be considered as follows:

- The external context is the environment within which an organization exists.
- Internal context refers to an organization itself.

The risk management context has already been described as the risk architecture, strategy and protocols or the risk management framework within an organization and explored in Chapter 6. As noted earlier, this framework must fulfil two functions: firstly, provide support for the risk management process within an organization; and secondly, ensure that the outputs from the risk management process are communicated to internal and external stakeholders.

External context

The external context is anything occurring outside of an organization, which cannot usually be directly controlled. This includes stakeholder expectations, industry regulations and regulators, the behaviour of competitors and the general economic environment within which an organization operates. These are the drivers and trends that can affect the success of an organization and its ability to achieve objectives.

Establishing the external context must take account of the expectations of external stakeholders. The critical importance of stakeholder expectations is considered in more detail in Chapter 11. For many organizations, the most important group of external stakeholders will be customers. Customers may also be described as consumers, services users, clients and so on. The external context for an organization will be significantly influenced by the nature of the customers and the products or services that they are being offered. Consideration of customers and the customer offering form an important part of the business model for an organization and the relevance of the business model to risk management is considered in more detail in Chapter 30.

The overall purpose of evaluating the external context is to consider what is going on in the world around an organization that makes it think that risks could occur. Putting it another way, it allows an organization to determine the level of riskiness associated with the external environment within which it operates, and to recognize its external opportunities and threats. This will enable an organization to validate the existing business model and develop strategy for the future, together with the tactics for implementing that strategy.

STAKEHOLDERS

An example of how important external and internal stakeholders are, especially from a risk perspective, is highlighted by some of the guidance provided by the Financial Reporting Council in the UK in its updated Corporate Governance Code Guidance.[1]

> Good stewardship by the board should not inhibit sensible risk-taking in pursuit of growth. However, the assessment of risks as part of the normal business planning process will support better decision making, ensure that the board and management respond promptly to risks when they arise, and ensure that shareholders and other stakeholders are well-informed about the principal risks and prospects of the company.
>
> The board should lead by example and demonstrate a commitment to integrity and the company's values. Its responsibility for the organization's culture is essential to the way in which risk is considered and addressed within an organization and with external stakeholders.

Internal context

The internal context is anything going on inside a team or direct sphere of influence, which can usually be managed, including the activities it undertakes, the range of skills and capabilities available within an organization, and how it is structured. Establishing the internal context of an organization must take account of the expectations of internal stakeholders. There will be a range of internal stakeholders, but the most important group will be the people on whom an organization directly depends. This will include members of staff and people providing services on an outsourced, contracted and/or supplier basis.

Internal stakeholders and their expectations are part of the internal context and operate within the culture of an organization. The internal context concerns objectives, the capacity and capabilities of an organization, as well as the business core processes that are in place. An important consideration regarding the internal context is how an organization makes decisions. These are the strengths and weaknesses within an organization and provide internal opportunities and threats.

Having identified the expectations of internal stakeholders, including the importance of these stakeholders to the operations and compliance activities of an organization, it will then be possible to view in more detail the factors that influence the internal context.

The purpose of reviewing the internal context is to understand what is going on within an organization that makes it think risk could occur. This is not just restricted to the internal stakeholders, but also to the activities an organization undertakes, its governance structure, the culture, the decision-making processes; basically, the 'way things are done around here'.

Tools and techniques for understanding context

Risks change depending on the internal and external context in which they are situated. As there are so many changes in the context in which organizations operate, and changes that occur quickly, the better models that an organization has of its context, the easier it is for it to adapt to those changes.

There are many different tools and techniques that can be used to understand both the internal and external contexts and how they change. These tools and techniques also enable organizations to understand and pre-empt changes in context, providing a more proactive approach to the management of risk, and giving an advantage over competitors or situations in general.

Some of the common tools and techniques to understand both the internal and external contexts have been split into four informal types: scoping; idea prompting; imagination; and perspective.

Scoping tools

Scoping tools explore the extent to which risk management is being applied, enabling the understanding of a situation, function, department, business unit or an organization as a whole, depending on what risk management is being applied to. These tools support teams in thinking in an interconnected manner about the activities and core processes that are undertaken, the key dependencies and stakeholder expectations.

Two common scoping tools are business process mapping and the extended enterprise. Business process mapping is considered in Chapter 30, where the link between risk management and strategy is explored in more detail.

The extended enterprise is a tool that produces a simple value chain of the area of an organization under consideration; that is, a description of the inputs and activities needed to create a product or service, and an understanding of the external influences that are or could influence that value chain.

The IRM (2014) Extended Enterprise paper[2] notes some key benefits of modelling the context with this approach:

- Identification of ultimate location of risk across the organizational network
- Understanding of the value chain
- Identification of key points in the network that controls the flow of information, products, etc.
- Identifying what can or can't be controlled
- Identifying gaps, overlaps and weaknesses
- Allowing scenario planning
- Improving response to future shocks
- Providing a framework, key dynamics of power, incentives, regulations, values and so on.

A simple approach to capturing the extended enterprise is shown in Figure 10.2:

Figure 10.2 Extended Enterprise tool

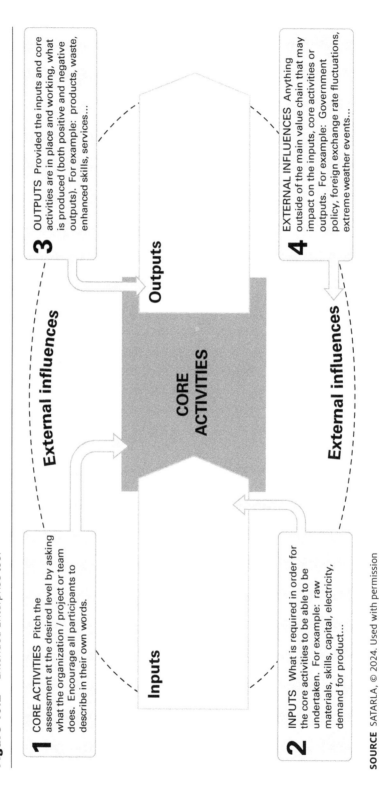

1 CORE ACTIVITIES Pitch the assessment at the desired level by asking what the organization / project or team does. Encourage all participants to describe in their own words.

2 INPUTS What is required in order for the core activities to be able to be undertaken. For example: raw materials, skills, capital, electricity, demand for product...

3 OUTPUTS Provided the inputs and core activities are in place and working, what is produced (both positive and negative outputs). For example: products, waste, enhanced skills, services...

4 EXTERNAL INFLUENCES Anything outside of the main value chain that may impact on the inputs, core activities or outputs. For example: Government policy, foreign exchange rate fluctuations, extreme weather events...

External influences

Inputs

CORE ACTIVITIES

Outputs

External influences

SOURCE SATARLA, © 2024. Used with permission

The outputs from considering the extended enterprise can also be used to inform business impact analyses that are carried out as part of business continuity management. This is another example of how risk management tools can be used for different purposes across an organization and, as the risk management process is explored, how different tools can be used for different stages in that process.

EXTENDED ENTERPRISE IN PRACTICE

The extended enterprise tool has been used in multiple risk workshops with a global manufacturing organization, enabling the different functional teams and business units to better understand the context in which they operate. Examples for each part of the extended enterprise model are provided for the legal regulatory and compliance team.

1 Core activities – handle enquiries from law enforcement agencies, investigate internal escalations, screen suppliers regarding sanctions and alerts and set policies in relation to know your customer (KYC), anti-money laundering (AML) and combating the financing of terrorism (CFT).

2 Inputs – data, key risk indicators, knowledgeable, experienced and skilled staff, external advisers, research tools, technology.

3 Outputs – external reporting, record keeping, AML and CFT assessments, protected and compliant organization.

4 External influences – political changes, regulatory changes, senior management approach, activities undertaken by other functions and business units.

Idea prompting tools

Idea prompting tools include checklists and categories, enabling an organization to identify the nature of the external and internal context within which it operates. Which classification system or checklist of questions is used is less important than the need to understand the context in which an organization operates. This will enable an organization to validate the existing business model, the resources required to deliver the business model, as well as the level of resilience within the existing business model.

The finance, infrastructure, reputation, marketplace (FIRM) risk scorecard provides a structure for carrying out a detailed evaluation of the context of an organization.

Using the FIRM risk scorecard, the financial and infrastructure components are primarily related to the internal context.

In summary, the financial component of the internal context of an organization defines the financial procedures and the means by which money is managed and profitability is achieved. In particular, when evaluating the financial component of the internal context, the following issues should be addressed:

- availability of adequate funds and future flows of funds to fulfil strategic plans;
- existence of robust procedures for correct allocation of funds for investment;
- nature of internal financial control environment to prevent fraud;
- availability of funds to meet historical and anticipated future liabilities.

The infrastructure component influences the nature of the processes undertaken within an organization. Infrastructure risks define the level of inefficiency and dysfunction that may arise during internal processes. In particular, when evaluating the infrastructure component of the internal context, the following issues should be addressed:

- senior management structure and the nature of the risk culture;
- availability of adequate people resources and skills, including intellectual property;
- availability of adequate physical assets to support operational activities;
- information technology infrastructure sufficient to achieve resilience and protect data;
- business continuity plans in place to ensure continuity of activities following major disruption;
- arrangements for service delivery and/or transportation and reliable communication infrastructure.

When considering the external context, the reputational component of the FIRM classification defines the external perception of an organization, the desire of customers to trade with an organization and the level of customer retention. In particular, when evaluating the reputational component of the external context, the following issues should be addressed:

- public perception of the industry sector in which an organization operates;
- corporate social responsibility standards achieved by an organization;
- governance standards and whether the sector is highly regulated;
- quality of products or services and/or after-sales service standards.

The other component of the FIRM risk scorecard relevant to the external environment is the marketplace and the level of presence of an organization within the marketplace. This will impact the level of customer trade or expenditure. In particular, when evaluating the marketplace component of the external environment, the following issues should be addressed:

- level of revenue generation in the marketplace and return on investment;
- presence of aggressive competitors and/or high customer expectations;
- level of economic stability, including exposure to interest rates and foreign exchange rates;
- complexity of the supply chain and volatility of raw material costs;
- exposure to disruption through either technology or geopolitical reasons (political risks, war and terrorism).

The FIRM risk scorecard offers one mechanism for evaluating the context of an organization, but other approaches may be employed, including PESTLE analysis or STOC, both of which are explored further in Chapter 14.

Other prompting tools can include using risk reports from other parts of an organization, or sector, industry or geographic trends or drivers. There is a wealth of information available for any organization to review and tailor for prompting of ideas around context.

Imagination tools

Imagination tools look further into the future to consider what the internal and external context might be for an organization. These types of tools are used more often than previously, following some of the major global context changes from 2020 onwards.

Imagination tools include such things horizon scanning, risk radars, what if analysis and scenario analysis. Most regulatory reporting requires organizations to consider not just their current principal risks, but also those that are emerging or that are on the horizon.

The IRM (2018) paper on horizon scanning[3] states that the technique helps people look at complexity, challenge assumptions and review multiple ways that events could unfurl, in order to increase the resilience and reliability of their organization.

Horizon scanning is not about predicting the future but helps organizations prepare for different versions of the future. The IRM (2018) paper also notes that horizon scanning can be used for identifying potential causes of risk, for identifying and exploiting opportunities and for ensuring organizations are adequately prepared and resilient. Horizon scanning is considered further in Chapter 32.

Scenario analysis has become an increasingly important tool in the risk management toolbox. It is an approach that enables the identification and analysis of possible events that can take place in the future. The international standard on risk assessment techniques, ISO 31010:2019[4] notes that scenario analysis relates to a range of techniques used to consider how the future might turn out, by building imaginary, but credible future situations. This technique, as with others, can be used to image what the context might look like in a number of years to come for an organization. It is one of the key risk management tools for exploring climate change, and in particular, for the UK, for understanding risks in relation to the Task Force on Climate-related Financial Disclosures (TCFD) requirements. Scenario analysis is considered further in Chapters 32 and 34.

Perspective/empathetic tools

Perspective or empathetic tools consider the context from a people or community perspective. These approaches include such things as social materiality studies or stakeholder mapping.

Materiality has historically been related to those issues that could impact on the financial health of an organization. In terms of corporate governance and annual reporting, it would be the inclusion of facts, that if excluded or misreported, could influence the decisions of users of financial statements made by an organization. These approaches are related to an organization and its financial prospects – an inward view of materiality.

The Sustainability Accounting Standards Board (SASB)[5] has widened this aspect of materiality to include those issues that are likely to impact on the financial condition or the operating performance of an organization. Social materiality considers not just how an organization is impacted by events, but also how an organization impacts society and the environment – an inward and outward view of materiality.

Social materiality gathers the views of those who represent an organization and external interested parties who are impacted by particular activities being undertaken by an organization. The different opinions are then compared to understand where there are common or conflicting views, providing useful information on what is considered material and indications of how to manage these material issues. More information on social materiality is provided in Chapter 33.

Stakeholder mapping provides an understanding of those people or organizations who can impact or influence the activities that are being undertaken by a company. Stakeholder mapping is explored further in Chapter 11.

Risk criteria

Another important consideration within this step of the risk management process is the establishment of risk criteria. ISO 31073[6] defines risk criteria as the 'terms of reference against which the significance of risk is evaluated'.

ISO 31073 goes on to note that risk criteria are based on the objectives of an organization and its internal and external context, but that they can also be derived from standards, laws, regulations or other requirements on organizations.

Risk criteria then help an organization understand how much risks matter, should they occur. As such, risk criteria include both the development of the impact scales for an organization, and the risk appetite and tolerance it needs to work within.

This will help an organization decide what controls should be put in place and whether the current level of risk is acceptable. It should also provide a means of establishing the overall total risk exposure so that this can be compared with the risk appetite of an organization and the capacity of an organization to withstand risk. Developing impact scales will be considered further in Chapter 15 and risk appetite and tolerance in Chapters 25 and 26.

Notes

1 FRC (2024) *Corporate Governance Code Guidance*, https://www.frc.org.uk/library/standards-codes-policy/corporate-governance/corporate-governance-code-guidance/#section.7eba31e6 (archived at https://perma.cc/24PW-T9TY)
2 IRM (2014) *Extended Enterprise: Managing risk in complex 21st century organisations*, https://www.theirm.org/media/7238/irm-extended-enterprise-resources-for-practitioners-full-document.pdf (archived at https://perma.cc/CT8Z-LSXY)
3 IRM (2018) *Horizon Scanning: A Practitioner's Guide*, https://www.theirm.org/media/7340/horizon-scanning_final2.pdf (archived at https://perma.cc/V86B-QCJH)
4 IEC 31010 (2019) *Risk management – Risk assessment techniques*, https://www.iso.org/obp/ui/en/#iso:std:iec:31010:ed-2:v1:en,fr (archived at https://perma.cc/PCT5-989L)
5 SASB (2017) *Sustainability Accounting Standards Board (SASB) Conceptual Framework*, https://sasb.ifrs.org/wp-content/uploads/2019/05/SASB-Conceptual-Framework.pdf (archived at https://perma.cc/5FSK-KU8Z)
6 ISO 31073 (2022) *Risk management – Vocabulary*, https://www.iso.org/obp/ui/en/#iso:std:iso:31073:ed-1:v1:en (archived at https://perma.cc/L4BD-APUM)

Stakeholders   11

Range of stakeholders

The term 'stakeholder' applies to the many constituencies impacted by an organization. ISO 31073 prefers the term 'interested party', but stakeholder is more readily accepted and an acceptable alternative. ISO 31073 defines an interested party (stakeholder) as a 'person or an organization that can affect, be affected by, or perceives itself to be affected by a decision or activity'. Understanding stakeholders is an important aspect in risk management, as they may bring risks to an organization and may also be instrumental in the management of those risks.

Stakeholders may have contradictory expectations of an organization; for the boards managing those organizations this can lead to an ethical dilemma. For example, a traditional 'theory of the firm' in economics suggests companies exist to maximize profit-making in any way that is legal. It has been argued that this attitude led to many corporate scandals. Certainly, it seems to have been the attitude that encouraged the high-risk strategy followed by HBOS (see Chapter 2). In this case the poor decision making of Mr Crosby hurt many millions of stakeholders.

Other examples can be found in manufacturing or chemical operations which were allowed, in the past, to discharge effluent and pollute rivers and lakes, making the water undrinkable and uninhabitable for fish and animals. Despite regulatory changes in most countries, there are still too many examples of water pollution around the world, whether in developed or developing countries.

For organizations in different sectors, the range of stakeholders will be different. For government agencies, the general public will be a major stakeholder. Specific groups within the general public will be stakeholders in different agencies, depending on the purpose of each particular agency. For organizations that have significant environmental interests or exposures, a different range of stakeholders would need to be considered.

Stakeholders can be less directly related to the operations of an organization than they initially expect; for example the taxpayers who funded the government rescue of banks during the financial crisis, and also funded businesses such as hospitality and events organizations during the health crisis, are all stakeholders.

Rio Tinto, one of the world's largest mining companies, wrestled with such an ethical dilemma, as shown in the next box.

DESTRUCTION OF A 46,000-YEAR-OLD ABORIGINAL HERITAGE SITE TO CREATE NEW MINE

In 2013, Rio Tinto received permission to conduct blasts at Pilbara mine site, Australia, under Section 18 of the WA Aboriginal Heritage Act. This removed the legal impediment to excavating ancient sites and legally allowed the destruction of ancient relics with proven genetic links to the present-day traditional owners, the Puutu Kunti Kurrama and Pinikura (PKKP) peoples. Archaeological digs conducted between 2013 and 2020 recovered richer finds than had been expected and the site was subsequently considered to be the oldest site of human occupation on the continent, with some of the earliest artefacts showing animal bones fashioned into tools.

In May 2020 the caves forming this ancient site were blown up to enable mining activity to take place. This act caused outrage in the wider community, leading to intense criticism on social media and damage to Rio Tinto's reputation. This also led directly to an investor backlash, which caused the board to request the resignation of Chief Executive Jean-Sébastien Jacques, the head of the business unit concerned and also the head of corporate affairs. These three senior executives were forced to leave within five months of the explosion taking place.

The chairman of Rio Tinto, Simon Thompson, was forced to apologize as he publicly stated the following: 'We have listened to our stakeholders' concerns that a lack of individual accountability undermines the group's ability to rebuild that trust and to move forward to implement the changes identified in the board review.'[1]

From the examples above it can be seen that the expectations placed on businesses have become wider than the pursuit of profit. There is now a greater need to balance the expectations of all stakeholders, and this has formed the basis of the international standard on governance, ISO 37000:2021, Governance of organizations – Guidance.[2] This standard considers improvement of long-term stakeholder value generation, effective stakeholder engagement and the provision of transparent, clear and concise reports and access to information to stakeholders.

These expectations have also been led by the investor community which, far from requiring greater profits for their own sake, is calling for sustainable profitability with more emphasis on the ethical dimensions to that profit. The requirement to balance different stakeholder needs is one that falls squarely on the board and one that, as we can see, has an impact on the reputation of an organization. It is clear from the many examples given that an organization's reputation is often its most valuable asset and therefore damage to this prized asset should be of concern to the risk management practitioner.

In March 2020, the Financial Conduct Authority (FCA) in the UK published proposals relating to the need for financial firms to disclose climate-related targets and their approach to investing in carbon activities and contributing to carbon reductions: the Task Force on Climate-related Financial Disclosures (TCFD). These requirements have extended beyond the financial community into all other organizations and boards have not only an ethical duty to take climate-related activity into account but, increasingly, a legal duty to do so. TCFD is explored further in Chapter 34.

Identifying stakeholders

In order to understand which stakeholders affect or can be affected by an organization and to engage with them effectively, they must be identified, taking into account those that are internal or external to an organization and the relationships between those stakeholders. Stakeholder mapping is a simple tool to do this.

Stakeholder maps can be used to inform strategy decisions, the identification and management of risks, the understanding of trends and drivers, the implementation of regulations, as well as enabling successful stakeholder engagement and management.

The Institute of Chartered Accountants in England and Wales (ICAEW)[3] note that there are three key principles of successful stakeholder engagement:

1 Listening, not just transmitting messages.

2 Recognizing that engagement is a reciprocal relationship.

3 Being willing to learn.

In order to build a stakeholder map, ICAEW suggest the first step is to establish its purpose, to understand why the exercise is being undertaken and how it will be used. Secondly, the different stakeholders should be identified, both the obvious and non-obvious, and the internal and external. Thirdly, these stakeholders need to be prioritized as not all are equal. A simple way to prioritize stakeholders is to use a Mendelow's matrix, as seen in Figure 11.1.

In addition to the lenses of level of interest and level of influence, it is useful to note whether the stakeholder is in favour of the activities being undertaken or against them. This can be done by simply putting a plus or minus next to the stakeholder. Most organizations will have stakeholder maps for different purposes, for example, for regulatory reporting, for engagement with shareholders, for different projects and so on. These existing stakeholder maps can also be utilized from a risk management perspective, rather than starting afresh each time.

Figure 11.1   Mendelow's matrix

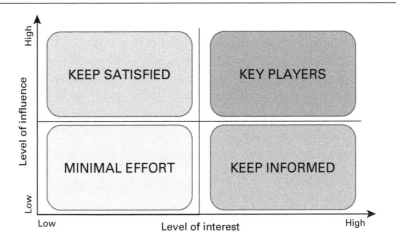

Stakeholder dialogue

The stakeholder mapping described above can then be used to develop communication plans. Dialogue with stakeholders should be based on a mutual understanding
of the objectives of an organization. The board is responsible for ensuring that the
dialogue is satisfactory. Although specific members of an organization may have the
day-to-day responsibility for communications with particular groups of stakeholders, the board will retain overall responsibility. Table 11.1 provides a summary of the
information that should be provided to shareholders of a company. This information
will focus on the provision of accurate financial data.

Table 11.1   Example data for shareholders

General	A clear statement of strategy and vision
	Corporate profile and principal markets
Financial data	Annual report and financial statements
	Archived financial information for the past three years
Corporate governance and CSR	Information related to compliance with Combined Code
	Information on the company CSR policies
Shareholder information	Shareholder analysis by size and constituent
	Information on directors' share dealings
Relevant news	Access to all news releases and presentations
	Developments that might affect the share value

The level and nature of dialogue with stakeholders will depend on the particular interests of the stakeholder in the operations of an organization. To obtain the fullest picture of the risks facing an organization, analysis of stakeholders and their expectations is necessary. The identification of stakeholder expectations is one output from the external evaluation stage of the business cycle. Different stakeholders may have expectations that are contradictory or even mutually exclusive in terms of the demands placed on an organization. The reporting of stakeholder engagement for larger companies has now been formalized, with Section 172 statements being required in strategy statements in the UK. Stakeholder dialogue in relation to reporting will be explored further in Chapter 22.

Stakeholders and core processes

Core processes deliver stakeholder expectations and are related to the internal and external context of an organization and as such both internal and external stakeholders should be identified, together with their short-term, medium-term and long-term expectations. Figure 11.2 provides a graphical illustration of the relationship between stakeholder expectations and the core processes of an organization. The figure illustrates that the core processes of an organization can be strategic, tactical, operational or compliance (STOC). Figure 11.2 shows compliance core processes as separate activities, although compliance core processes should also underpin and support the other types of core activities.

The relationship between core processes and stakeholder expectations is also considered in the attachment of risk in Chapter 12.

An approach based on stakeholder expectations has many advantages. It facilitates a full and thorough validation of the core processes of an organization in relation to the expectations that each stakeholder places on each core process. An important aspect of managing an organization is balancing the various stakeholder expectations. There are dangers and opportunities inherent in achieving this balance, and a risk identification procedure based on analysis of stakeholder expectations is the most robust way of ensuring that both are recognized, analysed and managed.

The analysis of stakeholder expectations is also one of the fundamental requirements of the business process re-engineering (BPR) approach. BPR is a technique to ensure that an organization has the most effective and efficient processes and operations. A starting point for many BPR exercises is to identify stakeholders and their expectations. The delivery of shared stakeholder expectations is then undertaken by the core processes of an organization. Core processes are the high-level collections of activities that are fundamentally important to an organization.

Figure 11.2 Importance of core processes

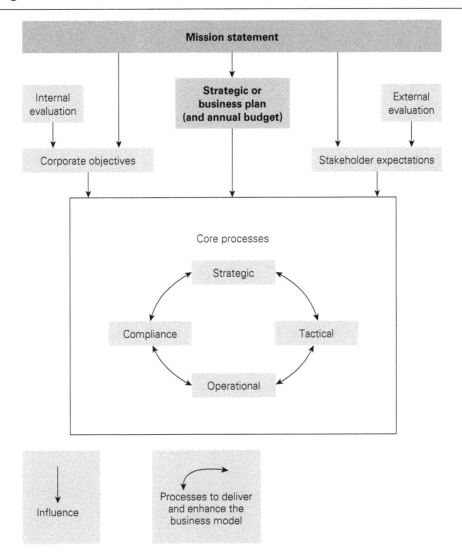

The stakeholders in the current and future activities of an organization can be identified. The expectations of each stakeholder in relation to each stated objective and
the corporate mission can then be evaluated. Shared expectations will emerge and
the core processes of an organization can then be defined (or refined) specifically in
terms of the delivery of these shared expectations. This approach is similar to social
materiality studies, which is explored further in Chapter 33.

Although the analysis of stakeholder expectations can be one of the most robust ways of identifying risks, there are implications in terms of the time and effort required for this approach to be successful. BPR can be a very time-consuming exercise when undertaken thoroughly. The benefits of taking a BPR or core processes approach include the ability to identify the core processes that are most vulnerable to risk events. This will enable the identification of stakeholders who are more likely to be dissatisfied because their expectations have not been delivered.

Stakeholders and strategy

It has been clearly established and demonstrated by research that incorrect risk management decisions related to strategy can destroy more value for an organization than incorrect risk management decisions associated with the operations or projects undertaken by an organization.

Stakeholder expectations are delivered by the core processes of an organization. The core processes that deliver stakeholder expectations can be strategic, tactical, operational or compliance (STOC). Strategic core processes need to be the most robust processes in an organization, and indeed this will be required by major stakeholder groups. Such stakeholders include financiers and other shareholders who are interested in the long-term success of an organization. These may be termed primary stakeholders. In using stakeholder analysis to inform strategy, all stakeholders should be identified who may affect relationships with primary stakeholders. For example, an environmental pressure group may influence customers by suggesting that the products made by an organization fail to meet ecological standards.

Stakeholders and tactics

Tactical stakeholders of an organization may be very different from those who are concerned with an organization's operations. If the tactics of an organization involve improvements to products, investment in new production techniques, response to technological changes or other developments that require a project, then finance is likely to be required. This means that financial bodies are likely to be key stakeholders in projects and similar tactical changes. Other stakeholders in projects, for example construction projects, may include building contractors and providers of other specialist professional support, such as architects.

The importance of employees in the implementation of tactics should not be underestimated. Staff will also have an interest in operational issues and be major stakeholders in an organization's operations. If changes to work practices or product features are to be successfully incorporated into the operations of an organization, then the support of staff is vitally important and good communication with them is essential.

It is important to consider the effect that changes, developments, projects and tactics will have on the full range of stakeholders. By considering the interests of stakeholders in detail, many unexpected surprises can be avoided, or, if beneficial, they could be exploited. The impact of the project, both in execution and after delivery, should be considered in detail. This consideration should extend both to internal and external stakeholders for whom the changes that the project will bring may be significant. These changes could relate to environmental factors during the construction project and after the work has been completed, as well as changes to the working arrangements for staff.

It may be a good idea to bring some people who are not directly involved in the activities of an organization into the project planning. This will enable an organization to fully understand the impact of the work that will be undertaken. When considering stakeholder management, the level of detail will often dictate whether engagement with stakeholders is successful. Even with successful projects, being able to minimize negative impacts by early attention to key stakeholders and their expectations may prove invaluable.

Stakeholders and operations

There may be many stakeholder groups involved in the operational activities of an organization. For example, pharmaceutical companies have a very diverse range of stakeholders, and especially so during the Covid-19 pandemic. Both AstraZeneca and Pfizer were involved in producing vaccines of different types for Covid-19 and had an obligation to ensure a constant availability of that medication. Governments were the main customers, but stakeholders included all patients and wider society as a whole.

The stakeholder groups that have an interest in the operational activities of an organization are likely to be customers, suppliers and others that may be affected by disruption to the normal efficient operation of an organization. For example, customers are likely to be affected if threats were to materialize. Likewise, suppliers are stakeholders in an organization and they will suffer if an organization is disrupted to the extent that their supplies/produce/components/services are no longer required.

Other stakeholder groups that are likely to be affected by threats will also have an interest in the continuity of the activities of an organization. For financial organizations such as banks, customers would be immediately affected if critical IT systems fail. The Bank of England, FCA and Prudential Regulation Authority (PRA)[4] published a policy statement on 'Operational Resilience: Impact tolerances for important business services' in March 2021, specifically referencing the need for organizations to:

- identify their important business services by considering how disruption to the business services they provide can have impacts beyond their own commercial interests;
- set a tolerance for disruption for each important business service;
- ensure they can continue to deliver their important business services and are able to remain within their impact tolerances during severe (or in the case of FMIs, extreme) but plausible scenarios.

The regulators also specifically require the board to approve the important business services identified for their firm and the impact tolerances that have been set for each of these.

Corporate governance models require the involvement of stakeholders and adequate stakeholder dialogue. In several countries, employees are recognized as stakeholders in an organization to the extent that employee representation on the board may be mandatory.

Communication and consultation with stakeholders are explored further in Chapter 22.

Notes

1 Rio Tinto (2020) Juukan Gorge, www.riotinto.com/news/inquiry-into-juukan-gorge (archived at https://perma.cc/E4NB-UK9V)

2 ISO 31000 (2021) Governance of organizations – Guidance, https://www.iso.org/obp/ui/en/#iso:std:iso:37000:ed-1:v1:en (archived at https://perma.cc/UCU9-GVV9)

3 ICAEW (2023) A guide to stakeholder mapping and engagement, https://www.icaew.com/technical/corporate-governance/new-boardroom-agenda/guide-to-stakeholder-mapping-and-engagement (archived at https://perma.cc/HDL3-WKVA)

4 Bank of England, PRA and FCA (2021) Operational Resilience: Impact tolerances for important business services, www.bankofengland.co.uk/-/media/boe/files/prudential-regulation/publication/2021/building-operational-resilience-impact-tolerances-for-important-business-services.pdf?la=en&hash=D6335BA4712B414730C697DC8BEB353F3EE5A628 (archived at https://perma.cc/MK4H-EM27)

Setting objectives 12

Strategy and objectives in standards

The various risk management standards that have been discussed in previous chapters all consider objective setting to be important. Both COSO and ISO have statements that are concerned with objective setting. The COSO (2017) ERM framework[1] goes further by explicitly stating the importance of considering risk in both the strategy-setting process and in driving performance. Objectives are then established to put the strategy into practice. The strategy and its associated objectives need to be clearly understood, to ensure the risk management process is effective.

It can be seen by considering these standards that ERM, strategy and objective setting are closely aligned and need to be integrated to work together in the strategic planning process. The ERM approach should ensure that an organization takes into account its risk appetite when framing its strategy. The strategy will in turn enable objectives to be designed and implemented and these objectives in turn will serve as a basis for identifying, analysing and managing to risk.

Again, in COSO 2017 the executive summary states, 'Enterprise risk management is as much about understanding the implications from the strategy and the possibility of strategy not aligning as it is about managing risks to set objectives'. Overall, therefore, the strategy is paramount: the ERM approach will inform strategy but strategy must come first. While easily said, this can still be challenging for the risk management practitioner for the following reasons.

Firstly, we should assume an organization has a consistent mission which is agreed upon by all senior management. From this it will be necessary to choose a range of suitable objectives that support the mission. This can be more challenging and will require consensus between senior management and the various stakeholders whose expectations need to be met. At this stage risk appetite will be an important factor in both making the choice of strategy and communicating that strategy to stakeholders.

Secondly, strategy does not exist in isolation: it will have been set according to the context of an organization at a point in time. That context will change, either gradually or through some form of disruptive activity caused by events such as technology failure. So, there will need to be a review of strategy at appropriate intervals, at which point it will be necessary to update and align the ERM approach to any newly aligned strategy.

Thirdly, in some organizations, and particularly large, geographically dispersed organizations, there may be different interpretations of the mission, and from that there may be a difference in the implementation of the strategy. This is where the culture of an organization will play a part and, as Peter Drucker the management educator said, 'culture eats strategy for breakfast'. By this he was meaning that the organization's culture is the dominant factor in its success and is clearly critical in terms of an agreed interpretation of the mission.

Fourthly, and linked to both the cultural issue discussed above and the requirement for consensus among management to the strategy, there is a need for the strategy to be accepted by all. There will be different agendas among management who have to deliver on the objectives that have been set and it will be important that those 'informal' objectives are aligned as far as possible to the formal objectives of an organization. Where they are not it can become toxic for an organization and at the extreme may need some 'fresh thinking' to deliver the objectives.

Lastly, it is important that the ERM approach does not overwhelm the setting of strategy, and therefore objectives. If ERM plays too great a role in the activity it may lead to an organization becoming overly risk averse and reducing its exposure to risk by being less ambitious in its strategy and setting too easily achievable targets.

Implementing objectives

The objectives once agreed will need to be cascaded in some form from the centre to each division or business unit that delivers the output of an organization and from there to each team or individual. It will be necessary to set some form of time period within which the objectives are to be achieved, and this should also be communicated at the organizational, divisional and team or individual level. Typically, organizations will seek to implement objectives over a one- to-three-year time horizon depending upon complexity. That time period will shorten as objectives are cascaded downwards, as shown in Figure 12.1.

Along with the time period in which to achieve objectives, it is important that there is a way of determining whether an objective has been achieved, and if so by how much. In other words, to be able to measure its realization in some way. Most organizations will have key performance indicators (KPIs) developed across an organization for a variety of reasons. One of those reasons should be to provide some measures that indicate whether objectives are being met. These KPIs can be used to help develop risk criteria, as noted in Chapter 10, and can also be used, where appropriate, to develop key risk indicators (KRIs) and key control indicators (KCIs), which will be explored further in Chapter 21.

From the tactical level this may be translated into quantitative terms in order to provide measurability. This may not be available for all objectives, however, and

Figure 12.1 Three levels of objective setting

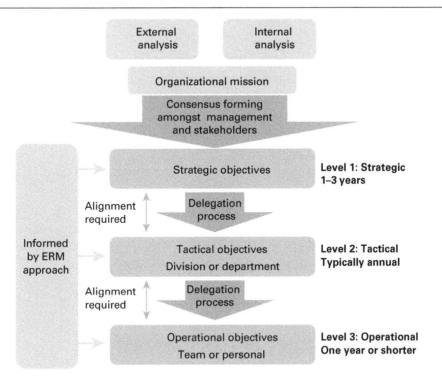

more qualitative aspects of managing risk may have objectives set around specific tasks to accomplish in a set period. For example, improving culture as a strategic objective may be translated to tactics such as running training or workshops. Measurability may be provided by some form of feedback scores from attendees. Care needs to be taken in more qualitative areas as they can provide an opportunity for 'gaming' the system by that individual, which would not achieve the stated intention of reducing risk.

Objectives need to be set in reality and with sufficient resources available to achieve them. And, finally, there must be a specific outcome to be achieved. The objectives will need to meet the SMART test as shown here. SMART objectives are:

- Specific – being clear about what needs to be accomplished.
- Measurable – having defined metrics that determine if the objective has been achieved.
- Achievable – having the tools and skills needed, and if not, ensuring they are gained.
- Relevant – ensuring the objective is aligned to the strategy.
- Time limited – providing a realistic date for delivering.

UK CABINET OFFICE: AN ESSENTIAL TOOL FOR DELIVERING OBJECTIVES

The Cabinet Office is the central ministry that brings a unifying focus to UK government activity. In its Annual Report and Accounts 2021–2022,[2] it states that 'Cabinet Office risk management and control environment management are essential tools used to minimise levels of uncertainty and to maximise the department's chances of successfully delivering its objectives, helping to inform both operational decision making and strategic planning.'

The publicly available report outlines the 'quarterly reporting cycle [is] established to review, report and escalate risks across the entire department, allowing ExCo, COARC and the Cabinet Office Board to remain informed on the key principal and emerging risks.' It also states that this quarterly reporting process is used 'to report overarching strategic risks that could have a significant impact on the department's ability to operate or meet its strategic vision.'

Aligning objectives to risk management principles

In Figure 12.1, it is noted that there needs to be alignment between each level of objective and the risk management perspective. This is because objectives are delivered by individuals, and different individuals respond to different criteria. There needs to be alignment between the longer- and shorter-term objectives, and between individual actions and organizational outcomes.

For example, how staff are rewarded according to the achievement of their objectives can have a significant effect on risk culture. Rewards that provide immediate and large bonus payments for the achievement of short-term gains may promote a culture of excessive risk taking, for instance by the aggressive selling tactics of banks prior to the global financial crisis. It was for this reason that 'clawbacks' were introduced to many financial services bonus arrangements in order to promote a longer-term perspective on risk taking. These clawbacks allow an organization to recover some element of previously paid bonuses should outcomes change over the longer term.

The Institute of Operational Risk[3] recommends that 'relevant professionals, from the operational risk function and the HR function, should be consulted about the organization's performance management and appraisal strategy to ensure that it promotes an appropriate risk culture'. They recommend, for example, that to help promote an appropriate risk culture, rewards are based on longer-term performance criteria such as customer satisfaction and retention, or profits over periods longer than one year, and that appraisals should reflect concern for operational risk and its management, as well as profit and sales growth.

Attachment of risks

Although most standard definitions refer to risks as being attached to corporate objectives, Figure 12.2 provides an illustration of the options for the attachment of

Figure 12.2   Attachment of risks

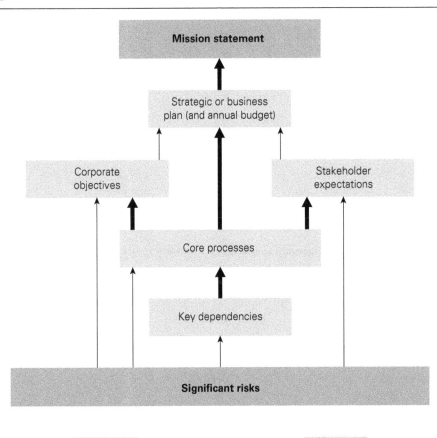

risks. Risks are shown in the diagram as being capable of impacting the key dependencies that deliver the core processes of an organization. Corporate objectives and stakeholder expectations help define the core processes of an organization. These core processes are key components of the existing nature and future enhancement of the business model and can relate to operations, tactics and corporate strategy, as well as compliance activities, as considered further in Chapter 11.

The intention of Figure 12.2 is to demonstrate that significant risks can be attached to aspects of an organization other than corporate objectives. Significant risks can be identified by considering the key dependencies of an organization, the corporate objectives and/or the stakeholder expectations, as well as by analysis of the core processes of an organization. For example, Arcadia, a clothes retailer in the UK, failed in 2020 because they had underinvested in online retailing and were unable to effectively maintain business operations (their core operations) when the Covid-19 pandemic disrupted their business model. The risk of underinvestment was magnified by the impact of the pandemic, which drove customers to online channels.

Another way of viewing the concept of attachment of risks is to consider, as alternative starting points for undertaking a risk assessment, those features shown in Figure 12.2. For example, a risk assessment can be undertaken by asking 'What do stakeholders expect of us?' and 'What risks could impact the delivery of those stakeholder expectations?'

One of the standard definitions of risk is that it is something that can impact the achievement of corporate objectives. This is a suitable definition, but to be useful the objectives should be presented as a full statement of the short-, medium- and long-term aims of an organization. Not only do the objectives need to be challenged to ensure that they are full and complete, but the assumptions that underpin the objectives should also receive careful and critical attention.

The 'objectives-driven' approach enables the analysis of the positive and negative aspects of risk. A drawback of reliance on using objectives is that they may fail to fully identify the strategic (or leadership), operational (or efficiency) and change (or competition) requirements of an organization. There is a danger of considering risks out of the context that gave rise to them if relying purely on this method, and a more robust analysis may be achieved when a 'dependencies-driven' approach to risk management is adopted.

Attachment of risks to key dependencies and stakeholder expectations is becoming more common. The importance of stakeholders and their expectations has been considered in more detail in Chapter 11. An organization will need to ask what features or components are key to success. Having identified key dependencies, an organization can then consider the risks that will impact these dependencies.

Core processes have been discussed in Chapter 10 and may be considered as the high-level processes that drive an organization. Risks may be attached to core processes, as well as being attached to objectives and/or key dependencies. Setting objectives for the ERM approach is intrinsically associated with the objectives for an organization as a whole. Making sure that the ERM objectives are aligned with an organization's objectives is therefore critical if the ERM approach is to be embedded correctly.

Therefore, a clear understanding of the organization's objectives is critical. Any misalignment of these objectives could be a risk in itself, as this could mean the risk management activity may support incorrect, unclear or vague objectives, leading to excellent risk management but of the wrong risks.

Notes

1 COSO (2017) *Enterprise Risk Management – Integrating with Strategy and Performance: Executive Summary*, https://www.coso.org/_files/ugd/3059fc_61ea5985b03c4293960642 fdce408eaa.pdf (archived at https://perma.cc/K8DB-5Y8L)
2 UK Cabinet Office (2022), Annual Report and Accounts 2021–2022, https://assets. publishing.service.gov.uk/media/639898b9d3bf7f3f7b333d83/CO_ARA21-22_WEB_ Final_121222.pdf (archived at https://perma.cc/DJ35-53KM)

Assessing risks – 13
risk identification
and articulation

Importance of risk assessment

The risk assessment step of the risk management process comprises both risk recognition and prioritization together with an understanding of whether anything further needs to be done to manage risks. It is defined in ISO 31000[1] as the overall process of risk identification, risk analysis and risk evaluation. Risk assessment is a key risk management input into strategy formulation and for this reason is a critical input to focus on for improved decision making.

Although risk assessment is vitally important, it is only useful if the conclusions of the assessment are used to inform decisions and/or to identify the appropriate risk responses for the type of risk under consideration. It should be considered an important part of the risk management process, but it is certainly not an end in itself. Managing risk is the priority rather than simply recording risk.

Approaches to risk assessment

There are a number of approaches that can be taken when planning how to undertake risk assessment. Before conducting the risk assessment, it is important to determine the participants in the risk assessment exercise. This can be achieved in one of two ways:

- senior management leading the process with information passed downwards for validation, as a top-down exercise; or
- by involving individual members of staff and local departmental management, as a bottom-up approach.

The opinion of the chief executive officer (CEO) is critically important, especially as it helps to define the overall attitude of an organization to risk. The CEO will be able to provide a structured view of the significant risks faced by an organization, but the CEO's focus is likely to be on external risks.

Technology such as 'crowd sourcing' software has become available in recent times and offers benefits of speed and a more dynamic approach to updating risks and monitoring emerging trends. Technology can provide additional information in the assessment of risk from different areas of an organization. If there is a broad spread of opinions, this needs to be explored, because it could represent a possible misunderstanding of the nature of the risk being discussed.

Table 13.1 provides examples of advantages and disadvantages of undertaking a top-down risk assessment exercise. A top-down risk assessment exercise will tend to focus on risks related to strategy, tactics, operations and compliance (STOC), in that order.

Table 13.2 provides examples of advantages and disadvantages of undertaking a bottom-up risk assessment exercise. A bottom-up risk assessment exercise will tend to focus on risks identified as threats and then as opportunities.

For most organizations, a combination of top-down and bottom-up risk assessments will be undertaken, with the risk manager collecting information from as many stakeholders as possible. Often, the main constraint in undertaking a bottom-up exercise is the greater time commitment that is required from the risk management department to attend and/or facilitate a series of risk assessment exercises.

Table 13.1 Top-down risk assessment

Advantages	Disadvantages
Likely to result in an enterprise-wide approach – the risks at the top will have impacts throughout the business.	Senior managers and directors tend to be more focused on risks external to an organization.
The most significant strategic risks for an organization can be captured quickly and there will be a manageable number.	Limited awareness of internal operational risks or interdependencies of risks within the business.
Shows risk management buy-in from the top, resulting in acceptance of risk management activities at all levels.	Danger that the approach becomes too superficial, because senior managers believe they can manage crises.
Since it originates from the top, there is likely to be consistent methodology throughout an organization.	New risks emerging from the operational activities of an organization might not be fully identified.

Table 13.2   Bottom-up risk assessment

Advantages	Disadvantages
Significant buy-in at all levels of an organization should be achieved.	There will be little focus on external risks or strategic risks.
Can be mirrored to an existing organization chart, and risk impacts beyond immediate operational risks can be discussed.	Time-consuming and may demotivate, if it takes longer to develop the overall enterprise results.
Operational staff have great awareness of local risks and their causes, which might elude higher levels of management.	Danger that the approach becomes too detailed and blinkered, resulting in a siloed approach to risk assessment.
Methodology can be varied according to local norms and culture, and this is useful for a multinational organization.	New risks emerging from the operational activities of the business might not be reported by operational staff.

Risk identification

Risk identification involves identifying, recognizing and acknowledging risks in relation to the context and objectives set (both opportunities and threats). In general, the overall approach by an organization to risk identification will be heavily influenced by the techniques that are selected. It is important that the approach that is adopted is consistent with the culture of an organization. For example, it should be considered whether an organization processes information best through workshops, or through written and structured reports.

Risk articulation

Before embarking on risk identification techniques, it worth spending some time considering how risks are articulated. This will support not just the risk identification process, but also the understanding of the risks once they are raised.

If risks are not articulated effectively, there is a high chance that others will make incorrect assumptions about what they mean. This can lead to incorrect analysis, and therefore wrong controls and monitors being put in place, and the real risk not being managed, either at all, or at least not effectively.

FIRE?

Quite often one word is included in a register to describe a risk. 'Fire' is a common example. This might be quite obvious to the author of the risk, but may not be clear to those who read the risk information in isolation. The author was thinking about a fire in the building leading to the destruction of the premises. The reader could have misinterpreted the risk to mean a small fire in the 'smoker's corner', or that a gun or ammunition might be fired, or someone might be fired from their job, or from a positive perspective, it might be putting the fire on because the room is cold, or firing up the barbeque so that we can have a party.

Many different possible risks flow from the use of one word.

The UK Government's Orange Book considers this further in Annex 5,[2] where it asserts that 'in stating risks, care should be taken to avoid stating consequences that arise as being risks themselves, i.e. identifying the symptoms without their cause(s).' The document goes further to note that care should also be taken not to define risks as the opposite to objectives, with the example given of 'failure to achieve the intended output/outcome' not being a risk.

Using the wider definition of risk from ISO 31000, Note 3 states that 'risk is usually expressed in terms of risk sources, potential events, their consequences and their likelihood.' As such, in describing a risk fully, one or two words will not suffice.

The risk source is usually considered the cause(s) of the risk. ISO 31000 defines the risk source as the 'element which alone or in combination has the potential to give rise to the risk'. The consequence or effect is usually considered the impact(s) should the risk occur, where positive impacts would signify an opportunity and negative impacts would signify a threat.

The Orange Book follows this format, suggesting the use of three separate parts to articulating a risk, through the terms cause, event (risk) and consequence, providing examples of all three parts.

The project world has also been using these three parts to tell the story of risks for many years, referred to as risk 'metalanguage'. In the third edition of *Practical Project Risk Management*, Hillson and Simon (2020)[3] describe risk metalanguage as a three-part structured description of a risk which separates cause, risk and effect, an adapted version of which can be seen in Figure 13.1.

In line with Figure 13.1 and ISO 31000, causes can be anything with the intrinsic potential to lead to the risk occurring. They can be direct or indirect and occur alone or in conjunction with one another. The causes should be facts, things that are

Figure 13.1   Describing a risk

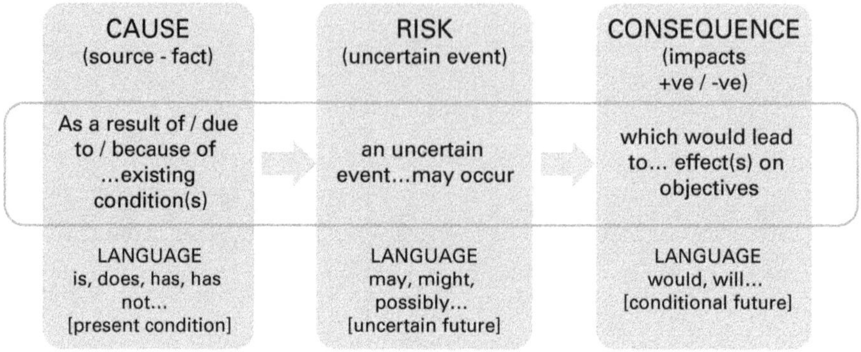

already in existence, such that they have happened or are happening. Understanding the context is helpful here as it provides an understanding of what is happening in the world around the team/organization that can inform whether a risk might happen. As such, the language used should be factual, using words such as 'is, does, has or has not'.

Risks are those uncertainties, that if they occurred would impact positively or negatively on what is trying to be achieved. As such, the language used should reflect the uncertainty, such as 'potential to', 'chance of', 'possibly', 'may' or 'might'. The risk ensures that uncertainty is involved, and that an issue is not being described instead – an issue being an unplanned event that has occurred.

Effects include anything that would reasonably happen as a result of the risk occurring. Although there may be some uncertainty in the impact, such as how big that impact could be, it is simpler to use language that signifies a conditional future, such as would or will. Using uncertain words in relation to consequence causes confusion as to which part of the sentence is the actual risk.

This technique has been used by many organizations to simplify and clarify the risk description. The reader then has more information to understand the risk and the suggested prioritization, ownership and management options. The causes inform how likely the risk is to occur, and what should be managed to either prevent the threat from occurring or enable the opportunity to occur. The effects inform the size of the impact the risk would have on objectives if it were to occur, and what should be in place to reduce the impact of the threat or enhance the impact of the opportunity.

Although this approach has originated in the project environment, it is an equally valid technique for describing any risk in any organization, whether threat or opportunity. Table 13.1 provides some examples of effective risk articulation.

Table 13.3 Examples of risk articulation

Cause	Risk	Effect
Because the team has not had the correct training for the new, highly complex equipment, …	…there is the potential for the equipment not to be used properly by those operating it, …	…resulting in patients not receiving the correct treatment, staff receiving injuries and damage to the hospital's reputation.
Due to the storing of flammable chemicals, staff being seen smoking in the storeroom and hot works being undertaken in a nearby vicinity, …	…a fire may start in the storage area, …	…leading to injuries, destruction to property, interruptions to day-to-day activities and legal action.
Due to the history between ourselves and key suppliers, …	…interface management on the new project may be better than expected, …	…which would lead to a reduction in the schedule and improvements in operational activities.
Because the onboarding process does not capture all staff, there are instances of poor culture regarding data collection, and often lack of support from management, …	…we may have poor quality data, …	…resulting in recurring incidents, incorrect labelling, rework, compliance breaches, reduction in performance and fines.
As a result of problems with suppliers and changing trends in customer requirements, …	…we might be able forge new relationships with other suppliers, …	…which would result in improved service, supply of essential products and more satisfied customers.

Known unknowns

Very much related to the articulation of risks, there is also the question of what information is being raised through the risk identification process.

There have been lots of discussions regarding things we know we know and those we don't. This concept was made famous in 2002, when the US Secretary of Defense, Donald Rumsfeld, remarked about 'known unknowns' when questioned about intelligence reports that did not back his assertion that Iraq was supplying weapons of mass destruction.

He stated that:

> as we know, there are known knowns; there are things we know we know. We also know there are known unknowns; that is to say we know there are some things we do not know. But there are also unknown unknowns – the ones we don't know we don't know. And if one looks throughout the history of our country and other free countries, it is the latter category that tends to be the difficult one.

SOURCE CNN (2002), Rumsfeld, Knowns, https://www.youtube.com/watch?v=REWeBzGuzCc

Donald Rumsfeld made a good point about different areas of risk, but putting these into a matrix, he missed one quadrant out – the unknown known. Figure 13.2 considers each part of a known unknowns matrix, which is loosely based on the Johari window.

The Johari window, created by psychologists Joseph Luft and Harrington Ingham in 1955, is a framework that assesses conscious and unconscious bias, in relation to self-awareness and the understanding of others. The matrix for the Johari window plots things that are known or not known to others against things that are known or not known to self, resulting in four quadrants described as the 'open area' (known to both), the 'blind spot' (known to others but not to self), the 'hidden area' (not known to others, but known to self) and the 'unknown' (not known to either).

As shown in Figure 13.2, the axes are simplified to 'known' and 'unknown'. Where everything is known about something – the known knowns – the quadrant is described as the 'facts'. Some people might term these facts as incidents or issues (unplanned events that have or are occurring). Things in this space are certainties. If it is thought that a 'fact' might happen again, then uncertainty is being introduced, which is termed as the known unknown quadrant. In this space, things are uncertainties, but they are recognized. As such these are the 'acknowledged risks' that are on risk registers and are being managed.

Moving round the quadrants, the next area denotes the unknown unknowns – the true surprises. Another term for things in this space is 'black swans', defined by Nicolas Taleb (2007)[4] in his book with the same name. The book explores random events or true surprises, from bestsellers to world disasters. The premise behind black swans is that the impact is large if they occur, but that they are impossible to predict, and that the human tendency is to try to rationalize them or to find simple explanations for them in their aftermath. A risk that has often been described as a black swan is the Covid-19 global pandemic. However, even Taleb[5] has denounced this, explaining that the pandemic was wholly predictable.

Risks such as Covid-19 are more akin to HILPs: high-impact, low-probability risks. These risks are often overlooked in registers and on risk matrices as they are

Figure 13.2   Known unknowns matrix

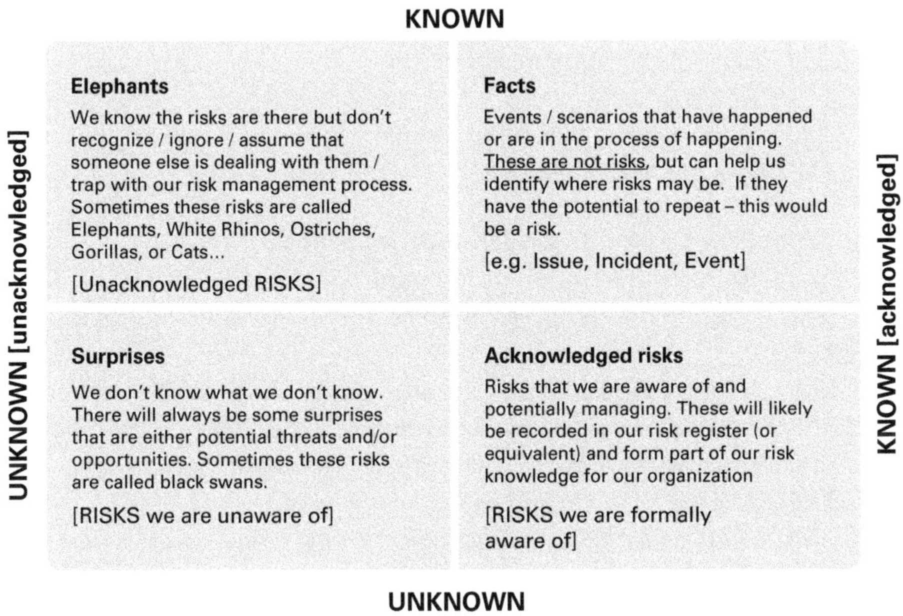

KNOWN

Elephants

We know the risks are there but don't recognize / ignore / assume that someone else is dealing with them / trap with our risk management process. Sometimes these risks are called Elephants, White Rhinos, Ostriches, Gorillas, or Cats...

[Unacknowledged RISKS]

Facts

Events / scenarios that have happened or are in the process of happening. These are not risks, but can help us identify where risks may be. If they have the potential to repeat – this would be a risk.

[e.g. Issue, Incident, Event]

Surprises

We don't know what we don't know. There will always be some surprises that are either potential threats and/or opportunities. Sometimes these risks are called black swans.

[RISKS we are unaware of]

Acknowledged risks

Risks that we are aware of and potentially managing. These will likely be recorded in our risk register (or equivalent) and form part of our risk knowledge for our organization

[RISKS we are formally aware of]

UNKNOWN [unacknowledged]

KNOWN [acknowledged]

UNKNOWN

SOURCE Adapted from Taylor, L (2014), *Practical Enterprise Risk Management*, Kogan Page, London, UK

not at the top of the list or in the top right-hand corner of a matrix, which would signify that they need to be considered further. Some organizations specifically focus on HILP risks to ensure that they are given the attention and management they deserve. However, many other organizations don't deal with them, perhaps putting them into the 'too difficult' pile. These kinds of risks, among others, drift into the fourth quadrant of the matrix.

Unknown knowns are uncertainties, which many in an organization will know about, but which are not recognized. As such these are 'unacknowledged risks', that even if on a risk register are being ignored and not managed. Risks in this space are often also known as elephants in the room, or ostriches with their head in the sand, or the cat that is under the table (depending on the country which provides the term).

Whichever animal is used, risks in this quadrant usually exists for a number of reasons: 1) they are too difficult to deal with; 2) they are about a sensitive subject that no one in an organization discusses; 3) it is assumed that someone else is managing the risk; or 4) the risk management process itself stops them being raised, for example, because an organization only focuses on the top five risks, or likelihood is not understood, or the system is too clumsy or difficult to input risks easily so people refuse to do so.

Risk practitioners should understand risks in all quadrants of the known unknowns matrix, but the real value comes from supporting an organization to recognize and manage those elephants, because if they occur, they usually result in a great deal of damage for organizations.

ELEPHANTS IN THE ROOM

When the Volkswagen (VW) emissions scandal became public, CEO Martin Winterkorn stated that he was unaware of the issue. The illegal 'defeat device' installed in US cars to trick US regulators, would have initially cost approximately $22m to fix.

However, nothing was done about it, and although VW admitted that Winterkorn was sent a memo explaining that some cars were actually producing 35 times the amount of nitrogen oxide allowed by the US regulations, the ex-CEO, at the time, denied all knowledge.

As of 2020, the emissions scandal has cost VW £33.3bn in fines, and Martin Winterkorn began a trial in September 2024 in Germany on charges of fraud and market manipulation in relation to the scandal.

SOURCE Yahoo News (2024) Trial of former Volkswagen CEO Winterkorn over diesel scandal set to start in September, https://uk.news.yahoo.com/trial-former-volkswagen-ceo-winterkorn-145844890.html?guccounter=1&guce_referrer=aHR0cHM6Ly93d3cuZ29vZ2xlLmNvbS88&guce_referrer_sig=AQAAAN7qa3kyFi7E6RqucCXESqnB1QX2RrnKzgHCSndgcEAiAbCVOZfZkEpRsCVyaOFXK9NDue2rl1HOFjmGFq0n9GQrrSUE_Wc8TTddpLdIpQhmQAcpuiI-0EjqDp2hYYlfCm7sAQK5t_dVgEHew_CWWO39QSuzV2dcfoQ3BZXW9ch5

Risk identification techniques

There are a wide range of risk assessment techniques available. The ISO International Standard IEC 31010:2019: Risk management – Risk assessment techniques provides detailed information on the full range of risk assessment techniques that can be used – for identification, analysis and evaluation. Table 13.4 lists the five key risk identification techniques that are commonly used and provides a brief description of each of these techniques.

Checklists and questionnaires have the advantage that they are usually simple to complete and are less time-consuming than other risk assessment techniques. However, this approach does have the potential disadvantage that any risk not referenced by appropriate questions may not be recognized as significant. A simple analysis of the advantages and disadvantages of each of the five common risk identification techniques is set out in Table 13.5.

Table 13.4 Techniques for risk identification

Technique	Brief description
Questionnaires and checklists	Use of structured questionnaires and checklists to collect information that will assist with the recognition of the significant risks.
Workshops and brainstorming	Collection and sharing of ideas at workshops to discuss the events that could impact the objectives, core processes or key dependencies.
Inspections and audits	Physical inspections of premises and activities and audits of compliance with established systems and procedures.
Flow charts and dependency analysis	Analysis of the processes and operations within an organization to identify critical components that are key to success.
Crowdsourcing technology	Use of mobile applications to enable individuals to upload their views on risks to a data platform.

Table 13.5 Advantages and disadvantages of risk identification techniques

Technique	Advantages	Disadvantages
Questionnaires and checklists	Consistent structure guarantees consistency Greater involvement than in a workshop	Rigid approach may result in some risks being missed Questions will be based on historical knowledge
Workshops and brainstorming	Consolidated opinions from all interested parties Greater interaction produces more ideas	Senior management tends to dominate Issues will be missed if incorrect people involved
Inspections and audits	Physical evidence forms the basis of opinion Audit approach results in good structure	Inspections are more suitable for hazard risks Audit approach tends to focus on historical experience
Flow charts and dependency analyses	Useful output that may be used elsewhere Analysis produces better understanding of processes	Difficult to use for strategic risks May be very detailed and time-consuming
Crowdsourcing technology	Speed of collection of data Analysis of responses enables a dashboard approach Diverse input enabled Encourages visual representation	Individuals may abuse the system maliciously, or find other ways to affect the system to produce incorrect outcomes

Given that risks can be attached to other aspects of an organization as well as or instead of objectives, a convenient and simple way of recognizing risks is to identify the key dependencies faced by an organization. Most people within an organization will be able to identify the aspects of the business that are fundamentally important to its future success. Identifying the factors that are required for success will give rise to a list of the key dependencies for an organization. The extended enterprise methodology considered in Chapter 10 would be useful for understanding these key dependencies.

Risk workshops are probably the most common of the risk identification techniques. Brainstorming during workshops enables opinions regarding the significant risks faced by an organization to be shared and a common view and understanding of each risk is achieved. However, the disadvantage can be that the more senior people in the room may dominate the conversation, and contradicting their opinions may be difficult and unwelcome.

One of the challenges when undertaking a risk workshop that covers both opportunities and threats is that perhaps a wide range of people will need to attend. Threats tend to be operational and compliance related, whereas opportunities tend to be associated with strategy and tactics. However, opportunities can be found in both operational and compliance activities, where improvements can be made, and there are always threats related to strategy and tactics.

In order to have a structured discussion at a risk identification workshop, several brainstorming structures are commonly used. These may be qualitative or quantitative, depending on the level of analysis of the risk that is required. The most common of the qualitative brainstorming structures are the SWOT and PESTLE analyses.

SWOT is an analysis of the strengths, weaknesses, opportunities and threats faced by an organization. The SWOT analysis has the benefit that it also considers the upside of risk by evaluating opportunities in the external environment. One of the strengths of the SWOT analysis is that it can be linked to strategic decisions. However, because it is not a structured risk classification system, there is a possibility that not all of the risks will be identified.

The other common qualitative approach is the PESTLE analysis that considers the political, economic, social, technological, legal and environmental/ethical risks faced by an organization. PESTLE is a well-established structure with proven results for undertaking brainstorming sessions during risk assessment workshops. Table 14.3, in Chapter 14, considers the PESTLE risk classification system in more detail.

Another option for brainstorming is to build a 'wall of risk'. This can be done in either a face-to-face or an online workshop, where each attendee is provided with a stack of Post-it notes and a pen (physically or virtually). Attendees are then given time to write a risk on individual Post-it notes, usually anywhere from two to 15 minutes depending on the length of the workshop. The facilitator then asks one person to share a risk, placing it on the wall (which has been prepared, either using a large whiteboard, or on to flipchart paper stuck to the wall). Other attendees are then asked whether they have similar risks or related risks. Risks are then posted on to the wall with lines drawn (carefully) between those that are related.

This technique allows attendees to write their own risks, provides more engagement with attendees, highlights the interconnectedness of risks, and assists in the development of themes. Further information on facilitation and workshops is explored in Chapter 41.

Many organizations will wish to undertake a more quantitative approach to identification of risks, usually in consideration of the possibility of a risk occurring. There are several techniques available for undertaking these quantitative evaluations. The most common are hazard and operability (HAZOP) studies and failure modes effects analysis (FMEA). Both techniques are structured approaches that ensure that few risks are omitted. However, the involvement of a wide range of experts is required in order to undertake an accurate quantitative analysis.

HAZOP and FMEA techniques are most easily applied to manufacturing operations. HAZOP studies are often undertaken of hazardous chemical installations and complex transport structures, such as railways. Also, HAZOP studies of complex installations, such as nuclear power stations, are often undertaken. They can also be applied to the analysis of the safety of products. In both cases, these are very analytical and time-consuming approaches, but such an approach will be necessary in a wide range of circumstances.

GOVERNMENT RISK ASSESSMENTS

The UK Government notes in its National Risk Register[6] that:

It will actively involve significant stakeholders, including members of the public, throughout the risk identification, assessment and management process. This will support timely and targeted action. Two-way communication will be used in all stages of policy development, risk assessment and risk management. Where there are differences in interpretation it will aim to clarify these through open discussion, and it will seek to balance conflicting views in a way that best serves the wider public interest. It will explain how views obtained through consultation have been reflected in its decisions.

In the document, the UK government also notes that they have been more transparent than ever, basing the register on their internal National Security Risk Assessment. The only information excluded from the register has been done so for specific purposes, such as national security or commercial confidentiality.

Emerging risks

All organizations are concerned about changes in the external and internal context that give rise to new challenges. These challenges can be considered to be the emerging risks facing an organization. The International Risk Governance Council[7] defines these risks as:

> a risk that is new, or a familiar risk in a new or unfamiliar context or under new context conditions (re-emerging). Emerging risks are issues that are perceived to be potentially significant but which may not be fully understood and assessed, thus not allowing risk management options to be developed with confidence.

Consideration of these risks can be difficult unless an organization clearly understands the nature of the emerging risks that it faces. Following the above definition emerging risks can be divided into three categories:

- new risks that have emerged in the external environment, but are associated with the existing strategy of an organization – new risks in a known context;
- existing risks that were already known to an organization, but have developed or changed circumstances have triggered the risk – known risks in a new context;
- risks that were not previously faced by an organization, because the risks are associated with changed core processes – new risks in a new context. This last category is where the risk manager will have the least confidence and will need to actively seek further information.

ISO/TS 31050 (2023)[8] goes further regarding the nature of emerging risks, with five different possible components:

- risks that have not been previously recognized or experienced by an organization;
- familiar risks in a new or unfamiliar context where the existing knowledge is not applicable;
- significantly evolving risk;
- systemic risks (those that are highly interconnected);
- a novel combination of risks.

The level of risk faced by organizations is constantly shifting, caused by challenges such as increased interconnectedness, new technology and increasingly complex supply chains. Some of these increasing risks will be under the control of an organization itself but many emerging risks will not be within the control of an individual organization, due to causes such as:

- government direction;
- climate change;

- sovereign debt;
- national security;
- changing demographics.

Depending on the activities of an organization, many of these emerging risks may be threats to an organization or represent opportunities for future development. In some cases, the emerging risks will simply represent additional uncertainties that need to be managed.

An important consideration when thinking about emerging risks is the speed at which they can become significant. Some risk management practitioners refer to the speed of development and change of risks as the risk velocity. Risk velocity will be considered further in Chapter 16.

A good example of emerging risk is nanotechnology.

THE RISKS OF NANOTECHNOLOGY

Nanotechnology is used extensively in the medical sector to conduct sensitive medical procedures and, to some extent, the cosmetics industry, to improve the effectiveness of cosmetic treatment of skin conditions. Whether any long-term risks will emerge from the use of nanotechnology has not yet been fully established. As nanotechnology is an emerging field, there is great debate regarding the extent that it will benefit or pose risks for human health. Nanotechnology's health impact can be split into two aspects: the potential for medical applications to cure disease, and the potential health hazards posed by exposure to nano-materials.

The extremely small size of nano-materials means that they are much more readily taken up by the human body than larger-sized particles. How these nano-particles behave inside an organism is not fully resolved and cannot be, without being applied at some scale. Health and environmental issues combine in the workplace of companies engaged in producing or using nano-materials and in the laboratories engaged in nano-science and nanotechnology research.

Notes

1 ISO (2018) ISO 31000: Risk Management – Guidelines, https://www.iso.org/obp/ui/#iso:std:iso:31000:ed-2:v1:en (archived at https://perma.cc/B69S-QYV4)
2 UK Government (2023) *The Orange Book: Management of Risk – Principles and Concepts*, https://assets.publishing.service.gov.uk/media/6453acadc33b460012f5e6b8/HMT_Orange_Book_May_2023.pdf (archived at https://perma.cc/QC37-YBWT)

3 Hillson, D and Simon, P (2020) *Practical Project Risk Management*, Berrett-Koehler Publishers Inc, Oakland, CA

4 Taleb, N (2007) *The Black Swan: The Impact of the Highly Improbable*, Penguin Group, London.

5 *The New Yorker* (2020) The pandemic isn't a black swan but portent of a more fragile global system, https://www.newyorker.com/news/daily-comment/the-pandemic-isnt-a-black-swan-but-a-portent-of-a-more-fragile-global-system (archived at https://perma.cc/NC48-GMWF)

6 HM Government (2023) National Risk Register – 2023 edition, https://assets.publishing.service.gov.uk/media/64ca1dfe19f5622669f3c1b1/2023_NATIONAL_RISK_REGISTER_NRR.pdf (archived at https://perma.cc/93VA-JYLK)

7 IRG (2019) Governance of emerging risks, https://irgc.org/risk-governance/emerging-risk (archived at https://perma.cc/XTE9-GV7T)

8 ISO/TS 31050 (2023) Risk management – Guidelines for managing an emerging risk to enhance resilience, https://www.iso.org/obp/ui/en/#iso:std:iso:ts:31050:ed-1:v1:en (archived at https://perma.cc/3SPE-RHJ2)

Classifying risks   14

Risk classification systems

There will be many identified risks facing an organization. The volume of these identified risks means there will often be too many risks to focus on any particular area and a structure to classify them will be required. Formalized risk classification systems enable an organization to identify where similar risks exist. Classification of risks also enables an organization to identify who should be responsible for setting strategy for management of related or similar risks. Appropriate classification of risks will enable an organization to better identify the risk appetite, risk capacity and total risk exposure in relation to each risk, group of similar risks or generic type of risk.

There are a number of classification systems available. They may sort the risks according to timescale of their impact or according to the nature of the risk, the source of the risk and/or the nature of the impact or size and nature of the consequences. Different systems have been devised in different circumstances and by different organizations; therefore, the categories are similar but not identical. For example, operational risk is referred to as infrastructure risk in the FIRM risk scorecard.

In describing different risk classification systems, Table 14.1 illustrates that many offer a combination of source, event, impact and consequences categories.

British Standard BS 31100[1] sets out the advantages of having a risk classification system. It states that the number and type of risk categories employed should be selected to suit the size, purpose, nature, complexity and context of an organization. The categories should also reflect the maturity of risk management within an organization. The advantages of having a risk classification system include:

- Accumulations of risk that could undermine a key dependency or business objective and make it vulnerable can be more easily identified.

- Responsibility for improved management of each different type of risk can be more easily identified/allocated if risks are classified.

- Decisions and knowledge about the type of control(s) that will be implemented can be taken on a more structured and informed basis.

- Circumstances where the risk appetite of an organization is being exceeded (or the risk criteria not being implemented) can be more readily identified.

- Categorizing risks according to a single risk classification system may not be sufficient to reveal all risks. Therefore, a combination of systems can be used to provide a complete picture.

Time to impact

Although not a formalized system, the classification of risks into short, medium and long term helps to identify risks as being related (primarily) to operations, tactics and strategy, respectively. This distinction is not clear-cut, but it can assist with further classification of risks.

A short-term risk can impact the objectives, key dependencies and core processes instantly. These risks can cause disruption to operations immediately the event occurs. They are predominantly threats, although this is not always the case. Short-term risks usually impact the ability of an organization to maintain effective and efficient core processes that are concerned with the continuity and monitoring of routine operations.

A medium-term risk can impact an organization following a (short) delay after the event occurs. Typically, the impact of a medium-term risk would be apparent within months, or at most a year after the event. Medium-term risks usually impact the ability of an organization to maintain effective and efficient core processes that are concerned with the management of tactics, projects and other change programmes. In information security risk, the phrase 'zero-day attack' indicates the day a system was breached and counting from that day to when organizations were aware of the breach can be between three and nine months.

A long-term risk can impact an organization between one and five years (or more) after the event. Long-term risks usually impact the ability of an organization to maintain the core processes that are concerned with the development and delivery of effective and efficient strategy. Risks that have the potential to undermine strategy can destroy more value than risks to operations and tactics.

Another consideration in relation to the time to impact and the short, medium and long timescale is when controls need to be put in place to manage the risks. Figure 14.1 indicates those that are considered short, sharp risks where the impact is felt quickly after a risk occurs, such as safety risks. There are others that take time to build up, some of which might then drop off and go away, such as a human resource risk where the lack of resource can take time to impact an organization, but could be treated and managed. The rest are often termed the slow burners, that take a long time to build up, but can have a large impact on an organization, for example, climate change. As such, it is not just considering how much impact a risk can have on an organization along a timeline, but when actions need to be taken to manage it.

Figure 14.1 Risks across different time horizons

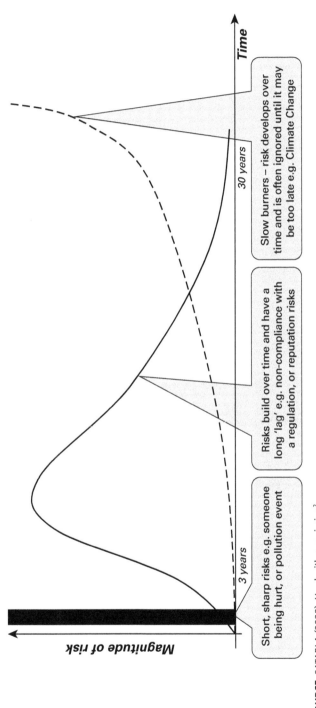

Short, sharp risks e.g. someone being hurt, or pollution event

Risks build over time and have a long 'lag' e.g. non-compliance with a regulation, or reputation risks

Slow burners – risk develops over time and is often ignored until it may be too late e.g. Climate Change

3 years

30 years

Magnitude of risk

Time

SOURCE SATARLA (2020). Used with permission[2]

VAPES

Lithium is an alkali metal which is becoming one of the most valuable commodities on the planet due its use in batteries, which power anything from electric cars to smartphones. Extracting lithium is very energy intensive and can have a large impact on the environment, but it is a very recyclable material. This is a quandary for society that in order to protect the environment, through the use of batteries, the environment in places will be damaged.

According to Material Focus, the not-for-profit organization campaigning for the better recycling of electricals, of the 500 million vapes sold each year in the UK, approximately 50 per cent of single use vapes are thrown away, the equivalent of just over one million every week. The lithium in the batteries contained in those vapes could power 1,200 electric vehicles.

In order to support and protect the environment, common sense would dictate that more is done to encourage the recycling of not just vapes but all electrical equipment and batteries, and the sooner the better to manage the 'slow burning' risk. In fact, many countries have already banned the use of disposable vapes or intend to do so in the near future.

SOURCE Material Focus (2022) One million single use vapes thrown away every week contributing to the growing e-waste challenge in the UK, https://www.materialfocus.org.uk/press-releases/one-million-single-use-vapes-thrown-away-every-week-contributing-to-the-growing-e-waste-challenge-in-the-uk/

SOURCE Earth.org (2023) The Environmental Impacts of Lithium and Cobalt mining, https://earth.org/lithium-and-cobalt-mining/#:~:text=Though%20emissions%20deriving%20from%20mining,and%20potential%20for%20groundwater%20contamination

Examples of risk classification systems

The more commonly used risk classification systems are highlighted in Table 14.1, provided in the main by international and industry standards and best practice.

It is for an organization to decide which risk classification system most fully satisfies its needs and requirements, or to tailor elements of systems into an individual framework.

FIRM risk scorecard

The FIRM risk scorecard builds on the different aspects of risk, and reflects the idea that every organization should be concerned about its finances, infrastructure, reputation and marketplace success. The attributes of the FIRM risk scorecard are set out in Table 14.2.

Table 14.1   Examples of risk classification systems

Standard or framework	FIRM risk scorecard	PESTLE	The Orange Book	Financial services sector	World Economic Forum Global Risk Report
Classification headings	Financial Infrastructure Reputational Marketplace	Political Economic Social Technological Legal Ethical/ Environmental	Strategy Governance Operations Legal Property Financial Commercial People Technology Information Security Project/ Programme Reputational	Market Credit Operational Strategic Liquidity Know your customer (KYC) Anti-money laundering (AML) Conduct risk	Economic Environmental Geopolitical Societal Technological

The FIRM risk scorecard can also be used as a template for the identification of corporate objectives, stakeholder expectations and, most importantly, key dependencies. Use of the FIRM risk scorecard facilitates robust risk identification by ensuring that the chances of failing to identify a significant risk are much reduced.

The inclusion of reputational risks as a separate category of risk in the FIRM risk scorecard is not universally accepted. It is often argued that damage to reputation is a consequence of other risks materializing rather than a separate risk category. It could be said, however, that the nature of reputation has changed in an era of social media. If a broad view of risk is taken, it becomes obvious that reputations can be burnished or damaged at a rapid pace.

PESTLE

Table 14.3 provides an outline of the PESTLE risk classification system. PESTLE is an acronym that stands for political, economic, social, technological, legal and environmental risks. This risk classification system is most applicable to the analysis of threats and is less easy to apply to financial, infrastructure and reputational risks.

The PESTLE risk classification system is often seen as most relevant to the analysis of external risks. External risk in this context is intended to refer to the external context that is not wholly within the control of an organization but where action can be taken to manage the risks. It is often suggested that the PESTLE risk classification

Table 14.2 Attributes of the FIRM risk scorecard

	Finance	Infrastructure	Reputation	Marketplace
Description	Risks that can impact the way in which money is managed and profitability is achieved	Risks that will impact the level of efficiency and cause dysfunction within the core processes	Risks that will impact the desire of customers to deal or trade, and level of customer retention	Risks that will impact the level of customer trade or expenditure
Internal or external risk	Internal	Internal	External	External
Quantifiable	Usually	Sometimes	Not always	Yes
Measurement (performance indicator)	Gains and losses from internal financial control	Level of efficiency in processes and operations	Nature of publicity and effectiveness of marketing profile	Income from commercial and market activities
Performance gap	**Procedures** Failure of procedures to control internal financial risks	**Process** Failure of processes to operate without disruption	**Perception** Failure to achieve the desired perception	**Presence** Failure to achieve required presence in the marketplace
Control mechanisms	Capex standards Internal control Delegation of authority	Process control Loss control Insurance and risk financing	Marketing Advertising Reputation and brand protection	Strategic and business plans Opportunity assessment

Table 14.3 PESTLE classification system

Category of risk	Description
Political	Tax policy, employment laws, environmental regulations, trade restrictions and reform, tariffs and political stability.
Economic	Economic growth/decline, interest rates, exchange rates and inflation rate, wage rates, minimum wage, working hours, unemployment (local and national), credit availability, cost of living, etc.
Sociological	Cultural norms and expectations, health consciousness, population growth rate, age distribution, career attitudes, emphasis on safety, global warming.
Technological	Technology changes that impact your products or services, new technologies, barriers to entry in given markets, financial decisions like outsourcing and supply chain.
Legal	Changes to legislation that may impact employment, access to materials, quotas, resources, imports/exports, taxation, etc.
Environmental	Environmental aspects, although many of these factors will be economic or social in nature.

system should be used in conjunction with an analysis of the strengths, weaknesses, opportunities and threats (SWOT) facing an organization.

There are several advantages and disadvantages to the PESTLE approach. The advantages are as follows:

- simple framework;
- facilitates an understanding of the wider business environment;
- encourages the development of external and strategic thinking;
- anticipates future business threats;
- helps identify actions to avoid or minimize impact of threats;
- facilitates identification of business opportunities.

However, there are certain disadvantages associated with the use of the PESTLE analysis as a means of identifying risks. These disadvantages are as follows:

- can oversimplify the amount of data used for decisions;
- needs to be undertaken on a regular basis to be effective;
- requires different people being involved with different perspectives;
- access to quality external data sources can be time-consuming and costly;

- difficult to anticipate developments that may affect an organization in the future;
- risk of capturing too much data that makes it difficult to identify priorities;
- can be based on assumptions that subsequently prove to be unfounded.

Some organizations extend the PESTLE classification system to include other categories, such as Ethics (STEEPLE), or International and Demographics (PESTLIED).

Orange Book (2023)

The PESTLE approach in the public sector has been expanded upon by the UK Government's Orange Book.[3] This provides 13 examples of risk categories, as follows:

- Strategy
- Governance
- Operations
- Legal
- Property
- Financial
- Commercial
- People
- Technology
- Information
- Security
- Project/programme
- Reputational

RISK CLASSIFICATION IN THE FINANCE SECTOR

There is no standard risk classification system that can be used by all types of organizations. Banks face a large number of risks and these are usually divided into three main categories of market risk, credit risk and operational risk. With enhanced regulation in all countries, compliance is becoming more common and may move from the legal function to the risk function. Often, the risk management framework and architecture will be different for the different types of risks.

Market risks are risks that occur due to fluctuations in the financial markets. The assets and liabilities of the bank are exposed to various kinds of market volatilities, such as changes in interest rates and foreign exchange rates. Market risk is primarily an opportunity that is embraced by the bank.

When the bank lends to a client there is an inherent risk of money not coming back, and this is the credit risk. Credit risk is simply the possibility of the adverse condition in which the client does not pay back the loan amount.

Operational risk relates to failure of internal systems, processes, technology and humans, and to external factors such as natural disasters, fires, etc. Compliance risks exist within this category since breaching the regulatory framework will be a failure to manage operations. Basel III defines operational risk as 'the risk of direct or indirect loss resulting from inadequate or failed internal processes, people and systems or from external events'. Operational risk has gained profile because of the need to quantify operational risk exposure, the increased use of technology and recognition of the critical role played by people in finance sector processes.

World Economic Forum

The first edition of the World Economic Forum's Global Risks Report[4] in 2006 grouped risks of global concern into five classes, which were based on criteria, such as:

- Economic – oil prices/energy supply, critical infrastructures, asset prices
- Environmental – earthquakes, climate change, loss of ecosystem services
- Geopolitical – terrorism, future hotspots
- Societal – regulation, crime, global pandemics
- Technological – nanotechnology, pervasive computing

Although the risks on the Global Risks Report have evolved, and the classification of those risks improved, the five categories have remained consistent across all reports.

Notes

1 British Standards (2021) BS 31100:2021 – TC: Risk management. Code of practice and guidance for the implementation of BS ISO 31000:2018. https://knowledge.bsigroup.com/products/risk-management-code-of-practice-and-guidance-for-the-implementation-of-bs-iso-31000-2018?version=tracked (archived at https://perma.cc/66J3-Q8JY)
2 Hillson, D (Ed.) (2023) *The Risk Management Handbook: A practical guide to managing the multiple dimensions of risk*, Kogan Page, London, UK

3 HM Treasury (2023) *The Orange Book: Management of Risk – Principles and Concepts*, https://assets.publishing.service.gov.uk/media/6453acadc33b460012f5e6b8/HMT_Orange_Book_May_2023.pdf (archived at https://perma.cc/G9XT-RFYE)

4 World Economic Forum (2024) The Global Risks Report 2024: 19th Edition, https://www3.weforum.org/docs/WEF_The_Global_Risks_Report_2024.pdf (archived at https://perma.cc/VX9T-TZYM)

Assessing risks – 15
risk analysis

Risk analysis

When undertaking a risk assessment, it is quite common to identify a hundred or more risks that could impact the objective, core process or key dependency that is being considered. This is an unmanageable number of risks and so a method is required to prioritize the risks so that the appropriate focus and effort can be applied to manage the risks effectively and efficiently.

Risk analysis is part of the assessing risk step and follows the risk identification process. Risk analysis is the process of prioritizing an organization's risks to determine those that require a greater level of attention and potentially more action.

ISO 31000 (2018)[1] states that the purpose of risk analysis is to 'comprehend the nature of risk and its characteristics, including, where appropriate, the level of risk'. The Orange Book (2023)[2] states that the 'risk analysis process should use a common set of risk criteria to foster consistent interpretation and application'. As such, the risk criteria explored in Chapter 10 are used here to prioritize the risks raised through risk identification.

Risk analysis is dependent on the availability and reliability of information, and influenced by opinions, biases, perceptions, judgements, assumptions, exclusions and constraints. As such, clear articulation of risks, including potential multiple causes and consequences, is key.

Risks are commonly prioritized using the combination of likelihood or chance of the risk happening, and impact or effect of the risk on overall objectives. ISO 31000 considers other factors that should be taken into account, including:

- complexity and connectivity;
- time-related factors and volatility;
- the effectiveness of existing controls;
- sensitivity and confidence levels.

Different lenses through which risks can be prioritized are considered in Chapter 16, including likelihood and impact, impact versus action, proximity, velocity and clock-speed.

Both ISO 31000 and the Orange Book note that risk analysis techniques can be qualitative, quantitative or a combination of these, depending on the circumstances and intended use. This book does not focus on the more quantitative risk analysis techniques, such as Monte Carlo Simulation, Bayesian analysis or Value at Risk (VaR). There are whole chapters or textbooks that can be found elsewhere on these approaches, which are usually focused on the sector which uses them; for example, project, programme or portfolio risk management often uses Monte Carlo Simulation to help calculate time or cost contingencies, and financial risk management often considers Value at Risk to help calculate the value of a loss that might occur within a defined time span. A useful source of information on these and other risk analysis techniques, whether qualitative, quantitative or both, is the International Standard on risk assessment techniques, ISO IEC 31010.[3]

The risk matrix

There are many different styles of risk matrix. The most common form is one that demonstrates the relationship between the likelihood of the risk materializing and the impact of the event should the risk materialize. Figure 15.1 is an illustration of a simple risk matrix, also referred to as a risk map or heat map. The risk matrix can be used to plot the level of risk, defined by ISO 31073[4] as the 'magnitude of a risk or combination of risks, expressed in terms of the combination of consequences [impacts] and their likelihood'. This supports an organization in deciding whether the risk is acceptable and within the risk appetite and/or risk capacity of an organization.

Throughout this book, a standard format for presenting a risk matrix has been adopted. In this edition of the book, the horizontal or x-axis is used to represent impact and the vertical or y-axis is used to indicate likelihood, as shown in Figure 15.1.

Figure 15.1   Risk likelihood and impact

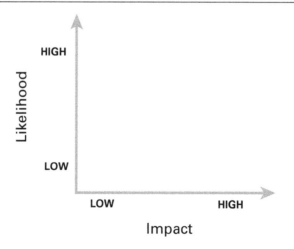

Figure 15.2   Risk matrix for opportunities and threats

Upside risk			Likelihood	Downside risk		
High	High	Medium	1:2 Probable	Medium	High	High
High	Medium	Low	1:10 Possible	Low	Medium	High
Medium	Low	Low	1:100 Unlikely	Low	Low	Medium
Major	Moderate	Minor		Minor	Moderate	Major
Consequence						
Multiple objectives exceeded beneficially	Objective delivered significantly early, better or cheaper	Objective delivered slightly early, better or cheaper	Objective-driven (customer, people, society or key performance)	Slippage and minor deviation	Failure to meet an objective	Extinction of organization

The risk matrix can be very simple, with a range from low to high, although this does not usually provide sufficient divisions or graduations to understand whether the impact of one risk is as high, or as low, as another. The common graduation for many organizations is having a five-by-five risk matrix: a range of very low, or 1, to very high, or 5, for both impact and likelihood, but some organizations use five-by-four, or six-by-four, and so on.

When seeking to identify opportunities, many organizations facilitate a risk assessment workshop that seeks to identify and analyse threats and opportunities at the same time. Figure 15.2 provides an example of a risk matrix that can be used to record the outcome of such a risk assessment workshop. The exact design of the risk matrix and the descriptors of impact and likelihood will vary between organizations. Figure 15.2 should be treated as one example or illustration of how to record the output from the risk assessment workshop.

Shading or colour coding is often overlaid onto the risk matrix to provide a visual representation of the importance of each risk under consideration. As risks move towards the top right-hand corner of the risk matrix, they become more likely and have a greater impact. Therefore, the magnitude of the risk becomes greater and the risk requires more attention, to ensure that effective risk control measures are in place, or are put in place, where necessary and where possible.

However, care should be taken when using shading or colouring in the risk matrix. There are some risks that reside in the top right corner of the risk matrix that may be acceptable to an organization, in other words, they are within its risk appetite. However, there is often a lack of understanding that this is possible, especially when the risk matrix is used to illustrate risk appetite and tolerance. An example of this misunderstanding is explored in the box below.

VEHICLE IMPACT RISK

Imagine a UK construction company whose core activity is to maintain and repair live highways or roads; those on which the public are still able to drive while the construction work is ongoing.

One of its principal risks is that a vehicle might be involved in an accident and hit the construction works, which would lead to damage to the works being undertaken, to the equipment or to the workforce. This risk has many existing controls in place and is constantly being reviewed to highlight whether any improvements or additional controls are needed. As such, the risk is deemed acceptable to the organization.

This risk, however, sits in the high impact and high likelihood, top-right, 'red' corner of the organization's risk matrix. During each risk meeting the board consider this principal risk, challenging why the risk is still in the 'red zone' if it is considered acceptable. The risk manager explains that the risk is being managed to the best possible extent, but that the likelihood remains high because, despite all best efforts, the general public who drive next to the construction works cannot be fully controlled, and accidents do happen.

The board have asked that this risk is managed to the 'green zone' on the risk matrix (low likelihood, low impact). The board thinks this represents the area where the risk would be acceptable for the organization and where all risk should be managed to within their risk appetite. The risk manager has explained that the likelihood of the risk occurring could be managed to a low level if the highways and roads were closed to the public during the construction works. This would only move the risk into the 'amber zone' (low likelihood, high impact) on the organization's risk matrix as construction vehicles could be involved in accidents on the sites. To move this risk to the 'green zone' or remove it from the register entirely, the risk manager explained that the only real option would be to stop undertaking construction works.

This is a simplified version of the story, but indicates that high-likelihood, high-impact risks can sometimes be acceptable, usually due to the nature of the work that is being undertaken and despite the many controls put in place to manage the risk. In addition, it highlights that not all risks can be brought into the lower, left-hand, 'green' corner of the risk matrix, often because every effort can be made to reduce the likelihood of a risk happening, but when it does, all aspects of the impact may not be able to be reduced.

One option to remove the misunderstanding around high-impact risks being acceptable is to remove the colours from the risk matrix. This may be controversial, but it is a quick fix. Another option is to change the lenses for prioritizing risk from likelihood and impact to another option, such as impact versus action, which is considered later in this chapter.

As well as, or instead of, the colouring of the boxes in a risk matrix, each box is usually given a 'score' that orders the risks when they are input to a risk register so that the risks can be ordered by magnitude. Some organizations number each box by multiplying the impact scale by the likelihood scale. For example, a risk rated as a five-impact and a five-likelihood scale would be given a score of 25 by multiplying both scales, and as such it is considered one of the most important risks.

However, by multiplying the axes, a risk with a five-impact and a one-likelihood would be given a score of five, and a risk with a one-impact and five-likelihood would also be given a score of five. This means that both of these risks are equally important, but most organizations would wish to prioritize a risk that is unlikely but would have significant impact on objectives over one that is highly likely but would have little impact on objectives.

A simple way of overcoming this issue is to put more weighting into the impact over the likelihood. The UK Charity Commission suggests that this can be achieved by multiplying the numbers representing likelihood by those representing impact, and then adding the number representing impact to provide the score, and therefore the order in which the risks are considered. However, this still leaves some duplication in the scoring. An even simpler option is to remove the numbers in both the x- and y-axes, and to score each box linearly in a diagonal line, from 1 in the bottom left corner to 25 in the top right corner, with 1 being the lowest score and priority and 25 being the highest, as shown in Figure 15.3.

Figure 15.3 Score of risk magnitude on the risk matrix

LIKELIHOOD	Very Low	Low	Medium	High	Very High
Very High	11	16	20	23	25
High	7	12	17	21	24
Medium	4	8	13	18	22
Low	2	5	9	14	19
Very Low	1	3	6	10	15

IMPACT

By removing the numbers in the axes and instead using the words from, such as, 'very low' to 'very high', the temptation to multiply the axes is removed, allowing the scoring to be accepted as a simple tool to prioritize the risks. This method for scoring also provides a rudimentary weighting to the impact over the likelihood. Using words such as 'very low' to 'very high' also removes some of the subjectivity in analysing risks which sometimes happens when words such as 'insignificant' or 'catastrophic' are used. In addition, words such as 'very low' to 'very high' also support the rating of opportunities, whereas words such as 'catastrophic' indicate threats only are being analysed.

However, many organizations will need to be more specific than these generic descriptions, depending on the type of risk and the size, nature and complexity of an organization.

Impact

As noted earlier, the effect that risk can have on the achievement of an organization's objectives can also be termed consequence, which is defined in ISO 31073 as 'the outcome of an event affecting objectives'. For the purposes of risk analysis, the effect or consequence is commonly known as the impact. Although risk analysis usually refers to likelihood and impact, impact is going to be considered first it usually has more weighting than likelihood.

As noted in Chapter 13, if the risk has a positive impact should it occur, this denotes an opportunity and where it would have a negative impact this denotes a threat. As such any risk impact criteria should be developed to allow the measurement of both.

Risk criteria was explored in Chapter 10, as part of setting the scope, context and criteria. Providing ranges for both impact and likelihood, for example, from very low or one, to very high or five gives an indication of the size of both axes. However, a very low impact for one person or group of people could be perceived as very high to another if no further information is given.

Because impact is used to describe the range of consequences and risk analysis is a subjective subject, it is important for an organization to describe the qualitative terms they use with some quantum or scales that can inform decisions made on the magnitude of the risk.

Impact scales for risk should ideally be based on an organization's objectives as a measure of how much a risk could impact on objectives should it occur. A useful place to start in developing the impact scales for an organization is a review of its objectives and the key performance indicators (KPIs) used to measure performance against those objectives.

REPURPOSING KPIs

Most organizations will have a variety of KPIs measuring everything from staff turnover to retention of customers to volume of sales or keywords in top 10 search engine results. Some of those KPIs set against an organization's objectives could be repurposed to set impact scales. For example, a housing association in the South of England used some of their KPIs to develop the impact scales for an organization.

In this example, the risk manager engaged with the owners of the five corporate objectives for an organization to explore which of the KPIs could be considered the core measure of performance against the objectives. In other words what were the one (or two) measures that would be fundamental to indicating a change in the objectives – the really 'key' key performance indicators, as it were.

These indicators were then repurposed to inform the measure of the impact a risk would have on these objectives should it occur. For example, the impact of a risk on their objective of customer support was measured by the reduction or increase in their net promotor score around the target set. For their objective regarding help for people needing work, the impact scale was based on their KPI for the number of funding streams they had aligned to learning, work or training initiatives, above or below the target. Of course, each organization will have its own objectives and its own ways of measuring performance against those objectives.

- The housing association found this approach beneficial in a number of ways: engagement with the owners of the objectives further embedded risk management in an organization as the individuals felt included in the process and empowered by owning the relevant impact scales.

- The impact scales were tailored to the organization and what it was trying to achieve.

- The impact scales were written in language colleagues within an organization recognized and understood.

- It was easier to link the risks to the organizational objectives.

Other examples in considering the impact a risk could have on objectives include those shown in Table 15.1, which are based on relevant KPIs against the FIRM risk scorecard.

The basis for impact scales will vary according to the nature of the risk and whether it is a financial or non-financial one. For large organizations, identifying a

Table 15.1   Sources of information for impact scales

FIRM risk scorecard	Sources of information for impact scales
Financial	Increase or reduction on balance sheet of 0.25% Profit and loss of 2.5% annual profit
Infrastructure	Disruption to normal operations of ½ day Increased or reduced cost of operation exceeds 10% budget
Reputational	Share price falls by 10% or rises by 5% Event is on national TV, radio or newspapers
Marketplace	Increase or reduction on balance sheet of 0.5% turnover Profit and loss impact of 1% annual profit

financial impact scale can be undertaken in a number of ways. Depending on the risk this could be:

- levels of authorization to spend money, often set out in a formal document referred to as a 'delegation of authority';
- level at which full board approval is required for expenditure in excess of a particular financial threshold;
- levels that external auditors consider to be material when compiling the accounts of an organization;
- use of financial metrics, for example a proportion of:
  - o the budgeted profit for the year (5 per cent), or
  - o the budgeted turnover for the year (0.5 per cent), or
  - o the value of the balance sheet or reserves of an organization (0.25 per cent).

The use of the FIRM risk scorecard can help some organizations set their impact scales, although others may find this too restrictive and not in line with the organizational objectives set.

Figure 15.4 provides further examples of impact scales. These impact scales have been graduated or divided into five ranges for the impact should a risk occur, from very low to very high, rather than single values provided in Table 15.1.

The impact scales provided in Figure 15.4 give examples of how negative and positive impacts can be captured so that both identified threats and opportunities can be prioritized against objectives.

When prioritizing risks the impact should be considered before the likelihood. This ensures that those involved understand the risk they are dealing with. It is common to find that some people think of the low likelihood risk with a big impact, whereas others may think of a high likelihood risk with a small impact. For example,

Figure 15.4   Example impact scales, with ranges

	IMPACT				
	Very Low	Low	Medium	High	Very High
SAFETY [Lives saved / lost]	First aid case	Medical treatment	LTI	Life	Multiple lives
FINANCIAL [$ made / lost]	<$10k	$10k – $100k	$100k – $1m	$1m – $10m	> $10m
PRODUCTION/ OPERATIONS [Production / operational hours saved / lost]	<3 hours	3hrs – 1 week	1 week – 1 month	1 – 6 months	>6 months
REPUTATION [Positive / negative comments]	<50 comments	50 – 100 comments	100 – 500 comments	500 – 1000 comments	>1000 comments
Etc. (other key objective areas for your business)					

there may be a risk of someone losing control of their car. In scenario one, there is a low likelihood of the loss of control leading to a major accident with the impact of serious injury and damage. In scenario two, there is a high likelihood of the loss of control leading to a minor accident with little or no injury and slight damage. By considering the impact first it will be clear in which of the two scenarios the risk is being prioritized.

Likelihood

The other common criterion for prioritizing risks is likelihood. This is defined by ISO 31000 as 'the chance of something happening'. The standard notes that likelihood is not easily translatable to all languages. 'Probability' is often used instead, although in English probability is usually associated with the mathematical or statistical term. In addition, the term 'frequency' is sometimes used, which can imply an event will definitely occur, and could occur more than once. Some organizations use 'likelihood' as the overall term dealing with chance of something happening, with 'probability' used for risks that could only happen once, such as a whole building burning down and 'frequency' used for risks that could happen more than once, such as flooding.

Figure 15.5 provides examples of likelihood scales, with ranges for both probability and frequency, from very low to very high, graduated or divided into five ranges, as with the impact scales considered earlier.

Figure 15.5 Example likelihood scales, with ranges

LIKELIHOOD		Probability	Frequency
	Very high	>80%	>Once a week
	High	50 – 80%	Once every month to once a week
	Medium	20 – 50 %	Once year to once every month
	Low	5 – 20%	Once every 10 years to once a year
	Very low	<5%	<Once every 10 years

Inherent, current and target levels of risk

An important consideration for risk managers when developing impact scales is the consequences that follow. For example, a large fire could occur that completely destroys a warehouse of a distribution and logistics company, which would signify the inherent or gross exposure to the risk. Although the impact of the event may be large, if sufficient insurance is in place, the impact in terms of financial costs for the company could be minimal. The impact on management time, lost reputation and potential future sales cannot be recovered; but if the company has effective business continuity plans to cope with such an event, the consequences for the overall business may be much less than would otherwise be anticipated. This would signify the organization's current or net exposure to the risk.

As well as likelihood and impact, other features of the risk can be represented on the risk matrix. For example, the scope for achieving further risk improvement is often represented using a risk matrix. In this case, the risk matrix will demonstrate the level of risk in relation to the additional measures that can be taken to improve the management of that risk, which would signify a target exposure for the risk. The common levels for risk rating are shown in Table 15.2.

Table 15.2   Levels of risk rating

Level of risk rating	Definition
Inherent (total, gross or raw)	The level of risk before controls are applied, or if all controls failed
Current (net or residual)	The level of risk after the application of existing controls, taking into account the current effectiveness of those existing controls
Target	The desired level of risk after the application of planned controls that bring the risk to an acceptable level

Care should be taken if using the term 'residual' when defining the level of risk. Some organizations consider 'residual' to mean the current level of the risk, taking into account the current existing controls and the current effectiveness of those controls. Other organizations consider it to mean the current level of the risk taking into account the existing controls *if* they were operating 100 per cent effectively. These could give a different and misleading perspective on the level of the risk. Either definition is acceptable, as long as all involved in the risk analysis process understand how they are prioritizing the risks, and that the definition is used consistently across an organization.

Different professions view these aspects of risk at different levels. For example, internal auditors will start with the inherent risk and audit the controls in place. Risk managers prefer to start with the current level of risk and review whether the risk is acceptable where it is or whether further action is needed to bring the risk to an acceptable level. Health and safety practitioners also prefer to undertake risk assessment with the current controls in place, that is, at the current level. This relies on the assumption that the current controls will always work to the assumed effectiveness. For example, if an assessment of an X-ray machine is being undertaken, the safety person will assume that the enclosure or cabinet is in good order and the risk should be assessed on that basis. The internal auditor will more easily recognize that the enclosure or cabinet is a vitally important control factor that has to be subject to a routine inspection.

The advantages of considering the inherent level of a risk are that it enables the effect of individual control measures to be identified. Figure 15.6 illustrates the effect of controls on the level of risk. Control 1 is an existing control which reduces the risk from the inherent level to the current (or residual) level and it can be seen that this control has its main effect on the likelihood of the risk materializing.

Control 2 in Figure 15.6 is an additional control that will be introduced to reduce the risk from the current level to the target level. It is intended to have a significant effect on the impact of the risk, but little effect on the likelihood of it materializing. The effect of the planned introduction of Control 2 is also illustrated, which is

Figure 15.6   Inherent, current and target levels of risk

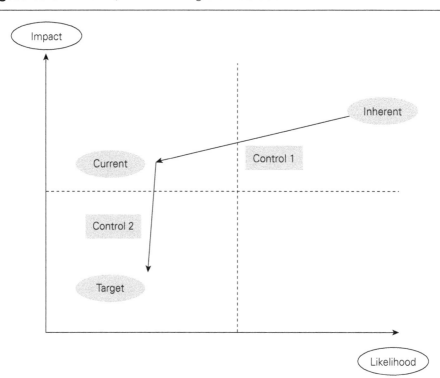

intended to reduce the impact of the risk. This is known as the target level of risk, which, in this case, brings the risk into the bottom left-hand quadrant of the risk matrix.

When seeking to establish the target level of risk, a concept that is often used by health and safety practitioners is to reduce the risk to a level that is 'as low as reasonably practicable' (ALARP). As noted earlier in this chapter, not all risks can be managed to the bottom left of the risk matrix. Although ALARP is one of the fundamental principles of risk management for health and safety risks, it is also relevant for consideration in the management of any risk, both threat and opportunity, as in most cases, it is not appropriate to manage a risk at any cost. It refers to managing risk to the point where the cost of additional controls would exceed the benefits.

Having placed the various risks on a risk matrix, the relative importance of the risks can easily be identified. Large organizations frequently make use of a risk matrix as a means of summarizing their risk profile. It can also be used to identify the type of risk response that is most likely to be employed.

Control confidence

While the target level of risk is indicated in Figure 15.6, it is not possible for an organization to be absolutely confident that controls will always be fully implemented or will be as effective as expected or required. Controls will need to be audited in order to allow confidence that the control selected has been properly implemented and is producing the desired effect.

The level of control confidence can also be illustrated on a risk matrix, as shown in Figure 15.7. If the effectiveness of a control is uncertain, a greater variability of the outcome may be expected. This can be demonstrated on a risk matrix by using a circle or ellipse to represent a risk, instead of representing the risk as a single point on the risk matrix. By doing this, the level of uncertainty or variability in the outcome can be illustrated in relation to both the likelihood and impact of the event materializing.

Two questions need to be asked: 'How confident are we that this is the correct control?' and 'How confident are we that it is fully implemented and effective in practice?' When there is limited confidence in the effectiveness of a control, it will be the role of internal audit to test the control and provide information on the likely level of variability of outcome, should the risk materialize.

Figure 15.7   Confidence in controls

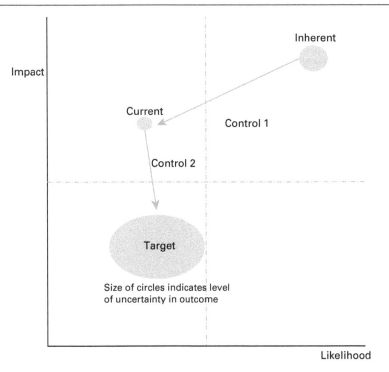

It is the responsibility of internal auditors to check that the correct controls have been selected and that they are working correctly in practice. Internal auditors refer to effective and efficient controls respectively when reviewing these points. The use of effective and efficient is also included in this book in relation to core processes of an organization. Undertaking the testing of controls is a key function fulfilled by internal audit, and the importance of the testing of controls should also be recognized by risk management practitioners.

Management needs to receive assurance of adequate control, and this can come from internal audit activities, or measurement of the outputs of activities and projects, as well as from management reports. The responsibility for designing and implementing controls and auditing the effectiveness and efficiency of controls should be allocated within the risk management documentation. Control confidence and effectiveness is explored further in Chapter 19.

Notes

1 ISO 31000 (2018) Risk management – Guidelines, https://www.iso.org/obp/ui/#iso:std:iso:31000:ed-2:v1:en (archived at https://perma.cc/64QY-LQBP)

2 HM Treasury (2023) *The Orange Book: Management of Risk – Principles and Concepts*, https://assets.publishing.service.gov.uk/media/6453acadc33b460012f5e6b8/HMT_Orange_Book_May_2023.pdf (archived at https://perma.cc/JEV5-FJP9)

3 ISO IEC 31010 (2019) Risk management – Risk assessment techniques, https://www.iso.org/obp/ui/en/#iso:std:iec:31010:ed-2:v1:en,fr (archived at https://perma.cc/G27N-CEC5)

4 ISO 31073 (2022) Risk management – Vocabulary, https://www.iso.org/obp/ui/en/#iso:std:iso:31073:ed-1:v1:en (archived at https://perma.cc/B8ZT-G7AX)

Different lenses for prioritizing risk   16

Impact and likelihood

As noted in Chapter 15, the most common way for organizations to prioritize their risks is by using impact and likelihood to understand the risk magnitude and to focus management attention and resources to those risks that need to be managed further to reach an acceptable level or to bring them within an organization's risk appetite.

However, there are other approaches or lenses through which to understand the effect risks may have on organizational objectives. Among the different prioritization lenses, those that are considered in this chapter are risk clockspeed, proximity, velocity, controllability/manageability, and impact versus action.

Risk clockspeed

In the IRM paper on horizon scanning,[1] risk clockspeed is defined as 'the rate at which information necessary to understand and manage a risk becomes available'. Where the information to manage either a threat or opportunity is available in advance of the potential risk occurring, this is termed slow clockspeed and an organization has time to plan and put controls in place. On the other hand, information for some risks only becomes available closer to the potential risk occurring, which is termed fast clockspeed.

This concept is also termed the 'time dimension' in ISO 31050,[2] where it is suggested that when describing emerging risks, consideration should be given to the rate at which information is available, using the same definition of risk clockspeed as the IRM Horizon Scanning paper.

Understanding the risk clockspeed can influence data collection and analysis and the creation of knowledge to support timely decision making. ISO 31050 also suggests key time indicators should be developed in relation to clockspeed and emerging risks, including such things as the:

- rate or speed of change in context;
- rate of development of the emerging risk;

- time to reach data maturity;
- time between changes in context and early warning signals;
- time from risk identification to the potential occurrence of the risk.

Understanding the time-related characteristics of emerging risks also influences the interpretation of the information gathered, the options for controlling the risks and the expertise required to do so.

Proximity

Proximity in relation to risk management is defined by the UK's Association for Project Management (APM)[3] as 'the nearness in time at which a risk is expected or predicted to occur'. This could be thought of as the time related to the cause of a risk.

This is a useful lens to prioritize risks that are closer in time, which highlights the sense of urgency against which management effort can be put in place. However, this may result in some risks not having sufficient attention because their impact has a much longer time horizon.

This concept is similar to that considered in Figure 14.1 in Chapter 14, in relation those slow-burning risks which develop over time, such as environmental risks.

Velocity

Velocity in relation to risk management is defined in Management of Risk: Creating and Protecting Value – M_o_R®4 (2022),[4] as 'how quickly the risk would have an impact on objectives should it occur'. This could be thought of as the time related to the impact of a risk.

This is considered to be a more useful lens to understand the urgency of risks, as it provides information on how much time there would be to react to a risk once it occurs.

In ISO 31050, velocity is used to describe the rate of change in condition or circumstances as one of the time indicators in relation to emerging risks. Clearly, as with many other aspects of risk management, the same terms are used for similar but different reasons, and care must be taken to communicate clear definitions across an organization to ensure consistency in understanding and use of risk management terms.

Controllability/manageability

If proximity is loosely related to the cause, and velocity is loosely related to the impact of a risk, controllability/manageability is more related to the management of a risk. Controllability is defined in the APM (2008)[3] paper as 'the degree to which an organization is able to control a risk's outcome', with manageability as a 'function of controllability and response [control] effectiveness'.

CONTROLLABILITY AND THE RISK MATRIX

An international mining company undertook many projects in different countries, with many risks facing each project. Due to the nature of the work being carried out in those countries, under different jurisdictions and pressures, there were some risks that were outside of the control of the projects.

In order to communicate this to more senior managers the risk matrix was used to depict a third lens of controllability. Each risk was illustrated on the organization's risk matrix, with threats having a triangular shape, and opportunities a circular shape. Where the risk was mostly uncontrollable by the project, but it was thought that it could be controlled by a different team within an organization, the outline of the risk was highlighted in a bold, dashed line, for example cybersecurity. Where the risk was mostly uncontrollable by the project, but it was thought it could be controlled by more senior management, the outline of the risk was highlighted in a bold, solid line, for example changes to the company structure. Where the risk was uncontrollable by the project, and it was thought it was mostly outside the control of an organization, for example changes in regulations, the outline of the risk was highlighted in a bold, solid, red line.

The term 'mostly outside the control of...' was used, because although those example risks could not be explicitly controlled by the projects, the teams involved were constantly monitoring the risks and the surrounding context and communicating with the relevant individuals to gain appropriate information, support or actions needed.

Impact versus action

Impact versus action is a different approach to prioritizing risks, where the likelihood measure and axis of the risk matrix is replaced by a measure of the amount of further action needed to manage risks to an acceptable level. As noted in Chapter 15, there are a number of issues when using likelihood to prioritize risks. In fact, Gerd Gigerenzer,[5] in his book, *Calculated Risks*, provides many more reasons why this is the case, including the lack of understanding of uncertainty, miscommunication of risk and the different ways people draw conclusions from statistics and numbers.

The impact versus action approach avoids the, often unnecessary, debate on likelihood, or probability, or frequency, and has a clear focus instead on action. The

Figure 16.1 Impact versus Action

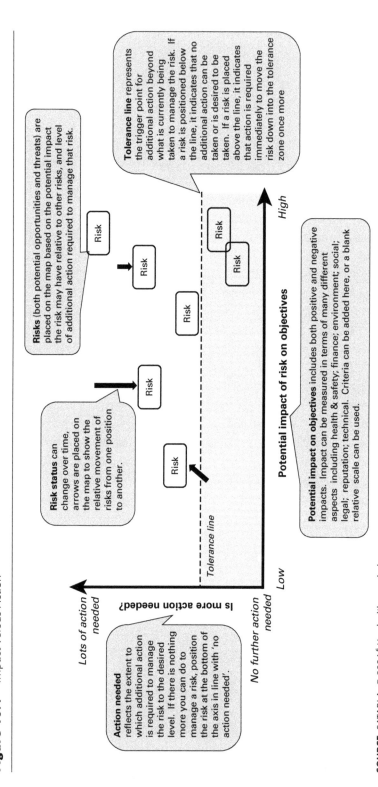

Risks (both potential opportunities and threats) are placed on the map based on the potential impact the risk may have relative to other risks, and level of additional action required to manage that risk.

Tolerance line represents the trigger point for additional action beyond what is currently being taken to manage the risk. If a risk is positioned below the line, it indicates that no additional action can be taken or is desired to be taken. If a risk is placed above the line, it indicates that action is required immediately to move the risk down into the tolerance zone once more

Risk status can change over time, arrows are placed on the map to show the relative movement of risks from one position to another.

Action needed reflects the extent to which additional action is required to manage the risk to the desired level. If there is nothing more you can do to manage a risk, position the risk at the bottom of the axis in line with 'no action needed'.

Potential impact on objectives includes both positive and negative impacts. Impact can be measured in terms of many different aspects including health & safety; finance; environment; social; legal; reputation; technical. Criteria can be added here, or a blank relative scale can be used.

Is more action needed?

Lots of action needed

Tolerance line

No further action needed

Low

High

Potential impact of risk on objectives

SOURCE SATARLA, © 2024.[6] Used with permission

approach clearly shows where further action is needed or where controls are currently weak, and highlights risks that are outside desired acceptance levels. It supports decision-making activities, including optioneering, allows changes to be tracked over time, and supports high-level reporting through the use of risk dashboards, which will be explored further in Chapter 22. It also supports accountability for decisions made in relation to the management of the risks.

Figure 16.1 illustrates the impact versus action matrix, where both threats and opportunities are mapped based on the potential impact the risk might have relative to other risks, and the level of additional action required to manage that risk.

The x-axis reflects the potential impact of the risk on objectives, which can be both positive and negative. The x-axis in Figure 16.1 simply flows from low to high, but can be divided or graduated further, as discussed in Chapter 15.

The y-axis, on the other hand, is used to reflect the additional action needed to manage the risk to an acceptable level. If no additional action can be taken or is desired to be taken to manage a risk further, it would be positioned at the bottom of the axis below the Acceptance line. Again, the y-axis ranges from low to high, but could be divided further, for example from very low to very high. The amount of further action needed is usually measured in terms of the number of potential actions or controls and additional resources required.

The Acceptance line represents the trigger point for additional action over and above the controls already in place, taking into account the effectiveness of those existing controls. This acknowledges that most risks are already being managed to some extent, and consideration is given to whether the risks are being controlled sufficiently at present or whether more effort is required. Where a risk does require additional effort, it would be plotted above the Acceptance line along the y-axis, depending on the amount of further action needed.

This approach has been applied by many different organizations, whether in the private, public or third sector. In most cases, engagement with users of the approach has been gained due to the focus on action, and the reduction in unhelpful conversations regarding likelihood that have been taken place at different levels of the organizations.

Notes

1 IRM (2017) Horizon Scanning: A Risk Practitioner's Guide, https://www.theirm.org/media/7423/horizon-scanning_final2-1.pdf (archived at https://perma.cc/PFR8-849J)

2 ISO 31050 (2023) Risk management – Guidelines for managing an emerging risk to enhance resilience, https://www.iso.org/obp/ui/en/#iso:std:iso:ts:31050:ed-1:v1:en (archived at https://perma.cc/93H7-5S6C)

3 Association for Project Management (2008) Prioritising Project Risk, Association for Project Management, Buckinghamshire

4 Axelos Ltd (2022) M_o_R®4 Management of Risk: Creating and Protecting Value, PeopleCert International Ltd, Cyprus

5 Gigerenzer, G (2002) *Calculated Risks: How to know when numbers deceive you*, Simon & Schuster, New York

6 Hillson, D (Ed.) (2023) *The Risk Management Handbook: A practical guide to managing the multiple dimensions of risk*, 2nd Ed., Kogan Page, London

Assessing risks –   17
risk evaluation

Evaluating risks and risk appetite

Once risks have been analysed it will be necessary to decide how to respond to them. Risk evaluation is, in effect, a decision point at which to decide whether to respond, or not to respond, to the risk.

In order to do so, this implies there is a threshold that the risk will need to cross before action is taken. An example of this threshold was illustrated in Figure 16.1, as the Acceptance line in the impact versus action matrix.

This Acceptance line or threshold can also be termed the 'risk appetite' of an organization, which is defined in the IRM's Risk Appetite and Tolerance[1] paper as the 'amount of risk that an organization is willing to seek or accept in pursuit of its long-term objectives'.

Risk appetite has six principles as expressed in the IRM's discussion paper on the subject, regarding the complexity, measurability, diversity of risk appetite and its relationship to an organization's risk management capability and risk culture, and the level at which risk appetite is to be applied. These principles have been condensed here into four overriding components:

- Acknowledging interconnectedness: What is acceptable in one division or business unit may be out of appetite in another and there needs to be a way of reconciling or dealing with this complexity.

- Measurability: The use of key risk indicators and key control indicators based on data available inside or from outside an organization is needed to apply risk appetite consistently. An organization's appetite needs to be practically applied, however, in terms that are realistic for an organization for the term to have any currency.

- Variability: While risks may be assessed consistently and scored against similar matrices there will be a range of appetites for different risks.

- Maturity: How adept an organization is at managing risk will have a bearing on the appetite of an organization for taking that risk. Confidence in its management of risk should not be misplaced, however, and may require some form of external validation to corroborate the internal view of risk management maturity.

In the corporate governance and assurance section of this book (Part Six) it will be seen that it is incumbent upon the board to evaluate its risk management capability. Good corporate governance requires the board to understand its risks and provide clarity in terms of its appetite and tolerance of risk. This is especially so, and mandated, for all listed companies.

There are some clear benefits to establishing risk appetite in a transparent fashion within an organization:

- It provides clear safeguards within which an organization can operate.
- It creates a framework for better decision making, by bringing clarity and structure to the process.
- It will allow the identification of issues at an early stage.
- It will facilitate the achievement of long-term objectives while respecting stakeholder views.

This transparency should ensure that all levels of an organization have a clear understanding of the appetite of an organization for risk and can ensure its application or raise a concern if it is felt to be breached. This also supports the risk evaluation process, in helping to understand which risks are acceptable, and how much more effort is required to bring the risk to an acceptable level, or within risk appetite. Risk appetite and tolerance are explored further in Chapters 25 and 26.

Further to the consideration of risk appetite, it is important that risk evaluation relates to the authority level needed to make decisions regarding the management of risks. This supports the escalation process regarding who should make decisions and provide accountability on how much further risks should be managed and at which level they will be accepted.

Answering the 'so what?' question

Following the analysis of risks, risk evaluation should support the answer to the 'so what?' question. Should any further action be taken to respond to the risk or not? Based on the prioritization of risks using the impact and likelihood, the decision made on whether to take additional action should be based on the difference between the current and target rating of the risk, but also considering the amount of effort needed to bring the risk to an acceptable level. It should not be based on which coloured 'zone' the risk sits in a risk matrix, as noted in Chapter 15.

There have been problems in some organizations in relation to this aspect of risk prioritization. Considering the high impact/low likelihood (HILP) risks, take for example a global pandemic, which may not have been given due attention. On the other hand, some organizations have struggled with those risks in the high impact/

high likelihood zone that are being managed to their best extent, such as the example of the vehicle impact risk, but are acceptable to an organization regardless of the size of the impact due to the nature of work they are undertaking.

Using the impact versus action matrix illustrated in Figure 16.1, the global pandemic risk (before Covid-19) would have been placed top right-hand corner of matrix, illustrating the high impact should the risk occur, and the fact that there were very few controls in place to manage the risk. A decision would then be needed to provide the additional resources to control the risk further to an acceptable level. If it were decided that no further action would be taken, which is what occurred in many countries and organizations, the risk would be placed below the dotted Acceptance line; this illustrates that the risk would be acceptable without further action taken. Using the impact versus action matrix, that decision then has an audit trail, where the person who makes the decision takes accountability for accepting the risk within an organization's risk appetite.

Using the matrix illustrated in Figure 16.1, the vehicle impact risks, on the other hand, would be placed in the bottom right of the matrix, under the Acceptance line, to illustrate that the risk was being sufficiently controlled at the current time, and that no further action was needed. However, the risk would be monitored for any changes in the context, risk or controls that might mean further action would be needed, when the risk would be moved above the Acceptance line.

In using this approach, one company has overlaid the likelihood lens to the matrix when reporting the risks in their annual report and accounts. In fact, any of the lenses for prioritizing risk can be overlaid onto each other, either through the outlines of the risk shapes on a matrix, as noted in the controllability/manageability lens discussed earlier or perhaps by enlarging the size of the risk shape, or changing its colour. Information can be illustrated using 'infographics', which is very useful when a great deal of information is often needed to be shared with limited space, such as a board report.

Whichever method of risk analysis used, or the number of lenses applied to that prioritization, risk evaluation is a key step in linking analysis with the management of risks, and at the same time, improving decision making and accountability in relation to the amount of effort needed to manage risks to an acceptable level.

Note

1 IRM (2011) Risk Appetite and Tolerance: Guidance Paper, https://www.theirm.org/media/7239/64355_riskapp_a4_web.pdf (archived at https://perma.cc/F6ZF-6D9P)

PART FOUR
Risk response and monitor, review and report

LEARNING OUTCOMES

Having studied this section readers will be able to:

- Explain the purpose of managing risk.
- Explain how to identify and develop real controls, considering control effectiveness.
- Describe the risk response options for both threats and opportunities in terms of eliminating uncertainty, involving others, changing the size of the risk and accepting the risk.
- Describe the main components of the risk bow-tie in understanding proactive and reactive controls for both threats and opportunities, and its relationship to loss control for threats.
- Describe ongoing monitoring, including the use of key risk indicators, and produce practical examples of key risk indicators to monitor both threats and opportunities.
- Explain ongoing review, in relation to the risk management framework, process, risks and their controls
- Explain how to verify the effectiveness of real controls, and produce practical examples of key control indicators to monitor those controls.

- Describe the link between risk controls and internal controls.

- Describe the process of learning from controls.

- Explain the importance of risk reporting, including communication and consultation and the range of risk reporting obligations placed on companies.

- Describe the purpose of internal reporting, including the 'ask' of the management level above and reporting formats.

- Describe the purpose of external reporting, including the perspective of listed companies, charities, public sector organizations and governments.

- Produce examples of risk reporting approaches adopted by different types of organizations, including companies, charities and government agencies.

Managing risk 18

Purpose of managing risk

There is a broad range of terminology available to describe risk response options. In fact, both the Orange Book[1] and ISO 31000[2] use the term 'risk treatment' as the more generic description. As treating a risk is considered by some organizations as a response method for responding to threats only, this book will use the terms 'manage' and 'management' instead of 'treat' and 'treatment'.

ISO 31073[3] defines this step as the process to modify risk, with ISO 31000 stating that the purpose of managing risks is to 'select and implement options for addressing risk'. An important point here is not just the selection, but implementation of options to manage risk. Both standards consider the management of risk to be an iterative process which includes:

- selection of options;
- planning for and implementing the chosen options;
- assessing the effectiveness of the options;
- deciding whether the remaining risk is acceptable;
- if not acceptable, then going back through the process again.

These options will then provide controls or improve on current controls. Control is then defined in ISO 31073 as the 'measure that maintains or modifies risk' and further staties that controls include, but are not limited to, any process, policy, device, practice or other conditions or actions.

FROGS ON A LOG

A risk practitioner colleague once posed a question of a team who were struggling with their risk management process. They had a comprehensive list of risks and related controls on their risk register, but yet risks seemed to be occurring quite frequently.

The question was, 'Five frogs are sitting on a log. Four frogs decided to jump off. How many frogs were left sitting on the log?' The team looked a little confused and after a while, the consensus was that one frog had been left on the log. The risk practitioner stated that that was not the right answer, at which point the team started to object. The risk practitioner then explained that there were still five frogs sitting on the log, because they had only decided to jump off and had not actually done so.

The lesson from this story is that deciding on controls to manage risks and putting them on a risk register does not mean that those controls have been implemented. Once controls are agreed upon, then they become part of 'business as usual' in managing activities. In other words, controls should not sit solely in a risk register, but should be included as part of the system of internal control, so that they are proactively implemented. The link between risk management and internal control will be explored further in Chapter 28.

Real controls

As noted previously, controls are measures to maintain or modify a risk. However, there are many instances in all organizations when chosen controls have not had the desired effect and changed the risk they are being applied to, an example of which is illustrated in the box below.

CONTROLLING THE SPREAD OF COVID-19

From early 2020, all countries struggled with the risk of the spread of Covid-19, with measures put in place to restrict the movement of and contact between people. In the UK, one of the key measures was to ask people to take regular 'lateral flow' tests to detect if they had Covid, especially if they had symptoms of the disease. If someone tested positive, they were given guidance on isolation and hygiene requirements.

The lateral flow test data was gathered nationally and shared with the general public to indicate how many people had the disease in different regions of the country.

If someone contracted the disease, they were initially advised to isolate themselves for 10 days, which involved not leaving their home, sleeping in separate rooms, using different towels, making and eating meals at different times than the rest of the people in the home, and ensuring they practised high hygiene standards such as washing hand and sanitizing surfaces.

However, what became clear is that, although people were undertaking lateral flow tests, they may have felt it was not in their interest to be honest about the results of the tests since the isolation required would affect them economically. This also meant that individuals were not then isolating themselves once they had tested positive. Or, in many cases, they were not testing even though they had symptoms of the disease. As such, the spread of Covid-19 was difficult to manage, especially following the relaxation of the earliest restrictions placed on the country where few people were allowed to leave their homes except for very specific reasons.

The COSO (2017) definition of risk management highlights this point by including the requirement for 'culture, capabilities and practices'. This is in recognition that having data and not using it or providing guidance and it not being implemented means that some risks will not be managed at all. This attitude to controlling risks, as well as many other examples of risks that were not being effectively managed, led to the development of the 'real controls' flowchart, illustrated in Figure 18.1.

When putting in place controls to manage risk, the collection of data, such as information for monitoring, inspections, audits, and so on, on their own, do not modify a risk. That data must be used in order to change a risk, such as recording and reporting lateral flow tests rather than ignoring the information.

Providing guidance, such as procedures, or training, putting in place alarms and so on, do not, on their own, modify a risk. The implementation of the requirements in the procedure, the following of the learning and the proactive response to alarms are what change the causes of the risk or the impacts.

Of course, data collection and guidance form part of the information required for a control to be effective, but relying on those parts of a control alone may give false assurance that a risk is being managed.

Identifying controls

It can be difficult to identify real controls, those that will modify either a threat or an opportunity. Having effective risk articulation, explored in Chapter 13, is a suitable starting point and will provide sufficient information for the identification of effective management of many risks.

Where the magnitude of risk is high, or where a risk is complex and in need of further understanding, the risk bow-tie is an effective method to examine the different aspects of the risk and where the control options will be most effective. Risk bow-ties display the understanding of a risk on one page, can be updated as knowledge regarding the risk increases, and are a useful communication tool that can support business cases and decision making on the most cost- and risk-effective controls.

Figure 18.2 highlights a simple risk bow-tie and its five different components, which unpack the causes and consequences of a risk and enable the exploration of the suite of controls that contribute to effective management of a risk.

Figure 18.1 Real controls

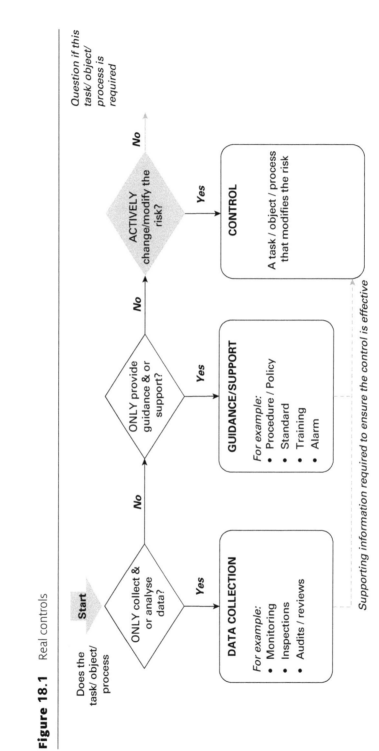

SOURCE SATARLA, © 2024.[4] Used with permission

Figure 18.2 Risk bow-tie

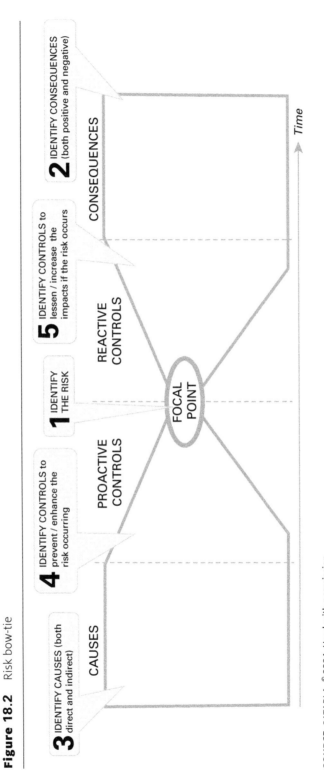

SOURCE SATARLA, © 2024. Used with permission

The first step is to place the identified risk into the middle of the bow-tie, using the uncertain part of risk articulation, that is that an uncertain event may, might, possibly, and so on, happen.

The second step is to move to the right of the bow-tie and list out all the plausible and rational consequences, which will confirm that the risk truly has an impact on objectives. These should include the plausible extremes of the consequences. Using the example of risks raised for a hospital, during a risk bow-tie exercise, the consequences for all health and safety risks included the death of an individual, even though this was not a plausible consequence for all risks. This meant that many colleagues involved in the risk management workshop became disengaged with the process, feeling that the prioritization of the risks was becoming disproportionate and management attention being focused in the wrong areas. On reflection, it was agreed that a death was not a reasonable extreme consequence for every health and safety risk in the hospital, with the example given that the reasonable extreme consequence of a risk such as slipping down one step would more reasonably be a sprain or broken bone.

At the same time, it is important to allow all plausible consequences to be listed to allow for 'outside of the box' thinking. For example, slipping down one step may also lead to claims for damages, lost time, reduction in performance, increased costs in paying for temporary staff, and so on.

The third step is to move to the left of the bow-tie, where the potential causes of the risk are listed. This explores those things that have happened or are happening now in the world around the activity in question that could cause the risk to occur. These should be facts, which can be informed by the internal and external context explored in Chapter 10 and the known knowns considered in Chapter 13.

By this stage, a detailed risk articulation is being developed, with the causes, risk and consequences identified. Note that risk bow-ties, even simple ones, can be quite detailed and that the full contents of a risk bow-tie do not need to be used to articulate a risk for a risk report. Care must be taken to consider those causes and consequences that make a risk significant enough to report on, and what controls are needed to manage a risk further. Risk reporting will be explored further in Chapter 22.

The fourth step is to identify those controls that will affect whether or not the risk will happen, in that they will manage the causes. For a threat these will act to prevent the risk from occurring and for an opportunity they will enable the risk to occur. These controls are termed 'proactive' controls in that they are put in place and are effective before the risk occurs.

The fifth step is to identify those controls that will affect the impact of the risk should it occur to manage the consequences. For a threat these will act to reduce the consequences and for an opportunity they will increase them. These controls are termed 'reactive' controls in that they are effective after the risk occurs, but should be put in place before the risk occurs.

In some organizations these controls are termed 'pre' and 'post' risk. In Chapter 20, these controls are termed preventive and corrective, which are based on threats only. Whatever terminology is used, the controls put in place before a risk happens may help to manage either a single or multiple causes, and those put in place after a risk occurs may help to manage one or more consequences.

It should be noted when considering controls to manage risks that some controls raised may already be in place and working effectively, some may be in place and need improvement and some may be new controls or different options to manage the risk. It is important to note the difference in these controls, as those involved in the management of the risk will be given a more accurate picture of the effort needed to bring the risk to an acceptable level, rather than being put off by the amount of perceived work involved. As such, this exercise should inform the risk analysis process to improve the prioritization of the risks.

It is also worthwhile noting which controls are considered critical to the effective management of the risk, that is, those that have the most effect on the risk. Even in a high-level, quick review, this can focus a team's attention when many existing and new controls might have been identified.

Developing a simple risk bow-tie can take anywhere from five to 15 minutes, depending on the individuals involved and the time allowed. Although, the term 'risk' bow-tie is used here, a bow-tie can be used to explore issues, problems, incidents and so on, to help understand what has happened in a situation. Other risk assessment techniques can be used to explore aspects of the bow-tie in more detail, for example using root-cause or Ishikawa (fishbone diagrams) to explore the causes, or event trees to explore consequences.

Control effectiveness

When considering the cost of implementation of controls, attention needs to be paid to the change in the level of risk that can be achieved by applying that control measure. This involves a review of the change from the inherent level of a risk (with no control measures in place) to the current level of risk (taking account of the control measures currently in place at their current effectiveness) and then to the target (the acceptable level of risk with current and new controls working effectively).

Figure 18.3 provides an illustration of the control effect or control vector in relation to a threat. In Figure 18.3, a series of lines are drawn for Risk A to represent the effect of each individual risk control measure. The longer the line, the greater the effect of the control. It is also the case that the longer the line, the greater the control effort, in terms of management time, effort and money.

For Risk A, three controls (Controls A1, A2 and A3) are required to get to the target level of risk. For Risk B, only one control is required (Control B1) and this

Figure 18.3   Illustration of control effect

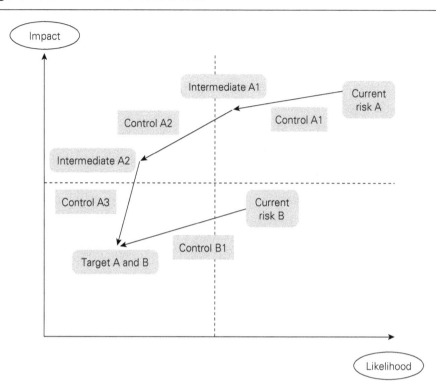

demonstrates that much more effort is needed to maintain Risk A at the target level of risk. Management and internal audit need to be aware of this, so that they can ensure that all of the controls (especially for Risk A) are operating in an effective and efficient manner.

A simple diagram, like Figure 18.3, provides an illustration of the distance between the current and target level of the risk. This simple illustration of control effort is important and demonstrates that there is value in undertaking a risk assessment at the current level of risk, so that the required control effort can be clearly identified and illustrated.

When considering the effort needed to control some risks, a business case may be required to expend that effort. Further detail on the effectiveness of the controls before they are designed is a useful start. Figure 18.4 illustrates some important questions regarding the proposed controls.

This diagram firstly provides levels of ease with which controls can be designed, implemented and maintained. These are measured in levels from one to five, which could include some quantum to describe further what these levels mean, if required. The control effectiveness is also measured in relationship to the change expected in the likelihood or impact of the risk, which should be based on the current and target

Figure 18.4 Control effectiveness

Control Effectiveness				
(1) Easy to design (easy to hard)				
1	2	3	4	5
(2) Easy to implement (easy to hard)				
1	2	3	4	5
(3) Easy to maintain/ keep in place (easy to hard)				
1	2	3	4	5
(4) Reduces (or increases) likelihood of risk (completely to hardly any)				
100–80%	80–60%	60–40%	40–20%	20–0%
(5) Reduces (or increases) impact of risk (completely to hardly any)				
100–80%	80–60%	60–40%	40–20%	20–0%
(6) Cost of control (minimal to very expensive)				
< £10K	£10–50K	£50–250K	£250–1M	>£1M

SOURCE Expert Partners, © 2024. Used with permission

levels and inherent level, where appropriate. Finally, the control effectiveness should be considered in terms of the cost, shown here in monetary terms, but could also include time or number of resources needed perhaps.

Cost of control

As noted above, when considering the current, intermediate (when more than one control is in place) and target risk levels, an organization should be aware of the cost involved in implementing controls. The cost of the control measures should be considered to be part of the total cost of risk for an organization. An organization can then evaluate whether the controls in place are cost-effective as part of a cost-benefit analysis.

If a calculation is undertaken of the risk exposure at the original level and a further calculation is undertaken of the risk exposure at the new level, the overall benefit of each control can be measured. Consideration of the cost of each control can then be undertaken, so that a cost-benefit analysis of individual controls may be completed. This will be an important exercise for an organization to undertake, so that cost-effective risk control priorities may be established.

Figure 18.5   Cost-effective controls

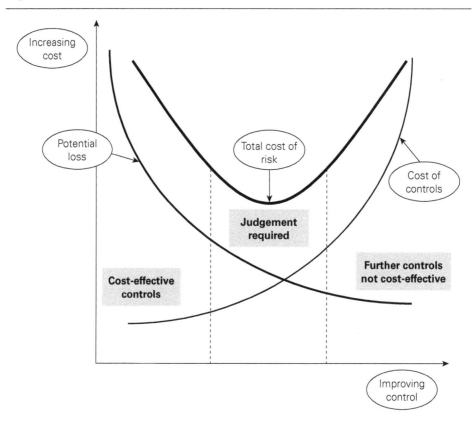

Figure 18.5 plots increasing the level of control (horizontal axis) against the increasing cost of controls (vertical axis). By adding the total cost of controls and the equivalent potential loss for each level of control, the figure illustrates that there is an optimum level of control that represents the lowest combined cost as a sum of the cost of control and the level of potential losses.

It can be seen in Figure 18.5 that a significant reduction in potential loss is achieved with the introduction of low-cost controls in relation to threats. This section of the diagram is labelled 'Cost-effective controls'. The centre section of the diagram illustrates that spending more on controls achieves a reduction in the net cost of risk up to a certain point. In this segment, judgement is required on whether to spend the additional sum on controls. On the right-hand side of the diagram, spending more on controls achieves only a marginal reduction in potential loss. In this segment, further controls are not cost-effective.

Notes

1 HM Treasury (2023), *The Orange Book: Management of Risk – Principles and Concepts*, https://assets.publishing.service.gov.uk/media/6453acadc33b460012f5e6b8/HMT_Orange_Book_May_2023.pdf (archived at https://perma.cc/F3HS-AXBZ)

2 ISO 31000 (2018) Risk management – Guidelines, https://www.iso.org/obp/ui/#iso:std:iso:31000:ed-2:v1:en (archived at https://perma.cc/3FZT-ZFMX)

3 ISO 31073 (2022) Risk management – Vocabulary, https://www.iso.org/obp/ui/en/#iso:std:iso:31073:ed-1:v1:en (archived at https://perma.cc/PW9H-QACF)

4 Hillson, D (Ed.) (2023) *The Risk Management Handbook: A practical guide to managing the multiple dimensions of risk*, 2nd Ed., Kogan Page, London

Controlling both threats and opportunities   19

Management options for controlling both threats and opportunities

In considering the options to manage risks using real controls, both ISO 31000[1] and ISO 31073[2] note that the options for modifying risk may involve one or more of the following:

- Avoiding the risk (threat)
- Taking or increasing the risk (opportunity)
- Removing the risk source (threat)
- Changing the impact (threat or opportunity)
- Changing the likelihood (threat or opportunity)
- Sharing the risk (threat or opportunity)
- Retaining the risk by informed decision (threat or opportunity).

In previous versions of the book, based on now superseded editions of the Orange Book and approaches to risk management, the options for managing threats were identified as the 4Ts. In addition, the 4/5Es were suggested as options for managing opportunities.

In order to align the management of both threats and opportunities and the ways to modify risks included in ISO 31000 and 31073, the options now suggested for managing risk are provided in Table 19.1, and are based on the approach used in the project environment[3] but are equally valid for any organization in any sector.

Different and/or additional responses may be appropriate, depending on the circumstances. For example, if high-impact/high-likelihood risks are embedded within mission-critical activities, they may be unavoidable. In this case, it will not be possible for an organization to eliminate the uncertainty in relation to those risks.

Table 19.1   Description of the options for managing risk

Eliminate uncertainty (previously terminate)	Some risks will only be manageable, or containable to acceptable levels, by eliminating uncertainty. For a threat, the controls put in place mean there is a zero per cent chance of the risk occurring or it has no impact should it occur. For an opportunity, the controls put in place mean there is one hundred per cent chance the risk occurs.
Involve others (previously transfer)	For some risks the best response may be to involve others in managing the risk. For a threat, the controls would be transferring the management of the risk (through contract) or its financial liability (through mechanisms such as insurance). For an opportunity, the controls would allow someone or another organization with a vested interest to manage the risk (through contract).
Change the size (previously treat)	By far the greater number of risks will be addressed in this way. The purpose of this option is to change the likelihood of the risk occurring (not to zero or one hundred per cent), or to change the impact should it occur. For a threat, the controls would reduce the likelihood or impact, and for an opportunity they would increase the likelihood or impact.
Accept (previously tolerate)	In this option, the exposure may be tolerable without any further action being taken. The ability to do anything about some risks may be limited, or the cost of taking any action may be disproportionate to the potential benefit gained; however, the decision is to accept the risk, whether a threat or an opportunity.

A practical difficulty for many organizations is that they may be forced to accept a risk that is recognized as being beyond the risk appetite, or even the risk capacity, of an organization. For example, a firefighting authority may have to accept circumstances where firefighters will be facing a very high level of impact in relation to health and safety risks that an organization has no choice but to accept, even though all possible controls have been implemented. Where organizations have to accept risks that have such large impacts if they occur, it is usual for enhanced monitoring of the risks to be put in place, as noted in the vehicle impact case study in Chapter 15. This will enable an organization to ensure that it takes the earliest opportunity of introducing any enhanced controls as soon as they become available.

Eliminate uncertainty

When a risk is both of high-likelihood and high-potential impact, an organization may wish to avoid the threat or exploit the opportunity, by eliminating the uncertainty.

In relation to threats, the controls will effectively avoid the risk, by eliminating the probability (to zero per cent) or reducing the impact to a negligible level. This can be achieved by such things as changing objectives or scope of activities, improving communication, obtaining expertise or by adopting familiar tools and techniques rather than trying something new.

For example, it may be that the risks of trading in a certain part of the world or the environmental risks associated with continuing to use certain chemicals are unacceptable to an organization and/or its stakeholders. In these circumstances, appropriate options would be to stop the process or activity or substituting an alternative activity that is associated with the risk.

An organization may wish to avoid a risk, but it could be the case that the activity that gives rise to it is fundamental to the ongoing operation of an organization. In such circumstances, an organization may not be able to eliminate the risk entirely and thus will need to implement alternative control measures.

It should be noted that the option of changing objectives may be severely limited in public sector organizations when compared to the private sector. There may be certain risks that have high likelihood and high impact, but an organization is unable to stop doing the activities giving rise to them. This may be because the activity is a statutory requirement placed on a government agency or public authority. The public service imperative may restrict the ability to cease the activity, so an organization will need to introduce control measures, to the greatest extent that is cost-effective.

In relation to opportunities, the controls may be similar to those for avoiding threats, but with the opposite effects. For example, making positive decisions to pursue improvements or to change the scope or objectives of activities undertaken to gain the opportunity.

Involve others

If a threat cannot be fully avoided or opportunity capitalized on, then the next option may be to involve others to help manage a risk. Traditionally, when the likelihood of a threat materializing is low, but the potential impact is high, organizations may have considered transferring the financial liability of the risk, which would usually be under the mechanism of insurance. However, the management of those risks with a high likelihood and low impact would usually be transferred via the mechanism of a contract.

In relation to threats, as noted above, the controls put in place would be to either transfer the financial liability of the risk or the management of that risk, or both. The transfer of financial liability is usually through insurance or could be through performance bonds or warranties.

Insurance is a well-established mechanism for transferring the financial impact of losses arising from threats. However, many risks cannot be transferred to the insurance market, either because of prohibitively high insurance premiums or because the risks under consideration have (traditionally) not been insurable, for example, reputation. The use of insurance as a risk transfer mechanism is considered in more detail in Chapter 36.

Risk transfer can be achieved also by contractual agreement. It may be possible to find a joint venture partner, a supplier or contractor, outsourcing, consultants or some other means of involving third parties who are better able to manage the risk and who have expertise that an organization might not. Risks transferred through the supply chain are considered further in Chapter 37.

The cost of risk transfer is a component of risk financing. Once again, there is variation in the definitions used. In relation to risk financing, BS 31100[4] states that risk financing involves the cost of contingent arrangements for the provision of funds to meet the financial impact of a risk materializing. Such arrangements are usually provided by insurance, and insurance is, therefore, finance that is contingent upon certain insured events taking place.

ISO 31000 also considers that the cost of risk financing should include the provision of funds to meet the cost of risk management. This is another example that illustrates that there is no universally agreed or common language of risk.

In relation to opportunities, transferring the financial liability of risks is not an option; however, allocating ownership to another party best able to obtain the opportunity by sharing the outcome is. In this case, the contractual route would reward the third party for helping to acquire the opportunity.

There is an issue of terminology with the use of the phrase 'risk transfer'. ISO 31000 recommends that risk sharing should be used in preference to risk transfer. The argument is that a risk can never be fully transferred, for example reputation and time, and whatever the intention of the parties, the risk will always be, to some extent, shared. This is an accurate analysis, but the choice of terminology used within an organization will also be influenced by other factors; for example, in relation to risk sharing, the insurance industry uses the terminology risk transfer.

Change the size

Controls that change the likelihood of a risk occurring and its impact should it occur are the most common method of managing a risk. This management option will often be undertaken with the risk at the inherent and/or current level, so that when the risk has been managed, the new current level or target level may become acceptable.

As noted earlier, there is an issue of terminology associated with this option for managing risk, as it is often termed 'treating' the risk, while at the same time, the likes of ISO 31000 consider that 'treat risk' is the main heading for this whole step in the process, to manage risk. In addition, the term 'mitigation' is common in describing how risks will be managed, but a dictionary definition of this term is to reduce the seriousness or severity of an occurrence, so relates to threats only.

In relation to threats, the aim is to reduce the likelihood of the risk occurring and/ or the impact of the risk should it occur. Actions to improve the standard of risk control will always be under constant review in an organization.

On a personal level, wearing a seat belt when driving a car or fitting an intruder alarm in a house are examples of threat reduction actions. Improvements to standards of risk control in relation to physical (insurable) risks are well known. Fitting sprinklers to buildings, providing enhanced building security arrangements and employee security vetting are all examples of risk improvement actions designed to better manage threats.

In relation to opportunities, risk exposure is modified by increasing the likelihood of the risk occurring or the impact should it occur, thereby enhancing the risk. This is often achieved by reinforcing the causes of the risk and taking direct action, and by maximizing the size of the impact.

Cost-effective controls will need to be selected, and the effect of different control measures can be shown on a risk matrix, such as that illustrated in Figure 18.3 in Chapter 18.

Accept

Risk acceptance relates to risk appetite, and whether an organization is willing to pursue a risk or to accept it. ISO 31073 also provides a definition of risk tolerance, noting that it is an organization's or interested party's readiness to bear the residual risk in order to achieve its objectives.

The standard then adds that risk tolerance can be influenced by legal or regulatory (compliance) requirements. The comment about legal or regulatory requirements is very relevant, in that organizations will often have to accept a risk because of legal or regulatory requirements, even in circumstances where an organization would otherwise not wish to accept that risk. It should be noted that tolerance in this instance relates to a specific or individual risk, rather than the more general approach represented by risk appetite.

When a threat is considered to be within the risk appetite of an organization, it will accept that risk. It is unusual for a threat to be accepted before any risk control measures have been applied, although this may be the case for those regulatory or legal risks noted above. Generally speaking, a risk only becomes acceptable when all cost-effective control measures have been put in place. Control effort for both threats and opportunities seeks to move the risk to target level.

Sometimes risks are only accepted as part of an arrangement whereby one risk is balanced against another. This is a simple description of neutralizing or hedging risks, but on a business level this may represent a fundamentally important strategic decision. For example, an electricity company operating independently in the northern part of the US may have to accept the impact of variation in temperature on electricity sales. By merging (or setting up a joint venture) with an electricity company in the southern states, the combined operation will be able to smooth the temperature-related variation in electricity sales. They will sell more electricity in the north during cold weather, when demand in the south is low. Conversely, they also sell more electricity for air-conditioning units in the south in the summer, when demand for electricity in the north may be lower.

Loss control

Another approach to managing threat, highlighted through a risk bow-tie, similar to the one explored in Chapter 18, is loss control. This includes loss prevention (proactive controls) plus damage limitation plus cost containment (reactive controls) and relates to threats only.

Although the most important component of loss control is loss prevention, threats can materialize despite the best efforts of organizations. Adequate assessment of threats is vital, so that appropriate pre-planning of during-the-loss and post-loss actions can be undertaken. Plans should be in place to ensure that the damage caused by the occurrence of a risk is kept to a minimum and the cost consequences of the event are also tightly controlled and contained.

Figure 19.1 illustrates the three components of loss control using the risk bow-tie. Before the event occurs, an organization will have controls in place to seek to achieve loss prevention. As the event is developing, steps should be in place to limit the damage that the event is causing. After the event, cost containment controls by way of business continuity and arrangements to reduce the cost of repair should be activated.

Figure 19.1 Loss control and the bow-tie

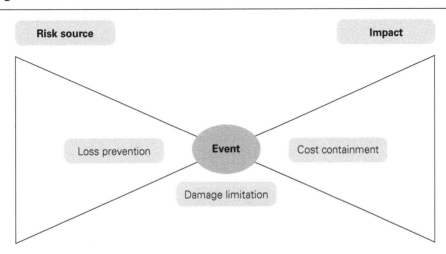

Disaster recovery plans will be relevant during both the damage limitation and the cost containment stages.

Another way of looking at loss control activities is that loss prevention is about reducing the likelihood of a threat occurring. Damage limitation is concerned with reducing the size of the risk when it does materialize. The contribution of damage limitation will be greatest if actions are planned that can be implemented rapidly as the event is taking place. Cost containment is concerned with reducing the consequences of the event. Effective cost containment will ensure the lowest cost of repairs, as well as business continuity management to ensure that an organization can continue operations following damage to the asset that has been affected.

Techniques for loss prevention, cost containment and damage limitation will vary according to the type of threat that is being considered. Examples of techniques in these three areas are highlighted in Table 19.2.

COST CONTAINMENT AND DEEPWATER HORIZON

The Deepwater Horizon oil spill in the Gulf of Mexico in 2010 provides many risk management lessons. One of the key issues was that the oil spill took some weeks to stop because the equipment for capping the damaged well was not immediately available. The oil industry has learned from this example and a sector-wide approach has now instituted the provision of specialist deep water oil well capping equipment at various places across the world, which is available to all operators.

Table 19.2 Examples of loss controls

Loss prevention	• Health and safety risks – elimination of the activity completely or ensuring that, for example, hazardous chemicals are no longer used
	• Security risks – security personnel; biometric scanners at building entry points to ensure only approved individuals gain access
	• Fraud/theft risks – segregation of duties; pre-employment screening; security tagging of expensive items in stores
Damage limitation	• Sprinkler systems; fire segregation within buildings; fire shutters
	• Well-rehearsed arrangements in place to remove, segregate or otherwise protect valuable items
	• Provision of first aid, emergency treatment or even medical facility arrangements
	• Crisis communications

(continued)

Table 19.2 (Continued)

Cost containment	• Arrangements for specialist recovery services
	• Decontamination services
	• Business continuity plans
	• Business interruption insurance (increased costs of working in bringing an organization back to pre-loss levels)
	• Notification of customers/product recall (if faulty goods are released)

COST CONTAINMENT AND PRODUCT RECALL

Any company or organization that manufactures, assembles, processes, wholesales or retails products could be financially impacted by the direct or indirect costs of a product recall. Direct costs can include wages for staff who have to implement the recall plan. Other direct costs include communications, and this could entail purchasing airtime on radio and television and notices in newspapers or industry publications.

Indirect costs can include lost production time for staff who must focus on the recall process, as well as the hiring of temporary employees to ensure continued production. However, the greatest indirect cost is the impact that adverse publicity could have on market share. A product recall should be designed to:

- protect the customer from bodily injury or property damage;
- remove the product from the market and from production;
- comply with specific regulatory requirements;
- protect the assets of the company.

PCDD

Preventive, corrective, directive and detective (PCDD) controls are a more detailed approach to loss control that were used widely in the public sector as part of 'changing the size' (treat) option for managing risks, although few organizations now use this approach as it is only related to one option for managing threats. These controls are listed in Table 19.3, again, linked to the risk bow-tie.

Table 19.3 PCDD controls

1	Preventive (proactive)	These controls are designed to limit the possibility of the threat being realized. The more important it is to stop a threat, then the more important it is to implement appropriate preventive controls.
2	Corrective (reactive)	These controls are designed to limit the scope for loss and reduce the consequences of threats that have been realized. They may also provide a route of recourse to achieve some recovery against loss or damage.
3	Directive (proactive and reactive)	These controls are designed to ensure that a particular outcome is achieved. They are based on giving directions to people on how to ensure that threats do not occur. They are important, but depend on people following established safe systems of work.
4	Detective (reactive)	These controls are designed to identify occasions when threats have been realized. Their effect is, by definition, 'after the event' so they are only appropriate when it is possible to accept that the loss or damage has occurred.

Developing real controls

Following consideration of different control types and in relation to the identification of real controls noted in Chapter 18, thought should be given to the development of those controls. Table 19.4 is the first half of an example control card that can be used to design controls, with the second half of the control card, including the verification criteria of those controls, considered in Chapter 22.

Table 19.4 Writing real controls

Control name	Unique name/number by which the control is identified
Control owner	Person who is responsible for ensuring the control is implemented effectively.
Risk the control is designed to help manage	Link to the originating risk.

(continued)

Table 19.4 (Continued)

Control user	Those in an organization who will be using the control, once implemented. This will identify who should be informed of, and be trained in using the control (where appropriate).
Stage of the control	This provides information on the lifecycle of the control, that is, is it in design (including the percentage completion), is it being implemented (including the percentage completion).
Purpose of the control	Information on what the control is designed to do and what is it changing in relation to the relevant risk, that is, which cause(s) or consequence(s) is it addressing.
Dependencies	Who or what is the control dependent on for its success, for example, money, approval, data, specialist knowledge, materials, time, and so on.

Writing real controls requires detail to ensure they are SMART (specific, measurable, achievable, realistic and timebound) and can be acted upon and implemented effectively.

These controls, when agreed, should form part of an organization's action planning process and internal control framework to ensure they are operating effectively. This will be explored further in Chapters 22 and 29.

Notes

1 ISO 31000 (2018) Risk management – Guidelines, https://www.iso.org/obp/ui/#iso:std:iso:31000:ed-2:v1:en (archived at https://perma.cc/FPZ5-KLPF)
2 ISO 31073 (2022) Risk management – Vocabulary, https://www.iso.org/obp/ui/en/#iso:std:iso:31073:ed-1:v1:en (archived at https://perma.cc/UH6W-LHA2)
3 Axelos (2022) M_o_R4® Management of Risk – Creating and Protecting Value, 4th Ed., PeopleCert International Ltd, Nicosia, Cyprus
4 British Standards (2021) BS 31100:2021 – TC: Risk management. Code of practice and guidance for the implementation of BS ISO 31000:2018, https://knowledge.bsigroup.com/products/risk-management-code-of-practice-and-guidance-for-the-implementation-of-bs-iso-31000-2018?version=tracked (archived at https://perma.cc/4V6Q-V3DV)

Ongoing monitoring

When considering how to respond to risk, it is important that it is not done as a 'once only' approach, but that the ERM approach is a continuous and dynamic exercise. This is especially so considering the constant changes in organizational contexts, in most cases from the external environment, which is often reflected in changes to the internal context.

ISO 31073[1] defines monitoring as the 'continual checking, supervising, critically observing or determining the status in order to identify change from the performance level required or expected'. ISO 31000[2] recognizes the importance of feedback through 'monitoring and review', which ensures that an organization monitors risk performance and learns from experience. Similarly, The Orange Book specifies that the effective monitoring of risks is essential in providing assurance that risks are being managed to acceptable levels.

THE ORANGE BOOK 2023 – SECTION D: RISK MONITORING

D10 – Monitoring should play a role before, during and after implementation of risk treatment [management]. Ongoing and continuous monitoring should support understanding of whether and how the risk profile is changing and the extent to which internal controls are operating as intended, to provide reasonable assurance over the management of risks to an acceptable level in the achievement of organizational objectives.

SOURCE HM Government (2020) *The Orange Book: Management of risk – principles and concepts.* https://assets.publishing.service.gov.uk/government/uploads/system/uploads/attachment_data/file/866117/6.6266_HMT_Orange_Book_Update_v6_WEB.PDF

The importance of monitoring

Risks are constantly changing as the external environment alters or internal systems change. It may be that since the initial assessment there have been changes to the regulations under which an organization operates or that new competitors or digital disruption have taken effect. Due consideration will also need to be given to economic factors or geopolitical concerns, which may have changed since last reviewed. In addition, there may be structural changes in an organization, such as a new chief executive, or a merger or acquisition.

Ongoing monitoring of the work that has been performed to assess and manage the risk should therefore be undertaken at regular intervals. This is especially important for risks that may occur over time if the speed at which they occur may be altered by management taken at the appropriate time.

This is particularly relevant when considering emerging risks. ISO 31050 notes that since emerging risks implicitly include change, monitoring the outcomes of the process is a key part of risk management.

NHS RESOLUTION: MONITORING

NHS Resolution is a UK government entity that administers and provides funding for clinical negligence in the NHS. It holds significant reserves and is charged with the prudent but fair delivery of outcomes for those injured as a result of treatment by the UK's health service. It performs a vital function to 'provide analysis and expert knowledge to drive improvement', or, in other words, to learn lessons from losses.

As an organization is essentially an administrative function, its key risks include IT infrastructure, cybersecurity and fraud. In its 2020 annual report, it is noted that an organization continually reviews and monitors the risks it faces and provides awareness training to staff to ensure it detects potential fraud and improves its control framework to reflect that fluctuating environment within which it operates.

The report also recognized that clinicians operate in a dynamic and fast-changing policy environment, which presents challenges, especially in monitoring and responding to the changes, a key one of which was the organization's reaction to Covid-19.

SOURCE NHS Resolution (2020) *Annual Report and Accounts 2020/21*, https://resolution.nhs.uk/wp-content/uploads/2021/07/NHS_Resolution_Annual-Report-2021.pdf

---

Monitoring risks on an ongoing basis will enable reassessments, when appropriate, to assure the risk practitioner that the risk remains within appetite. This will enable reporting to management if risks have expanded beyond the appetite of an organization. Alternatively, while monitoring a risk, it may be found that the appetite of an organization for that risk may have also changed.

In addition, it may be that new risks have emerged that require management and that some may in fact have reduced as threats and do not require the same allocation of resource as previously, and so on.

The monitoring process considers changes, which requires an understanding of the status of the risks and their controls. Much of this information can be gathered through the iterative nature of the risk management process. There are other tools available to the risk practitioner to focus attention on those risks that require monitoring and to obtain early warnings of changes that could signify changes to the risks or controls.

Risk status

Through the monitoring process, some organizations consider the lifecycle of a risk, and its status at different stages of that lifecycle. Hillson (2018)[3] provides a number of different risk status values. These lifecycle stages, or status values, can be condensed to ease understanding of which risks need to be monitored more regularly, and where lessons can be learnt, as can be seen in Table 20.1.

Table 20.1   Risk statuses

Status	Description
Draft/unapproved	Risks that have been raised but are not yet fully understood or formally approved for inclusion in the relevant risk register.
Active/open	Risks that have been approved and assessed, but where controls are not yet fully implemented to bring them to an acceptable level, so require regular monitoring to ensure the controls have been implemented effectively.
Ongoing	Risks that have been managed to an acceptable level, but are still relevant to an organization, so will be monitored for any changes.
Closed – managed	Risks that have been closed because they have been successfully managed, where the threat no longer exists, or the opportunity has been realized. Information gathered on how the threats or opportunities have been managed successfully can inform lessons learnt – success stories.
Closed – occurred	Risks that have been closed because they have not been successfully managed, where the threat has caused a problem for an organization, or the opportunity has not provided the benefits expected. Information gathered on how the threats or opportunities have been managed unsuccessfully can inform lessons learnt – failures.

Key risk indicators

Monitoring is considered to be a process of continually gauging the pulse of an organization's risks. Taking this analogy a little further, just checking on the health of a risk at a set time does not always catch changes to the risk, or at least does not provide information in a timely manner to understand whether the risk needs further attention or not.

One way to recognize changes to risks without constant formal monitoring of them, is to use indicators of change that are already being gathered in an organization. Most organization will have key performance indicators (KPIs) to help measure different targets or objectives. As considered in Chapters 10, 15 and 26, these KPIs can inform the risk criteria for setting risk appetite and impact scales when understanding and analysing risks.

The COSO (2010) paper[4] on key risk indicators (KRIs) defines them as 'metrics used by organizations to provide an early signal of increasing risk exposures'. These indicators can be used individually to track evolving risks signalling the need for further action to be taken or can be aggregated to highlight emerging events that may lead to new risks.

KRIs should provide useful insights about risks that could affect an organization's objectives, meaning that clear objectives and metrics related to them are fundamental; for example, changes in business performance such as an increase in sales in retail, or passenger numbers in the airline industry. KPIs such as financial, accounting

Table 20.2 Key risk indicators

Causal indicators	Effect indicators
Number and type of causes identified in loss event or near-miss data collection	The direct financial cost of operational loss events (asset writedowns, provisions for liability claims)
Staff turnover as a percentage of staff	The indirect costs of operational loss events (e.g. lost market share, goodwill payments to customers, fines, etc.)
Staff morale (collected from staff surveys)	Duration of staff absence due to health and safety incidents
Number of IT patches not implemented	Customer satisfaction scores
Number of attempted IT hacking attacks	Number and duration of disruptions to operational processes and systems
Number of overdue internal audit actions	Number of negative press reports following a loss event
Number of manual interventions to correct automated process failures	Number of negative social media posts following a loss event

or business management performance indicators may function as risk indicators; for example, a high level of business growth can put pressure on governance systems and internal controls, increasing the potential for fraud, human error, and so on. Indicators that relate to the performance of organizational systems, processes and human resources may also signal a change in operational risk.

A change in the value of the KRI will signal a change in a risk. In this regard, KRIs may relate to the causes or effects of risk. Table 20.2 contains some examples of cause-and-effect indicators from the Institute of Operational Risk's paper on KRIs.[5] Causal indicators tend to be leading indicators, which provide valuable early warning signs that risks are changing before they occur. Effect indicators tend to be lagging indicators, in that they provide information once risks have occurred.

The COSO (2010) paper provides some examples of how these indicators relate to risks, as highlighted in Table 20.3.

Table 20.3   Use of KRIs

Risk	Sample KRIs
Economic downturn might affect retail rental demand and real estate values	Actual and projected retail store occupancy rates Commercial real estate rental market information
Economic downturn might result in deteriorating customer base	Employment statistics Consumer spending
Competition increases	Change in number of similar businesses in the area Announcements of expansion by other similar businesses Significant price reductions by competitors

Risk datasets

Many organizations rely on information that they produce internally, gathered by teams within an organization, such as the Compliance, Procurement or People teams to provide performance metrics.

An article in the IRM's Enterprise Risk Magazine (2021),[6] notes that organizations are dealing with, and have access to, far larger datasets than ever before. There is also technology available that can use this information to identify trends and anomalies to inform the indicators used to measure performance, such as satellites measuring carbon emissions, or the Internet of Things that can measure the movement of equipment or people.

The ISACA (2023)[7] article on AI states that use of artificial intelligence (AI) is also gathering pace as a useful tool in gathering and utilizing data to provide indicators

Figure 20.1   Sources of data and datasets

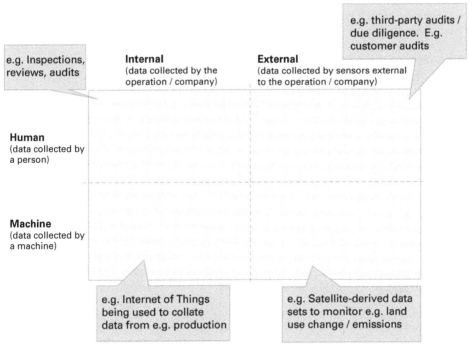

SOURCE © SATARLA (2024). Used with permission

of change or by recognizing patterns in unstructured data that can be used to develop risk predictors.

There are four key sources of datasets that can be considered by organizations to inform their metrics, both in relation to performance and risk, as shown in Figure 20.1.

Not all datasets will be useful in all circumstances, but organizations should use all available data that could be developed as key indicators, whether that data can be found within an organization and external to it:

- Internal sources of information: These will include reports available as part of general organizational management information such as sales, revenue, customer retention, cost of goods sold and similar performance metrics. These will have a bearing on how the risk has changed since it was previously considered. Key risk indicators are usually internal metrics. Internal audit reports should also be sought to assist in the risk monitoring process, since they will be evaluating whether business units are taking the agreed-upon actions.

- External sources of information: It is critical to this process that the monitoring process looks outside an organization to establish the up-to-date position with the risk concerned. This is necessary to ensure that 'groupthink', where assumptions are unchallenged, does not arise. Such external sources of information will be readily available and can include: news aggregators such as Google News; data mining, which may be readily available from external sources such as third-party suppliers, consultants, brokers or trade associations; and sector publications and professional institutes' websites.

ISO 31050[8] on emerging risks explores the risk intelligence cycle and the importance of gathering information on risks, whether at strategic, tactical or operational levels, to build and enhance knowledge. As emerging risks are partly defined by the lack of knowledge about them, then the more information that can be gathered during the monitoring process the more robust that decision making will be.

The ISO standard also notes that intelligence is gained by continually gathering, analysing and interpreting data, information and knowledge, forming an intelligence cycle. The application of the intelligence cycle not only requires the gathering and analysis of the data, but that it is used to inform decision making, especially relating to emerging risks where there are limitations on the availability of data and information.

Frequency of update

The schedule for monitoring risks will vary depending upon the nature of the risk and of an organization, which will have been decided when considering the risk architecture explored previously in Chapter 6. For some organizations, an annual monitoring process for the significant corporate risks may suffice but most organizations now operate in a much more fast-paced environment and are subject to more rapid alterations of environment, requiring a more agile approach to monitoring. In project management, for example, the project may require weekly monitoring of the risk register to take account of the work and findings from the previous week.

Much of the risk information will be captured at different levels of an organization, supporting a top-down and bottom-up approach, will be reflected in the frequency of reporting at operational, tactical and strategic levels, and should also reflect regulatory requirements. Whichever frequency is decided upon, it is important to have the time scheduled for all interested parties to be aware of the frequency and to contribute to the monitoring process.

Responsibility for update

Each risk should have a risk owner who should have the responsibility for ensuring their risks are regularly monitored for changes, whether using KRIs or not, and ensuring the risk information is kept up to date, at and between formal monitoring time-frames.

If an organization has an ERM function, this will be responsible for facilitating the ongoing monitoring of risks at a higher level, which should include a collaborative approach to consider where risks cross over more than one team and to consider external sources of information in order to challenge established assumptions held within an organization.

Notes

1 ISO 31073 (2022) Risk management – Vocabulary. www.iso.org/obp/ui/ en/#iso:std:iso:31073:ed-1:v1:en (archived at https://perma.cc/PSC2-5P99)

2 ISO 31000 (2018) Risk management – Guidelines, www.iso.org/obp/ ui/#iso:std:iso:31000:ed-2:v1:en (archived at https://perma.cc/PSC2-5P99)

3 Hillson, D (2018) Risk Doctor Briefing: The lifecycle of a project risk. https://risk-doctor. com/wp-content/uploads/2020/05/124-The-lifecycle-of-a-project-risk-DH.pdf (archived at https://perma.cc/SAS4-JCPG)

4 COSO (2010) Developing Key Risk Indicators to strengthen enterprise risk management, www.coso.org/_files/ugd/3059fc_6b2928dffbdf481dbf32971b3e9b9c85.pdf (archived at https://perma.cc/D9K6-SJXL)

5 The Institute of Operational Risk (n.d.) Key Risk Indicators – Operational Risk Sound Practice Guidance, www.theirm.org/what-we-say/thought-leadership/sound-practice-guides/operational-key-risk-indicators/ (archived at https://perma.cc/CH58-UVW3)

6 IRM (2021) Enterprise Risk – Summer 2021: Digital innovation is powering an evolution in risk management, https://issuu.com/irmglobal/docs/enterprise-risk-summer-2021 (archived at https://perma.cc/ZD2D-CCD2)

7 ISACA (2023) Can AI be used for risk assessments?, www.isaca.org/resources/news-and-trends/industry-news/2023/can-ai-be-used-for-risk-assessments (archived at https://perma. cc/7BS8-4L2A)

8 ISO 31050 (2023) Risk management – Guidelines for managing an emerging risk to enhance resilience, www.iso.org/obp/ui/en/#iso:std:iso:ts:31050:ed-1:v1:en (archived at https://perma.cc/PSC2-5P99)

Ongoing review   21

Risk review is similar to monitoring, where changes are considered. However, risk review focuses on the effectiveness of the processes or controls put in place as part of risk management. ISO 31073 (2022)[1] defines review as the 'activity undertaken to determine the suitability, adequacy and effectiveness of the subject matter to achieve established objectives'. It goes on further to note that review can be applied to the risk management framework, process, risk or risk control.

Reviewing the risk management framework

In the UK, the updated Corporate Governance Code (2024),[2] requires that an organization's risk management framework should be reviewed at least annually to check on its effectiveness. ISO 31073 provides a definition of a review or audit in this area as the 'systematic, independent and documented process for obtaining evidence and evaluating it objectively in order to determine the extent to which the risk management framework, or any selected part of it, is adequate and effective'. More information on audit and the requirements of corporate governance are provided in Chapter 29.

The risk management framework, as noted in Chapter 6, maps the implementation of risk management in light of the structure of an organization through its risk architecture. It should be reflected in the purpose of risk management and the tone from the top through its risk strategy. It should be supported by the methodologies, tools and techniques available to effectively implement risk management through its risk protocols.

The internal context of an organization is subject to change, as there can be regular and high-level changes brought on by major changes in the external context. These changes must be reflected in the risk management framework to ensure that roles and responsibilities, reporting lines and key documentation are up to date and fit for purpose.

Reviewing the risk management process

The risk management process should be tailored to suit the needs of an organization and to ensure it works effectively and protects, maintains and adds value. It may be that the process designed for an organization does not provide the value expected when it is used at the different levels within Łan organization. For example, workshops designed to assess risk may be too bureaucratic, or not robust enough, or the tools and techniques used to identify or analyse risks may not provide the breadth and depth of data needed to manage the risks effectively.

The review of the risk management process may form part of the annual review of the risk management framework or may form part of a less regular review. Many organizations use external experts to provide a review of the implementation of risk management, including considerations of the maturity of both risk management and risk culture, to identify areas of good practice and those in need of improvement. These reviews are usually benchmarked against international standards, such as ISO 31000 or the COSO ERM framework, and industry best practice. Continual improvement in risk management is explored further in Chapter 39.

Reviewing risks

Risks should be reviewed on a more regular basis than the risk management framework or process. As noted in Chapter 20, some organizations include an annual review of their strategic or corporate risks in line with their annual reporting; however, most now have quarterly or even more regular strategic risk reviews.

Within an organization, reviews of risks support the monitoring process. Reviews will be more formal in nature, whereas monitoring will provide more real-time data regarding the status of risks. For example, when reviewing opportunities, such as new markets, the factors that influence the uncertainty of the opportunity may change quite quickly, such as a new country becoming available to do business in, due to a change in sanctions policy. This may cause a review to take place to identify the areas that should be exploited and the factors that need to be in place to optimize the return.

When actively reviewing risks, a defined process should be undertaken that is appropriate for an organization concerned. This could be a formal review process requiring discussion papers to be prepared before risk committee meetings, or it may involve less formal, but still documented meetings where risks are discussed as an agenda item in already planned, regular team or management meetings. That agenda item should be near the top of the list, to emphasize the importance of risk management, but also to ensure that risks are discussed in the meeting, as items near the end of an agenda are often skipped if meetings run over time.

Whichever type of review is undertaken, the process will usually involve two stages:

1 Categorizing which risks require review and at what interval. Not all risks should be reviewed at regular intervals, as their ability to change will be limited and the benefit of undertaking such action would be negligible and waste the time of those providing input. For example, the risk of product substitution or competitor action may occur less frequently and be subject to annual review. Conversely, some risks will already be under constant and continuous review; for example, risks of cyberattack will probably be monitored by means of automated processes taking feeds from external sources, or an outsourced protection supplier may be involved. This categorization may use the risk status noted when monitoring risks explored in Chapter 20. Included in the categorization process should be an awareness of how any change to the prioritization of the risk may push it outside of acceptable limits.

2 Identifying and accessing all sources of information that may be appropriate for the review. These will include those sources that contributed to the initial review, but in addition datasets that may be gathered internally or externally, manually or by 'machine', as noted in Figure 20.1.

Figure 21.1 provides an example of the lifecycle of risk review within an organization, indicating the regularity of those reviews and how they inform the reviews at higher levels within an organization.

Point A on Figure 21.1 notes the regular, business-as-usual embedding of risk review with an organization. Point B notes escalation of key risk information to more formal team meetings, with the example given here of two-weekly meetings, which may be more or less frequent. Point C indicates the escalation of key risk information to more senior management meetings, feeding into board or board committee meetings shown in Point D. Point E highlights the importance of risk information being fed back down within an organization regarding decisions made.

Reviewing controls

Any review should also include a re-evaluation of any controls to ensure the assumptions that were applied when deciding upon the controls remain applicable. Without this regular review the control itself may become an unconscious risk which is naively being accepted.

Figure 21.1 Example of the lifecycle of a risk review

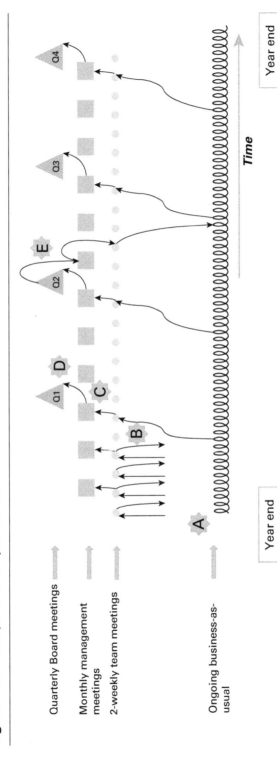

Quarterly Board meetings

Monthly management meetings

2-weekly team meetings

Ongoing business-as-usual

Year end

Year end

Time

SOURCE SATARLA (2024) Used with permission.

Table 21.1   Verification of real controls

Verification information	Activities involved
Maturity of control	Description of stage of development of control, such as designed, implemented, maintained, decommissioned
Trigger(s) for verification	Description of the desired state when the control is working effectively and fully implemented, including metrics (where possible)
	Description of triggers indicating whether a control is failing, including how triggers are monitored and who monitors them
Verification criteria	Description of how the control is monitored, including evidence that controls are working effectively or failing
How to action change if required	Process for reporting or escalating control failures and opportunities for improvement
Independent assurance	Link to formal audits or assurance activities and findings from both

Verification of real controls

Further to the initial development of controls included in Chapter 19, Table 21.1 is the second half of an example control card, which considers the verification of and verification criteria for real controls.

VERIFICATION OF REAL CONTROLS – DATA PROTECTION

A university had put together detailed online training for all staff regarding general data protection regulations (GDPR), which had to be undertaken each year to ensure staff were aware of the requirements and any changes to them.

   This training included assessment questions throughout and at the end to ensure that information was understood by staff. The university had good scores from this training and its assessment questions, thereby showing this control had a 98 per cent effectiveness, which they were continually working to improve. The university were assured that this risk was being managed effectively.

   One of the lecturers undertook the online training, the fourth year of doing so, achieving a full pass mark on the assessment, as usual. She went home that evening with her personal laptop, which did not have password protection or encryption on the data held, but which did have personal details of her students, and she left the computer on the train going home.

Thankfully, the laptop was returned to the lecturer the next day from lost property at her local train station, as an honest member of the public found the computer and handed it in.

The university thought that the risk was being managed but providing training without checking that the learning was followed and used, means that they were getting and giving false assurance.

Internal control

ISO 31073 defines risk control as 'a measure that maintains and or modifies a risk'. It also states that controls include any process, policy, device, practice, or other conditions and/or actions which maintain and/or modify risk. ISO 31073 also makes the important point that controls may not always exert the intended or assumed modifying effect.

However, not all controls within an organization are linked to live risks on risk registers. Some controls will be in place to manage risks that have been closed, have been developed as part of the way that an organization operates its activities, or are in place as part of regulatory requirements, for example. In these cases, the controls are already in place within an organization and usually referred to as internal controls.

Internal control is concerned with the methods, procedures and checks that are in place to ensure that a business or organization meets its objectives. One simple definition of internal control is the actions taken by management to plan, organize and direct the performance of sufficient actions to provide reasonable assurance that objectives will be achieved. There are alternative definitions of internal control and some of the key definitions are set out in Table 21.2.

When referring to internal control activities, it is important to have a single definition within an organization.

Internal control incorporates the organizational and hierarchical structure, as well as planning and objective setting. The scope of internal control extends to evaluation of controls designed to support an organization in achieving objectives and executing strategy, but it also applies to the controls that ensure an organization does not miss business opportunities.

When designing effective internal controls, an organization should look at the arrangements in place to achieve the following:

- maintenance of reliable systems;
- timely preparation of reliable information;
- safeguarding of assets, both physical and cyber, including data;
- optimum use of resources;
- preventing and detecting fraud and error.

Table 21.2 Definitions of internal control

Organization	Definition
COSO (2013) Internal Control Framework[3]	A process, effected by an entity's board of directors, management and other personnel, designed to provide reasonable assurance regarding the achievement of objectives in the following categories: • effectiveness and efficiency of operations; • reliability of financial reporting; • compliance with applicable laws and regulations.
Institute of Internal Auditors[4]	A process, effected by an entity's board of directors, management, and other personnel, designed to provide reasonable assurance regarding the achievement of objectives in the following categories: • effectiveness and efficiency of operations; • compliance with applicable laws and regulations.
Association of Chartered Certified Accountants[5]	The policies, processes, tasks, behaviours and other aspects of an organization that taken together: • Facilitate effective operation by enabling it to respond in an appropriate manner to significant business, operational, financial, compliance and other risks to achieve its objectives. This includes safeguarding of assets and ensuring that liabilities are identified and managed. • Ensure the quality of internal and external reporting, which in turn requires the maintenance of proper records and processes that generate a flow of timely, relevant and reliable information from both internal and external sources. • Ensure compliance with applicable laws and regulations and with internal policies.

Purpose of internal control

The primary purpose of internal control activities is to help an organization achieve its objectives. Typically, internal controls have the following purposes:

• safeguard and protect the assets of an organization;

• ensure the keeping of accurate records;

• promote operational effectiveness and efficiency;

• adhere to policies and procedures, including control procedures;

• enhance reliability of internal and external reporting;

- ensure compliance with laws and regulations;

- safeguard the interests of shareholders/stakeholders.

There is a very clear link between risk management and internal control. It is surprising, therefore, that many organizations operate separate risk management and internal control frameworks. This often means that controls to manage risks remain on a risk register and not embedded into the business-as-usual operation of an organization. As such, controls may not be fully implemented or monitored and there may be duplication of effort and a waste of resources. Further information on requirements for risk management and internal control frameworks to provide assurance that organizations are operating, and their risks are being managed effectively, are included in Chapter 29.

Key control indicators

Key risk indicators (KRIs) were considered in Chapter 20 as early indicators of changes in risks. Key control indicators (KCIs) are similar in nature but instead provide early indication of changes in controls. The Institute of Operational Risk[6] defines KCIs as 'metrics that provide information on the extent to which a given control is meeting its intended objectives'. It also states that KCIs indicate the effectiveness of a particular control at a particular point in time, meaning that KCIs are only a snapshot in time, and as with the ERM in its entirety, they should be updated frequently.

KCIs should be developed in line with the development of controls and will form part of the control card providing metrics relating to the desired state when the control is working effectively or providing triggers when the control is failing.

As noted in Chapter 20, KRIs tend to be leading indicators of change providing data on whether or not risks are more or less likely to occur (causal indicators) or how much an organization might be affected by a risk once it has occurred (effect indicators). KCIs tend to be more lagging indicators, as they provide data on whether or not controls are working effectively. However, they could be repurposed as indicators in change in risks also, as some of those controls will be in place to manage live risks.

Lessons learnt

Throughout the risk review process, information will be gathered on both the successful management of risks, and where mistakes have been made and failures have occurred. It is important to learn lessons from both.

Large failures, that have a detrimental impact on organizations, are often subject to deep dives or in-depth investigations into the root causes of the issue, so that mistakes are learnt and not repeated in the future. These investigations may be as a result of failures occurring in an organization, but many organizations will review their own controls in light of failures in competitor organizations. However, few organizations undertake investigations into successful management of risks, which could provide best practice for the future. As noted in Chapter 20, more granular information on the successful or unsuccessful management of risks can be captured in the risk status.

Lessons learnt should also be captured from near misses, risks which occur but do not result in the large impact that could have resulted from the occurrence of the risk. For example, a small fire in a building that was detected early or a small breach in security that was blocked quickly. Learning lessons from near misses enables organizations to understand why the incident occurred, whether it was identified as a risk, and whether it had been correctly prioritized during the risk analysis process.

It is as important to learn lessons from near misses as it is to learn from risks that occur.

Notes

1 ISO 31073 (2022) Risk management – Vocabulary, www.iso.org/obp/ui/en/#iso:std:iso:31073:ed-1:v1:en (archived at https://perma.cc/PSC2-5P99)
2 FRC (2024) *UK Corporate Governance Code*, https://media.frc.org.uk/documents/UK_Corporate_Governance_Code_2024_kRCm5ss.pdf (archived at https://perma.cc/YY3D-93M2)
3 COSO (2013) *Internal Control – Integrated Framework: Executive Summary*, www.coso.org/_files/ugd/3059fc_1df7d5dd38074006bce8fdf621a942cf.pdf (archived at https://perma.cc/7C35-AXGS)
4 IIA (2020) Official IIA Glossary, www.theiia.org/globalassets/documents/certifications/the-iia-official-glossary/official-iia-glossary-english.pdf (archived at https://perma.cc/7RA2-HWB4)
5 ACCA (2024) Internal controls, www.accaglobal.com/uk/en/student/exam-support-resources/fundamentals-exams-study-resources/f1/technical-articles/internal-controls.html (archived at https://perma.cc/9E59-NGR9)
6 The Institute of Operational Risk, n.d., *Key Risk Indicators – Operational Risk Sound Practice Guidance*, www.theirm.org/what-we-say/thought-leadership/sound-practice-guides/operational-key-risk-indicators/ (archived at https://perma.cc/8WQN-DFK6)

Reporting on risk management 22

Reporting

Chapter 8 introduced risk reporting as a key tool in decision making. ISO 31073[1] defines risk reporting as a 'form of communication intended to inform particular internal or external interested parties by providing information regarding the current state of risk and its management'. ISO 31000[2] goes further to note that reporting is an integral part of corporate governance, which should enhance dialogue with those interested parties, supporting senior managers and the board in meeting their responsibilities.

Communication and consultation

As noted in Chapter 8, communication and consultation is the first step in the ISO 31000 risk management process, and forms an important part of reporting on risks and risk management. ISO 31000 notes that communication and consultation assist in the understanding of risks, thereby supporting decision making. Considering both aspects then enables factual, timely, relevant, accurate and understandable exchanges of information. At the same time, that information should be used with integrity and confidentiality, as well as respecting the privacy rights of individuals. It is important to note that risk information is generally not non-disclosable from a legal perspective, even within the corporate risk register. Furthermore, establishing communication and consultation forms part of the risk management framework and stresses that consultation involves participants providing feedback.

The stakeholder mapping exercises explored in Chapter 11 are the foundation for developing communication plans, which then informs the nature of the risk reporting required. ISO 31000 notes that communication and consultation are not just about delivering risk information, but that they should ensure different views are considered and there is a sense of inclusiveness and ownership among those affected by risk. This requires some empathy with the receiver of the information in relation to the style and format of the delivery, and also the message provided, and the feedback required.

In more simple terms, reporting should consider the what, when, to who, by who, how and more importantly the why of communication. Reporting should not be done just for reporting's sake; there should be clear reasons for reporting and a clear understanding of the feedback from that process. In many organizations, a great deal of time and effort is taken to produce different risk reports at different levels of an organization. In more mature organizations, this effort is reduced by the regular monitoring and review of risks and controls, where information is kept up to date on an ongoing basis, meaning reporting is less onerous. Regardless, if feedback is not given on decisions made or accountability taken for risks and related controls, engagement with those providing risk information will reduce.

Internal reporting

Internal reporting should provide clear and transparent information that gives appropriate assurance, or not, to management levels above and to the board, that risks are being managed effectively so that the organizational objectives can be met. The format and style of internal reporting is not usually governed by law or regulations.

Reporting on risks should be in line with the risk review lifecycle noted in Chapter 21, embedded into the business-as-usual reporting process. The reporting of regularly monitored and reviewed risks will vary depending upon the urgency and importance of the findings. Clearly, any review which establishes that risks have changed to become outside of the agreed risk appetite will be escalated to the appropriate level of management, or, perhaps a non-executive director, who need to consider the actions required to bring such a risk back to within acceptable parameters at the earliest possible juncture. More regular findings will probably form part of a management information pack that provides regular updates to enable the management of an organization.

The 'ask'

Reporting should encompass the last arrow in the simple four-step risk management process; as such, it should answer the question regarding the ability to achieve objectives. If, given the context in which a team is operating and the objectives it is trying to meet, the risks it faces, and the ability it has to manage those risks, that team feels able to achieve its objectives, then risk reporting should state that fact, with evidence to prove it.

However, if the team feels it is unable to meet its objectives because of the risks it faces and its ability to manage those risks, then reporting should provide information on those risks. In this situation, reporting should also include the 'ask' of the management level above. ISO 31000 notes that reporting should provide information for

Table 22.1   The 'ask' in risk reporting

First request	For more time, money and effort to manage particular risks to an acceptable level (or within risk appetite) in order to achieve objectives. If this request is denied because an organization cannot or does not want to put more time, money, or effort in to manage particular risks, then the second request may be made.
Second request	To change the objectives or even the context in order to make it easier to achieve the objectives. If this request is denied, then the third request should be made.
Third request	For someone at the relevant level of management to accept the particular risks and take responsibility and accountability for them, and their potential occurrence, as such bringing those risks into the risk appetite.

decision making, as part of improvements in risk management activities and in relation to responsibility and accountability for those activities.

Essentially, the 'ask' of the management levels above forms part of an escalation process, where support, decision making and accountability are required, which is usually covered by three separate requests, noted in Table 22.1.

These important aspects of decision making, responsibility and accountability are often missing in the reporting process, where risk information is provided as a requirement of governance, with no expectation of actions to be taken or challenges to be made.

Reporting formats

Regular reports may involve a simple dashboard or similar report showing changes to the risks, or alterations to controls and profile which had been seen previously. It will be important not to overload management with reports that may be immaterial, in that risks have changed insignificantly. Ultimately, this will weaken the position of the risk management function in the eyes of senior management in that the ERM function may appear to be overly bureaucratic.

A risk dashboard can provide sufficient information on one page to inform decision making and accountability taking in relation to the 'ask' of the management level above. Figure 22.1 illustrates an example risk dashboard that indicates key risks on a risk matrix, using the impact versus action approach, although any format of matrix could be included, such as impact and likelihood. To the right of the matrix, a list of the key risks for management's attention is provided, with an indication of which objectives the risks affect. The objectives for the relevant team or corporate objectives are then listed with an indication of whether those objectives can be achieved due to the risk affecting them. At the bottom of the page is a list of the 'asks'

Figure 22.1   Example risk dashboard

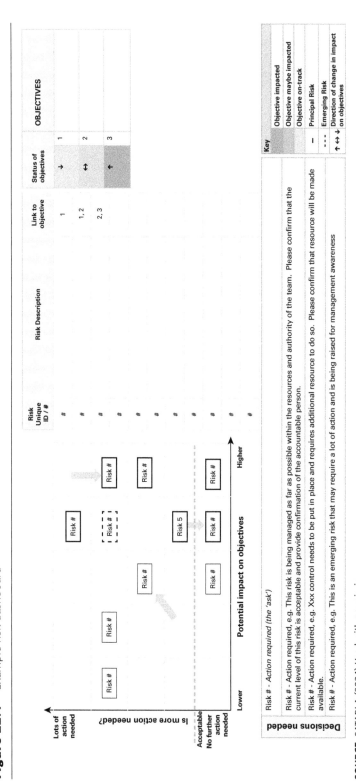

SOURCE SATARLA (2024) Used with permission

or requests for support to manage the risks further, to change the objectives or context, or to accept the risk and take accountability for it.

Further supporting documentation should be provided in addition to the risk dashboard but should be related to the information on the dashboard itself. Risk management documentation in its many forms is not required for reporting, but different sources do inform effective reporting depending on the message needing to be shared. It should be noted that it is not necessary to provide the risk register as the risk report; indeed, that should not be the case, although it may form part of supporting information. Management level above should be aware of the key strategic risks relevant to the particular activities being undertaken, the status of those risks, and the status of the controls, but do not need to be made aware of all risk information.

A RISK REGISTER IS NOT A RISK REPORT

In their first report to the board of a global engineering organization, the head of risk management included the full corporate risk register in the board papers. One of the executive team asked why all the risks on the risk register needed to be brought to the attention of the board. At that point it was agreed that only risks that should 'keep the board awake at night' would be included in the board report, either because of interest in an opportunity or worry about a threat.

It may also be possible to automate risk reporting on a more continuous basis using technology, especially if an organization uses digital processes in its ordinary course of working.

Risk performance and certification reports include operational management reports as well as more formal declarations and certified reports to stakeholders. In certain cases, certification of the financial results of operations of an organization will be undertaken as a formal attestation by a third party. Typically, this third-party attestation will be undertaken by an external auditor. Such a written attestation will also include an evaluation of the effectiveness of the control activities related to financial reporting.

Provision of risk assurance is explored further in Chapter 29.

External reporting

External stakeholders require assurance that their 'stake' in an organization is being effectively risk managed and they can reasonably expect to be reassured on that fact. External reporting is often governed by law and regulations.

Reporting requirements have become increasingly detailed, and it is sometimes necessary for organizations to produce separate reports for different regulatory authorities. Also, some organizations may decide to issue specific reports to achieve a high profile for certain aspects of their organization. In particular, several organizations issue separate sustainability reports to highlight their achievements in this important area. For example, there may be specific requirements that apply, such as the Sarbanes–Oxley Act when an organization is listed on the New York Stock Exchange. However, that organization may also be listed on another stock exchange with different requirements. Additionally, an organization may have subsidiaries that are registered as a charity, or operate as (for example) an insurance company, perhaps a captive insurance company.

Listed companies

Companies that are listed on the UK stock exchange are required to disclose risk information as part of the corporate governance requirements. The UK Corporate Governance Code Guidance (2024)[3] notes the following risk-related disclosure requirements to be included in an organization's annual report and accounts:

- information on the main features of the risk management and internal control framework;
- how the Board has monitored and reviewed the effectiveness of the risk management and internal control framework;
- a declaration of the effectiveness of material controls, and/or improvements in controls;
- information on the principal risks and how they are managed;
- information on procedures to identify and manage emerging risks.

In considering material information the guidance notes that the definition of material financial information from the International Financial Reporting Standards (IFRS) could also be applied to non-financial information:

> Information is material if omitting, misstating or obscuring it could reasonably be expected to influence the decisions that the primary users of general purpose financial statements make on the basis of those financial statements, which provide financial information about a specific reporting entity.

The UK Corporate Governance Code considers principal risks as risks that

> should include, but are not necessarily limited to, those that could result in events or circumstances that might threaten the company's business model, future performance, solvency or liquidity and reputation. In deciding which risks are principal risks companies should consider the potential impact and probability of the related events or circumstances, and the timescale over which they may occur.

Table 22.2   Reporting information that investors want to understand

Governance and processes	The who, what, how and when in relation to understanding risks, uncertainties and opportunities.
Nature	Understanding of an organization's context, the rating of risks and how risks are identified and categorized.
Approach	How risks are linked to objectives and how risks are being tangibly managed in relation to an organization's risk appetite.
Scenarios and stress-testing	Understanding emerging risks and how they are integrated into an organization's risk management process. This should also include information on scenario and stress-testing exercises.

In addition, the FRC's Reporting Lab (2021)[4] issued a report outlining what information investors want to understand in relation to risks (threats), uncertainties, opportunities and scenarios. Table 22.2 highlights the four key areas from the report that investors want information on in order to be assured that an organization is viable and will be resilient for the longer term.

More information on corporate governance and the requirements of different regulatory bodies is provided in Chapter 27.

Companies that are listed on a US stock exchange are required to make extensive disclosures about risk factors. These risk management reports are intended to be forward-looking, rather than a commentary on the risks that have materialized in the past. The reports are contained in the periodic Form 10-K or Form 20-F filings that should include industry, economic and environmental risks. Each of the listed risks would usually be described in more detail, by way of a detailed explanation of up to half a page.

In addition, the Sarbanes–Oxley Act (SOX) (2002) was passed in response to a range of corporate scandals in the US. These scandals involved misrepresentation of the financial status of various organizations, leading to misleading financial statements. The primary purpose of SOX is to ensure that information disclosed by companies listed on the stock exchanges in the US is accurate. SOX is explored further in Chapter 29.

Charities

Risk reporting by charities is compulsory in most countries in the world. In general, there is an expectation that charities should have detailed risk management procedures broadly equivalent to those required of government departments or of companies listed on a stock exchange. A shortened version of the advice on risk reporting set out in the UK Charity Commission[5] guidance is as follows:

> The form and content of the statement is likely to reflect the size and complexity of an individual charity's activities and structure. The commission is not seeking 'template'

reporting, or requiring a detailed analysis of the processes and results. A narrative style that addresses the key aspects of the requirements is acceptable.

This means:

- an acknowledgement of trustees' responsibility;
- an overview of the risk identification process;
- an indication that major risks have been reviewed or assessed;
- confirmation that control systems have been established.

It is recognized that some charities, particularly larger charities or those with more complex operations, might expand on this basic approach to reporting. The Charity Commission notes that where more information is used in reporting, the following broad principles are addressed:

- linkage between the identification of major risk and the operational and strategic objectives of the charity;
- procedures that extend beyond financial risk to encompass operational, compliance and other categories of identifiable risk;
- linkage of risk assessment and evaluation to the likelihood of its occurrence and impact should the event occur;
- ensuring risk assessment activities and monitoring are ongoing and embedded in management and operational procedures;
- trustees' review and consideration of the principal results of risk identification, evaluation and monitoring.

Public sector

Attention to risk management in government departments and other areas of the public sector is mandatory in most countries. Much of the information on risk management in government bodies is freely available on websites and this information forms very useful reference material. However, because the information is publicly available, there is often no specific mention of the risk reporting to external stakeholders. The UK Treasury (2021)[6] has produced a paper on risk reporting, which is part of the suite of risk management guidance, including the Orange Book (2023). The risk reporting guidance notes that:

> To maximize the benefits of this guidance, organizations should recognize that risk reporting will best enhance decision making when:
>
> Objective, priorities and delivery outcomes are clearly understood across the organization
>
> Effective partnership working arrangements are in place between departments, arm's length bodies and other delivery bodies

Risk identification processes are in place to capture new and emerging risks

Risk management is an integral element of day-to-day activities underpinned by good governance and leadership

Risk management is conducted as a collaborative process integrated with other key governance and oversight mechanisms, including but not limited to planning and performance processes

Risk management reporting is considered through formal governance mechanisms on a regular basis

Robust risk analysis takes place to ensure risk causes and consequences are properly understood, and control activity is directed effectively

The organization has set and understands its risk appetite

The risk culture embraces openness and clear communication, supports transparency, welcomes constructive challenge and promotes collaboration, consultation and co-operation

There are processes in place to enable the aggregation and escalation of risks to the appropriate management level

Governments

One of the biggest steps forward in risk communication in recent times has been the willingness of governments to be more open about security threats. Many governments undertake a national security threat analysis and publish the results. For example, the UK government published in 2011 a document entitled the *National Security Strategy of the United Kingdom*. More recently, the UK Cabinet Office (2023) published the *National Risk Register*.[7]

In addition, the UK government (2021) published its report on Global Britain in a Competitive Age: The integrated review of security, defence, development and foreign policy. Within this analysis, there was review of key objectives or dependencies of the UK.[8]

In the US, the Federal Emergency Management Agency has produced the National Risk Index for Natural Hazards, which is an online tool illustrating the communities most at risk for 18 natural hazards across the country. The US Department of the Treasury (2024) also published the National Risk Assessments for money laundering, terrorist financing and proliferation financing.

These reviews by the governments are interesting examples of the detailed risk assessment being undertaken at national level. It demonstrates that risk management is now embedded into the heart of national government. The fact that risk management has been embraced by national governments indicates that the importance of risk management is recognized at the highest level.

However, this does not always mean that action is taken regarding risks raised. For example, the UK government identified the critical issue facing national security as pandemic human disease. In 2016 the government conducted Exercise Cygnus, to test its preparedness for the outbreak of a pandemic (using a flu virus). Reports suggest many of the 57 recommendations were not acted upon, including a need to increase critical care capacity and a review of how the social care and health service interface. Despite being recognized as a critical risk, the political will did not seem to exist at the time to take any action on this. This is further evidence perhaps that the culture of an organization is critically important in applying risk management lessons.

Notes

1 ISO 31073 (2022) Risk management – Vocabulary, www.iso.org/obp/ui/en/#iso:std:iso:31073:ed-1:v1:en (archived at https://perma.cc/PSC2-5P99)
2 ISO 31000 (2018) Risk management – Guidelines, www.iso.org/obp/ui/#iso:std:iso:31000:ed-2:v1:en (archived at https://perma.cc/PSC2-5P99)
3 FRC (2024) *Corporate Governance Code Guidance*, www.frc.org.uk/library/standards-codes-policy/corporate-governance/corporate-governance-code-guidance/#reporting-in-the-annual-report-3c75fda8 (archived at https://perma.cc/WQ7T-N83B)
4 FRC Reporting LAB (2021) *Reporting on risks, uncertainties, opportunities and scenarios*, https://media.frc.org.uk/documents/Risks_uncertainties_opportunities_and_scenarios.pdf (archived at https://perma.cc/GG85-TTLV)
5 UK Charity Commission for England and Wales (2010) *Charities and risk management (CC26) - Guidance*, https://assets.publishing.service.gov.uk/media/5a81b552e5274a2e8ab556ee/CC26.pdf (archived at https://perma.cc/6SKX-BVFD)
6 UK Treasury (2021) Good Practice Guide: Risk Reporting, https://assets.publishing.service.gov.uk/media/611642cfe90e070541075731/Good_Practice_Guide_Risk_Reporting_Final.pdf (archived at https://perma.cc/3ATJ-2JN3)
7 UK Cabinet Office (2023) *National Risk Register – 2023 edition*, https://assets.publishing.service.gov.uk/government/uploads/system/uploads/attachment_data/file/1175834/2023_NATIONAL_RISK_REGISTER_NRR.pdf (archived at https://perma.cc/KW9L-7EH9)
8 HM Government (2021) Global Britain in a Competitive Age: The integrated review of security, defence, development and foreign policy, https://assets.publishing.service.gov.uk/government/uploads/system/uploads/attachment_data/file/975077/Global_Britain_in_a_Competitive_Age-_the_Integrated_Review_of_Security__Defence__Development_and_Foreign_Policy.pdf (archived at https://perma.cc/CWU2-YLL4)

PART FIVE
Risk strategy and culture

LEARNING OUTCOMES

Having studied this section readers will be able to:

- Describe the people aspect of risk-based decision making.
- Explain risk predisposition, risk perceptions and risk bias, and how they affect decision making.
- Explain risk culture in relation to organizational culture.
- Describe the key features of a risk-aware culture (LILAC) and how the key components are defined.
- Describe the key features of the ABC and Double S risk culture models.
- Describe a successful risk culture.
- Explain how risk culture can be measured and improved.
- Describe the importance of risk appetite and its related concepts of risk tolerance, risk capacity and risk universe.
- Explain how risk appetite can be developed, and used to measure risk appetite against objectives, risk categories and/or risks
- Review the nature of risk appetite statements and how these can be used to influence decision making within organizations.
- Explain the use of qualitative and quantitative risk appetite statements for use with internal and external stakeholders

Culture and behaviours

Making risk-based decisions

The previous chapters regarding the risk management process, in Parts Three and Four, considered how to understand and manage risks related to the context an organization is operating in and the objectives it is trying to achieve. Chapter 22 explored how to provide information and assurance to management levels above to support decision making in achieving those objectives.

The COSO (2017) definition of risk management provided in Chapter 1 noted that the framework needs to consider the culture, capabilities and practices of risk management within an organization. This recognizes that risk management is not just a function or department, but that it requires all within an organization to have the appropriate level of risk awareness. In addition, failures in risk management, despite there being risk protocols and risk strategies in place, highlight the fact that the right attitudes, behaviours and risk culture are needed for risk management to be effective.

RISK CULTURE AND FINANCIAL CRISIS[1]

The financial crisis started on September 15, 2008, with Lehman Brothers filing for bankruptcy, followed quickly by Merrill Lynch being acquired and AIG being bailed out by the US Federal Reserve. By 17 September 2008, financial markets around the world were in chaos, with governments having to intervene to prevent a worldwide depression.

There were many causes of this catastrophic failure in the financial sector, but investigations have raised findings and lessons learnt that affect organizations from any sector or industry. Three key lessons that emerged relate to the need for more proactive risk management, heightened expectations for boards of directors and the emphasis on culture and the 'tone from the top'.

All three of these findings require more risk awareness, challenges and accountability at the senior management levels, with the encouragement of appropriate engagement, communication and behaviours throughout an organization. This would support a top-down and a bottom-up approach to risk management, providing the 'tone from the top' and the 'echo from the bottom'.

Clearly, people have a part to play in making effective risk-based decisions related to the information provided. This section of the book considers this people aspect of risk-based decision making, exploring how to get relevant individuals or groups in an organization to make decisions and take actions.

Based on the stakeholder analyses considered in Chapter 11 and the communication plans covered in Chapter 22, an additional aspect should be the consideration of individuals' different decision-making styles. These styles typically measure an individual's preferences along two spectrums. The first is a range of tolerance for ambiguity and the second is a range in ways of thinking (rational and task focused, to intuitive and people focused). The product is four core styles of decision making, which are directive, analytical, conceptual and behavioural, explored in more detail in Figure 23.1.

These decision-making styles at leadership level will also provide an insight into the potential risk culture within an organization.

Figure 23.1   Decision-making styles

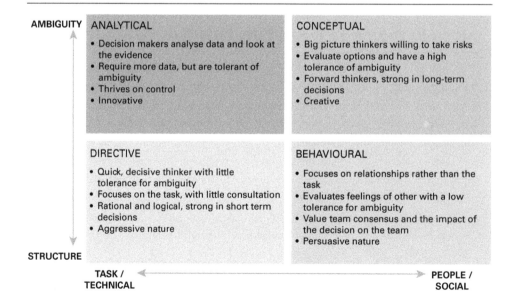

Risk culture

Risk culture is an important part of embedding risk management effectively into an organization. The development of the risk management framework can be undertaken in a relatively short space of time, but the effective implementation of risk management often requires a change in people's risk culture. One of the eight principles in ISO 31000[2] specifically notes that 'human behaviour and culture significantly influence all aspects of risk management at each level and stage'.

Risk culture is also a key aspect of the updated UK Corporate Governance Code,[3] where the guidance states that boards should lead by example, demonstrating a commitment to integrity and company values. It notes that the board is responsible for the culture, which affects the way risks are identified, analysed and managed, and the promotion of risk awareness, the acceptance of challenge and the encouragement of open communication regarding risk-taking across an organization.

Risk culture is a subset of an organizational culture and is defined by the IRM's risk culture paper[4] as the 'values, beliefs, knowledge and understanding about risk shared by a group of people with a common purpose'. ACCA (2024)[5] define risk culture in similar terms as 'the values, beliefs, knowledge, attitudes, conduct, behaviours, and understanding about risk and the level of accepted risk shared by a group of people who have a common purpose'.

A good risk culture will be the product of individual and group values and of attitudes and patterns of behaviour. This will lead to a commitment to the risk management objectives of an organization. Organizations with a risk-aware culture are characterized by communication founded on mutual trust and a shared perception of the importance of risk management, including a sharing of confidence in the selected control measures and a commitment to adhering to the established risk control procedures.

A risk-aware culture requires good communication of risk information from and to senior management. Good communication also requires that reports from all employees, as well as reports from outside an organization, are welcome and well received. Information on risk performance should be included in the communication activities.

ISO 31000 places considerable importance on the context within which an organization operates. Information is provided in the standard on the importance of the external context, internal context and risk management context for an organization. Context is closely related to risk management culture and the benefits that will be derived from enhanced risk management within an organization.

The first component in the COSO ERM framework (2017)[6] relates to governance and culture, with its underlying principles requiring the defining of desired cultures. The second component refers to analysis of the business context, rather than the control environment that is described in the COSO internal control cube (2013).[7]

The control environment and the internal context are measures of the risk culture and the level of risk awareness within an organization.

An overall improvement in risk performance will be achieved through improvements in the internal context, risk management context, control environment or internal environment.

Chapter 24 explains the ABC model of risk culture, which is the attitudes, behaviours and culture regarding risk and risk management within an organization. These start with individuals and their predisposition towards risk, their perceptions and their biases.

Risk predisposition

Risk predisposition is the level to which people are sensitive towards risk. This relates to their resilience, cautiousness, pessimism or optimism and ranges from risk averse to risk seeking. Risk predisposition can be measured by risk personality profiling tools, which, similar to the approach to gauging an individual's decision-making styles, look at comfort levels in taking risk, and the amount of preparedness a person needs to do so.

An understanding of those who are risk averse or risk seeking, and those needing to be prepared or are willing to be spontaneous, can provide an insight into the risk culture in an organization. However, everyone is capable of flexing their behaviour from their personal predisposition; that is, they can work outside of their comfort zone for a period of time. However, asking a risk-averse person to work in a sales position, or risk-seeking person to work in a compliance role may push them too far out of their comfort zones if they work in those roles for too long.

From a leadership perspective, risk predisposition can have a significant impact on an organization's strategic direction and decision making. It is important to have a balance of risk predisposition at leadership level, to ensure effective challenge and risk-taking takes place. A famous quote related to this balance from William Wrigley Jr (of the chewing gum company), is sometimes misstated as, 'When two [people] in business always agree, one of them is unnecessary'.

Risk perceptions

Risk perceptions are subjective judgements that individuals make about the characteristics and size of risks and their response to risks. Hillson and Webster (2007)[8] note that risk perception is best understood if considered as two extremes, where a situation is perceived as good or neutral, or where a situation is seen as bad.

Where a situation is perceived as good or neutral, a more positive and proactive approach is taken towards the risk and its management, for example acquiring a new organization without robust due diligence because a potential new market looks promising. Where a situation is perceived as bad and more negative, a reactive approach is taken, for example the instinctive fight, flight or freeze response in relation to personal safety.

As such, risk perception will have an effect on risk culture and the management of risks. Risk perception can affect any part of the risk management process. For example, whether a situation has any risks associated with it (risk identification), how big those risks are (risk analysis), whether to do anything about the risks (risk evaluation), how much effort to put in to managing the risks (risk management), and whether to keep the risk information up to date (monitor, review and report).

Risk bias

Risk bias or cognitive bias relates to the mental shortcuts individuals use to make decisions on situations, usually when there is little information about a situation, or when a situation is first encountered. There is a great deal of research around bias, and how it affects decision making around risk.

Some of the common cognitive biases are noted in Table 23.1.

Table 23.1   Cognitive biases

Availability	Treating more memorable events as more significant. For example, terrorist attacks in London may discourage tourists, even though those attacks have been rare, and if they occur, do not take place across the whole of the capital.
Representativeness	Stereotyping as an indicator of significance. For example, being scared of young males wearing hoodies in public, where, in fact, this is usually more of a fashion choice than indicator of behaviour.
Anchoring and adjustment	Remaining with an initial estimate and being unable to change an opinion relating to that estimate even though there is no evidence of fact. For example, being told a 'best estimate' cost for managing a risk, and making a judgement on that even though very little information was provided in relation to the estimate.
Confirmation trap	Assuming an answer, looking for evidence to support it, and not being able to consider opposing evidence. For example, the MMR scandal in 1998 in the UK, where a fraudulent research paper was published in a prestigious medical journal claiming a link between the measles, mumps and rubella (MMR) vaccine and autism in children. The claim was refuted and retracted in 2010, but is still used as evidence by those who are against the vaccine.

(continued)

Table 23.1 (Continued)

Group think	Accepting a situation or decision as a group consensus, even though some individuals do not agree. For example, agreeing to the strategic direction of an organization, even when some individuals do not think it is the right choice.
Halo effect	Following the example of a charismatic person even though it contradicts the personal preferences of individuals in a group. For example, agreeing to business trips in socio-political unstable areas because a key team member is comfortable doing so, even though members of the team may be risk averse.

Whether considering personal predisposition, perception or cognitive bias, individuals and groups have an important influence on the risk culture within an organization. This should be considered in embedding and implementing effective risk management and ensuring objective risk-based decisions are being made, or at least understanding where they are not.

Notes

1 Harvard Law School Forum on Corporate Governance (2018) *The Financial Crisis 10 Years Later: Lesson Learned*, https://corpgov.law.harvard.edu/2018/10/05/the-financial-crisis-10-years-later-lessons-learned/ (archived at https://perma.cc/47BZ-U39A)

2 ISO 31000 (2018) Risk management – Guidelines, www.iso.org/obp/ui/#iso:std:iso:31000:ed-2:v1:en (archived at https://perma.cc/GEZ8-ESYW)

3 FRC (2024) *Corporate Governance Code Guidance*, www.frc.org.uk/library/standards-codes-policy/corporate-governance/corporate-governance-code-guidance/#section.7eba31e6 (archived at https://perma.cc/44F8-9K97)

4 IRM (2012) Risk Culture – Under the microscope guidance for Boards, www.theirm.org/media/4703/risk_culture_a5_web15_oct_2012.pdf (archived at https://perma.cc/89PU-DBDW)

5 ACCA (2023) *Risk culture: Building resilience and seizing opportunities*, www.accaglobal.com/content/dam/ACCA_Global/professional-insights/riskculture/PI-RISK-CULTURE%20v8.pdf (archived at https://perma.cc/38U6-M89W)

6 COSO (2017) *Enterprise Risk Management: Integrating with Strategy and Performance – Executive Summary*, www.coso.org/_files/ugd/3059fc_61ea5985b03c4293960642fdce408eaa.pdf (archived at https://perma.cc/XXB5-M7FU)

7 COSO (2013) *Internal Control: Integrated Framework – Executive Summary*, www.coso.org/_files/ugd/3059fc_1df7d5dd38074006bce8fdf621a942cf.pdf (archived at https://perma.cc/9VZ6-QBYP)

8 Hillson, D and Murray-Webster, R (2007) *Understanding and Managing Risk Attitude*, 2nd Ed., Gower Publishing Limited, Aldershot, UK

Risk culture models and success factors

Risk culture models

The culture of an organization is often difficult to describe. However, it is generally accepted that it is a reflection of the overall attitude of every component of management within a company. The culture of an organization determines how individuals will behave in particular circumstances. It will define how an individual feels obliged to behave in many circumstances.

As noted in Chapter 23, the risk culture of an organization determines how individuals will behave in relation to risk and risk management. There are different models that can help organizations describe their risk culture, some of which are included in this chapter.

LILAC

Table 24.1 sets out the components of a risk-aware culture. These components are suggested by the UK's Health and Safety Executive (HSE)[1] through their research into safety culture following several rail disasters in the 1980s and 1990s. The components can be simplified as leadership, involvement, learning, accountability and communication, making the acronym LILAC. Creating a culture where effective risk management is an integral part of the way people work is a long-term aim for most organizations and LILAC is a model that can be used to understand risk culture in relation to any specialist area or industry.

A risk management initiative cannot be successful unless the culture of an organization is receptive to it. In order to be receptive, a risk-aware culture is required in an organization. A high level of maturity in relation to leadership will require senior management to actively promote a risk-aware culture and act in ways that support this. This will include setting risk management performance targets and ensuring that the commitment of senior management to the risk-aware culture is clear.

Table 24.1   Risk-aware culture

A risk-aware culture is achieved by LILAC	
Leadership	Strong leadership within an organization in relation to strategy, projects and operations
Involvement	Involvement of all stakeholders in all stages of the risk management process
Learning	Emphasis on training in risk management procedures and learning from events
Accountability	Absence of an automatic blame culture, but appropriate accountability for actions
Communication	Communication and openness on all risk management issues and the lessons learnt

In addition, involvement can be achieved by adequate training, so that ownership of risks is fully understood. Specialist risk functions should play an advisory or consultancy role. There should be feedback mechanisms in place to inform staff about any decisions that are likely to affect them.

The existence of a learning culture is vital to the success of a risk-aware culture. A learning culture enables organizations to learn, and to identify and change inappropriate risk behaviour. In-depth analysis of incidents and good communication of feedback enables a learning culture to develop.

Accountability is vitally important if the risk-aware culture is to be successful. However, it is not the same as a blame culture. An organization should ensure that it moves from a blame culture to a non-discriminatory culture based on accountability. When investigating incidents, management should demonstrate care and concern towards employees. Employees should feel that they are able to report issues and concerns without fear that they will be blamed or disciplined personally.

A risk-aware culture requires good communication of risk information from senior management. Good communication also requires that reports from all employees, as well as reports from outside an organization, are welcome and well received. Information on risk performance should be included in the communication activities.

The next box provides an example of risk awareness and the embedding of risk management into the culture of an organization.

RISK AWARENESS CAMPAIGN

The embedding of risk management into an organization has been undertaken by following three routes: a risk awareness campaign, the implementation of new risk identification processes at directorate level, and the ongoing development of existing risk processes at a strategic level.

The primary aim of the awareness campaign was to make staff realize their responsibilities towards risk. This took for the form of training at different levels in an organization.

At board level, a two-hour risk appetite workshop was undertaken, including explanations of the risk management process as it was being applied to the assessment and management of risks in relation to corporate objectives during the workshop.

At functional and project level, risk workshops were undertaken with each team, again including training on the risk management process as it was being practised in the workshop, and the policy, framework and register in place to support risk management.

At operational level, training was developed in short, 20-minute e-learning sessions, that could be accessed by existing and new employees, and where appropriate, with key stakeholders in the supply chain.

ABC

The IRM (2012)[2] paper on risk culture includes two risk culture models that can be helpful in describing risk culture within an organization. The first of these is the ABC model, relating to attitude, behaviour and culture.

The ABC model is based on organizational culture, which is then considered through a risk lens to take account of risk attitude, risk behaviour and risk culture, helping organizations understand how risk culture works in practice. Risk attitude is defined as the chosen position adopted by an individual or group towards risk, influenced by risk perception and predisposition. Risk behaviour is defined as the external, observable risk-related action, including risk-based decision making, risk processes, communications, and so on.

The model recognizes that risk culture is not static, where risk attitude can shape risk behaviour and risk behaviours then form the risk culture. Risk culture can then in turn influence risk behaviours and risk attitudes. The ABC approach is cyclical and when managed well forms a 'virtuous' circle, and when managed poorly, can form a vicious circle.

A VICIOUS OR A VIRTUOUS CIRCLE

Research into problems with the Boeing 737 airplane is identifying lessons to be learnt, including those related to risk management and risk culture. Recent findings by Cagan (2024)[3] note that:

- cutting costs with suppliers can result in cutbacks in quality and supply;

- culture is important and employees should feel empowered to highlight potential issues;
- top-down initiatives should incorporate bottom-up reviews.

Clearly Boeing had been operating in a vicious cycle that went as far back as 2001, when warnings on outsourcing and quality control were ignored, followed by stories of cost-cutting pressures leading again to quality issues, and the loss of expert, experienced employees.

An example of this cultural cycle was found when Boeing employees stated in interviews that they could go 'inspector shopping', seeking those inspectors who were willing sign off work without too much investigation or challenge.

Double S

The second risk culture model from the IRM paper, is the Double S model developed by Goffee and Jones (1998). This model is again based on organizational culture but is overlaid with the risk perspective. Figure 24.1 indicates the two key dimensions in the model:

- Sociability – people focus based on how people interact socially.
- Solidarity – task focus based on goal orientation and team performance.

The model identifies four organizational cultures which are:

- Mercenary – where the focus is on the task and not on people.
- Fragmented – where there is no focus on either the task or people.
- Networked – where there is a focus on people and not the task.
- Communal – where there is a focus on both the people and the task.

From a risk perspective, the Double S model is an indicator of the health of the risk culture within an organization. For example, a focus on people ensures a sense of cohesion and common purpose, which would indicate more openness and transparency when discussing risk and working together to manage risks. A focus on the task ensures that management of actions is undertaken, and therefore, risk controls implemented.

Where there are weaknesses in either aspect of the model, it indicates that there may be barriers to the effective implementation of risk management and both the solidarity and sociability aspects of the model would need strengthening. As noted earlier, risk culture is not a static concept, and there may be times when either aspect of the model is focused on to achieve a particular outcome.

Figure 24.1   Double S model

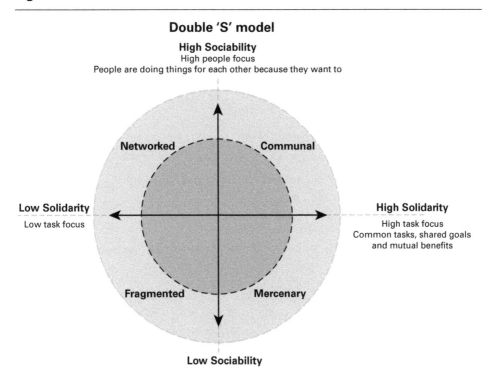

Double 'S' model

High Sociability
High people focus
People are doing things for each other because they want to

Networked

Communal

Low Solidarity
Low task focus

High Solidarity
High task focus
Common tasks, shared goals
and mutual benefits

Fragmented

Mercenary

Low Sociability

For example, during Covid-19, organizations initially focused on the task to ensure people could work from home by providing laptops and allowing access to organizational systems, or, as within the UK, perhaps by providing the furlough scheme to staff (where organizations could retain and continue to pay staff). After the initial rush to deal with employment issues, the focus for many organizations moved to people. As the effects of isolation from the workplace were better understood, organizations started by setting up such things as weekly community calls with employees perhaps asking what had made them smile that week, or individual calls with staff members who appeared to be struggling.

There are different models that organizations can use to understand risk culture, but that requires an understanding of what a successful risk culture should look like, which then supports ways to measure risk culture.

Successful risk culture

There are many views on what a successful risk culture does or doesn't look like. The ACCA (2023)[4] report on risk culture notes that risks associated with bad conduct include excessive risk taking, abusive behaviour, profiting from dishonesty, or not talking (or caring) about culture.

The IRM (2012) risk culture paper considers what a successful risk culture would include, comprising 10 key points:

1 Distinct and consistent tone from the top.

2 Commitment to ethical principles.

3 Common acceptance of the importance of continuous management of risk.

4 Transparent and timely risk information flow.

5 Encouragement of risk event reporting.

6 Risks understood despite complexity, obscurity or size of process or activity.

7 Appropriate risk-taking behaviours rewarded and encouraged.

8 Risk management skills and knowledge valued, encouraged and developed.

9 Consistent and rigorous challenge of the status quo.

10 Alignment of culture management with employee engagement and people strategy.

It is worthwhile reviewing the risk culture in any organization to understand where there might be weaknesses in or absences of any of the features of a successful risk culture. It is also important to consider the views from the top of an organization and those from within an organization – a top-down and bottom-up assessment. Quite often senior managers believe they have a successful risk culture whereas those lower down in an organization may disagree. The IRM paper on risk culture also includes 10 important questions a board should ask itself, relating to a successful risk culture, such as how accountabilities are established and how the board responds to whistleblowers and genuine concerns raised.

AN UNSUCCESSFUL RISK CULTURE

A research report from the Chartered Institute of Management Accountants (2010)[5] considered current practice in the reporting and management of risk across different sectors. One of the businesses included in the paper was the Royal Bank of Scotland (RBS), with research into what went wrong with the business during the financial crisis. Risk culture formed a key cornerstone in its failings.

There were two changes of chief risk officer after 2007, which clearly complicated matters at a crucial period for the bank. The CEO, whose opinions on risk management may have gone unchallenged, was a dominant figure.

An aggressive risk culture seems to have permeated down through the organisation. Ron den Braber was working in the bank's London office in 2003 when he became worried that the bank's models were underestimating exposure to credit risk. When his bosses failed to listen to his message, he left the bank.

Measurement of risk culture

It can be difficult for an organization to gauge risk culture, but this area is so important that measurements need to be taken. The ACCA (2023) report states that measurement of risk culture is difficult because it relies on participation across the breadth and depth of an organization and that human behaviour is, itself, difficult for organizations to define and measure.

Audit committees will often ask how seriously a department or location takes risk management. In general, it will be easy to answer this question on a qualitative basis by reviewing the quality of the policy and details of the procedures contained in the risk guidelines or protocols. This will give an indication of the risk culture of an organization, although only in relation to data collection and guidance provided, but not perhaps in the effective implementation of risk management.

However, quantitative measurements should be developed to identify and focus on areas of weakness and enable appropriate improvement actions to be planned. Frameworks for measuring culture can be found in, for example, audit committee evaluations and the level of risk culture maturity. Chapter 29 explores the role of the audit committee and Chapter 39 considers risk maturity models in more detail. However, there are more focused methods of measuring risk culture.

The IRM has developed its own model for measuring risk culture; the Risk Culture Aspects model.[6] This model provides an organization with key indicators of the health of its risk culture, measured across eight aspects of risk culture that are grouped into four main themes. This is supported by a simple questionnaire that can be sent across an organization, or which can be used as part of structured interviews with key individuals. The eight aspects and four themes are noted in Table 24.2.

The analysis of risk culture undertaken through this model identifies areas of strengths and weaknesses, and tangible actions to improve the risk culture where necessary. It also helps identify areas of vicious and virtuous risk culture circles that need to be amended or enhanced.

Table 24.2 Risk Culture Aspects model

Tone from the top	• Risk leadership – clarity of direction • How an organization deals with bad news
Governance	• The clarity of accountability for managing risk • The transparency and timeliness of risk information
Decisions	• Well-informed risk decisions • Appropriate risk taking rewarded and performance management linked to risk taking
Competency	• The status, resources and empowerment of the risk function • Risk skills – the embedding of risk management skills across an organization

A further important point raised in the IRM paper is that improvements in risk culture can drive positive change for organizations, which can be managed as a change project in its own right. Change management, whether in relation to risk management maturity or in order to reach a desired risk culture, is explored further in Chapter 39.

Improving risk culture

For many organizations, improving risk culture is a valid strategic risk objective. This will be especially true when areas of weakness in the level of risk awareness have been identified.

When undertaking actions to improve the risk culture within an organization, it is important to acknowledge that improving the risk management processes must lead to improvements in risk management outputs. This, in turn, should have a positive impact that delivers greater benefits from risk management.

There is little point in improving the risk management processes as a means of improving the risk culture of an organization if the overall effectiveness of the risk management effort is not enhanced. There is a danger that enhancing and improving the risk management process in an organization is automatically assumed to have improved the risk culture.

It is possible for the risk management process to be enhanced without the risk culture of an organization being improved. For example, a more aggressive internal audit programme may improve compliance standards, but that does not guarantee that the risk culture of an organization has been enhanced. Improvements to the risk management process may not deliver any additional benefits, whereas improvements to the risk culture should be expected to at least provide an enhanced level of risk assurance.

Notes

1 Health & Safety Executive (2005) A review of safety culture and safety climate literature for the development of the safety culture inspection toolkit, www.hse.gov.uk/research/rrpdf/rr367.pdf (archived at https://perma.cc/9PQT-XETW)

2 IRM (2012) *Risk Culture – Resources for Practitioners*, https://www.theirm.org/media/7230/risk-culture-resources-for-practitioners.pdf (archived at https://perma.cc/GT8T-ZPAY)

3 Cagan, P (2024) *Columbia School of Professional Studies – Risk management Lessons Learned from the Boeing 737 Max 9 Incident*, https://sps.columbia.edu/news/risk-management-lessons-learned-boeing-737-max-9-incident#:~:text=However%2C%20these%20high%2Dlevel%20efforts,should%20be%20prioritized%20and%20remediated (archived at https://perma.cc/VN6U-WZ8F)

4 ACCA (2023) *Risk Culture: Building resilience and seizing opportunities*, https://www.accaglobal.com/content/dam/ACCA_Global/professional-insights/riskculture/PI-RISK-CULTURE%20v8.pdf (archived at https://perma.cc/78L2-VLZ2)

5 CIMA (2010) *Reporting and managing risk: A look at current practice at Tesco, RBS, local and central government*, https://issuu.com/cimaglobal/docs/r267_manage_risks (archived at https://perma.cc/NBF5-6SM3)

6 IRM (2012) *Risk culture aspects scorecard*, https://www.theirm.org/what-we-say/thought-leadership/risk-culture/ (archived at https://perma.cc/EV7Q-LXQ4)

Risk appetite and tolerance

Nature of risk appetite

In Chapter 17, the evaluation of risks was explored. As mentioned, this is the point at which an organization must decide whether to respond, or not to respond, to the risk, depending on whether it is or is not within its risk appetite.

Risk appetite is the willingness of an organization to undertake an activity that involves risk, be that a threat or an opportunity. It is a vitally important concept in the implementation of risk management. However, it is difficult to precisely define and apply in practice.

One of the fundamental difficulties with the concept of risk appetite is that, generally speaking, organizations will have an appetite to continue a particular operation, embark on a project or embrace a strategy, rather than a direct appetite for the risk itself. Most risk management standards say that risk should be managed within its context and, as such, an organization's risk appetite can only be answered within the context of the strategy, tactics, operations and compliance activities. Decisions on risk appetite should be taken within the context of other business decisions, rather than as a stand-alone evaluation.

In addition, an organization should be able to decide how much value it wishes to put at risk and agreeing this will ensure that it does not put too much (or too little) value at risk. The risk capacity of an organization needs to be fully understood and utilized to ensure that risk taking is at the optimal level and delivers maximum benefit.

Another way of describing risk appetite is that it is the total value of the corporate resources that the board of an organization is willing to put at risk. A range of definitions of risk appetite is shown in Table 25.1, all of which show similarities.

The similarity in the definitions can cause problems with understanding and applying risk appetite. For example, the IRM (2011) paper includes the willingness to seek or accept risk, with the ISO 31073 definition including the willingness to pursue or retain. The IIA, COSO and UK Corporate Governance Code definition include the preparedness only to accept risk.

Table 25.1   Definitions of risk appetite

Organization	Definition
COSO (2020)[1]	The types and amount of risk, on a broad level, an organization is willing to accept in pursuit of value.
IIA (2023)[2]	The level of risk that an organization is prepared to accept in pursuit of its objectives.
IRM (2011)[3]	The amount of risk that an organization is willing to seek or accept in the pursuit of long-term objectives.
ISO 31073 (2022)[4]	The amount and type of risk that an organization is willing to pursue or retain.
UK Corporate Governance Code Guidance[5]	The amount of risk that a company is willing to accept in pursuit of its strategic objectives.

On the other hand, the UK HM Treasury (2021) paper on risk appetite[6] splits the concept of pursuit and acceptance by considering risk positions:

- Optimal risk position – the level of risk with which an organization aims to operate, informed by an organizational mission and strategic objectives.
- Tolerable risk position – the level of risk with which an organization is willing to operate, given current constraints. It notes that the tolerable risk position is not the same as tolerating a risk as part of a risk response strategy.

These differences may in part reflect the two sides of risk as both a threat and an opportunity, and perhaps as part of understanding strategic objectives and the opportunities inherent in those objectives.

Other terms in this area are important in understanding whether or not risks are acceptable to an organization but are often used interchangeably. The COSO (2020) paper notes that this interchangeable use of the terms can cause confusion as the concepts, although related, are different. However, as long as an organization decides which definitions it wants to use, and uses them consistently, that problem should be avoided. For the purposes of this book, risk appetite and related terms of risk universe, risk capacity and risk tolerance, based on the IRM (2011) paper, are noted in Figure 25.1.

Risk universe

Risk universe is the dark, outer circle in Figure 25.1, which considers the full range of risks which could impact, either positively or negatively, on the ability of an

Figure 25.1   Risk universe, capacity, tolerance and appetite

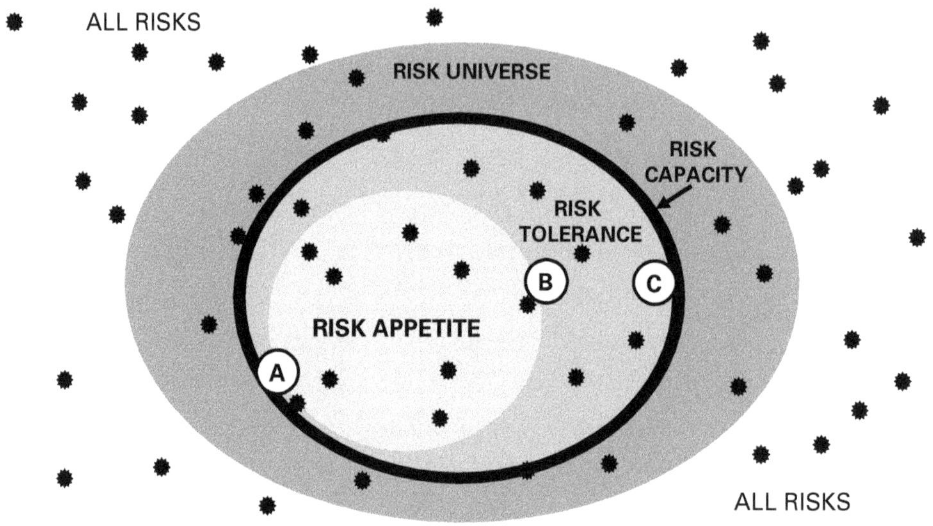

SOURCE Expert Partners and Satarla 2022:[7] Adapted from the Financial Stability Board. Used with permission

organization to achieve its long-term objectives. This covers all risks, both opportunities and threats that an organization could take but does not want to.

For example, a pharmaceutical organization that produces non-branded, generic products that are already licenced. If that organization were to move into the field of research and unlicenced medicine, the threats could jeopardize its viability as a business, whereas the opportunities may not provide the value expected. As such, risk universe is often related to an organization's capability to take risks.

Risk capacity

There are several aspects that are important when an organization is deciding how much risk to take. An important measure of risk is the risk capacity or capability of an organization. This is a measure of how much risk an organization should take or can afford to take, shown as the black, bold outline of risk tolerance in Figure 25.1.

In simple terms, the risk appetite of the board should be within the risk capacity of an organization. It would be inappropriate for an organization to embark on a project that could exhaust all of its resources. Similarly, an organization should not put more value at risk than is appropriate, given the sector in which it operates and prevailing market conditions.

The capacity of an organization to accept risk will depend on such things as its financial strength, the robustness of its infrastructure, the strength of its reputation and brands and the competitive nature of the marketplace in which it operates. It is important to consider changes in the internal and external context that can affect financial, infrastructure, reputational and marketplace risk capacity.

The more rapidly the marketplace is changing, the greater the capacity for risk an organization may be required to have available. For example, if an organization is facing a significant change in technology, the strategic options may be limited. Consider an organization that was involved in the manufacture of DVD players when it became obvious that streaming technology was taking over. This organization would have faced a significant risk related to the change in technology and would have needed to develop a new business model. It would have needed to acquire new production equipment, new skills and new distribution patterns. It may be that the transition to the new technology and the risks that it involves are outside the resources and risk capacity of an organization. If that is the case, an organization may need to explore strategic options, including seeking a joint-venture partner, locating a buyer for the business or simply withdrawing from the marketplace.

In addition, risk capacity will be affected by an organization's risk management maturity and its ability to understand and manage risks. Many circumstances will arise where organizations are faced with risks that could destroy them if those risks materialized, such as major physical damage to assets, regulatory breaches, cyber-attacks, risks that negatively impact on reputation, and so on. For some organizations, there may be several individual and even independent risks, each of which could destroy an organization. In these circumstances, the challenge for the risk management function will be to focus on the circumstances that could trigger one or more of these risks.

Risk tolerance

Risk tolerance considers the boundaries of risk taking outside of which an organization is not prepared to venture in the pursuit of its long-term objectives. The IRM (2011) paper also notes that risk tolerance relates to those risks which, 'if push came to shove', organizations might put up with. These two terms mean that risk tolerance is, in practice, a range between risk appetite and risk capacity as indicated on Figure 25.1.

In this zone, an organization can tolerate risks up to the risk capacity for a certain amount of time but will be working actively to bring the risks to an acceptable level or within risk appetite. Point A on Figure 25.1 highlights risks that an organization has very little tolerance for and will be working hard to bring them to an acceptable level as quickly as possible. For example, organizations often have a very low tolerance for data privacy risks.

The range between points B and C on the diagram relates to those risks that an organization can tolerate for a longer period of time. For example, an organization's incident reporting system may not be working effectively, and plans are in place to bring in a new system. While that system is being implemented an organization may tolerate more manual workarounds than it wishes until the new incident management system has been implemented. Those risks that sit closer to the risk capacity at the outer edge of the risk tolerance zone will require further and more immediate attention than those that are closer to the risk appetite.

Risk appetite

Risk appetite can be defined in a number of ways, as explored earlier in this chapter, but for the purposes of this book, it is the amount of risk that an organization is willing to seek or accept in pursuit of its long-term objectives, shown as the circle in the middle of Figure 25.1.

Most organizations, just like individuals, do not actively seek risk. An individual may be described as a risk taker, but the reality will be that such a person enjoys activities that have a high level of risk attached. It is the activity that appeals to the individual in the first instance, not the actual risk. In other words, risk taking has to be seen within the context of the activity and the intended rewards.

Organizations are similar in that it is the strategy, project or activity that appeals to the board, not the actual risk. An organization may embark on a risky strategy, approve a risky project or be operating risky activities or core processes. However, it is the business drivers and imperatives that are the primary concern for board members, not the level of risk involved. It is more often the case that the level of risk comes with the defined strategy, rather than the risk appetite defining the strategy.

As noted in Chapters 8 and 22, where risks are not acceptable, effort will be needed to manage a risk further or changes to objectives will be needed. Where it is decided that an organization cannot or does not want to manage a risk further, nor to change the objectives, the risk is then, effectively, accepted at its current level. In this case, the risk appetite 'circle' changes shape, moving into the risk tolerance zone to absorb that risk. Following some of the world events or shocks at the beginning of the 2020s, such as Covid-19, the risk appetite of some organizations has had to change quite dramatically.

The COSO (2020) paper notes that risk appetite must be flexible enough to adapt to changing conditions, which means that organizations should broaden their view on risk appetite to align it with objectives and performance expectations. Approaches to measuring risk appetite will be explored in Chapter 26.

CHANGES IN RISK APPETITE

In the UK, guidance on managing the risk of electrical shock, burn or fire from portable electronic equipment is provided by the Health and Safety Executive in its paper on 'Maintaining portable electrical equipment', and is usually referred to as PAT testing. During Covid-19, a large manufacturing organization could not have portable equipment in its facilities PAT tested, as the electricians were prohibited from visiting the sites during lockdown. An organization had to accept the risk of shock, burns or fires for that short period of time.

Many other organizations around the world managed the risks related to internal networking and team dynamics by insisting that all employees work in organizational offices or facilities. During Covid-19, large numbers of employees were forced to work from home due to lockdown requirements. Since the end of the global pandemic, many organizations accept that staff work from home all or some of the time, whereas other organizations are being forced (usually by staff themselves) to accept at least a measure of homeworking by staff, which is a long-term change in risk appetite.

Risk appetite related to the upside of risk is usually the opportunity within an investment that an organization is willing to embrace. Organizations will be willing to invest resources in opportunities if it is felt they are likely to produce a positive gain. However, it should be recognized that value put at risk in this way could also result in losses. Incorrect strategic decisions regarding opportunities have sometimes destroyed more value than threats for organizations.

An organization may have an appetite for investing resources in an opportunity, but it needs to be sure that it has the capacity to endure any loss that may result. It also needs to be sure that the total amount invested, or value at risk, is not beyond the capacity of an organization. The turbulence in the UK energy sector over the last five years or so has led to the failure and acquisition of many organizations. In turn, some of those acquiring organizations have failed or left the market, providing examples of firms overreaching their ability to absorb investments in the market. For example, in the UK, Gnergy were acquired by Bulb in 2020, who were themselves acquired by Shell Energy in 2021, who then left the market, selling on their business to Octopus Energy in 2023. Careful identification of the nature of the risks and calculation of the actual risk exposure associated with an opportunity should clearly be undertaken.

The identification of the risk appetite for an organization requires judgement, and this judgement can be exercised at different levels within an organization. Risk appetite should be set at board level to direct an organization in relation to how much risk is acceptable. Risk appetite is likely to be an operational constraint at line-manager level because line managers will be expected to operate within the risk appetite policy that has been established by the board.

At the individual level, it is likely that consideration of risk appetite will be a behaviour regulator. This is because individual members of staff should only operate within the risk appetite framework that has been developed at board level and is implemented by line managers.

The topic of risk appetite is a key aspect of risk-based decision making and of corporate governance, and risk management practitioners should have a good understanding of what this concept means and how it can be applied. The UK Corporate Governance Code Guidance[8] notes that the board should ensure that risk appetite is:

- appropriately defined and articulated;
- aligned with strategy and embedded at various levels of decision making;
- regularly reviewed and evaluated;
- communicated at the appropriate levels throughout the company in a timely manner, including any changes to it.

The IRM (2011) paper notes that setting risk appetite can be difficult, and that risk appetite:

- can be complex, and oversimplification is not the best approach;
- needs to be measurable to enable it to be used and understood at all levels of an organization;
- is not a single, fixed concept, because context, objectives, risks and controls change;
- should be developed in relation to the capability and maturity of an organization, in that clarity in what risk management should deliver and how it should be delivered is needed before risk appetite can be effectively set;
- should be considered at all levels of an organization, whether strategic, tactical, operational or compliance, where different and more detailed measures of risk appetite will be needed for an organization to operate against. In some ways, risk appetite is already embedded in part in many organizations through delegated levels of authority;
- must be integrated with the control culture of an organization, as part of a balance between the propensity to take risk and the propensity to exercise control. This, again, will be an aspect in the development of delegated levels of authority.

Notes

1 COSO (2020) *Risk Appetite – Critical to Success*, https://www.coso.org/_files/ugd/3059fc _1607e24e43ad44bf96f725765cb8e78a.pdf (archived at https://perma.cc/9Z7T-FLQV)

2 IIA (2023) *Tone at the Top: Adjusting the Risk Appetite for Non-Financial Measures*, https://www.theiia.org/globalassets/site/resources/research-and-reports/tone-at-the-top/2023/tatt_april_2023_final-revised.pdf (archived at https://perma.cc/3446-SUS4)

3 IRM (2011) *Appetite & Tolerance: Guidance Paper*, https://www.theirm.org/media/ 7239/64355_riskapp_a4_web.pdf (archived at https://perma.cc/E4FH-4EPW)

4 ISO 31073 (2022) Risk management – Vocabulary, https://www.iso.org/obp/ui/ en/#iso:std:iso:31073:ed-1:v1:en (archived at https://perma.cc/TS3W-Z8QL)

5 FRC (2024) *Corporate Governance Code Guidance*, https://www.frc.org.uk/library/ standards-codes-policy/corporate-governance/corporate-governance-code-guidance/ #establishing-the-risk-management-and-internal-control-framework-9c034f8e (archived at https://perma.cc/V73E-HQ58)

6 HM Treasury (2021) *Risk Appetite Guidance Note*, https://assets.publishing.service.gov. uk/media/61239758e90e0705481fc085/20210805_-_Risk_Appetite_Guidance_Note_ v2.0.pdf (archived at https://perma.cc/4NXU-AU8W)

7 Crawley, J and McAneny, E, (2023) Enterprise Risk Management. *The Risk Management Handbook*, D H (ed.) London, Kogan Page

8 FRC (2024) *Corporate Governance Code Guidance*, https://www.frc.org.uk/library/ standards-codes-policy/corporate-governance/corporate-governance-code-guidance/ (archived at https://perma.cc/YWD4-HNTP)

Risk appetite criteria and statements

In Chapter 10, risk criteria were considered as understanding how much risks matter, should they occur. In Chapter 15, risk criteria were used to measure the impact of risk as part of the prioritizing process in risk analysis. In this chapter, risk criteria will be explored in helping to understand and measure risk appetite and develop risk appetite statements.

Risk appetite criteria

It was noted in Chapter 25 that risk appetite should be developed in relation to an organization's risk management capability and maturity. The COSO (2020)[1] research paper on risk appetite suggests that as organizations become more experienced in the application of risk management their measurement of risk appetite becomes more precise. At the same time, however, some organizations may find that the use of broader, less precise measurement or terminology, such as low or high, is sufficient, often depending on the level of an organization risk appetite is set at.

Where organizations have reached an appropriate level of maturity and capability, and dependent on the level of an organization it is being set at, more precise criteria for risk appetite can be developed. This can, once again, be based on an organization's existing performance indicators rather than an development of a new set of metrics. The use of existing data and existing language further embeds the understanding of risks and their impact on an organization's objectives. For example, measurements of staff turnover may not only provide early warning signals of changes in risks around retention or recruitment of talent but could also be used as a measure of risk appetite against an objective for an organization to be an employer of choice.

To ensure the effective use of organizational indicators to set appetite criteria, it should not be up to one individual to decide which metrics are chosen. The COSO

(2020) paper suggests that the approach should include facilitated discussions with key individuals to ascertain which metrics would be most appropriate.

Risk appetite criteria are often developed against one or more of three different foundations, namely objectives, risks and risk categories.

Risk appetite criteria against objectives

As risk can be defined as the effect of uncertainties on objectives, it is clear that risk appetite criteria should have a relationship to the successful achievement of objectives. The COSO (2020) research suggests that organizations adopt an objective-focused approach, unless other regulatory or business requirements dictate otherwise.

Risk appetite set against objectives supports decision making around, and delivery of, an organization's strategy. This firmly puts risk appetite into the centre of what an organization wants to achieve and its strategic direction, allowing flexibility and adaptability in relation to the increasingly changing internal and external context in which it operates.

Risk appetite set against objectives tends to be qualitatively based. This is usually because risk appetite at the strategic level is communicated to both internal and external stakeholders. Although an organization will want to, and may be required to, express its risk appetite externally, it is often not in its best interest, commercially, to state more tangible or quantitative measurements of what it is willing to accept or take in pursuit of its objectives.

However, when the risk appetite is communicated internally, more tangible metrics are needed to ensure an organization understands more clearly what risks or levels of risk are acceptable. As most organizations have clearly set objectives and related KPIs, with targets and tolerances around those, setting risk appetite criteria against objectives should be relatively straightforward.

OBJECTIVES AND RISK APPETITE STATEMENTS

A charity in the UK was struggling to develop their risk appetite. This was the first task for the new head of risk. As part of fact finding and to better understand an organization, the head of risk requested meetings with the owners of each of the strategic objectives. The agenda for the meetings included detailed discussion on the objectives and how an organization measured performance.

During those discussions, it was clear that the performance measures developed for each objective included targets for performance. The owner of each strategic objective was asked which of the performance measures would best indicate whether risks being considered were within their risk appetite. For example, one objective was to maintain the organization's reputation, and a measurement of performance against that objective was the net promoter score (a metric measuring the satisfaction of users of the services provided). The charity had a target for the net promoter score, with a range around that target of five points reduction and 10 points increase. These measures were then used to reflect the board's risk appetite and tolerance in relation to the organization's reputation, and therefore the risk appetite statements that were used internally.

Risk appetite criteria against risk categories

Some organizations focus their risk appetite criteria against categories of risk, such as talent, regulatory, supply chain or health and safety. Where these categories are related back to an organization's objectives, this supports the communication and implementation of risk appetite at tactical and operational levels.

Risk appetite criteria set against risk categories is usually quantitively based. For example, the risk appetite against talent may be based on the number of unfilled vacancies, whereas against supply chain it may be based on the stock levels operating within contractual limits.

Problems often arise when risk appetite criteria are developed against risk categories, but these categories are not truly related to the objectives of an organization. The risk categories may have been developed historically, but no longer reflect the strategic direction of an organization. In heavily regulated sectors, such as financial services, the requirement to report on risks against categories means that organizations commonly develop risk criteria against categories, such as credit, liquidity and conduct risk, which although important, may not reflect the individual strategies of the organizations.

Risk appetite criteria against risks

As organizations develop an understanding of their principal risks, many develop appetite criteria against them. These criteria are usually quantitative, providing a clear understanding of the level of risk that is acceptable by the board.

However, developing risk appetite criteria purely against risks does have its pitfalls:

- the criteria are only related to those particular risks and do not provide an overall picture of what is acceptable across the breadth of an organization;
- not all risks have associated performance measures that can be used to develop quantitative risk appetite criteria; as such, additional work is required to create metrics;

- unfortunately, in some organizations, not all risks are related to its objectives, meaning that risk appetite criteria may not be aligned to the strategic direction;

- the lifecycle of some risks is quite short, meaning that the associated risk appetite criteria may need to be updated more regularly than if set against objectives.

The COSO (2020) paper suggests that risk appetite criteria should be based on an organization's objectives, which then cascades into more detailed criteria against risk categories or individual risks.

Risk appetite and the risk matrix

Some organizations expand on risk appetite criteria against individual risks, by using their risk matrix to set risk appetite, where risks that are prioritized in the 'red' zone of a red, amber, green (RAG) matrix are considered unacceptable, while those in the green zone are considered to be within risk appetite. As noted in Chapter 15, this can result in unhelpful conversations when risks are prioritized in the 'red' zone but are actually acceptable to an organization.

However, using the risk matrix as a proxy for initially setting risk appetite can be useful. As organizations' risk management maturity improves, some may use swim lanes, where different impact levels reflect risk appetite. For example, a medium impact or below on reputational impact is noted as being within risk appetite, but high or very high is outside of appetite, whereas only a very low health and safety impact may be within risk appetite. These swim lanes can be adjusted if there are significant changes in internal or external context that necessitate an alteration.

This may still result in unnecessary conversations, where a health and safety risk may be in the green zone of a RAG matrix but is not within risk appetite. To counteract these conversations, some organizations remove the colours from the risk matrix. Other organizations remove the colours from the risk matrix, but colour the risks themselves on the matrix, indicating which risks are within or outside of risk appetite.

Using the risk matrix as a proxy for risk appetite does provide an overall profile of the risks and the number of risks that may be within or outside of risk appetite. However, a true understanding of what is acceptable may be misunderstood, and some of the disadvantages of setting risk appetite against risks alone remain. The UK government's guidance on risk appetite[2] notes that metrics used to inform risk appetite should be separate from scales used to assess the likelihood and impact of a risk.

Risk appetite and total cost of risk

Total cost of risk calculations were commonplace in the 1980s and were often undertaken by organizations or their insurance brokers. The calculation was limited to insurance risks only but did enable an organization to determine the total cost of threats to it. The calculation was comprised of insurance premiums, cost of claims not covered by insurance, and money spent on loss-control actions. Tables were published for this type of total cost of risk in various organizations so as to benchmark the performance of an organization against others in the same sector. This type of risk calculation was often used as a justification for setting up an in-house or captive insurance company, as discussed in Chapter 36.

The difficulty with this type of calculation was its 'backward-looking' nature, as it depended on historical information, which was not necessarily a good guide to future loss performance. The approach also drove organizations to seek the lowest immediate cost for the management of threats, rather than an optimized approach across time.

As noted earlier, organizations should be aware of the limitations of these total cost of risk calculations, which only apply to the management of threats in relation to insurance purchase. Buying too much insurance could represent the lowest risk position for an organization but will be achieved at a high overall cost.

The type of total cost of risk calculation that is now undertaken by organizations is somewhat different. It consists not just of those risks that can be insured but will include all types of risks. The actual risk exposure in this calculation is used to identify the level of risk that an organization is willing to accept. The risk appetite of the board can then be compared with the actual risk exposure that an organization faces.

As discussed in the introduction and throughout this book, it should be recognized that the business environment is more volatile, and processes undertaken by organizations are being disrupted by the opportunities that technology presents. Under these conditions, all organizations are forced to increase their risk exposure. As a consequence, risk management has become more important, and boards are faced with the reality of increasing the total value that they are willing to put at risk or to find mechanisms to reduce the total risk exposure.

When an organization decides whether to embark on a merger or acquisition, its risk exposure will be affected. Organizations need to undertake an opportunity analysis of all acquisition opportunities, and this analysis should include consideration of at least the following features of the acquisition opportunity:

- financial strength and reputation of the proposed acquisition;
- potential for developing further revenue/profit from the acquisition;

- risks associated with suggested purchase contract terms and conditions;
- anticipated profitability and sustainability of the proposed acquisition;
- investment required to deliver the anticipated future plans for the acquisition;
- impact on existing investment and business development plans.

Risk exposure is the cumulative total at risk, but is often calculated on a risk-by-risk basis, without consideration of whether the risks are correlated, as noted earlier in this chapter. When calculating the total actual risk exposure of an organization, it is important that the cumulative total of the values at risk is adjusted to take account of whether risks show any correlation.

Risk appetite statements

As noted in Chapter 25 and earlier in this chapter, risk appetite will normally relate to a range of possible outcomes which can be considered as zones of risk exposure or levels of risk. This is usually referred to as the risk tolerance range for exposure to that particular risk. The COSO (2020) paper notes that risk tolerance refers to the boundaries of acceptable variation in performance in relative objectives.

For some organizations, risk appetite is the driver of strategy. This will be true for organizations such as banks and other financial institutions. For banks, risk is at the heart of the business and the appetite of an organization; for example, to lend money to particular companies or groups of people will be a reflection of its risk appetite and will be the main driver of the business. If risk appetite is a driver of the business, then an organization will wish to embrace risk in order to gain the benefits.

For other organizations, risk is not a driver of the business, but it is a consequence of the strategy, tactics, operations and compliance core processes that they undertake. In this case, risk appetite is unlikely to be a driver for an organization but will be a planning mechanism for it to decide whether it wishes to adopt certain tactics, given the risks that would be embedded within those tactics, projects or changes. Where an organization is using risk appetite as a planning tool, it will wish to operate within certain tolerance levels and manage the uncertainty associated with risk.

In other circumstances, risk appetite may simply reflect the constraints that are placed on staff in an organization. Authorization levels, expenditure limits and other constraints are often established in a delegation of authority within an organization. Levels of authority are a clear indication of the risk appetite of an organization. In these circumstances, exposure to risk is a consequence of the size, nature and complexity of an organization, and it will wish to set limits that define risk appetite and thereafter manage the risk exposure and possible impact and consequences.

In simple terms, if risk management is about achieving the most favourable outcome and reducing uncertainty, then risk appetite is about identifying the optimum level of risk that will achieve the most favourable outcome.

Many organizations have attempted to produce statements about their risk appetite without clearly focusing on whether risk is a driver, planning guide or set of operating constraints. If all three approaches are applied, the risk appetite statement will reflect the complexity of that approach. The COSO (2020) paper suggests that risk appetite should be developed for both senior-level management and those involved in the day-to-day operational activities.

Developing risk appetite statements

The stages that would be involved in developing a risk appetite statement are as follows:

1 Identify stakeholders and their expectations, making reference to the possible range of stakeholders.

2 Define the company-wide risk exposure through an analysis of strategy, tactics, operations and compliance.

3 Establish the desired level of risk exposure that will lead to a risk appetite statement that provides a set of qualitative and quantitative statements.

4 Define the range of acceptable volatility or uncertainty around each of the types of risks, leading to a statement of acceptable risk tolerances.

5 Reconcile the risk appetite and risk tolerances with the current level of risk exposure and plan actions to bring exposure in line with risk appetite.

6 Formalize and ratify a risk appetite statement, communicate the statement with stakeholders and implement accordingly.

The IRM (2011)[3] and COSO (2020) papers on risk appetite suggest similar approaches, in facilitating discussions with relevant stakeholders to develop risk appetite statements, aligning risk appetite to strategy and objectives, developing metrics that can be used at strategic and operational levels, and validating and improving risk appetite.

Stakeholder engagement is an important aspect of developing risk appetite statement, as it allows debates regarding what a board is comfortable with, such as what is too high or too low, or what the board want to see an organization doing. It can be useful to ask the board what behaviour or stories in the news that they would want to see, and what they would not want to see.

The COSO (2020) paper also notes that it is appropriate to engage with a wider cohort of stakeholders, especially when considering sustainability and the effect that an organization's actions can have on communities and the environment. For example, should an organization produce cheaper products during national and global economic crises when customers may prefer quality and also have environmental concerns?

UK GOVERNMENT GUIDANCE NOTE ON RISK APPETITE STATEMENTS

Risk appetite statements should:

- Provide a structure for an organization to work within. When correctly applied, statements describe acceptable outcomes relating to decisions being taken.

- Drive thinking about results and outcomes an organization seeks to realize, as well as about what would need to change if outcomes were not acceptable.

- Describe the organization's typical challenges and the basis on which different outcomes are justified.

- Describe the organization's acceptable behaviour in reasonable circumstances. In circumstances where a decision is to be made and there are no directly comparable situations, risk appetite statements can provide illustrative guidance that can be adapted, documented and applied.

- Be set against a sliding scale, with descriptors which are relevant to an organization. This scale should demonstrate and reinforce the range of outcomes that are acceptable in different situations. These scales should be separate from scales used to assess the likelihood and impact of a risk.

- Be dynamic and updated as necessary to reflect any significant changes in the context their organizations operate within, whether driven by societal, economic or political changes, for example.

SOURCE Government Finance Function (2021) *Risk Appetite: Guidance note V2.0*, https://assets.publishing.service.gov.uk/government/uploads/system/uploads/attachment_data/file/1012891/20210805_-_Risk_Appetite_Guidance_Note_v2.0.pdf

---

Qualitative risk appetite statements

As noted earlier, risk appetite statements may be qualitative or descriptive in nature, dependent on the maturity and needs of an organization, and the audience they are communicated to. Table 26.1 provides a set of example narrative or qualitative risk appetite statements that could be in place for a college or educational establishment.

Some organizations use a four-point scale as noted in Table 26.1. The UK Government (2021) guidance provides a descriptive five-point scale, from averse and minimal, through to cautious, open and eager.

Table 26.1   Risk appetite statements for a college

Assessment	Description
High risk appetite	The college accepts opportunities that have an inherently high risk that may result in reputation damage, financial loss or exposure, major breakdown in IT systems, significant incidents of regulatory non-compliance or high potential risk of injury to staff and students.
Moderate risk appetite	The college is willing to accept risks that may result in reputation damage, financial loss or exposure, major breakdown in IT systems, significant incidents of regulatory non-compliance, potential risk of injury to staff and students.
Modest risk appetite	The college is willing to accept some risks in certain circumstances that may result in reputation damage, financial loss or exposure, major breakdown in IT systems, significant incidents of regulatory non-compliance, potential risk of injury to staff and students.
Low risk appetite	The college is not willing to accept risks in circumstances that may result in reputation damage, financial loss or exposure, major breakdown in IT systems, significant incidents of regulatory non-compliance, potential risk of injury to staff and students.

Quantitative risk appetite statements

In order to operationalize and embed risk appetite statements, and to give clarity and understanding regarding the acceptable level of risk taking, quantitative risk appetite statements should be developed. This approach is again a reflection of the maturity and needs of an organization, and should be regularly reviewed and improved, especially in light of changes in context, risks and controls.

Table 26.2 shows a set of example quantitative risk appetite statements from a manufacturing organization.

Table 26.2   Risk appetite for a manufacturing organization

Business component	Risk appetite statement
Target credit rating	Maintain a credit rating of at least BBB+
Earnings per share	Maintain an earnings per share level within the upper quartile of the peer group
Target capital ratio	Maintain a debt-to-capital ratio in the range 45% to 50%
Self-sustaining growth	New business will not dilute target capital ratio and maintain a capital working ratio in the range 1.5% to 2%
Financial strength	Maintain an earnings-before-interest and taxes-to-interest ratio between 5% and 7.5%
Customer dependence	No single customer will exceed 15% of total sales
Regulatory compliance	Score in the upper quartile of the peer set in regulatory reviews
Social responsibility	Seek a position in the upper quartile of the peer group in a social responsibility index

Notes

1 COSO (2020) *Risk Appetite – Critical to Success: Using risk appetite to thrive in a changing world*, https://www.coso.org/_files/ugd/3059fc_1607e24e43ad44bf96f725765cb8e78a.pdf (archived at https://perma.cc/UMG5-Q84J)

2 Government Finance Function (2021) *Risk Appetite: Guidance note V2.0*, https://assets.publishing.service.gov.uk/government/uploads/system/uploads/attachment_data/file/1012891/20210805_-_Risk_Appetite_Guidance_Note_v2.0.pdf (archived at https://perma.cc/42NY-H222)

3 IRM (2011) *Risk Appetite and Tolerance Guidance Paper*, https://www.theirm.org/media/7239/64355_riskapp_a4_web.pdf (archived at https://perma.cc/LJ79-JGM3)

PART SIX
Corporate governance and assurance

LEARNING OUTCOMES

Having studied this section readers will be able to:

- Explain the importance of corporate governance and the principles and rules-based approaches.
- Summarize the influences on corporate governance in relation to the UK FRC, the OECD, the US Sarbanes–Oxley Act, ISO 37000 and stock exchanges.
- Explain the structure and responsibilities of boards in relation to risk management and internal control.
- Describe the nature and purpose of internal control and the contribution that internal control makes to risk management.
- Summarize the importance of the control environment in an organization and provide a structure for evaluating the control environment, including the COSO internal control framework and the UK government's risk control framework.
- Summarize the importance of risk assurance and identify who requires assurance, who provides assurance and how assurance can be given.
- Describe the activities involved in an ERM initiative and how these can be allocated to internal audit, risk management and line management.
- Describe the activities of a typical internal audit function and the relationship between internal audit and risk management as part of the three lines model.

Introducing corporate governance

Corporate governance

Most countries in the world place corporate governance requirements on organizations. Corporate governance requirements should be viewed as obligations placed on the board of an organization by legislation and by various codes of practice. ISO 37000[1] defines the governance of organizations as the 'human-based system by which an organization is directed, overseen and held accountable for achieving its defined purpose'. Much of the corporate governance requirements around the world have been developed as a response to the poor management of organizations. As such, these obligations have been developed to ensure organizations are successful and sustainable and that directors are held accountable for their actions.

The requirements are particularly strong in relation to companies quoted on stock exchanges, organizations that are registered charities and government departments, agencies and authorities. However, they are followed as best practice guidelines by many smaller, privately owned organizations.

WHAT HAPPENS IF CORPORATE GOVERNANCE IS WEAK?

Better practices in corporate governance were called for in the UK from the 1980s following the unexpected collapsed of a number of companies: Bank of Credit, Commerce & Industry, the Mirror Group, Polly Peck International and Barings Bank. In each case, there were serious accounting and financial reporting irregularities and inadequate internal controls and risk management.

However, in 2001 these examples were eclipsed when a company in the US called Enron collapsed with a loss to shareholders of $74 billion, caused by the main executives withholding information on company debt that should have been reported to investors and employees. The fraudulent activity was reported by a whistleblower and had not been revealed by auditors. This scandal led to the successful prosecution of the chair of the board and imprisonment of the chief executive, chief accounting and chief financial officers, the establishment of the Sarbanes–Oxley Act and the demise of Arthur Andersen, who were at the time one of the main global accounting firms.

There are two main approaches to the enforcement of corporate governance standards: principles based and prescriptive based.

Principles-based approach

Some countries have adopted a regulatory, principles-based approach, where corporate governance requirements are treated as a 'comply or explain'. In other words, an organization should comply with the requirements or explain why it was not appropriate, necessary or feasible to comply. If appropriate, an organization could explain that an alternative approach was taken to achieve the same result. In these countries, the requirements may be regarded as one means of achieving good practice, but equally effective alternative arrangements are also acceptable. This principle-based approach is applied in countries such as the UK and Australia, and in the European Union.

Prescriptive-based approach

Some countries require full compliance with detailed requirements, although limited alternatives for achieving compliance are sometimes included within these requirements. In this approach, corporate governance requirements are treated as a 'comply and sign'. In these countries, such as the US, detailed compliance is mandatory and exceptions would not be acceptable.

Influences on corporate governance

Corporate governance is concerned with systems, procedures, controls, accountabilities and decision making at the highest level and throughout an organization.

Because corporate governance is concerned with the way that senior management fulfil their responsibilities and authority, there is a large component of risk management contained in the overall corporate governance structure of every organization. Corporate governance is concerned with the need for openness, integrity and accountability in decision making, and this is relevant to all organizations, regardless of size or whether in the public or private sector.

Those countries that place corporate governance requirements on organizations will be influenced by legal, regulatory, standards or industry requirements, which are explored below.

UK Financial Reporting Council and the UK Corporate Governance Code (2024)

The UK Financial Reporting Council was first established in the 1980s as a private sector body to promote high quality financial reporting. It took on formal responsibilities for audit and accounting regulation in 2004 and for actuarial oversight in 2006. In 2011 it became an independent regulator of auditors, accountants and actuaries, setting UK corporate governance and stewardship codes. It is funded by a levy on companies, the audit profession and local authorities in the UK.

In the UK, corporate governance is defined by the Financial Reporting Council (2024)[2] as the system by which companies are directed and controlled. There are five sections in the UK Corporate Governance Code (UKCGC) developed by the FRC, which cover:

1 Leadership – Every company should be headed by an effective and entrepreneurial board which is collectively responsible for the long-term success of the company.

2 Division of responsibilities – There should be a clear division of responsibilities between the leadership of the board and the executive leadership of the company's business.

3 Composition, succession and evaluation – The board and its committees should have a combination of skills, experience and knowledge. Annual evaluation of the board should consider its composition, diversity, inclusion and equal opportunity, and how effectively members work together to achieve objectives.

4 Audit, risk and internal control – The board should establish procedures to manage risk, oversee the internal control framework, and determine the nature and extent of the principal risks the company is willing to take in order to achieve its long-term strategic objectives.

5 Remuneration – Remuneration policies and practices should be designed to support strategy and promote long-term sustainable success. Executive remuneration should be aligned to company purpose and values, and be clearly linked to the successful delivery of the company's long-term strategy.

The main focus on risk management is within section 4 of the UKCGC, with particular reference in principle O, which states:

> The board should establish and maintain an effective risk management and internal control framework, and determine the nature and extent of the principal risks the company is willing to take in order to achieve its long-term strategic objectives.

A key change in the updated UKCGC is that the board should not just establish an effective risk management and internal control framework, but also maintain it. In addition, that framework should also be reviewed at least annually, as noted in Chapter 21. The linkage between risk management and internal control will be explored further in Chapter 29.

OECD principles of corporate governance (2023)

The Organisation for Economic Co-operation and Development (OECD) is an international body helping governments tackle the economic, social and governance challenges of a globalized economy. The OECD (2023)[3] published its set of principles for corporate governance, which are summarized in Table 27.1. These principles focus on the development of an effective corporate governance framework that pays due regard to the rights of stakeholders.

Table 27.1 OECD principles of corporate governance

Principle	Definition
I. Ensuring the basis for an effective corporate governance framework	Promote transparent and fair markets, efficient allocation of resources and be consistent with the rule of law and support effective supervision and enforcement.
II. Rights and equitable treatment of shareholders and key ownership functions	Protect and facilitate the exercise of shareholder rights and ensure equitable treatment of all shareholders, including minority and foreign shareholders, with the opportunity to obtain effective redress for violation of their rights at a reasonable cost and without excessive delay.
III. Institutional investors, stock markets and other intermediaries	Provide sound incentives throughout the investment chain and provide for stock markets to function in a way that contributes to good corporate governance.
IV. Disclosure and transparency	Ensure that timely and accurate disclosure is made on all material matters, including the financial situation, performance, ownership and governance of the company.

(continued)

Table 27.1 (Continued)

Principle	Definition
V. Responsibilities of the board	Ensure strategic guidance of the company, the effective monitoring of management by the board and board accountability to the company and the shareholders.
VI. Sustainability and resilience	Provide incentives for companies and their investors to make decisions and manage their risks, in a way that contributes to the sustainability and resilience of the corporation.

US Sarbanes–Oxley Act (2002)

In the US, corporate governance is enshrined in the Sarbanes–Oxley Act of 2002.[4] The Sarbanes–Oxley Act (SOX) was passed in response to a range of corporate scandals in the US. These scandals involved misrepresentation of the financial status of various organizations, leading to misleading financial statements. The primary purpose of SOX is to ensure that information disclosed by companies listed on the stock exchanges in the US is accurate and that senior executives are held accountable. The two key risk management requirements in SOX relate to sections 302 and 404.

Section 302 requires that all data produced by an organization must be validated. In relation to financial statements, detailed analysis of risks that could result in misrepresentation of the financial results of an organization has to be undertaken. It states that the chief executive officer and chief financial officer are directly responsible for the accuracy, documentation and submission of all financial reports and the internal control structure.

Section 404 requires that the risk assessment is designed to identify weaknesses in the financial reporting structure. It states that all annual financial reports must report that management are responsible for an 'adequate' internal control structure, and an assessment by management of the effectiveness of that structure, with any weaknesses being reported. This is a very detailed procedure that requires considerable work by the internal audit department.

In addition, under section 404, the financial results of an organization and the evaluation of the financial reporting structure have to be reviewed by external auditors, who have to provide an attestation that they consider the results to be accurate. The procedures for compiling financial information and attestation of the financial disclosures by external auditors (as required by section 404) are very detailed and are considered by some to be extremely onerous and costly to undertake.

SOX requirements state that an approved risk management framework should be used to evaluate risks to accurate financial reporting. The framework recommended for ensuring the accuracy of financial disclosures is the COSO internal control cube (2013), which will be considered in Chapter 29. The SOX requirements apply to subsidiaries of US companies operating in other countries. They also apply to organizations based in other countries if the company has a listing on a US stock exchange. Therefore, the internal control version of COSO is used by companies in many countries in the world.

In order to comply with the requirements of Sarbanes–Oxley, many organizations have decided to set up a disclosures committee to validate all information disclosed by an organization. Because of the extensive application of SOX, many companies based in countries other than the US have also been obliged to set up disclosures committees. The risk architecture shown in Figure 6.2 for a large corporation includes a disclosures committee.

Compliance with the requirements of the Sarbanes–Oxley Act of 2002 is a costly and time-consuming exercise. Questions have been asked about whether the Act has been effective in improving the accuracy of reports from companies that are listed on US stock exchanges. These criticisms are relevant, given that the SOX requirements relate primarily to accuracy of reporting, rather than the achievement of enhanced risk management standards. A summary of some of the views of the CEOs of some US companies is presented in the box below.

IS SARBANES–OXLEY EFFECTIVE?

Chief executives across the US view the Sarbanes–Oxley law as reactionary and overburdensome. Yet they still cite 'improper accounting practices' as the number one ethical issue facing business today. A 2023 survey of CEOs on business ethics by Georgia State University polled nearly 300 chief executives at both private and public companies. Among its findings, most executives agreed that the Sarbanes–Oxley Act strengthened public and investor trust in corporate America, although it had done nothing to improve ethical standards at their businesses. Many suggested that the Act was an overreaction to the ethical failures of a handful of executives and has proven burdensome and unnecessary.

However, examples remain of inaccurate, misleading and potentially fraudulent activity of senior management, which Sarbanes–Oxley was designed to prevent. Among these examples are when General Electric, one of the founding companies of the Dow Jones Index, agreed to pay US$200 million to the SEC for misleading investors about the source of profit in its power and insurance businesses in 2020.

ISO 37000 (2021): Governance of organizations – guidance

There have been a number of standards published on corporate governance, including ISO 37000, which states 'The pursuit of purpose is at the centre of all organizations and is, therefore, of primary importance for the governance of organizations. Good governance of organizations lays the foundation for the fulfilment of the purpose of an organization in an ethical, effective and responsible manner in line with stakeholder expectations'.

This approach means that the scope of the code goes beyond the avoidance or mitigation of threats. It defines the principles of governance and accountabilities of the governing body, which should result in responsible stewardship, effective performance and ethical behaviour. The principles, similar to other corporate governance requirements are:

- Stakeholder engagement
- Leadership
- Data and decisions
- Risk governance
- Social responsibility
- Viability and performance over time.

Stock exchanges

In order to list on stock exchanges around the world and gain access to shareholder capital these exchanges require adherence to guidelines. The London Stock Exchange (LSE) produced guidance on corporate governance in 2013, the focus of which is on the effectiveness of the board. In the view of the LSE, good corporate governance is also about strong leadership, a positive culture and robust risk management.

The LSE governance activities are centred on the board of an organization with the corporate governance framework having two main components: 1) the responsibilities, obligations and rewards of board members; and 2) the fulfilment of stakeholder expectations, rights, participation and dialogue.

The New York Stock Exchange (NYSE) also produced a Corporate Governance Guide (2014), viewing corporate governance as an enabler of long-term value creation and protection, based on accountability and agility, the promotion of behaviours and compensation that reinforces a long-term perspective, and a rich dialogue between companies and investors.

There is much guidance available on corporate governance to support organizations in ensuring they are effectively managed for long-term sustainability and success, whether an organization is required to implement regulatory or mandatory obligations or not. Whatever approach is taken, there appears to be consensus that it should be tailored to each organization to ensure value creation and protection. It should also be noted that having a corporate governance system in place does not guarantee effective governance, but it does encourage and support positive organizational values and behaviours.

For commercial organizations, corporate governance and risk management are designed to assist an organization to achieve its objectives, including commercial or marketplace objectives. The motivation for government departments to ensure good standards of corporate governance is narrower and is often focused on accountability.

In government agencies, the driving principles include value for money and avoidance of inappropriate behaviour. Corporate governance is often seen by government agencies as establishing a framework of control that supports innovation, integrity and accountability and encourages good management throughout an organization.

The box below is an extract from the guiding principles for risk management set out by the UK government in *The Orange Book* under the section concerned with governance and leadership.

THE ORANGE BOOK 2023 – GOVERNANCE AND LEADERSHIP

Main principle

Risk management shall be an essential part of governance and leadership, and fundamental to how an organization is directed, managed and controlled at all levels.

Supporting principles

Each public sector organization should establish governance arrangements appropriate to its business, scale and culture. Human behaviour and culture significantly influence all aspects of risk management at each level and stage. To support the appropriate risk culture, the accounting officer should ensure that expected values and behaviours are communicated and embedded at all levels.

SOURCE UK Government (2023), *The Orange Book: Management of risk – principles and concepts*, https://assets.publishing.service.gov.uk/media/6453acadc33b460012f5e6b8/HMT_Orange_Book_May_2023.pdf

---

Structure of the board

The focus of corporate governance is on the board – its effectiveness and accountability. The board has overall responsibility for an organization in terms of setting strategy and ensuring satisfactory governance. Management of an organization is the responsibility of the executive management, and top management, by way of the executive directors of an organization, will often be members of the board.

As noted in Chapter 7, boards consist of both executive and non-executive directors (NEDs), with guidance usually requiring more NEDs than executives on the board. As NEDs are not full-time employees and should have independence from the running of an organization, their role is restricted. Other than their responsibilities as members of the board, they will only be involved in the committees of the board.

When executive and non-executive directors are members of the same board, this is referred to as a unitary board, which is common in some countries, such as the UK and US. In other countries, the board comprises non-executive directors only, and is referred to as the supervisory board. Where a supervisory board is in place, the executive directors will meet as an executive committee. The separating of non-executive and executive directors into separate committees is sometimes referred to as a two-tier board structure.

The two-tier board structure is common in some countries in the European Union, and often includes representation from the workforce as a mandatory requirement for large companies. It is usual for a two-tier board structure to be in place in charities and public sector organizations. Regardless of whether the structure is unitary or two-tier, the board will have a range of responsibilities. It is standard practice for the board to identify those issues where it will retain ultimate authority and responsibility. These issues are usually referred to as matters reserved for the board. A key area of risk responsibility for the board that is usually not delegated is setting the risk appetite of an organization, although this will be often be supported by the risk function.

Having decided the matters that are reserved for the board, it will then be necessary to decide how authority and responsibility will be delegated in respect of other issues. It is common for large organizations to produce a statement of the delegation of authority, which will be an important document related to the governance structure in an organization.

Committees of the board

An organization should set up appropriate committees with established terms of reference and membership of each of these committees, which may be established as committees or sub-committees of the board. Reports on corporate governance standards, concerns and activities should be received at every board meeting, and these papers will often be presented by the company secretary.

Since many organizations in the UK operate with unitary boards, the guidance on the UKCGC[5] recognizes that board committees play an important part in supporting this approach. It is expected that boards have at least nomination, audit and remuneration committees, but many organizations now also have risk and/or sustainability committees. The responsibility of the audit committee is considered in more detail in Chapter 29.

These board-level committees should comprise NEDs only, although executive directors and other relevant personnel will be invited from time to time to attend meetings. For example, the head of audit or the chief financial officer will attend the audit committee meetings to discuss the findings of audits reports or the financial results, when necessary.

Evaluation of board performance

Evaluation of board performance is a critically important part of the corporate governance arrangements for any organization. The guidance on the UKCGC provides a series of questions and concepts for the board to consider across all aspects of corporate governance, that the board can use to stimulate discussion of whether it is performing effectively. Some of the questions include:

- What proportion of board time is spent on financial performance management versus other matters of strategic importance?
- Is the balance between the focus on immediate issues and long-term success appropriate?
- Is sufficient board time allocated to idea generation, opportunity identification and innovation?
- How do we demonstrate ethical leadership and display the behaviours we expect from others?
- How well are our values and desired behaviours embedded in our human resources policies, processes and practices?
- Have we sought input from enough stakeholders and what impact has this had on our decisions?
- Do our directors have the right level of expertise to oversee risks to an organization?
- What are the sources of the assurance we receive, and can these be considered objective?
- How has the board assessed whether employees have the knowledge, skills and tools to manage risks effectively?
- Does the company communicate what is expected of the workforce in relation to its risk landscape; for example, business continuity, financial and narrative reporting and compliance with applicable laws and regulation and internal policies?

Future direction of corporate governance

The various codes that define good corporate governance are under constant review. From a UK perspective, the UK Corporate Governance Code has been updated every two or three years since 1992. A proposal to replace the FRC with a
statutory body accountable to parliament was made in 2019, but changes to the
corporate governance in the UK have not gone as far as expected – to date. Needless
to say, risk practitioners should keep up to date with all changes to corporate governance requirements in their relative jurisdictions.

Notes

1 ISO (2021) ISO 37000: *Governance of organisations – Guidance*, https://www.iso.org/
   obp/ui/en/#iso:std:iso:37000:ed-1:v1:en (archived at https://perma.cc/5ZSQ-BRAX)
2 FRC (2024) *UK Corporate Governance Code*, https://media.frc.org.uk/documents/
   UK_Corporate_Governance_Code_2024_kRCm5ss.pdf (archived at https://perma.cc/
   R5T8-YV6V)
3 G20/OED (2023) *Principles of Corporate Governance*, https://www.oecd-ilibrary.org/
   governance/g20-oecd-principles-of-corporate-governance-2023_ed750b30-en (archived
   at https://perma.cc/9JPJ-FQB7)
4 Sarbanes Oxley 101 (2024) *Sarbanes Oxley 101*, https://sarbanes-oxley-101.com/
   (archived at https://perma.cc/4T3G-PDDC)
5 FRC (2024) *Corporate Governance Code Guidance*, https://www.frc.org.uk/library/
   standards-codes-policy/corporate-governance/corporate-governance-code-
   guidance/#additional-organisational-committees-f3baf13c (archived at https://perma.
   cc/7KU8-UDNN)

Compliance and the control environment

28

Nature of internal control

Chapter 21 explored internal control as all the elements, processes, functions, activities and people that support the achievement of an organization's objectives. This overall system of internal control is an important component in the successful management of an organization and its risks.

The internal control system includes internal control activities and the structure and responsibilities that relate to them. The purpose of an internal control system is to enable directors to drive an organization forward with confidence, in both good and bad times. A further purpose of the internal control system and internal control activities is to safeguard resources and ensure the adequacy of records and systems of accountability.

The internal control framework

In Chapter 27, the need for corporate governance to ensure organizational sustainability and successful performance was considered. In the UK, a key risk-related corporate governance requirement is for organizations to have a risk management and internal control framework. The risk management framework and its associated process have been detailed in earlier sections of this book. The most commonly used internal control framework, COSO (2013), along with the risk control framework from the UK Government (2023), are considered below.

COSO Internal control framework (2013)

The COSO Internal Control – Integrated Framework (2013)[1] aims to support organizations to develop agile systems of internal control, manage risks to acceptable levels and support sound decision making and governance, effectively and efficiently.

It notes that the system of internal control is not just about complying with policies and procedures, but that it also requires judgement regarding:

- How much control is enough – by management and boards of directors
- The selection, development and deployment of controls – by management and other personnel
- The monitoring and assessment of the effectiveness of the system – by management, internal auditors and other personnel.

The internal control framework is intended to operate across the depth and breadth of an organization, irrespective of whether it is considering operations, reporting or compliance objectives, and regardless of where it is being applied. It has five key components with related principles representing the fundamental concepts associated with each component, as indicated in Table 28.1.

Table 28.1 Components and principles of the COSO Internal Control Framework

Control environment	1. Commitment to integrity and ethical values
	2. Board independence from management
	3. Establishment of structures, reporting lines and appropriate authorities and responsibilities by management
	4. Commitment to attract, develop and retain competent personnel
	5. Holding individuals to account from their internal control responsibilities
Risk assessment	6. Clear objectives developed to enable identification and assessment of risks
	7. Identification, assessment and evaluation of risks enterprise wide
	8. Consideration of potential fraud in assessing risk
	9. Identification and assessment of changes in relation to the system of internal control
Control activities	10. Selection and development of control activities to manage risks to an acceptable level
	11. Selection and development of control activities over technology
	12. Deployment of control activities through policies that establish what is expected and procedures that put policies into action
Information and communication	13. Collection and generation of relevant, quality information
	14. Internal communication of information, including objectives and responsibilities for internal control
	15. External communication with external parties
Monitoring activities	16. Selection, development and ongoing validation of effectiveness of internal control
	17. Timely evaluation and communication of internal control deficiencies

The link and overlap between internal control and risk management is clear in this framework, although there is a distinct and different focus between each.

UK Government Risk Control Framework (2023)

The Risk Control Framework (RCF)[2] forms Part II of the UK Government's Orange Book, explored in earlier chapters. The purpose of the framework is to help accounting officers (essentially the CEOs of public sector organizations) be confident in their control activities, to support prioritization of control improvements and to strengthen decision making, leading to more effective and efficient risk management.

In consultation with the UK Government Internal Audit Agency, the RCF covers all controls, including those related to legislation, standards, codes and practices, functions, and local operational controls. It consists of four pillars, captured in Table 28.2, which are underpinned by an effective culture and the operation of a three lines of assurance model, which will be considered further in Chapter 29.

Table 28.2   The four pillars of the Risk Control Framework

Pillar 1: Governance and Management Framework	Each organization should have a governance framework which complies with expected standards of conduct, requirements of efficiency and transparency in delivery.
Pillar 2: Roles and Accountabilities	Roles and accountabilities should be defined and assigned to people with appropriate seniority, skills and experience. All individuals need to be clear on their roles and responsibilities in the management of their organization's risks and controls and discharge of duties.
Pillar 3: Strategy, Planning & Reporting	Public sector organizations should take short, medium- and longer-term approaches to planning and when doing so should ensure risks to strategy and business objectives are visible and mitigated effectively. Performance and risk reporting should be designed and operated to inform and enable effective risk-based decision making.
Pillar 4: Standards, Policies & Procedures	Approvals should be given, and decisions made and implemented in a timely manner in accordance with the organization's governance and management framework (including financial management controls and delegations of authority), government policy and regulations and the organization's strategy.
	Local organizational processes should have appropriate controls attached to them which reflect the scale, nature and complexity of an organization.

The control environment

The phrase 'control environment', rather than internal controls, is preferred by internal auditors. The purpose of the control environment is to ensure consistent responses to risks that materialize. A well-developed control environment will also ensure that pre-planned responses to a crisis situation are efficiently and effectively implemented.

Linking risk management, governance and controls

As noted above, internal controls are the actions taken by management to plan, organize and direct the performance of an organization with sufficient actions to provide reasonable assurance that objectives will be achieved. These actions may be:

- part of the business-as-usual activities that an organization operates by;
- controls that have been developed to manage risks that are now considered closed or within risk appetite and, as such, embedded in the business as part of day-to-day operations; or
- new controls to manage 'open' or current risks.

The development of real controls was explored in Chapter 19, which is applicable to all controls, whether related to open risks or not. Ensuring these actions, activities or controls are implemented as part of business as usual is commonly part of the compliance management of an organization. The COSO (2020)[3] paper on compliance risk management considers the interrelationships between compliance and risk management and how they both support each other for the successful achievement of objectives. That interrelationship is demonstrated by applying the COSO ERM Framework (2017) to compliance risk.

COSO (2020) suggests that organizations have a chief compliance officer or the equivalent, who should have oversight of compliance and ethics in an organization, bringing together all relevant information on controls relating to the application of laws, regulations, contractual terms, standards and internal practices. Although this is not appropriate for many organizations, having oversight on compliance and ethics issues is an important aspect of good governance and organizational success.

The US Office of Compliance Ethics and Governance (OCEG) has developed a framework for combining governance, risk and compliance (GRC) in its GRC Capability Model,[4] or Red Book (2023). It notes that, for an organization to perform effectively against objectives it must co-ordinate capabilities that address governance, the management of risks and compliance with both mandatory and voluntary requirements; each in consideration of the other.

The Red Book suggests that organizations develop an approach that ensures the 'right people get the appropriate and correct information at the right times, that the right objectives are established, and that the right actions and controls necessary to address uncertainty and act with integrity are in place'.

This means that functions and operational activities should not be undertaken in siloes, but have central repositories for information, standardized procedures and templates, and consistent terminology and communication.

Much of the GRC Capability Model, its components and elements are similar to the risk management process and components of internal control in understanding context (Learn), aligning with objectives and understanding risks (Align), managing issues and risks (Perform), monitoring, reviewing and reporting (Review).

PRACTICAL LINKS – ORGANIZATIONAL

A large organization was getting numerous complaints from staff who were being asked for the same information by different departments, causing confusion and frustration. It appeared that both the compliance and risk management teams were undertaking workshops to understand risks and their required controls. In addition, business continuity and audit were requesting information already developed during these workshops but in different formats.

The company considered how to bring the requirements together in one workshop. It was discussed and agreed that using tools from the risk management process would help. The steps would be:

Step 1 – the extended enterprise tool was used to understand the internal and external context and also inform the business impact analysis (risk management and business continuity management).

Step 2 – risks were identified, including those related to compliance, then prioritized using the risk assessment prioritization scales, to highlight which risks to address further. This informed all four teams.

Step 3 – risk bow-ties were used to unpack the causes and effects of the key risks. Options to manage the causes and effects to bring the risks to an acceptable level were considered, noting which controls were existing and those that needed to be developed or improved. In addition, the most material controls were identified; those that were the most effective in managing the risks. This informed all four teams.

Step 4 – the monitoring, review and reporting were undertaken following the risk workshops, but were informed by the preceding steps. This informed all four teams.

Applying different models for risk management and internal control may be appropriate for some organizations. However, as highlighted above, there is a considerable overlap with each other. As noted in the COSO (2013) internal control framework, there is a different focus between the two, but that does not mean that they should be dealt with separately.

PRACTICAL LINKS – PROJECTS

A multi-billion-euro project was on site and implementing the risk management process. Risks and controls were being identified, which were held on the risk database. The project also had an action management system in place to track day-to-day project activities, which were reviewed on a weekly basis against the project plan.

Controls to manage risks, once agreed upon, became part of the project, but were being treated in a risk management 'silo' and were not being as actively managed or regularly reviewed as the project actions. To better embed risk management into the project a link was developed between both systems whereby agreed controls to manage risk were captured and kept up to date in both the risk database and the action management system but were actively managed and reviewed through the latter.

One final consideration of the relationship between risk management and internal control comes from the UK Corporate Governance Code (2024).[5] In previous versions of the code there has been a requirement relating to risk management and internal control frameworks. The updated code refers throughout to a combined, singular risk management and internal control framework, which should encompass policies, processes, culture, behaviours and other aspects of an organization related to strategy, operational activities, reporting and compliance. It suggests the framework should be:

- Tailored to an organization
- Part of the strategy and purpose
- Embedded into operations and form part of the culture
- Agile
- Regularly updated
- Not just a periodic compliance exercise, but integral to business-as-usual
- Able to escalate significant concerns, including the appropriate action being taken.

This implies that a framework for risk management and internal control can be developed by organizations to reduce frustration, duplication, gaps and overlaps, as long as the sufficient focus is provided to the relevant aspects of a combined framework

Expectations of internal control

As noted in the guidance on the UK Corporate Governance Code, an effective risk and control framework reduces, but cannot eliminate, 'the possibility of poor judgement in decision making, human error, control processes being deliberately circumvented by employees and others, management overriding controls, and the occurrence of unforeseeable circumstances'.

A sound system of internal control, therefore, provides reasonable, but not absolute, assurance that an organization will not be hindered in achieving its business objectives, or hindered in the orderly and legitimate conduct of its business, by circumstances that may reasonably be foreseen. A system of internal control cannot provide protection with certainty against an organization failing to meet its business objectives or against all material errors, losses, fraud, or breaches of laws or regulations. This has been highlighted in the link between internal control and compliance, and is the reason why internal control systems are audited, which is considered further in Chapter 29.

The future for control processes

Traditionally, the control processes discussed above are, on the whole, backwards looking, seeking to monitor controls and determining whether something has happened. It has often been described as 'driving a car looking in the rear-view mirror'.

The growth of technology, analytical processes, real-time and continuous monitoring of systems is starting to provide sufficient data to enable a form of preemptive control, where risks are more effectively anticipated. Integrating different datasets with monitoring can form analysis which is capable of spotting the leading indicators for potential failure. In so doing, control measures become proactive rather than reactive.

Notes

1 COSO (2013) *Internal Control – Integrated Framework: Executive Summary*, https://www.coso.org/_files/ugd/3059fc_1df7d5dd38074006bce8fdf621a942cf.pdf (archived at https://perma.cc/8EP7-EGWC)

2 UK Government (2023) *The Orange Book: Management of Risk – Principles and Concepts*, https://assets.publishing.service.gov.uk/media/6453acadc33b460012f5e6b8/HMT_Orange_Book_May_2023.pdf (archived at https://perma.cc/9SS7-L8P8)

3 COSO (2020) *Compliance Risk Management: Applying the COSO ERM Framework*, https://www.coso.org/_files/ugd/3059fc_5f9c50e005034badb07f94e9712d9a56.pdf (archived at https://perma.cc/7M49-UBQE)

4 OCEG (2023) *GRC Capability Model – OCEG Red Book: Guidance for people who govern, audit, and manage performance, risk and compliance*, https://www.oceg.org/grc-capability-model-red-book/ (archived at https://perma.cc/5ULX-APHS)

5 FRC (2024) *Corporate Governance Code Guidance*, https://www.frc.org.uk/library/standards-codes-policy/corporate-governance/corporate-governance-code-guidance/#risk-and-internal-controls-overview-abcc1f06 (archived at https://perma.cc/H7AY-8NJS)

Risk assurance 29

Assurance

Assurance relates to the comfort or level of confidence that can be taken from assessing the effectiveness of risk controls. The Chartered Institute of Internal Auditors (2023)[1] defines assurance as 'an objective examination of evidence for the purpose of providing an independent assessment'.

Risk assurance is an important component of the overall risk management process, as part of risk review, considered in Chapter 21, and the verification of real controls in Table 21.1. Assurance is required regarding internal controls, whether financial, operational, reporting or compliance, and is needed for both open risks and/or operational management of an organization, as noted in Chapter 28.

Why is assurance required?

As noted above, assurance provides comfort regarding particular aspects of organizational activities. Overall, assurance is provided so that organizations can demonstrate to relevant 'audiences' that they are able meet their objectives, are a going concern and are sustainable in the longer term.

The UK Corporate Governance Code (UKCGC)[2] requires organizations to state whether they have a reasonable expectation that they will be able to continue in operation and meet their liabilities as they arise over the period of their viability assessment. This period is expected to be significantly longer than 12 months from the approval of financial statements, but recognizes that the longer the period, the lower the degree of certainty.

Viability statements are considered further in Chapter 32.

Who requires assurance?

Assurance can be provided at any level of an organization; however, corporate governance more formally relates to assurance in relation to material controls. It is difficult to find a definition for a material control, as each organization is different, and materiality can be affected by an organization's size, complexity, operations, strategy and structure. However, the FRC in its guidance on the UK Corporate Governance Code[3] notes that when determining which controls are material, the board should consider how a deficiency in a control could impact the interests of an organization and its stakeholders.

The Code makes clear the board's accountability for effective internal controls including the requirement for a reporting declaration on the matter, which provides a stronger basis for organizations to provide evidence of the effectiveness of those controls.

The Board

Overall assurance on risk management and internal controls is required by the boards of organizations to ensure they have effective oversight regarding the successful achievement of objectives.

THE BOARD'S ULTIMATE RESPONSIBILITY FOR RISK AND INTERNAL CONTROL

Guidance on the UK Corporate Governance Code (2024) notes five core responsibilities for the board in relation to risk management and internal control:

1 Establishing and maintaining an effective risk management and internal control framework.

2 Determining the nature and extent of the principal risks and those risks which an organization is willing to take in achieving its strategic objectives (determining its 'risk appetite').

3 Agreeing how the principal risks should be managed or mitigated to reduce the likelihood of their incidence or their impact.

4 Monitoring and reviewing the risk management and internal control frameworks, and the management's process for this, and satisfying itself that they are functioning effectively, and that corrective action is being taken where necessary.

5 Ensuring effective external communication on risk management and internal control.

Item four on this list is the key consideration for this chapter in that the board should be able to satisfy itself that the risk management and internal control framework is functioning effectively.

> The guidance also notes that the board should not rely solely on the embedded monitoring but should conduct its own monitoring to better understand risks to organizational objectives and the controls in place to manage those risks. In addition, it is suggested that the board uses its professional judgement and scepticism in relation to the assurance provided by an organization; challenging information given rather than just blind acceptance.

Section 302 of the Sarbanes Oxley Act[4] also states that the CEO and CFO are directly and personally responsible for the accuracy, documentation and submission of all financial reports as well as the internal control structure, including:

- establishing and maintaining internal controls designed to ensure that material information is made known to such officers by others within those entities;
- evaluating the effectiveness of the internal controls; and
- presenting conclusions about the effectiveness of internal controls based on their evaluation.

This is a further example of the requirement for assurance on risk management and internal control at the board level.

The audit committee

An increasing number of organizations have decided that it is appropriate to have an audit committee, and for those publicly listed in the UK, it is a requirement of the UK Corporate Governance Code. Almost invariably, the audit committee consists of non-executive directors, with senior executive directors also in attendance at audit committee meetings. It is chaired by a non-executive director, often referred to as the lead non-executive director, who should be able to demonstrate competence in audit reviews. This lead NED is not usually the non-executive chairman of an organization.

Although the audit committee may be considered to be the guardian of compliance within an organization, the terms of reference are usually much broader than just compliance.

The audit committee is in a position to evaluate the governance standards within an organization, ensure that risk management receives appropriate attention, and seek assurance on the levels of compliance achieved within an organization. The role of the audit committee may be much broader than this and includes evaluation of the arrangements for governance of the board itself.

In reviewing the effectiveness of the board, the audit committee will also evaluate the effectiveness of the subcommittees. Given this role, the audit committee will retain its position as the ultimate monitor of governance, risk and compliance throughout the whole operation. The audit committee will seek assurance relating to all aspects of the strategy, tactics, operations and compliance of an organization.

The outcomes and impact of risk management activities are often reported to an audit committee in a large organization. Audit committees have a range of responsibilities, including the obligation to obtain adequate risk assurance in an organization. The audit committee is also concerned with internal control in an organization.

Table 29.1 provides a list of typical responsibilities of the audit committee. Audit committees should be non-executive bodies that do not have executive responsibility

Table 29.1 Responsibilities of the audit committee

External audit	Recommend the appointment and reappointment of external auditors. Review the performance and cost-effectiveness of the external auditors. Review the qualification, expertise and independence of external auditors. Review and discuss any reports from the external auditors.
Internal audit	Review internal audit and its relationship with external auditors. Review and assess the annual internal audit plan. Review promptly all reports from the internal auditors. Review management response to the findings of the internal auditors. Review activities, resources and effectiveness of internal audit.
Financial reporting	Review the annual and half-year financial results. Evaluate annual report against requirements of the governance code. Review disclosure by CEO and CFO during certification of annual report.
Regulatory reports	Review arrangements for producing the audited accounts. Monitor and review standards of risk management and internal control. Provide assurance that proposed regulatory and legislative changes are being adequately considered for all aspects of an organization, particularly in a global context. Develop a code of ethics for CEO and other senior management roles. Annually review the adequacy of the risk management processes. Receive reports on litigation, financial commitments and other liabilities. Receive reports of any issues raised by whistle-blowing activities.

for risk management. Similarly, they should not have responsibility for the identification of significant risks or the identification and implementation of material controls.

The function of the audit committee is to seek risk assurance and check that the procedure for the identification of significant or material risks is appropriate. The audit committee should validate that the significant risks have been correctly identified, as well as seeking assurance that material controls have been correctly designed and implemented.

A UK Corporate Governance Code (2024) requirement for those organizations listed on the UK Stock Exchange is that where a company does not have an internal audit function, it should provide an explanation for the absence, how assurance has been achieved, and how the absence has affected the work of external audit.

The audit committee also provides assurance to the board, and through its reporting disclosures, to external stakeholders too.

Management

In addition to the more formal requirements for assurance at more senior levels in an organization, management will also need assurance that risks are being managed and controls operated effectively within the business-as-usual activities.

As noted in Chapter 27, Section 404 of SOX requires organizations to state the responsibility of management for establishing and maintaining an adequate internal control structure, including an assessment of the effectiveness of the internal control structure, again placing the requirement for assurance also at the management level and reinforcing the relevant responsibilities. In this situation, management requires assurance in relation to risk management and internal control from within an organization, in order to provide assurance themselves.

Who gives assurance?

Any organization can be divided into three layers, being senior management (directors), middle management (managers) and staff/employees, all of which have some responsibility for both risk management and internal control.

Three lines model

To ensure responsibility, both risk management and internal control is appropriately delegated and to gain effective assurance, many organizations use the 'three lines model' developed by the Institute of Internal Auditors (2020).[5] Executive directors, managers and staff represent the three levels of management within an organization,

Figure 29.1 The three lines model from a public body perspective

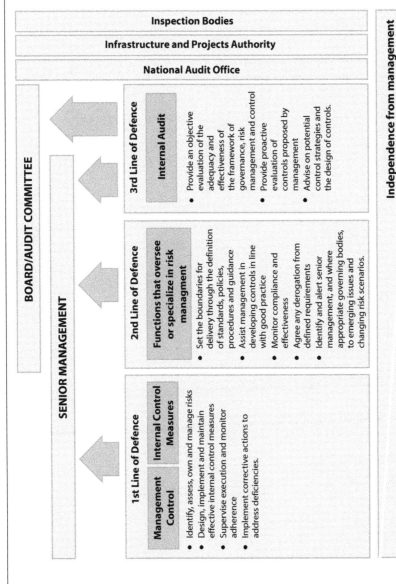

SOURCE HM Government (2020) *The Orange Book: Management of Risk – Principles and Concepts*, p 33, https://assets.publishing.service.gov.uk/government/uploads/system/uploads/attachment_data/file/866117/6.6266_HMT_Orange_Book_Update_v6_WEB.PDF

and together these are the first line in ensuring satisfactory standards of governance, including risk management and internal control. Specialist risk oversight functions within an organization provide expertise, support, monitoring and challenge and advice to management in their role, as the second line. Internal Audit provide independent advice and assurance to management and the governing body regarding the effectiveness of risk management and internal control, and act as the third line.

This model is an update of the IIA's Three Lines of Defense Model, which addresses some key issues with the previous version:

- more clarity on the role of the governing body (e.g. the board), including integrity, leadership and transparency;
- recognition that risk includes both opportunity and threat, and opportunities should not be defended against;
- understanding that the first and second lines are not mutually exclusive and that the separation between those who operate an organization and those who provide advice is often blurred, although some regulatory requirements require a level of independence.

The UK Government's Orange Book (2023)[6] considers responsibility for and assurance on risk management and internal control using the three lines model, noting where the responsibility sits and where assurance can be gained, both internally and externally, and the level of independence in the assurance given, in Figure 29.1.

The Institute of Internal Auditors paper (2020) also gives guidance on the oversight and assurance provided through the three lines model:

- Governing body – relies on reports from management (in both first and second lines), internal audit and others to exercise oversight and achievement of objectives
- Management (first line) – provides assurance on outcomes, risk management and internal control
- Specialist functions (second line) – provide additional assurance on risk-related matters
- Internal audit (third line) – provides independent assurance, carrying the highest degree of objectivity and confidence in the assurance it provides
- External providers – provide further independent assurance.

The three lines model is not appropriate or applicable for all organizations, although all organizations are required to ensure assurance and oversight are provided, no matter what form it is given in. The Four Lines of Sight paper from Walde (2024)[7] expands on the three lines model, considering the different directions that an organization should be looking in to gain a holistic picture of the management of and assurance on risks and internal controls through oversight, insight, foresight and hindsight, as shown in Figure 29.2.

Figure 29.2   The Four Lines of Sight

SOURCE Walde, J (2024). Used with permission

The Four Lines of Sight provides clarity around roles and responsibilities for risk management and internal control, strengthening risk governance and organizational resilience:

1 Insight *develops* from within an area of expertise, with knowledge and experience on current risks and related controls, facilitating understanding of risks and informing risk perception – looking at the current state.

2 Foresight is *exercised* by strategy setters driving an organization forward, with an understanding of emerging risks and those on the horizon, fostering risk awareness and informing decision making – looking forward.

3 Hindsight is *gained* through evidence of actual performance on the management of risks and implementation of internal controls, checking the current risk perception through evidencing controls and promoting learning – looking back.

4 Oversight is *applied* to connect the overall risk picture using insight, foresight and hindsight, enabling risk governance and effective resource application according to risk appetite – looking across the whole picture.

Internal audit

The role of internal audit is to provide independent assurance that an organization's risk management, governance and internal control processes are operating effectively. Internal audit, in the third line of providing assurance, is mainly involved in gaining hindsight. However, they will also review risk and internal control information that is developed through insight and exercised through foresight.

Generally, there will be a long-term risk-based audit plan in place, which will identify areas that pose the key risks to achieving organizational objectives and should therefore be audited within specific times. The plan should, therefore, include coverage of the material controls of the principal risks and be drawn up with input from the ERM team. Usually, an annual plan will sit within a larger three- or five-year plan that ensures all critical process are reviewed. The annual plan should be approved by the board or audit committee, and 'audit sponsors' shall be identified who represent the client for the audit.

Undertaking an internal audit exercise involves a number of steps involving planning, fieldwork, reporting and follow-up. As part of the audit exercise, the auditor should collect information relevant to the audit that is to be undertaken.

Analysis of the information that has been collected will enable an auditor to determine and agree the priorities and objectives of the review. For example, an audit of the supply chain will require the auditor to collect information on the contracts that are in place with suppliers.

In many ways, the fieldwork is the most important part of the audit exercise. The auditor may need to visit locations, including supplier locations if the audit is concerned with the supply chain. The purpose of the fieldwork is to understand the risks and their related controls.

Testing will then be undertaken to ensure the efficiency and effectiveness of the controls that are in place. As noted in Chapter 21, this testing or validating should consider whether the controls have been designed, operated and maintained effectively and as expected. Testing of these controls will be based on discussions with the managers and staff, as well as observation and evidence of the activities as they are carried out.

Based on the fieldwork that has been undertaken, the auditor will produce the audit report. The audit report will contain comments on the efficiency and effectiveness of the controls that are in place and recommendations for further improvement, if considered necessary.

The internal auditor will need to form an independent opinion of the level of control that has been achieved so that assurance can be provided to the audit committee, to the extent that this is justified. Also, if the audit report sets out recommendations, these should be agreed with the management of the unit. This collaborative approach should increase uptake and implementation of recommendations. If the controls are inadequate and local management does not accept these conclusions, escalation of the issue will be required, up to the audit committee, if appropriate. These recommendations will be followed up to ensure any findings are resolved.

Establishing audit priorities is an important function of internal audit. In relation to risk management activities, internal auditors will need to establish their priorities for the testing of controls. There is an important interface between risk management and internal control. Risk management professionals are very good at assessing risks and identifying the appropriate type of control that should be in place. The risk register will often record current controls and make recommendations for the implementation of additional controls.

Figure 29.3   Role of internal audit in ERM

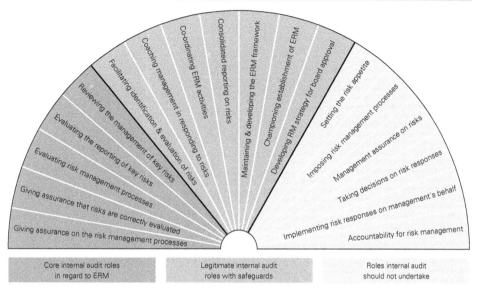

Core internal audit roles
in regard to ERM

Legitimate internal audit
roles with safeguards

Roles internal audit
should not undertake

SOURCE *Position paper: Risk management and internal audit*, reproduced with the permission of the Chartered Institute of Internal Auditors – UK and Ireland, https://www.iia.org.uk/resources/risk-management/position-paper-risk-management-and-internal-audit/

Figure 29.2 illustrates those activities that are core to the work of the internal audit. These activities include reviewing the management of key risks, evaluating the reporting of those risks and evaluating risk management processes.

The diagram also identifies activities that internal audit should not undertake, generally around taking decisions about and managing risk. Those activities in the middle of Figure 29.2 require safeguards before internal audit get involved but they have a legitimate reason to do so.

ADDED VALUE OF INTERNAL AUDIT

Although what constitutes value-added activity will vary based on many factors, there are some general rules that apply across the board. Four factors that can help auditors determine what will add the most value to their organization are:

- knowledge of an organization, including its culture, key players and competitive environment;

- courage to innovate in ways stakeholders don't expect and may not think they want;

- ability to adapt to an organization in ways that exceed stakeholder expectations;
- knowledge of those practices that the profession, in general, considers value-added.

Three of these factors (organizational knowledge, courage and ability to adapt) are competencies and personal qualities that, for the most part, are self-explanatory. However, knowledge of the practices that the profession considers value-added is a continuing professional challenge for internal auditors.

Risk management and internal audit

There needs to be a close working relationship between the risk management function and internal audit. The responsibilities allocated to each of these functions will vary according to the nature, type and size of an organization. This is an important working relationship, because successful management of risk depends on the important risk-based outputs considered previously in Chapter 5 and summarized as MADE2:

- mandatory as required by laws, customers/clients and standards;
- assurance for the management team and other stakeholders;
- decision making based on the best information available;
- effective and efficient core processes throughout an organization.

It is clear that if these outputs are to be successfully delivered, all stakeholders need to work together, and that includes cooperation between risk management and internal audit.

Internal control is concerned with the methods, procedures and checks that are in place to ensure that an organization meets its objectives. Because internal control is concerned with the fulfilment of objectives, there is a clear link with risk management activities. Internal control activities within a large organization are likely to be evaluated by internal audit. In some cases, internal audit may be outsourced to an external accountancy firm, but it should not be the same company that undertakes external auditing for an organization.

Internal audit is primarily concerned with risk assurance and in validating the controls and procedures in place to manage risk. It is generally considered inappropriate for internal auditors to fulfil an executive function by assisting management with the identification, design and implementation of those risk control measures, as will be seen below. Managing risk, however, is critical to the success of an organization and therefore considered an executive function.

Although there is a distinction between the approach and activities of internal audit and of risk management, as noted in Figure 29.2, there are areas of common interest. For example, having identified the critically important controls, the auditor will need to check that they are implemented in practice and that they are correct and effective. The outcome of testing of controls is to ensure that the intended level of risk is actually achieved in practice, as highlighted in Chapter 21 and Figure 18.1, and not just a collection of data that is not used or guidance that is not followed. In other words, the control actually moves the level of risk from the inherent level to the intended target level in the way that was planned.

If the control is not effective and efficient, it will need to be modified; another area where risk management and internal audit share expertise. Although these discussions on controls can be facilitated by risk management and internal audit, the ultimate decisions on the controls and their anticipated effectiveness have to be made by the members of line management who are responsible for the controls.

External audit and other assurance providers

External audit provides additional verification, creditability and reliability to the assurance reports produced by an organization. As outsiders to an organization, they are seen to be independent and able to provide different and valuable perspectives regarding the effectiveness of risk management, internal controls, processes, guidelines, policies and so on.

External audit provides assurance to stakeholders outside of an organization's governance 'boundary', that is, shareholders or perhaps heads of government departments. For example, Section 404 of SOX (2002) requires registered external auditors to attest to the accuracy of an organization's assertion that internal accounting controls are in place, operational and effective. However, the work of external audit is also of interest to the senior management and boards of the organizations being audited.

External assurance is not related to just financial reporting but can be provided in relation to other specialist topics. For independent and credible assurance, the provider of the assurance should be recognized experts in their field, benchmarking against recognized standards. For example, these include rating agencies who assess the financial strength of organizations and government entities, licensed sustainability assurance providers who review an organization's practices in relation to ESG or expert risk management consultants who review risk management frameworks and practices.

How is assurance given?

Depending on the risk priorities of an organization, the board or audit committee may require annual reports on certain operational threats. Because of the importance of health and safety at work, boards usually receive annual reports on safety performance. Likewise, the audit committee will wish to receive an annual report on the incidents of fraud that have been detected within an organization.

At the tactical level, the successful completion of projects is often the subject of a review by the board or audit committee. Within large organizations, it is typical to have a post-implementation review of a project. For example, if the board of a retail company has authorized the opening of a new store, the audit committee will require a review of the completion of the project for opening the store. This post-implementation review will evaluate whether the project was delivered on time, within budget and to specification. It is also common for the audit committee to require a further post-implementation review of the first 12 months' trading of the new store.

Risk assurance related to strategy is somewhat less well developed. However, a review of changes in strategic direction, such as mergers and acquisitions, can provide important information and lessons learnt, in both areas of success and failures.

Regardless, the audit committee and board will seek assurance that all significant risks are being adequately managed and that all material controls are effective and that they have been efficiently implemented.

There are a number of sources of assurance available within organizations and examples of these are set out in Table 29.2, some or all which may be depended on, subject to the nature of an organization.

Assurance will also be required in relation to the risk management activities themselves. When working together, risk management and internal audit should always concentrate on the outputs from the risk management process and the impact that is sought. The contribution of risk management is to ensure a greater chance of achieving the objectives of an organization, and this is also a stated intention of internal audit activities. The review and monitoring stage of the risk management process is usually represented as an information and experience loop that provides feedback to the beginning of the process.

Risk and control self-assessments (RCSA)

As well as undertaking physical audits, internal audit departments will often facilitate a procedure of self-certification of controls. Self-certification of controls is an arrangement whereby local senior management complete a regular (often annual) return confirming details of the level of risk assurance that has been achieved in the department.

Table 29.2   Sources of risk assurance

Culture measurement	By use of a recognized framework such as COSO to gain a quantitative evaluation of the control environment.
Audit reports	Produced by internal audit and external auditors on a range of issues including risk assessment, implementation, compliance and training.
Unit reports	On such issues as risk performance indicators, risk and control self-assessment (RCSA), response to audit recommendations and reports on incidents that have occurred.
Performance of the unit	On risk-related issues, losses, significant weaknesses in control measures and details of any material losses suffered by the unit.
Unit documentation	On topics such as the risk management policy, health and safety policy, business continuity plans and disaster recovery plans.

This type of self-certification is generally known as risk and control self-assessment (RCSA), or sometimes control and risk self-assessment (CRSA), and it is frequently undertaken as an electronic return for an organization. The questionnaire for the RCSA can be based on the criteria set out in the COSO internal control or any other relevant framework, such as the risk guidance from the UK Financial Reporting Council.

As well as providing confirmation of adequate levels of risk and internal control assurance, the RCSA return can also provide details of situations where significant weaknesses in controls have been identified. This information will enable the internal auditors to identify areas where additional controls may be required. Also, in addition to identifying significant weaknesses, the RCSA returns can require information on any material failures that have occurred. Disclosures around failures and improvements implemented are a requirement of the UK Corporate Governance Code (2024).

APPROACHES TO RCSA

The executive has recommended the use of an annual RCSA exercise, to be conducted by internal audit, as part of the annual review of corporate governance. Each year a sample of the governance policies will be chosen by the governance panel for inclusion in the RCSA exercise. Policy custodians will be required to help formulate questionnaires and report back on the feedback received from services to internal audit.

The findings from the RCSA exercise, together with the assessment of compliance against each of the supporting principles and work carried out by internal audit in accordance with the annual audit plan will be drawn together into the annual governance statement, for review by the governance panel, the audit committee and the executive committee.

Assurance mapping

Assurance mapping is a structured means of identifying and understanding the main sources and types of assurance across an organization in a co-ordinated way. It provides a connection between risk management and internal control, providing oversight across an organization in relation to the strategic, operational, reporting and compliance activities.

Assurance mapping enables evidence to be gathered of organizational governance, the successful management of risks and the improvements of controls in all areas of a business. This mapping may be carried out in line with the assurance providers through the three lines model, or against business entities or functional activities, all to align with the organizational structure.

The mapping should also be informed by risk management to provide risk-based assurance. This will support the design of an appropriate plan of where audits have been, or should be carried out, based on information from such sources as RCSAs, audit reports, risk registers, and so on, ensuring there are no unnecessary overlaps or gaps in assurance.

The Institute of Auditors in England and Wales (ICAEW)[8] considers 10 steps in preparing an assurance map including the scope, the amount of assurance required, the assurance activities and providers, the gaps and overlaps and the next steps in taking any necessary remedial or improvement action:

1 Identify the sponsor

2 Determine the scope

3 Assess the required/desired amount of assurance for each element

4 Identify the assurance providers

5 Identify the assurance activities

6 Reassess the scope

7 Assess the quality of the assurance activities

8 Assess the aggregate amount of assurance for each element

9 Analyse the gaps and overlaps in assurance for each element

10 Determine the course of action

Benefits of risk assurance

Corporate governance is a major concern for all organizations and their stakeholders. Therefore, risk assurance should not be an administrative or box-ticking exercise. Organizations need to demonstrate that corporate governance is a priority for management. Many organizations recognize the need for openness of risk reporting. This requires effective communication activities to be in place at all times.

Having established good communication activities, an organization needs to ensure that there are positive messages to be communicated to stakeholders. Undertaking risk assurance activities will provide assurance to all stakeholders, including employees, suppliers, customers, government departments, external audit and internal audit.

Obtaining risk assurance is an important part of the corporate governance arrangements for all organizations. The benefits of adequate risk assurance are that it:

- builds confidence with stakeholders;
- provides reassurance to sponsors and financiers;
- demonstrates good practice to regulators;
- prevents financial and other surprises;
- reduces the chances of damage to reputation;
- encourages a virtuous risk culture within an organization;
- allows more secure delegation of authority.

Notes

1 Chartered Institute of Internal Auditors (2023) *Assurance Definitions*, https://www.iia.org.uk/resources/technical-blog/assurance-definitions/ (archived at https://perma.cc/FN8X-R6QL)
2 FRC (2024) *UK Corporate Governance Code*, https://media.frc.org.uk/documents/UK_Corporate_Governance_Code_2024_ofM100g.pdf (archived at https://perma.cc/QQF4-K6ΛV)
3 FRC (2024) *Corporate Governance Code Guidance*, https://www.frc.org.uk/library/standards-codes-policy/corporate-governance/corporate-governance-code-guidance/#risk-and-internal-controls-overview-abcc1f06 (archived at https://perma.cc/HAK9-DXQ4)
4 Securities and Exchange Commission (2024) *Sarbanes-Oxley 101*, https://www.sarbanes-oxley-101.com/sarbanes-oxley-compliance.htm (archived at https://perma.cc/8YNG-ZS83)
5 Institute of Internal Auditors (2020) *The IIA's Three Lines Model: An update of the Three Lines of Defense*, https://www.theiia.org/globalassets/documents/resources/the-iias-three-lines-model-an-update-of-the-three-lines-of-defense-july-2020/three-lines-model-updated-english.pdf (archived at https://perma.cc/4W7P-USLU)
6 UK Government (2023) *The Orange Book: Management of Risk – Principles and Concepts*, https://assets.publishing.service.gov.uk/media/6453acadc33b460012f5e6b8/HMT_Orange_Book_May_2023.pdf (archived at https://perma.cc/68AB-Y2CH)
7 Walde, J (2024) *Four lines of risk sight – A new risk management model can help businesses assess and control risk more effectively*, https://abmagazine.accaglobal.com/global/articles/2024/sep/business/four-lines-of-risk-sight.html (archived at https://perma.cc/A8AF-PEN6)
8 ICAEW (2018), *Assurance mapping: A vital governance and management tool*, https://www.icaew.com/technical/audit-and-assurance/assurance/assurance-mapping/10-steps-to-prepare-your-assurance-map#step_10 (archived at https://perma.cc/8AAC-GJN7)

PART SEVEN
Organizational environment, resilience and sustainability

LEARNING OUTCOMES

Having studied this section readers will be able to:

- Explain the purpose of strategy for organizations and the board's role in defining it.
- Describe how strategy is formulated and implemented.
- Explain and produce examples of strategy models that are appropriate for designing, validating, implementing, and reviewing and repurposing an organization's strategy.
- Summarize the links between strategy and risk management in creating value.
- Describe organizational resilience and provide examples of disruptors.
- Explain the testing tools for resilience, including emerging risks, horizon scanning, resilience indicators, scenario testing and stress testing.
- Explain long-term viability in relation to resilience.
- Summarize the links between resilience and risk management in protecting value.

- Explain business continuity management and its role in resilience.
- Describe business continuity planning, including business impact analysis.
- Summarize the links between business continuity management and risk management in maintaining value.
- Describe sustainability and its evolution.
- Explain double materiality in considering the perceptions of organizations and wider society.
- Summarize the links between sustainability and risk management in creating, maintaining and protecting value.
- Explain climate change and its role as part of ESG.
- Produce examples of climate change risks in relation to the categories of physical, transition and liability risks.
- Explain the different standards and frameworks in relation to climate change.
- Describe the role of risk management within climate change, including the use of tools such as scenario analysis.

Strategy and risk management 30

Strategy

Strategy is an important starting point for enterprise risk management. Setting and understanding organizational objectives follows on from the strategy, and risk management focuses on the uncertainties associated with the achievement of those organizational objectives.

Strategy is highlighted in ISO 31000[1] as part of the scope, context and criteria step, and in the second component of the current COSO ERM Framework[2] relating to strategy and objective setting, which have been considered in previous chapters. It also forms part of the risk management (RASP) framework covered in Chapter 6.

Understanding the mission, vision and core values of an organization and the development of strategy and objectives is key to ensuring that relevant risks are identified, understood and managed within an organization's risk appetite.

There are numerous definitions of strategy. In the context of strategy and risk management, Table 30.1 provides the most relevant definitions.

Strategy, as a business discipline, has been the focus of plenty of study and observation. Some notable observations or quotations relating to strategy include:

- Lee Bolman[3] – 'A vision without a strategy remains an illusion'
- Lewis Carroll[4] – 'If you don't know where you are going, any road will get you there'
- Stephen Covey[5] – 'Begin with the end in mind'

This chapter goes into further detail on strategy and objectives, introducing methods for formulating business strategy and building on that knowledge to assess the interconnectivity between risk and strategy processes. Finally, the role of risk in a series of strategy models will be evaluated.

Table 30.1   Definitions of strategy

Source	Definition
Dictionary definition	A plan that is intended to achieve a particular purpose.
Strategic Thinking Institute	The intelligent allocation of resources through a unique system of activities to achieve a goal.
Robert M Grant in *Contemporary Strategy Analysis* 10th Edition	Strategy is a key ingredient of success for both individuals and organizations. A sound strategy cannot guarantee success, but it can improve the odds. Successful strategies tend to embody four elements: clear long-term goals; profound understanding of the external environment; astute appraisal of internal resources and capabilities; and effective implementation.

The board's role in defining strategy

Chapter 27 dealt with governance structures. One of the key aims of a governance structure is to ensure that an organization's strategy is delivered upon. Strategy starts with an organization's shareholders, members or trustees. In founding and continuing to mandate the existence of an organization they define the core purpose of an organization. They also entrust the governance oversight of delivering this purpose to a board of directors, who set the strategic objectives. The board in turn, using their authority to delegate power to the executive, charge the executive with creating an implementation plan to deliver on these strategy objectives, as can be seen in Figure 30.1.

Figure 30.1   Governance oversight

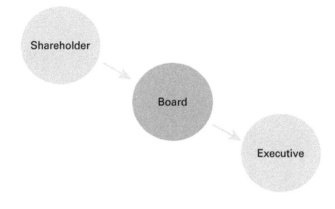

Therefore, when considering risk management in this context it is important to understand and regularly revisit the strategic objectives set by the board on behalf of the shareholders, members or trustees.

Organizations will typically have a three-to-five-year strategy to deliver on the vision and mission which is set by the shareholders. This strategy is approved by its board. Organizations then typically have an annual plan and financial budget which is a subset of the three-to-five-year strategy and focuses on the near-term objectives. The three-to-five-year strategy documents and annual plans are often for internal use and not published by organizations. Many organizations will publish a strategy statement or report that can be found in their annual report each year. In large organizations there may be a regulatory or legal requirement to report on strategy, such as the UK FRC guidance on the application of the strategic report requirements of the Companies Act 2006.[6]

GUIDANCE ON THE STRATEGIC REPORT

In the UK, the Financial Reporting Council (FRC) has produced a paper regarding Guidance on the Strategic Report. This guidance sets out the elements that must be included in an organization's strategic report to ensure that shareholders are provided with a holistic and meaningful picture of an organization's business model, strategy, development, performance, position and future prospects.

The guidance also requires that a description of the principal risks that an organization faces is included and how those risks might affect future prospects. Although the FRC guidance relates specifically to companies listed on the UK Stock Exchange, it has also become generally accepted best practice in other countries and organization types.

How strategy is formulated and implemented

Organizations have both strategic and business objectives. Often these are documented separately, and the risk management process undertaken will need to view both of these sets of objectives and explore the relationship between them. Business objectives will often relate to the annual budget of an organization and comprise details such as the anticipated sales as income and the cost of sales as expenditure.

Underpinning the business objectives of an organization will be the business development model (or business model for short) that an organization has developed. The risks that are attached to business objectives are associated with the robustness of the business model and the efficiency of the business model. The essence of the business objectives normally relates to an organization as it currently exists.

Figure 30.2 identifies the essential features of a business model. The business model is underpinned by the business objectives and the annual business plan. An organization will also have plans to develop and enhance the business model in line with long-term strategy. Figure 30.2 describes how the existing business model is developed by implementing the tactics that achieve that long-term strategy. The existing business model is defined by the existing operations or 'where an organization is now'.

Most organizations recognize that changes in the external environment mean that 'current' business models will not always be successful. If business objectives are to be sustainable in the long term, then an organization will need to develop.

In order to place risk management within the context of business operations, it is necessary to consider the business development model. The first stage for an organization is to decide the strategy that it is seeking to deliver. The strategic aims will be determined by considering the mission statement of an organization, the corporate

Figure 30.2   Business development model

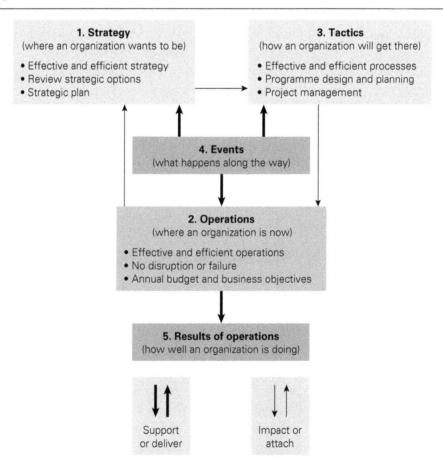

objectives and the stakeholder expectations. The strategy should be capable of delivering the mission statement of an organization.

Once the overall strategy is established, the tactics that will deliver it need to be identified. If the strategy requires changes to core processes or the introduction of new core processes, then projects or programmes of work will be required. The tactics introduced by an organization should ensure that effective and efficient core processes to deliver the desired outcomes in the most cost-effective manner are in place. In relation to operations, the desired state of an organization is the continuity of normal efficient operations with no unplanned disruption.

Organizations will have a business model that represents how they deliver the customer/beneficiary offering. Organizations that are public sector, third sector or would otherwise consider themselves to be non-commercial will still have a means of delivering their vision and/or mission statement. The means of delivering the defined customer offering is the business model of an organization. In summary, customers receive the offering from an organization because it utilizes the resources that it has available. The customer offering is underpinned by the resilience of an organization and by arrangements to ensure that an organization remains sustainable.

Figure 30.3 illustrates the components of the business model as customer, offering, resources and resilience (CORR), which can be summarized as follows:

- Customer includes analysis of customer segments, recruitment and retention, as well as how products or services will be delivered.

- Offering refers to the customer value proposition and the related benefits that are delivered to those customers.

Figure 30.3 Components of the business model

Customer	**Resources**
• Customer segments and targets • Marketing and sales activities • Customer servicing and support • Distribution routes and channels	• Data, capabilities and assets • Partnerships and networks • Organizational structure • Activities and core processes

Offering
Alignment of available resources and capabilities to deliver the intended customer value proposition and related benefits

Resilience
- People, commitment, purpose, capability, culture, leadership and governance
- Ethos, organizational activities and values, standards, ethics and reputation
- Expenditure based on development, infrastructure, sales and support costs
- Revenue streams based on sales volume, profit and cash flow requirements

- Resources include the data, capabilities and assets of an organization, as well as partnerships and networks.

- Resilience of an organization is reputational (based on ethos and culture) and financial (based on expenditure and revenue).

Having identified the business model and undertaken a risk assessment, an organization will then need to decide whether the existing business model is sustainable. All business models have to be sustainable, and this is normally represented by financial sustainability of resources and the need to balance expenditure against revenue streams. Sustainability has a wider context and has grown to include environmental considerations. For example, in order to contribute to climate change sustainability, there is scope to address the business model to make this contribution. Sustainability is considered further in Chapter 31. The scope of the sustainability requirements of an organization and its business model will need to be included in the risk assessment.

Where changes are required the enhanced business model becomes the strategy of an organization. The means by which the business model is modified to achieve the strategy can be considered to be the tactics of an organization and these tactics will be implemented by way of projects and/or programmes of work that achieve the required changes.

A component of a successful business model is recruiting of new customers and drawing them into a deeper relationship with an organization, so that the relationship is sustained and becomes more secure. Enhancements to the business model, therefore, need to not only recruit additional customers, but also retain existing customers at a constantly increasing level of customer satisfaction.

Strategy models

Organizations are beginning to make better use of enterprise risk management in their strategy-setting processes. Rather than setting strategy and asking what risks this gives rise to, they are using risk as part of strategy setting.

The COSO (2017) ERM Framework notes that strategy is 'about making choices and accepting trade-offs' and recognizes that risk management plays a key role in supporting decision making around these choices and trade-offs.

As noted in previous chapters, COSO (2017) emphasizes that this role is not just related to the execution of strategy, which is the approach taken in many organizations, but is also fundamental to the selection of that strategy. Some of the questions that boards should be asking or risks they should be considering are around the customer, offering, resources and resilience that make up the strategy.

Table 30.2   Common strategy models

Stage	Models
Design – the creation of strategic options that an organization could pursue The design phase typically arises in the following scenarios: • The startup of a new organization – depending on the size and complexity of the new organization, designing the strategy can be a very structured formal process or a more informal undertaking that evolves as the idea for a new organization takes shape • The development of a new product or service offering, or • A significant change in the internal or external context of an organization	• Ansoff model • Business model canvas • CORR (customer, offering, resources and resilience)
Validation – the testing of the strategic options an organization has identified to enable it to select the most appropriate strategy	• SWOT (strengths, weaknesses, opportunities and threats) • Porters 5 forces • PESTLE (political, economic, social, technological, legal, environmental)
Implementation – the translation of the chosen strategy into objectives and tasks	• VMOST (vision, mission, objectives, strategy and tactics) • Value chain analysis
Review and repurpose – the periodic review of existing strategies and objectives to ensure they remain fit for purpose	• The BCG Matrix • Kotter: Our Iceberg is Melting • McKinsey: 7s Model

Strategy evolves over time and its focus is different depending on the stage that an organization is at in its lifecycle. Organizations use many different management models to provide a structure for the formulation and consideration of strategy. Table 30.2 highlights commonly used strategy models that support organizations through the processes of strategy design, validation, implementation and review.

Strategy and reputation

A key focus area within strategy is how an organization deals with its reputation. Reputation is fundamentally important to organizations, and they should make sure that they understand the foundations of their reputation. Reputation is based on the size, nature and complexity of an organization, but it is useful to put more structure into what makes a good reputation. It is necessary also to assess from where an organization's reputation is being viewed.

Table 30.3 shows the components of reputation, which are also illustrated as a spidergram in Figure 30.4. The four main components of reputation (CASE) are as listed below.

An organization will offer a range of services and products, and the standards of service and service delivery will be a critical component of reputation. An organization will also have business ethics that demonstrate its integrity, illustrated, to some

Table 30.3 Components of reputation

Component	Comments
Capabilities	Does an organization have a clear purpose or resolve, together with the commitment, vision, capabilities and resources to deliver that purpose?
Activities	Which sector and what activities does an organization undertake, and does it have the financial resources and stability to support those activities?
Standards	What range of services or products does an organization offer, and what are the standards of quality, delivery, support, execution, innovation and investment?
Ethics	Does an organization adhere to appropriate sustainability, integrity, values and governance, and continuously monitor performance to learn and achieve improvements?

Figure 30.4 Mapping the components of reputation

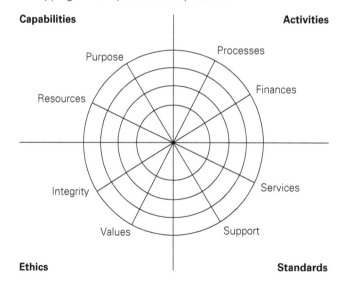

extent, by the monitoring of performance in order to learn and achieve continuous improvement in performance.

The use of a chart, such as that shown in Figure 30.4, will enable an organization to map its overall reputation, within the context of the sector in which it operates. For each of the four segments, or eight attributes, an organization should be able to plot its current status in a ranking of 1 to 4, representing poor (1), adequate (2), good (3) and excellent (4). It will then be possible for an organization to identify the areas on the map that represent the greatest threats to its reputation.

This chapter has considered the importance of reputation in general and used integrity as an example of one of the main pillars of reputation. However, reputation is a broader issue than just business ethics. Indeed, customers will often trade with an organization even though they do not believe it to have a particularly ethical business model. Although only a cursory insight and discussion of reputation has been included in this book, the overriding importance of reputation is fully acknowledged, especially in relation to risk management.

DIFFERENT PERCEPTIONS OF REPUTATION: AMAZON

The traditional view of reputation can be enhanced by the use of technology to provide more nuance around the topic. In this case study, technology has been used to identify various different groupings and their view of the reputation of Amazon.

In 2024, Amazon was ranked as the fifth largest company globally by market capitalization, the 'fourth most valuable brand' and regularly features in the top three most admired companies. Different reputation consultancies rank Amazon among the top one or two in their indices, while others, such as the Reputation Institute,[7] indicate that although Amazon's reputation is improving, it is still ranked at number 72 out of the top 100 most reputable companies.

It is becoming increasingly clear with the availability of sophisticated data analysis that 'multiple reputations' can be discerned among the various components of reputation.

How strategy influences the management of risk

The strategy adopted by an organization can influence the way that risk is managed in an organization. The strategy that an organization adopts is generally influenced by the lifecycle stage that an organization is at, as shown earlier in the book in Figure 1.3 of Chapter 1.

For example, at start-up and growth stage the strategic focus tends to be on expansion and growth. At this stage operations tend to be very lean and agile, and the management of risk is primarily situated at the front lines with minimal central support.

By contrast, at the mature stage the strategic focus has often moved to increasing margins for existing products or services and encouraging innovation to develop new offerings. At this stage organizations have typically developed more formal risk management infrastructure with a robust professional risk function in the second line of defence. Therefore, as an organization moves through the stages in its lifecycle there is an opportunity for risk management to also mature.

Risks arising from strategy

Chapter 8 introduced the simple four-step iterative process for the management of risk. An organization's strategy can be mapped to this four-step process as follows:

- Step 1 – Consider the context, strategy and objectives, and set the amount of risk that an organization is willing to seek or accept to achieve these objectives (risk appetite).
- Step 2 – Identify and assess the risks associated with the achievement of the strategy and objectives.
- Step 3 – put in place the controls and actions needed to manage these risks.
- Step 4 – monitor and review the risks and controls and report to stakeholders on the implications for the achievement of the strategy and objectives.

A review of the strategy may be required if the proposed management is not in keeping with the amount of risk an organization is willing to take (risk appetite). There are two choices in this situation: change the strategy/objectives and/or the risk appetite; or increase the level of management, for example, invest further in controls.

Figure 30.5   The board and strategic risks

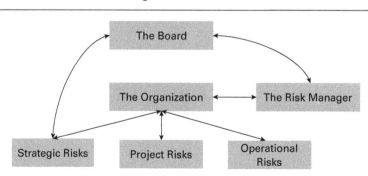

In considering how strategic risk is managed in organizations, it is important to understand that the board should own or closely oversee an organization's strategic risks. In some organizations there is a separate strategic risk register that is usually operated by the chief risk officer or similar. Figure 30.5 indicates the relationship between the board and the risk information within an organization.

The following strategic risk areas are indicative of the risks that are commonly found in strategic risk registers:

- Succession planning for CEO/key C-suite staff

- Competition risk

- Industry existential threats/evolution

- Shareholder exit arrangements

STRATEGIC QUESTIONS FOR THE BOARD

In *Practical Enterprise Risk Management*, Taylor (2014)[8] asks four key strategic questions that boards should consider in relation to the risks to the strategic plan:

1 How do we integrate ERM with an organization's strategic direction and plan?

2 What are our principal business risks both coming from the strategic plan and those that threaten/enhance that plan?

3 Are we taking the right amount of risk?

4 Do we know which risks, if managed well, will increase, or decrease the value of, or results for, our organization?

These are part of a suite of board questions that can be asked to focus discussions on whether risk management processes and frameworks are appropriate to ensure achievement of the right ERM objectives, rather than the focus being on whether the processes and framework are being followed.

Risk management tools and the development of strategy

As noted earlier, the risk management process can be effectively applied to both the selection and execution of strategy. In doing so, existing risk management tools and techniques can be applied successfully, regardless of the strategy models in place, to form an assessment on how likely it is that the various strategies being considered or employed by an organization will be successful.

Figure 30.6 Strategy versus Realization matrix

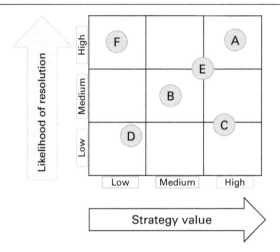

However, as with the whole risk management process, some of those tools may need to be tailored to enable understanding and evaluation of different strategies and contexts. An example of a modified risk management tool is provided in Figure 30.6, where a risk matrix has been used to illustrate the potential success of different strategies.

The matrix in Figure 30.6 creates a continuum to assist the strategy deliberations of an organization from a risk perspective. When interpreting this matrix consideration should also be given to the effort or resources required to manage the risks.

Notes

1 ISO 31073 (2022) *Risk management – Vocabulary*, https://www.iso.org/obp/ui/en/#iso:std:iso:31073:ed-1:v1:en (archived at https://perma.cc/TLD2-B853)

2 COSO (2017) *Enterprise Risk Management: Integrating with Strategy and Performance – Executive Summary*, https://www.coso.org/_files/ugd/3059fc_61ea5985 b03c4293960642fdce408eaa.pdf (archived at https://perma.cc/5AZY-K6JP)

3 Bolman, L (2021) *Reframing Organizations: Artistry, choice and leadership*, 7th Ed., John Wiley & Sons, New Jersey, USA

4 Carroll, L (1865) *Alice's Adventures in Wonderland*, Macmillan & Co. Ltd, London, UK

5 Covey, S and Covey, SR (2020) *The 7 Habits of Highly Effective People: Revised and Updated*, Simon & Shuster, London, UK

6 FRC (2023) *Guidance on the Strategic Report*, https://www.frc.org.uk/library/standards-codes-policy/accounting-and-reporting/annual-corporate-reporting/guidance-on-the-strategic-report/ (archived at https://perma.cc/9JSK-QHAC)

7 RepTrak (2024) *Global RepTrak 100 – 2024*, https://www.reptrak.com/globalreptrak/#2 zzmhhdAPWprMriaiKHNlc (archived at https://perma.cc/R932-MXSV)

8 Taylor, L (2014) *Practical Enterprise Risk Management: How to optimize business strategies through managed risk taking*, Kogan Page, London, UK

Resilience and risk management

Disruptors

Recent years have seen a marked increase in disruptive events, defined by ISO 22300(2021)[1] as an 'occurrence or change that interrupts planned activities, operations or functions, whether anticipated or unanticipated'. Examples of disruptive events include natural disasters, cyber-attacks, new technologies such as AI and climate change.

Not only are these events more frequent, but they are also increasing in scale and complexity. This is evident from the Covid-19 pandemic. The unprecedented disruption to economies, health care systems, organizations and individuals tested the ability of organizations to both withstand sudden shocks and to adjust organizational priorities to best manage a changed environment. It revealed gaps and shortcomings in the capability of organizations to cope with uncertainty. In the 2024 World Economic Forum Global Risk Report[2] respondents were asked to characterize their outlook for the world over the next 10 years across five categories from calm to stormy. There were 63 per cent of respondents who felt the global outlook is stormy or turbulent.

Organizational resilience

Resilience as a concept evolved from information technology around the 1990s, expanding into business continuity in the mid-2000s. In the US, the International Consortium for Organizational Resilience was founded in 2006. The British Standards Institute issued its *Guidance on Organizational Resilience* in 2014 and the International Standards Organization created its standard, ISO 22316, in 2017. There is a clear trend here to ensure organizations are fit to withstand future shocks. ISO 22316 (2017)[3] defines organizational resilience as 'the ability of an organization to absorb and adapt in a changing environment to enable it to deliver its objectives and to survive and prosper.'

Organizational resilience, ERM and business continuity

As noted in Chapter 19, loss control considers how to prevent threats (loss control), how to reduce the size of the threat as it materializes (damage limitation) and how to limit the overall consequences of the threat once it has occurred (cost containment). However, resilient organizations are characterized by their ability to anticipate, resist, recover and adapt to both threats and opportunities stemming from sudden or gradual changes in their environment. ERM and business continuity management (BCM) have a pivotal role to play in the achievement of organizational resilience.

The IRM (2021)[4] paper on organizational resilience considers resilience to be a combination of proactive ERM processes and BCM focused on maintaining continuity of operations if faced with disruption. It goes beyond BCM by its focus on the long-term viability of an organization and so could be said to have two legs, operational and strategic, which are discrete but connected.

Business continuity is event oriented, whereas ERM focuses on the enterprise as a whole, but they both have roots in being preventive, that is, trying to stop threats from occurring. They also both have proactive and reactive components. In other words, they are both about managing the causes and consequences of threats. ERM processes determine when proactive or reactive resilience measures should be implemented through defining the significance of the risks. By applying risk analysis and evaluation techniques an organization should be able to prioritize actions within commonly understood concepts of risk appetite and tolerance.

Agility and ERM

Agility in an organizational context is defined by the COSO (2022)[5] paper on the matter as the ability of an organization to mobilize its 'processes, people and technology to anticipate, see, understand and respond to a dynamic fast-changing world.' At a strategic level, choosing to invest in agility when operating in markets or geographies with very high uncertainty could mean that an organization is best placed to avoid threats and exploit opportunities where anticipating change in advance is difficult.

The adoption of agile practices, such as cross-divisional empowered teams collaborating with external partners to problem solve, enables an organization to move much more quickly. This increased speed of operation puts more pressure on the ERM systems to function efficiently. In an organization where pivoting, adapting and accelerating are prioritized it is not sufficient to have an ERM process that operates on an annual cycle. Operating at speed creates risk at all levels in an organization and requires an ongoing, adaptive and responsive risk management and internal control framework to ensure that an organization can take and accept risks as safely as possible.

Testing tools

It is important that an organization is aware of its level of resilience prior to a disruptive event. A key element of this level will be the effectiveness of an organization's BCM processes, which are considered in the next chapter. There are a number of other resilience testing and monitoring tools that can be utilized, including:

- Emerging risks
- Horizon scanning
- Resilience indicators
- Scenario analysis
- Stress testing.

Emerging risks

A key aspect of resilience is an organization's ability to anticipate risks. Resilient organizations seek to develop good early warning mechanisms or indicators that can signal when there is a change in the internal or external context that could impact an organization. Emerging risks have been considered in Chapter 13, as those risks that are new, or a familiar risk in a new or unfamiliar context or under a new context. If potential emerging risks can be identified as early as possible this gives an organization more time to assess these risks and to put preventative and recovery mechanisms in place.

According to ISO/ TS 31050 (2023),[6] emerging risks are defined by their novelty, by limited data, and not enough verifiable information and knowledge to enable informed decision making. The term emerging risk covers a broad spectrum and includes risks that an organization has not experienced before, and risks that an organization may be aware of, but which are quickly evolving or are developing in a different context where existing knowledge is no longer relevant.

Figure 31.1 Risk radar

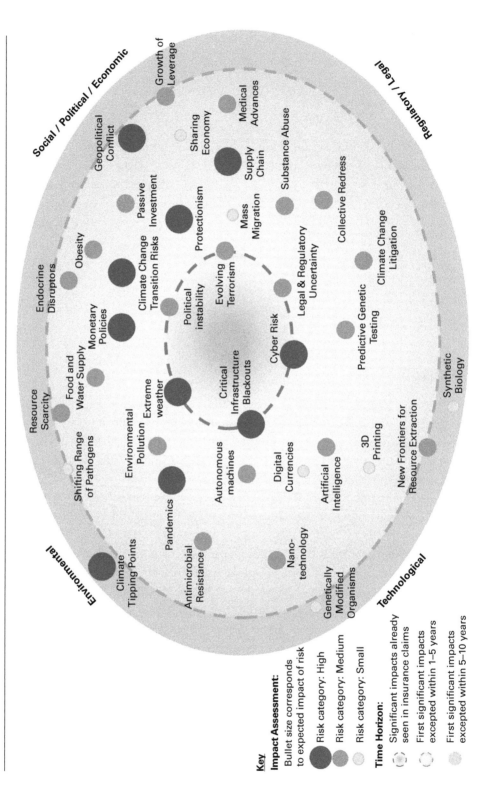

Key

Impact Assessment:
Bullet size corresponds
to expected impact of risk

Risk category: High

Risk category: Medium

Risk category: Small

Time Horizon:

Significant impacts already
seen in insurance claims

First significant impacts
excepted within 1–5 years

First significant impacts
excepted within 5–10 years

Horizon scanning

As noted in Chapter 10, the IRM (2018)[7] has published a practitioner's guide to horizon scanning, advising organizations to consider multiple sources of information and time horizons. Horizon scanning is defined as 'a systematic method for spotting potential causes of uncertainty, ensuring adequate preparation, exploiting opportunities and surviving threats.'

Continuous scanning of the internal and external context aids in detecting minor changes in data, circumstances and behaviours, as well as the intervals between these changes and their potential impact on an organization and its goals. Identifying subtle changes in context and the rate of observed change during systematic reviews (the monitoring and review phase of the ERM process) can provide early warnings or indicators of potential emerging risks, whether they pose threats or opportunities to organizational objectives.

The IRM's practitioner's guide to horizon scanning also shows how horizon scanning information can be presented using a risk radar, as illustrated in Figure 31.1.

Resilience indicators

It is important for an organization to monitor its level of resilience capability. ISO 31050 notes that this can be done using indicators. Unsurprisingly, it is easier to identify and monitor lagging indicators by tracking how an organization has reacted to changes in context in the past. This can be benchmarked against how other organizations responded and adapted to the same change.

Leading indicators of resilience can be focused on the level of preparedness and the capabilities present in an organization to anticipate and manage changes and shocks. This means monitoring the implementation and testing of the emerging risk process, BCM process and scenario analysis exercises. An organization can also monitor staff training and skill building in areas that build resilience capabilities. Key risk indicators may be useful in understanding resilience, and were considered in Chapter 20.

Scenario analysis

To achieve resilience there needs to be a focus on the future and an understanding of how an organization might become vulnerable to future trends. This involves scenario planning, introduced in Chapter 10, which is an important component of business continuity and has broader implications for the successful implementation of enterprise risk management. For financial institutions, scenario planning extends to evaluation of the balance sheet capital that would be required by the financial institution in the event of disturbances in the economy and is usually referred to as 'stress testing'. Stress testing usually considers one variable, whereas scenario analysis usually considers a number of variables.

Organizations in all sectors are also using scenario analysis to understand changes in context related to climate change, in addition to the use of the tool to understand changes in relation to other sustainability requirements. As noted in Chapter 10, scenario analysis can be used to consider how the future might turn out, by building imaginary, but credible future situations, which can be utilized by any organization in any sector.

Scenario planning needs to take account of the external and internal context of an organization, as well as the business impact analysis. It requires input from all parts of an organization. This can cause tension among competing elements or divisions and requires clear and robust governance structures to maintain focus and ensure the process pays off.

There is a strong relationship between scenario planning and crisis management. Disaster recovery planning and business continuity planning can take account of foreseeable incidents, but it is more difficult to foresee every crisis that might arise. Therefore, a useful aspect of scenario planning is that it anticipates highly unlikely circumstances and then challenges senior management to develop successful responses.

The lessons from scenario planning can then be used to take actions that will increase the resilience of an organization. The next box describes an approach to scenario planning supported by the Cabinet Office of the UK government, in relation to disruption of national infrastructure, such as the electricity supply network.

REASONABLE WORST-CASE SCENARIOS

Event standards can be established to set a level of resilience against an extreme event so that the network or system should be able to continue to operate without widespread loss or disruption to the essential services. Describing reasonable worst-case scenarios for hazards will enable infrastructure owners and operators to identify and assess their resilience and consider any gaps in resilience of an asset or network between the event and the actual or current design and service standards.

The ability and capability to manage and respond to events greater than these reasonable worst-case scenarios is dependent upon their generic organizational resilience. Alongside this, infrastructure owners should consider, in their business continuity plans, the speed with which they expect to be able to restore services in the event of supply being disrupted for whatever reason, including events that are not specifically itemized, or which are more serious or extreme than those covered in the reasonable worst-case scenarios.

SOURCE Cabinet Office (2020) Guidance: National Resilience Standards for Local Resilience Forums (LRFs), www.gov.uk/government/publications/national-resilience-standards-for-local-resilience-forums-lrfs

Stress testing

As noted earlier, stress testing is usually connected to the financial sector, where financial institutions are required to assess their ability to meet capital and liquidity requirements in stressed conditions. In other words, checking the financial health of an organization to determine whether it can cope in the event of disruptions. The focus on stress testing gained momentum following the 2008 global financial crisis, when organizations in the financial sector lost vast sums of money, leading to company failures and governmental bailouts.

Similar to scenario analyses, stress testing considers plausible worst-case scenarios, which will help determine the amount an organization will need as a financial reserve to cover for the risks identified. This financial reserve is considered further in Chapter 36.

Stress testing is not just the preserve of financial institutions and financial contingencies but is being used by different organizations for different reasons. For example, stress tests are used to the robustness of materials or systems through constant use. All are relevant dependent on the context and activities of an organization to understand risks, their controls and the resilience of an organization, or parts of it.

Long-term viability

In finance and audit there is a long-standing concept of going concern that is intended to provide assurance to stakeholders and investors that an organization is financially stable enough to meet its obligations and continue to operate for 12 months from the date that the annual financial statements are signed.

Despite the assurance of going concern, organizations continue to fail without warning and in 2014 the UK's financial reporting council (FRC) introduced a new requirement that directors of companies must include in their annual report an assessment of their organization's longer-term viability taking into account the key risks of an organization, as discussed in Chapter 29.

This requirement introduces an element of risk assurance for stakeholders when dealing with an organization. While the FRC's directives apply to larger listed organizations in the UK this linking of viability over longer time periods and risk management can also be seen in the ISO Guidance on Governance of organizations (ISO 37000)[8] which was published in 2021.

ISO 37000 – GUIDANCE ON GOVERNANCE OF ORGANIZATIONS

Paragraph 6.11.3.4 of ISO 37000 considers the governance for organizational viability over time:

The governing body should ensure that an organization protects and restores those systems on which it depends. In this regard, the governing body should consider and manage risk associated with those decisions it makes that can impact the natural environmental, social and economic systems (see 6.9). While doing so, the governing body should ensure that relevant stakeholders are consulted and engaged (see 6.6). This should provide clarity regarding the impact the governing body's decisions have, over time, on those aspects on which an organization is:

- directly dependent;
- not directly dependent but whose ability to be sustained will be affected by the governing body's decisions.

Embedding organizational resilience into governance mechanisms should ensure that the management of the risks posed by disruptive events is considered by the board. The needs of organizational resilience would thereby inform strategic investment and procurement decisions, risk management and discussions with supply chain partners.

It would enable infrastructure owners and operators to improve their understanding of the resilience of their infrastructure, measure the success of the strategy at regular intervals, and make necessary amendments to secure delivery or to match changing organizational priorities.

Notes

1 ISO (2021) *ISO 22300 – Security and Resilience – Vocabulary*, https://www.iso.org/obp/ui/#iso:std:iso:22300:ed-3:v1:en (archived at https://perma.cc/KUZ3-VEQF)

2 World Economic Forum (2024) *Global Risk Report 2024*, 19th Ed., https://www.weforum.org/publications/global-risks-report-2024/ (archived at https://perma.cc/2NZS-8AE9)

3 ISO (2016) *ISO 22316 – Security and resilience — Organizational resilience — Principles and attributes*, https://www.iso.org/obp/ui/#iso:std:iso:22316:ed-1:v1:en (archived at https://perma.cc/PF94-KECL)

4 IRM (2021) *Organisational Resilience: A risk manager's guide*, https://issuu.com/irmglobal/docs/organisational_resilience_-_a_risk_manager_s_guide (archived at https://perma.cc/4XSE-DQZ7)

5 COSO (2022) *Enabling Organizational Agility in an Age of Speed and Disruption*, https://www.coso.org/_files/ugd/3059fc_cef1343e024a43c0b65d23ad0178d41e.pdf (archived at https://perma.cc/6EX8-S7XJ)

6 ISO (2023) *ISO/ TS 31050 Guidelines for managing an emerging risk to enhance resilience*, https://www.iso.org/obp/ui/#iso:std:iso:ts:31050:ed-1:v1:en (archived at https://perma.cc/8JXL-8NGB)

7 IRM (2018) *Horizon Scanning: A Practitioners Guide*, https://www.theirm.org/media/7340/horizon-scanning_final2.pdf (archived at https://perma.cc/QKJ7-5VS9)

8 ISO (2021) *ISO 37000 – Governance of organizations — Guidance*, https://www.iso.org/obp/ui/#iso:std:iso:37000:ed-1:v1:en (archived at https://perma.cc/65YM-AEAF)

Surviving shocks and disruption   32

ERM, BCM and resilience

Business continuity management (BCM) is an integral part of resilience and risk management. In simple terms, BCM is how an organization prepares for future incidents that could disrupt operations and jeopardize its existence. The range of incidents that should be covered will include everything from local events like fires through to regional disorder and global events such as earthquakes, terrorism and pandemics.

The international standard for BCM is ISO 22301 (2019),[1] which defines BCM as the 'capability of an organization to continue the delivery of products and services within acceptable time frames at predefined capacity during a disruption'. This standard also describes a plan-do-check-act (PDCA) approach that is similar to the plan, implement, measure and learn (PIML) approach used throughout this book and described in detail in Chapter 9.

Business continuity management (BCM)

As with loss control, considered in Chapter 19, many organizations see BCM as having three components:

1 Business continuity planning – The creation of business continuity, crisis management and disaster recovery plans and procedures. Ensuring that these plans are tested frequently and that all staff are familiar with what is required of them.

2 Crisis management – Implementation of crisis management procedures to contain the crisis and ensure the appropriate responses are taken while fully engaging stakeholders to avoid/reduce damage to reputation.

3 Disaster recovery – Execution of recovery measures to ensure operations continue as before, or better than before (if possible).

Business continuity planning (BCP)

ISO 22301 identifies a business continuity planning lifecycle that has the following five components related to the business continuity management system:

- Identify crucial risk factors already affecting an organization.
- Understand the needs and obligations of an organization.
- Establish, implement and maintain the organization's business continuity management system.
- Measure the overall capability to manage disruptive incidents.
- Guarantee conformity with stated business continuity policy.

Figure 32.1 provides a model for BCP that is consistent with ISO 22301, in: understanding an organization and the business impact from disruption; determining appropriate BCM strategies; developing appropriate responses; establishing an appropriate BCM culture; and testing and implementing improvements.

Figure 32.1   Model for business continuity planning

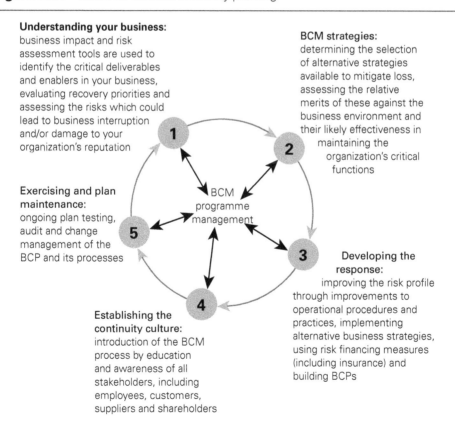

Understanding your business: business impact and risk assessment tools are used to identify the critical deliverables and enablers in your business, evaluating recovery priorities and assessing the risks which could lead to business interruption and/or damage to your organization's reputation

BCM strategies: determining the selection of alternative strategies available to mitigate loss, assessing the relative merits of these against the business environment and their likely effectiveness in maintaining the organization's critical functions

Exercising and plan maintenance: ongoing plan testing, audit and change management of the BCP and its processes

BCM programme management

Developing the response: improving the risk profile through improvements to operational procedures and practices, implementing alternative business strategies, using risk financing measures (including insurance) and building BCPs

Establishing the continuity culture: introduction of the BCM process by education and awareness of all stakeholders, including employees, customers, suppliers and shareholders

Table 32.1   Key activities in business continuity planning

1	Assess company activities to identify critical staff, materials, procedures and equipment required to keep the business operating.
2	Identify suppliers, shippers, resources and other businesses that are contacted on a daily basis.
3	Plan what to do if any important buildings, plant or store were to become inaccessible.
4	Identify necessary actions to ensure continuity of critical business functions, especially payroll.
5	Decide who should participate in compiling and subsequently testing the emergency plans.
6	Define crisis management procedures and individual responsibilities for disaster recovery activities.
7	Co-ordinate with others, including neighbours, utility suppliers, suppliers, shippers and key customers.
8	Review the emergency plans annually and when the business changes and/or new members of staff are recruited.

Table 32.1 provides a checklist of the key activities involved in BCP. Having business continuity plans is recognized as essential by most large organizations. Indeed, many governments take an active role in encouraging businesses (especially small businesses) to develop and implement adequate business continuity plans.

Business impact analysis

A critical part of ensuring that adequate business continuity plans are in place is completion of a business impact analysis (BIA). The BIA will identify the critical nature of each business function by assessment of the impact of interruption to that activity. This information will be required in order to identify appropriate continuity strategies for each function.

The BIA is similar to both the understanding of an organization's context and risk assessment that is undertaken as part of the overall risk management process. However, the critical difference from risk assessment is that the emphasis of a BIA is the identification of the relative importance and criticality of each function, rather than just understanding the context or identifying the events that could undermine that particular function.

Therefore, risk assessment and the BIA are related and could well be undertaken together as suggested in Chapter 10 in relation to the Extended Enterprise tool. Risk assessment will help in identifying the risks that might threaten the achievement of the business continuity objectives. For a television company for example, broadcasting continuity is the target and may even be a requirement imposed by the licensing authority. Both risk assessment and BIA require a structured and systematic approach.

The business impact analysis has three clear purposes, as follows:

1 Identify mission-critical activities and the required recovery time in the event of disruption. This identification activity will establish the time frame within which the critical functions must be resumed after the disruptive event.

2 Establish the impact potential and the resource requirements for recovery within the agreed timescale. The business requirements for recovery of the critical function must be established.

3 Determine whether the likely impact is within the risk appetite of an organization as the basis for business continuity strategy. The technical requirements for recovery of the critical function also need to be established.

Once the sources of disruption that face the operations of an organization are identified, undertaking a BIA will become simpler. The focus of a business impact analysis, however, is likely to be on processes within an organization and how these may be disrupted. This is especially relevant as continuity of business processes safeguards the interests of key stakeholders, reputation, brand and value-creating activities.

Crisis management and disaster recovery

Figure 32.2 provides a practical example of crisis management and disaster recovery and seeks to illustrate a crisis management and disaster recovery timeline and costs. This example is based on a broadcasting organization that suffers a major disruption at its main broadcasting facility at point A on the timeline. The business continuity plan and procedures will ensure that broadcasting resumes within a short space of time, but this may only be an emergency broadcast. The emergency broadcast starts from point B on the timeline. Note Figure 32.2 does not include the cost of repairing or restoring the facility that has been damaged.

After a short period of emergency broadcasts, an organization will be able to commence full broadcasting of its normal service from an alternative location. For example, the broadcaster may move the London broadcast facilities to studios in Manchester. In order to do this, however, the Manchester capability will be lost. Therefore, Figure 32.2 shows that the level of service is much improved at point C, which is the move to Manchester, but because the Manchester broadcast facility has been lost, the level of service is not up to the previous level.

There will be an increased cost of operation from the time of the incident. There will be a cost associated with implementing the disaster recovery plan and further

Figure 32.2   Disaster recovery timeline and costs

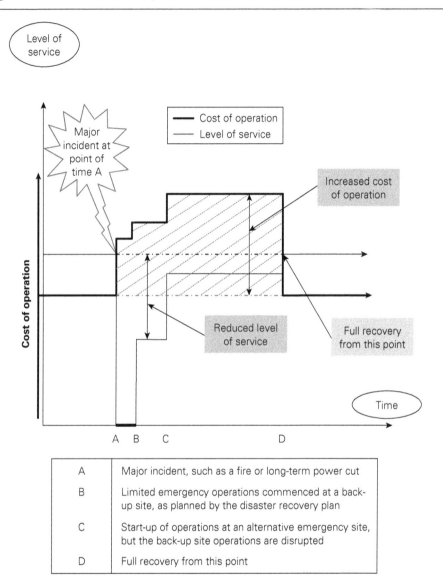

A	Major incident, such as a fire or long-term power cut
B	Limited emergency operations commenced at a back-up site, as planned by the disaster recovery plan
C	Start-up of operations at an alternative emergency site, but the back-up site operations are disrupted
D	Full recovery from this point

costs associated with emergency broadcasting and then the move to Manchester. During the period of broadcasting from Manchester, increased costs will be involved by way of temporary accommodation for staff and increased technical facilities. Eventually, from point D on the timeline, the facilities in London have been repaired and full recovery has been achieved.

Figure 32.2 represents a typical set of circumstances for an organization that suffers a major incident. The impaired level of service will continue for some time and increased cost of operation will be involved. Insurance may be available for the increased cost of operation, provided that it does not exceed the indemnity period (duration of the disruption) quoted in the insurance policy. It is unlikely that insurance cover will be available to cover any losses associated with a reduced level of service from the time the incident occurs until the point of full recovery, unless specific types of costs or losses are identified and insured.

Every time an incident occurs that requires the BCM plan to be used an organization should ensure that a lessons learnt exercise takes place. Depending on the severity of the incident this could be a workshop or a more detailed investigation. The BCM plan should then be updated to incorporate the lessons learnt.

Business continuity and risk management

Determining a BCM strategy will require the identification of risks to the business and decisions about how likely it is that the risks will materialize. It is also necessary to understand the impact of risks on the business. These assessments should then be used to prioritize treatment of the risks and to agree the likelihood and impact of the risks materializing.

Developing and implementing a BCM plan and appropriate controls for each of the identified risks will require decisions on the appropriate risk responses, considered in Chapters 18 and 19.

It is important to note that the implementation of the BCP is likely to have secondary impacts on an organization. For example, if the time and attention of senior leaders is consumed by managing an ongoing crisis it is likely that the quality of business-as-usual management may suffer. ERM can be used to explore the potential unintended consequences of invoking BCM processes.

Successful business continuity management

To ensure that implementation is successful BCM needs to be:

- comprehensive;
- cost-effective;
- practical;
- effective;
- maintained;
- practised.

In addition, it is necessary to build and embed a business continuity management culture in an organization. All stakeholders will need to be engaged and involved in the business continuity activities and will need to understand the reasons for the development of the BCM plan. The important role of all employees in the avoidance of incidents that could result in major disruption should be emphasized.

It is important that BCM should cover all the operations and premises of the organization to ensure that the plans and procedures can facilitate a complete resumption of normal business operations. It is also important that the BCM is cost-effective and proportionate to the risk exposures.

The BCPs must be practical and easily understood by staff and others who are involved in the execution of the plan. Overall, BCM must be effective in that it will recognize the urgency of certain business components or functions and identify responsibilities for ensuring timely resumption of normal work.

In order to guarantee that BCM will be effective, it needs to be tested, maintained and practised. All members of staff need to be familiar with the intended operation of the BCPs and training will need to be provided. The lessons learnt during testing and practice of the BCP should be incorporated into the plan so that it becomes more effective.

Testing BCPs is an essential component of ensuring that they will be appropriate and effective. Testing plans can be time-consuming and, in some circumstances, disruptive and costly. However, given the increasing uncertainty in the world around us, it may be more damaging for an organization to have ineffective BCM measures.

CIVIL EMERGENCIES

In many countries, there is an obligation placed on local government to ensure the continuity of local businesses in the event of a major civil emergency. The emergency may be triggered by a natural disaster such as flooding or an earthquake. Alternatively, it could be caused by terrorism, civil unrest or, as we have seen, by a pandemic. The ISO 22300 series of standards relate to societal resilience and the increasing importance of this series of standards is also considered in Chapter 31.

Many civil authorities publish guidance for businesses to assist them with their BCM. For example, the US government provides valuable information on its Federal Emergency Management Agency (FEMA) website.[2] Also, several trade associations and small business associations offer practical guidance on BCM, including appropriate actions in the case of civil emergency.

Most local authorities have statutory responsibility for responding to civil emergencies. Factories and warehouses may have equipment and facilities that could be useful in the event of a civil emergency. Likewise, retail shops will have food and other goods that may be required for distribution as emergency supplies.

The products that may be useful in a civil emergency will include food, bottled water, clothing and blankets. Also, schools and other civic buildings may be required as accommodation in the event of a civil emergency, such as the wide area floods that have become more frequent in several European countries.

Encouraging organizations to make arrangements to ensure business continuity will benefit local authorities in charge of civil emergencies, because there will be fewer problems and issues for them to take into account at the time of the emergency.

As noted earlier, business continuity and risk management have overlapping activities and can use similar techniques, but the focus for both will be slightly different.

Notes

1 ISO (2019) ISO 22301 – Security and resilience — Business continuity management systems — Requirements, https://www.iso.org/obp/ui/#iso:pub:PUB100442 (archived at https://perma.cc/DV9U-K8J3)

2 FEMA (2024) Continuity Policy, Doctrine and Guidance, https://www.fema.gov/emergency-managers/national-preparedness/continuity/documents#:~:text=The%20purpose%20of%20a%20continuity,the%20threat%20or%20hazard%20faced (archived at https://perma.cc/WR8Y-Q2GB)

Sustainability and risk management 33

Optimizing the balance of the world in which we live has allowed humans to thrive on our fragile planet. This optimization has required an inbuilt drive to experiment and take risks, but at the same time, an understanding of what may break the system, and therefore the risk tolerance should be tested. The discipline of sustainability focuses on the ability to preserve the balance of nature and people, while acknowledging that the context in which they reside changes constantly. The manner in which ongoing sustainability can be achieved therefore requires significant risk taking and optimization, with rapid feedback loops and openness to acknowledge and respond to failures, as well as celebrate successes.

This chapter will explore what sustainability truly is, different forms of governance that are being constructed to ensure it becomes a core part of all organizations, and the role of risk management to ensure that sustainability becomes a reality rather than a box-ticking exercise.

What is sustainability?

Sustainability as a term means different things to different people. To some it is synonymous with resilience and refers to the long-term viability of an organization. To others it is linked solely to the environment, and the sustaining of all its components. Here the alignment will be with the broader definition of sustainability, where it refers to the long-term balancing and optimization of people, the planet and prosperity of all components where possible. Different definitions relating to sustainability are provided in Table 33.1.

Evolution of sustainability

The Brundtland Commission (1987) defined sustainable development as being that which 'meets the needs of the present without compromising the ability of future generations to meet their own needs'. Three areas of focus were identified as being required to fulfil these needs:

- Environmental components – including the need for robust biodiversity, clean air and water, and acknowledgement of the carrying capacity of the planet.

Table 33.1 Definitions relating to sustainability

Term	Definition
Sustainable development[1]	'Development that meets the needs of the present without compromising the ability of future generations to meet their own needs'.
Sustainability[2]	'Sustainability integrates natural systems with human patterns and celebrates continuity, uniqueness and placemaking'.
ESG[3]	ESG stands for environmental, social and governance and refers to a set of standards used to measure an organization's environmental and social impact.
CSR[4]	Corporate social responsibility is a self-regulating business model built on the belief that businesses should act in a way that benefits the well-being of society and the environment.
	ISO 26000 is seen as a widely adopted CSR set of standards, describing itself as guidance to those who recognize that respect for society and environment is a critical success factor. It explicitly links CSR with sustainable development, by defining it as 'the responsibility of an organization for the impacts of its activities on society and environment, through transparent and ethical behavior that contributes to sustainable development [...]'.
Triple Bottom Line[5]	The idea that companies should focus on social and environmental concerns as much as they do on profit. The term was coined in 1994 by corporate responsibility strategist John Elkington.
Impact vs. Outcomes[6]	**Outcomes**: The likely or achieved short-term and medium-term change and effects of intervention outputs.
	Impact: Positive and negative, primary and secondary, long-term effects produced by development interventions.
	Impacts are often the cumulative long-term effect of an outcome or number of outcomes.
Resilience[7]	Resilience is a growing term and can be defined in several ways. Generally, the concept describes a system's ability to 'bounce back' in response to external factors/disruptions/changed circumstances.
Greenwashing[8]	Greenwashing is making misleading claims about the environmental (and/or social) impacts or benefits of products and services to create a false sense of sustainability.

- Social components – including the need for equity, participation, empowerment of all people, social mobility and cultural preservation.

- Economic components – including the responsible distribution and use of resources, industrial growth, meeting of household needs and efficient use of labour.

This structure also provided the grounding for what became known as the 'triple bottom line' of people, planet and profit/prosperity (PPP) established by Elkington, which has been built on by many individuals and organizations, seeking to measure and manage value through more than just financial mechanisms.

A focus on human rights forms the core of significant bodies of work in this area, including the United Nations Millenium Goals, launched in 2000. This greatly influenced the concept of corporate social responsibility (CSR) which began to emerge in the late 1990s. CSR provided the mechanism through which organizations began to formally measure and manage their potential impact on both their own employees, as well as any other stakeholder group who may be impacted positively or negatively by the organization's activities. This evolved into being known as an organization's licence to operate, with various alternatives being used within different sectors and geographies.

In the early 2000s, carbon markets began to take form. Driven by the scientific understanding that elevated concentrations of greenhouse gases (GHGs) were causing the earth to warm beyond its natural levels, the solution identified was to reduce the volume of GHGs in the atmosphere through reduction in emissions and removal through capture and storage (sequestration). The enhanced management of gases such as carbon dioxide and methane through the optimized management of peat bogs, soils and trees, began to take shape, and as of 2023, the World Bank estimated that the carbon market could be valued at 104 billion USD.

In 2015, the United Nations launched their sustainable development goals (SDG).[9] Consisting of 17 ambitious goals, and supported by thousands of underpinning targets and measurements, these goals have driven significant focus into key areas such as the eradication of poverty, gender equality and climate action.

The scope and importance of sustainability components such as those outlined by the Brundtland Commission, the triple bottom line, CSR through to the UN SDGs, has led to their most recent packaging, in the form of environment, social and governance, or ESG, as illustrated in Figure 33.1. ESG takes on different meanings for different people. For some it is the mechanism through which the status of sustainability can be measured. For others it is synonymous with a new form of commercial enterprise that seeks to capitalize on our desire to be more sustainable. No matter what the interpretation, the underpinning theory of ESG still stands, with the environment and social components being updated forms of that which was explored in the 1980s through the Brundtland Commission, and the governance providing the accountability, culture and trust to hold it all together and ensure that positive impact is created through ESG initiatives.

Figure 33.1   ESG components with example aspects

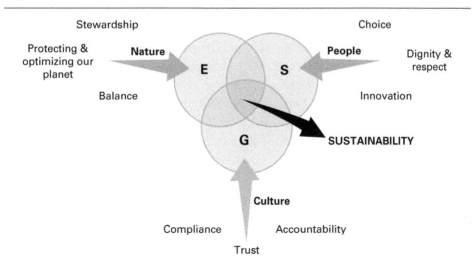

SOURCE SATARLA (2022).[10] Used with permission

Table 33.2   European Sustainability Reporting Standards

Cross-cutting	ESRS 1 – General requirements ESRS 2 – General disclosures
Environmental	ESRS E1 – Climate change ESRS E2 – Pollution ESRS E3 – Water and marine resources ESRS E4 – Biodiversity and ecosystems ESRS E5 – Resource use and circular economy
Social	ESRS S1 – Own workforce ESRS S2 – Workers in the value chain ESRS S3 – Affected communities ESRS S4 – Consumers and end-users
Governance	ESRS G1 – Business conduct

Regulation and legislation are now catching up to the ambitions of the 1980s to 2020. Driven by the ticking clock, that is the speed with which our climate is changing, climate-focused government and industry-level requirements are now mandatory in many jurisdictions, which is explored in Chapter 34. Consolidation and alignment of many of the international sustainability standards and guidance providers has led to the International Sustainability Standards Board (ISSB) releasing its clear expectations regarding climate change metrics and targets that should be established by a company. The European Union has taken it a step further, including a full array of sustainability key areas of interest in its requirements for companies wishing to operate in or trade with the EU. In 2023, the Corporate Sustainability Reporting Directive (CSRD) came into force, bringing in a new ESG reporting regulation.[11]

Forming part of the EU Green Deal,[12] the CSRD is the next evolution of the Non-Financial Reporting Directive (NFRD) and ensures companies that fall under the remit of the CSRD report sustainability risks and opportunities in line with the European Sustainability Reporting Standards (ESRS),[13] which are highlighted in Table 33.2. The ESRS framework also takes into consideration guidelines from the ISSB and the Global Reporting Initiative (GRI) to ensure alignment between the EU and global standards. These new guidelines and reporting standards allow for greater transparency and assessment of a company's efforts in identifying challenges and opportunities arising from sustainability risks.

Guidance, regulation, legislation, and expectations placed on organizations by customers and suppliers will continue to evolve. In all cases, risk management is key, be it to support an organization to identify which areas are most material to them, through to using risk management to help scenario plan which controls may provide the most valuable support in the future.

Ethics and risk tolerance

Sustainability is nothing new. The ability to recognize where societies may be negatively impacting aspects of the environment, or groups of people, and then do something about it, may be difficult, but it has been achieved multiple times.

For example, in the 1980s, sulphuric acid falling as acid rain down-wind of industrial facilities was common in all industrialized regions of the world. This was recognized as a problem, and research was undertaken to understand how and why the acid was forming, resulting in chimneys being fitted with scrubbers to remove the sulphur dioxide before it was emitted from industrial sites, removing its potential to mix with water to form acid rain.

Similarly, in the 1980s and 1990s the hole in the ozone layer grew progressively year by year over Antarctica. Again, research was undertaken, resulting in the understanding that chlorofluorocarbons (CFCs) were to blame. Decades later, and with the banning of CFCs, it has been observed that the ozone layer is recovering.

There are many other examples; however, in each case, something had to go very recognizably wrong before concrete action was taken. In other words, the risk tolerance had to be breached for enough countries, organizations and individuals, for action to be taken.

In some cases, knowledge is not available about the damage that is being done. In other cases, a potential threat may be recognized, but is not actively acknowledged, nor is there action taken to proactively manage it, as illustrated in the Rio Tinto case study in Chapter 11.

Unfortunately, in some cases, there is active use of sustainability and ESG to drive greenwashing.

DEUTSCHE BANK

In 2023, Deutsche Bank was accused of fraud for overstating the sustainability credentials of their investment products. The bank marketed certain products as being leading in ESG; however, they were accused of not implementing certain policies as they were sold to investors. The US Securities and Exchange Commission (SEC) fined the bank 25 million USD for the 'greenwashing' that had been carried out, building on a precedent it had set in 2022 when it fined Goldman Sachs and BNY Mellon with fines for similar indiscretions.[14]

The role of risk management in sustainability

Sustainability includes many uncertainties, from areas of science about which there is little understanding, through to perceptions of different cultures that have not yet been acknowledged. In fact, many sustainability risks can be categorized as 'emerging'.

Many of these uncertainties compete and conflict with one another, often on different timescales or across different time horizons, as highlighted in Figure 14.1. What might be a threat to one individual or organization may be an opportunity to another. This can be seen in Figure 38.1, which provides an example network of illustrative themes of sustainability risk, showing the positive and negative aspects, and how they impact one another.

The first step is to understand the context in which an organization is working, focusing on the large-scale system in which it sits. Then, within that system, to work out what are the 'sustainability superpowers' that an organization can bring to the system in order to optimize it. While the ultimate goal is to solve all of the problems outlined in the UN SDGs, in reality, organizations can probably make a significant difference to only a handful of them. The second step is therefore to understand where the potential threats or opportunities are that organizations have the potential of addressing within the broader system. Step three is to take action, while step four is the ongoing monitoring, reviewing and communication to ascertain if what is being done is making a difference. This in itself is just risk management, as outlined by the four-step model illustrated in Figure 8.1.

There is one vital difference between this interpretation of the risk management process, and how it is often used, and that is the direction of impact. Rather than the traditional view of how the external world may impact on an organization, sustainability also requires organizations to acknowledge how they may impact the world around them. This is one of the interpretations of double materiality. The other interpretation refers to the inclusion of both the potential financial impact of a risk or an issue when compared to the 'sustainability' impact of a risk or issue.

Figure 33.2 Double materiality

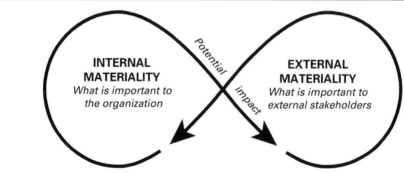

INTERNAL
MATERIALITY
*What is important to
the organization*

EXTERNAL
MATERIALITY
*What is important to
external stakeholders*

Potential

impact

SOURCE SATARLA (2022). Used with permission.

Double materiality assessment: two interpretations

A material item of knowledge is that which would influence a stakeholder's opinion or decision regarding an organization, such as whether to invest in or gain employment with that organization. Materiality assessments are a common requirement in sustainability standards and certifications, all of which rely on the ability to identify areas of issue and risk relating to an organization. However, there are two key interpretations of double materiality: one from the perspective of interval vs external, and one which focuses on financial vs sustainability impacts.

Double materiality interpretation 1: Outside World In, Inside World Out

This interpretation of double materiality requires material issues to be viewed from two perspectives, as shown in Figure 33.2:

1 Outside World In: This outlook emphasizes how external risks impact an organization (internal materiality). These external impacts are viewed as direct risks to an organization's performance, operations and overall long-term viability.

2 Inside World Out: This perspective focuses on how an organization's activities influence and impact external stakeholders, including the environment, economy and society. External materiality analyses how an organization's decision making and actions impact all external entities

This interpretation is often referred to as the importance of a risk or an issue to the business versus its importance to external stakeholders.

Figure 33.3   Financial vs Sustainability materiality

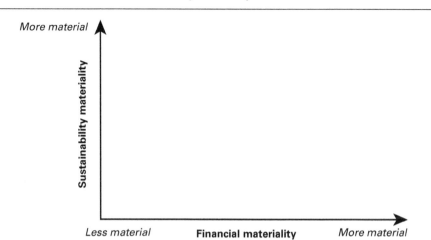

SOURCE SATARLA (2022). Used with permission.

Double materiality interpretation 2: Finance Impact vs. Sustainability Impact

This interpretation of double materiality again requires material issues to be viewed from two perspectives, but this time with a more focused view, as shown in Figure 33.3:

1 Financial Impact: This element of materiality highlights how sustainability issues financially impact an organization's performance. This approach considers how sustainability risks and opportunities impact an organization's operational efficiency, financial health and ultimately market value (financial materiality). Because financial materiality has direct influences on an organization's overall valuation, it is largely of interest to investors.

2 Sustainability Impact: This aspect of materiality has a broader approach. The impact on sustainability examines how an organization's activities affect the broader community of the economy, environment and society. This dimension is of interest to a more extensive range of stakeholders from citizens to consumers to civil society organizations and NGOs.

Sustainability can either be viewed as a specific discipline when it comes to risk management, or a myriad of disciplines being woven together. Similar to the role of integrated enterprise risk management, shown in Figure 38.2, sustainability departments within organizations are often integrated across multiple teams and/or require multiple skill sets such as finance, environmental, legal, social, reputation, engineering and communication.

A wide range of risk management tools are typically used within sustainability risk management, including scenario analysis, which is especially vital for climate change risk management, considered in Chapter 34.

Risk management is often the starting point for many sustainability guidance documents and regulatory requirements. For example, the Task Force for Climate-related Financial Disclosure (TCFD) and the Task Force for Nature-related Financial Disclosure (TNFD) – both start with understanding an organization's strategy followed by its risks. A robust risk assessment, including both the potential threats and opportunities posed by an organization on its surroundings and vice versa, is key for the vast majority of management and reporting documentation pertaining to sustainability.

The purpose of more recent guidance and expectations on sustainability, such as those being outlined in European expectations, for example, ESRS and CRSD, considered earlier in this chapter, through to ISSB and other specific guidance on climate change, is that organizations are expected to become more proactive in dealing with sustainability.

As a result, increased governance has been explored and implemented, in some cases focusing on all aspects of sustainability as a combined unit, and in others, focusing on only one key aspect. This ambition for sustainability to become more proactive allows for opportunities to be realized and threats minimized. As a result, risk management is at the heart of sustainability management and governance.

Risk management as a tool to hold organizations to account regarding sustainability

The continual referring back to the status of the risks posed to the achievement of an organization's objectives, as well as those unwritten objectives that an organization may achieve for the surrounding environment, allows for an element of accountability to be maintained.

The integration of sustainability risks into the broader ERM portfolio also allows for sustainability risks to be compared and contrasted with those that may be more directly linked to organizational activities. In addition, the accountability of boards to ensure the effective management of both current and emerging risks, is noted across Section 6 of the book in relation to corporate governance. In many cases, an integrated management approach may lead to opportunities being identified and realized for both financial and sustainability areas of risk.

Notes

1 Brundtland, G (1987) *Report of the World Commission on Environment and Development: Our Common Future*, United Nations General Assembly document A/42/427

2 Early, D (1993) *What Is Sustainable Design*, Berkley: Society of Urban Ecology

3 Krantz, T and Jonker, A (2024) What is ESG? IBM, https://www.ibm.com/topics/environmental-social-and-governance (archived at https://perma.cc/FDX4-Q8YA)

4 ISO (2010) *ISO 26000 — Guidance on social responsibility*, https://www.iso.org/obp/ui/en/#iso:std:iso:26000:ed-1:v1:en (archived at https://perma.cc/7P4D-NFTA)

5 Elkington, J (2018) '25 Years Ago I Coined the Phrase "Triple Bottom Line". Here's Why It's Time to Rethink It'. Harvard Business Review, https://hbr.org/2018/06/25-years-ago-i-coined-the-phrase-triple-bottom-line-heres-why-im-giving-up-on-it (archived at https://perma.cc/A3ZP-6LMT)

6 Organization for Economic Co-operation and Development (2002) *Glossary of key terms in evaluation and results-based management*, https://www.oecd.org/dac/evaluation/2754804.pdf (archived at https://perma.cc/J5DL-85TK)

7 Kochskämper, E et al. (2023) *Resilience and the Sustainable Development Goals: A scrutiny of urban strategies in the 100 Resilient Cities initiative*, https://www.tandfonline.com/doi/full/10.1080/09640568.2023.2297648 (archived at https://perma.cc/4TUC-APRD)

8 UN (2022) 'Zero tolerance for greenwashing', Guterres says at report launch, https://www.un.org/en/delegate/%E2%80%98zero-tolerance-greenwashing%E2%80%99-guterres-says-report-launch#:~:text=The%20report%20slams%20greenwashing%20%E2%80%93%20misleading,and%20weak%20net%2Dzero%20pledges (archived at https://perma.cc/7GA3-QWEY)

9 UN Department of Economic and Social Affairs (2024) *The 17 Goals*, https://sdgs.un.org/goals (archived at https://perma.cc/3X5A-W4MV)

10 Gordon, S (2023) Environmental, societal and governance risk management. Hillson, D (ed.), *The Risk Management Handbook*, Kogan Page, London

11 EC (2024) *Corporate sustainability reporting*, https://finance.ec.europa.eu/capital-markets-union-and-financial-markets/company-reporting-and-auditing/company-reporting/corporate-sustainability-reporting_en#legislation (archived at https://perma.cc/B647-XLLH)

12 EC (2024) *The European Green Deal – Striving to be the first climate-neutral continent*, https://commission.europa.eu/strategy-and-policy/priorities-2019-2024/european-green-deal_en (archived at https://perma.cc/XM7D-QJTS)

13 KeyESG (2023) *CSRD and ESRS: the relationship explained*, https://www.keyesg.com/article/csrd-and-esrs-the-relationship-explained (archived at https://perma.cc/R7K4-JA45)

14 Reuters (2022) *CEO of Deutsche Bank's asset manager steps down after 'greenwashing' raid*, https://www.reuters.com/business/german-police-raid-deutsche-banks-dws-unit-2022-05-31/ (archived at https://perma.cc/U8CY-64HH)

ESG and climate change   34

Climate change as part of environment, social and governance (ESG)

The risks relating to the changing climate are seen by some as existential for humanity. They are often prioritized ahead of other sustainability or ESG risks as they are complex, global and urgent given the impact of non-compliance.

While each individual may be impacted in different ways by climate change, attempts to manage aspects of it proactively and reactively require large-scale collaboration across geographies and cultures. This chapter will explore climate change and its role within ESG, with specific focus on what climate change means to risk management.

What is climate change?

According to the UN (2024)[1] climate change refers to long-term shifts in temperatures and weather patterns that may be natural or caused by human activities. Climate change has occurred throughout Earth's history and can be viewed and measured in the geological record. This record shows alternating warmer and cooler periods, caused by a variety of factors.

In the last two hundred years, the burning of fossil fuels for energy and clearing of vegetation for purposes such as agriculture, has meant that atmospheric levels of greenhouse gases (including carbon dioxide, methane and nitrous oxide) have risen sharply. The World Economic Forum (2021)[2] states that the Earth's average surface temperature has risen every year by 0.07°C (0.13°F) since 1850, which may not seem much, but is significant when added together. In addition, that yearly rise has increased since 1981 to 0.18°C (0.32°F).

As a result, atmospheric carbon dioxide levels have increased steadily from pre-industrial revolution levels at 280 parts per million (ppm) to post-industrial revolution levels of 300ppm. These levels have continued to rise to over 420ppm

Table 34.1 Example climate change risks and opportunities

Category	Risk	Opportunity
Physical risks	Extreme weather events (flood, wildfires)	Development of resilient infrastructure
	Rising sea levels impacting coastal operations	Investment in flood defences and coastal protection
Transition risks	Regulatory changes increasing compliance costs	Access to new markets for low carbon technologies
	Carbon pricing increasing operational costs	Incentives for renewable energy adoption
Liability risks	Litigation and settlement costs to defend or settle actions for past alleged negligence in contributing to climate change	Support for strategy to transition to low carbon technologies

in 2024. This rapid rise in carbon dioxide levels has enhanced the greenhouse effect, leading to a range of environmental impacts including rising global temperatures, melting ice caps and glaciers, rising sea levels, and increased frequency and severity of extreme weather events.

Typical climate change risks (and opportunities)

Much of the guidance published regarding climate change refers to risks as being negative, as do other specialisms in risk management. It is therefore common for climate change-related literature to refer to 'risks and opportunities'.

Robust guidance is freely available to support organizations in the management of their climate change risks. This guidance typically categorizes climate change risks as being either physical (those related to the physical impacts of climate change) or transition (those related to the changing social and economic environment), examples of which are provided in Table 34.1. More financially oriented guidance also refers to liability risks as a category of climate change risk.

THE TENSION BETWEEN CLIMATE CHANGE AND OTHER ESG RISKS

Climate change is one of many ESG risks. The management strategies for climate change can sometimes have the potential to also impact on the management of other ESG risks. These impacts can, in turn, be either positive or negative for those other ESG risks. For example:

- The introduction of a ban or significant reduction in emissions may lead to coal power-reliant nations, such as India, being unable to provide enough electricity to its population, which may result in a slowing of the country's development. This is part of the reason that India has often challenged commitments to cease the use of coal power in forums such as the climate change-focused Conference of the Parties (COPs) to the United Nations Framework Convention on Climate Change (UNFCCC).

- As a result of efforts to improve efficiency, a company whose manufacturing operation uses significant quantities of water in a water-scarce region may implement water-saving technologies internally, while working with external ecological groups and communities to create net positive watershed management and increase the availability of water to those in the wider community. These improvements and opportunities may not be instigated if the manufacturing company was not present in the region.

- All forms of renewable power generation technology, including wind turbines and photovoltaic batteries require significant volumes of minerals and metals that have never been needed in vast quantities before. These materials need to be extracted from the ground or recycled, both of which pose significant sustainability risks to the surrounding environments and people if processes and facilities are not managed appropriately. If undertaken responsibly, the extraction of natural materials from the ground can bring significant wealth and value to a region, allowing for robust development, as was seen in, for example, the UK during the industrial revolution.

It is therefore imperative that climate change be managed in an integrated fashion with other ESG and broader organizational risks. Climate change risks may be prioritized, but should not be managed in isolation.

Climate change standards and frameworks

Climate change-related guidance, expectations and reporting disclosures have evolved significantly since 2020, and will continue to evolve rapidly over the coming years. As a result, there are a number of different acronyms used regularly, which have been listed below for ease of reference in Table 34.2, and are included in the Appendices.

Figure 34.1 shows the alignment and interconnections of the common climate-related frameworks and standards with regards to the Financial Reporting Standards (IFRS).

Table 34.2 Climate change standards and frameworks

Acronym	Standard or framework
CDP	not for profit charity helping organizations with disclosures on environment impacts
CDSB	Climate Disclosure Standards Board
COP	Conference of Parties
IFRS	International Financial Reporting Standards
IIRC	International Integrated Reporting Council (now retired)
ISSB	International Sustainability Standards Board
NGFS	Network for Greening the Financial System
SASB	Sustainability Accounting Standards Board
TCFD	Task Force on Climate-Related Financial Disclosures
TIFD	Task Force on Inequality-Related Disclosures
TNFD	Task Force on Nature-Related Financial Disclosures
TPT	Transition Plan Task Force
UNFCCC	United Nations Convention on Climate Change
VRF	Value Reporting Foundation

Figure 34.1 highlights the following key elements:

1 IFRS Integration (S1 and S2): the purpose of these standards is to integrate sustainability and financial reporting.

   a. IFRS S1 (Sustainability): combination of VRF and CDSB.

   b. IFRS S2 (Climate Change): integration of TCFD and other relevant disclosures.

2 Foundational Frameworks:

   a. VRF, leveraged by the ISSB and housed by the IFRS, which is a consolidation of the SASB, the IIRC and CDSB to provide the base for sustainability reporting. Climate reporting integrates recommendations from the TCFD, also housed by the IFRS, and other relevant disclosures.

Figure 34.1 Summary view of Financial Reporting Standards (IFRS)

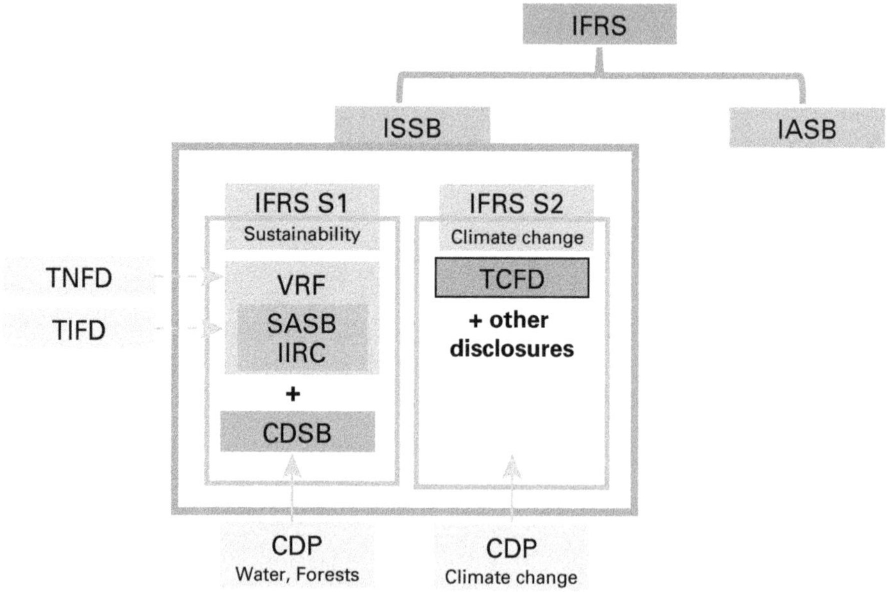

SOURCE SATARLA (2024). Used with permission

3 Broader alignment across the industry:

a. additional entities, such as CDP (for water, forests and climate change) and TNFD have signed agreements to work closely with the ISSB and inform them of disclosures. TIFD may do the same in the future.

The role of risk management within climate change

While each standard and framework is written for its own purpose and therefore in its own style, risk management is usually included as an integral part of the guidance to categorize the array of typical climate change risks to an organization making use of the standard. The manner in which risk management is applied is generally left to an organization itself, with guidance regarding what the desired outputs should be being suggested by the relevant standard or framework, an example of which is included in the box below.

RISK MANAGEMENT WITHIN TCFD

The Task Force on Climate-related Financial Disclosures (TCFD) is a framework to help organizations disclose climate-related risks and opportunities in a consistent and comparable manner. There are four pillars to TCFD[3] that provide a useful backbone for most subsequent sustainability regulations, including climate, nature and broader sustainability factors, as can be seen in Figure 34.2.

Figure 34.2   Four pillars of TCFD

The four pillars of governance, strategy, risk management, and metrics and targets are replicated in other frameworks such as the Task Force on Nature-related Financial Disclosures (TNFD). By understanding the risks and what can be done to manage them, organizations can formulate strategies, which can be measured to assess progress against targets set. Organizations can then be held to account through governance arrangements.

Managing climate change – transition plans

It is acknowledged that the management of climate change is a long-term global challenge, which will require the design of meaningful plans, allowing countries, regions and organizations to improve their climate change performance in a measurable way. These plans are generally known as transition plans and take many forms, allowing for material climate change risks to be managed through their implementation, while outlining a practical plan for achieving any climate change targets which have been set.

In the UK, the Transition Plan Task Force (TPT) was launched by HM Treasury (2022)[4] with the aim of developing a gold standard for private sector climate transition plans. The Task Force engaged with financial institutions, real economy corporates (those involved in the production, purchase and flow of goods and services), policymakers, regulators and civil society to develop their materials. They have published a Disclosure Framework, which sets out good practice for robust and credible transition plan disclosures. This is built on the three principles of ambition, action and accountability. The TPT has said transition plans should take a strategic and rounded approach which explains how an organization will meet climate targets, manage climate-related risks, and contribute to the economy-wide climate transition. Transition planning is an iterative process and organizations should have already started implementing them.

EXAMPLE TRANSITION PLAN: AVIVA

Aviva's climate ambition and targets are underpinned by five strategic pillars:[5]

1 Managing our operational footprint:
   a. Achieve Net Zero operations by 2030.
   b. Source 100 per cent renewable electricity by 2025.
   c. Transition to a fully electric or hybrid vehicle fleet by 2025.
2 Reducing our supply chain emissions:
   a. Engage suppliers to adopt science-based targets.
   b. Increase the percentage of suppliers with verified emission reduction commitments.
   c. Include carbon management clauses in supplier contracts.
3 Transitioning our investments:
   a. Reduce the carbon intensity of our investment portfolio by 25 per cent by 2025 and 60 per cent by 2030.
   b. Divest from companies that do not meet climate standards.
   c. Tilt investments towards low-carbon and green assets.
4 Advancing our insurance underwriting:
   a. Integrate climate considerations into underwriting and claims management.
   b. Increase underwriting volumes for low-carbon assets.
   c. Develop and offer renewable energy insurance products.
5 Using our influence:
   a. Advocate for systemic change in financial markets.

b. Participate in climate-focused alliances and initiatives.

c. Use our influence to drive broader industry and societal transitions towards Net Zero.

Scenario analysis

Scenario analysis, also considered in Chapters 10 and 31, is often cited as the risk management tool of choice by many of the climate change frameworks and standards. Scenario analysis is a process which evaluates and explores potential risks and impacts of different climate outcomes on an organization's operations. Typically, this includes the following steps as set out by Accounting for Sustainability:[6]

- Objectives and scope – establish the governance and objectives of the exercise and understand the material risk drivers and the key stakeholders
- Scenario design – determine the scope of climate risks and select the scenarios and the time intervals
- Impact assessment – assess the potential effects
- Use and communicate results – disclose outcomes and improve risk awareness and risk management

A wide range of 'standard' scenarios have been developed, which are often used as a starting point by organizations when undertaking their own scenario analysis for climate change. For example the Network for Greening the Financial System (NGFS) scenarios are freely available and include robust datasets for more quantitative forms of analysis. The NGFS[7] includes four key scenarios, which consider the applicability and materiality of both physical and transition risks, highlighted in Table 34.3.

Table 34.3   NGFS climate change scenarios

Orderly	Climate policies are introduced early and become more rigorous, meaning that physical and transition risks are controlled
Disorderly	Climate policies are delayed or different across countries and sectors, meaning that transition risks and carbon prices are higher
Hot house world	Climate policies are implemented in some countries, but global efforts do not halt global warming, meaning that there are severe physical risks
Too little, too late	Climate policies are delayed and are different across countries and sectors, meaning that transition risks are high in some countries leading to high physical risks in all countries

While there are no defined methodologies for the type of scenario analysis that should be undertaken, the outputs from the scenario analysis should enhance an organization's understanding of how climate change will affect it, and enhance the quality of the transition plan required to manage the most important risks to that organization.

Metrics and targets

'1.5 to stay alive' was the slogan chanted on the streets of Glasgow during the 2021 COP26. This referred to the target established at the Paris Climate COP six years earlier which outlined the 'tipping point' of the maximum increase in average global temperature beyond pre-industrial levels that it is felt by some the Earth can tolerate. After this, it has been suggested that it will be difficult to stop the melting of the ice caps and shifts in ocean currents, or reverse the increase in the frequency of extreme weather events.

According to the European Union's Copernicus Climate Change Service,[8] the average temperature for 2023/2024 was measured at 1.52°C higher on average compared with between 1850 and 1900. The tolerance level of 1.5°C has therefore been breached. If this is sustained in the coming years, we may begin to see significant changes and variations across the planet.

While the target of staying below 1.5°C is a good target for the planet, it is not tangible for a single organization. As a result, it is more common for organizational targets to be more practical, focusing on the immediate output of an organization's management actions. Example targets from different organizations are provided in Table 34.4.

Table 34.4   Example climate targets

Company	Carbon neutral or net zero goal	Renewable energy goal	Waste reduction goal	Other commitments
Apple	Every product carbon neutral 2030	100% renewable	Zero waste to landfill for all products	Supplier clean energy programme
Amazon	Net zero 2040	100% renewable energy by 2035	50% of all shipments net-zero carbon by 2030	Investment in reforestation
Unilever	Net Zero emissions 2039	100% renewable energy	Halve food waste in operations by 2035	Plastic reduction and circular economy initiatives

(continued)

Table 34.4   (Continued)

Company	Carbon neutral or net zero goal	Renewable energy goal	Waste reduction goal	Other commitments
IKEA	Climate positive by 2030	100% renewable energy	Zero waste to landfill	Use only renewable and recyclable materials in products by 2030
Patagonia	Carbon neutral by 2025	100% renewable energy	Increase renewable energy in supply chain	Using recycled material in its products

As organizations mature in their understanding of what is required to improve their performance in managing climate-related risks, it is common to see them re-evaluating their targets, and often restating those targets. Commitments to be 'net zero by 2025' have often been moved out to 2030 or beyond as the difficulty to achieve such a feat is acknowledged. What is truly meant by these targets can be confusing as the terminology used is often unclear, with examples shown in the box below.

NET ZERO VERSUS CARBON NEUTRAL?

Although often used interchangeably, net zero and carbon neutral have different meanings and implications.

- **Net zero** refers to reducing greenhouse emissions as much as possible, then balancing remaining emissions by offsetting through undertaking activities to sequester carbon. The term 'net zero' is used because the goal is for a company to reach a point where they are contributing nothing (zero) to overall atmospheric greenhouse gases. Net zero therefore requires reductions in all scopes of emissions:

  o Scope 1: direct emissions from sources owned or controlled by an organization, such as combustion from vehicles, boilers and so on

  o Scope 2: indirect emissions not directly owned or controlled by an organization, but related to its purchased energy, such as electricity, heating, cooling and so on

  o Scope 3: all other indirect emissions from activities outside of an organization's own operations, but related to them, such as emissions from those in the supply chain, transportation of goods, employee commuting and so on.

- **Carbon neutral**, on the other hand, involves balancing the emitted carbon with an equal amount of carbon offsets; essentially, compensating for emissions by

> investing in environmental projects. Unlike net zero, carbon neutrality does not involve reducing emissions, but primarily involves the offsetting technique.
>
> Net zero is therefore regarded as being more robust than carbon neutral as it requires an organization to prioritize reducing its emissions before filling in the gap with offsetting.

Perspectives on climate change

Depending on the outcome of climate change, some individuals stand to make or lose significant value on their assets depending on where, when and how the climate will change in the future. It is not unsurprising that there is a wealth of different perspectives, and the topic can be incredibly emotive.

Risk management can be used as an unemotional and objective tool through which this diversity of perceptions is acknowledged and welcomed. Scenario analysis or a 'what if' analysis can be undertaken even in situations where there is a range of perspectives in the room. Therefore, risk management can be the safe haven through which an organization can tackle topics as divisive as climate change, resulting in tangible plans of action that can be taken no matter what the future holds.

Notes

1 UN (2024) *What is Climate Change?* https://www.un.org/en/climatechange/what-is-climate-change (archived at https://perma.cc/2F6S-95QP)

2 World Economic Forum (2021) *Since 1985, these historical events have accelerated climate change,* https://www.weforum.org/agenda/2021/02/global-warming-climate-change-historical-human-development-industrial-revolution/ (archived at https://perma.cc/BV8E-UF6C)

3 TCFD (2017) *Recommendations of the Task Force on Climate-related Financial Disclosures,* https://www.fsb-tcfd.org/recommendations/ (archived at https://perma.cc/26TK-8XMZ)

4 TPT (2024) *Background information about the Transition Plan Taskforce,* https://transitiontaskforce.net/about/ (archived at https://perma.cc/FT4L-XL47)

5 Aviva (2024) *Acting on climate change,* https://www.aviva.com/sustainability/climate/ (archived at https://perma.cc/3RLQ-ZTU6)

6 A4S (2021) *TCFD climate scenario analysis: A guide for finance teams on frequently asked questions*, https://www.accountingforsustainability.org/content/a4s/corporate/en/knowledge-hub/guides/tcfd-climate-scenario-analysis.html (archived at https://perma.cc/3HQU-F6MN)

7 NGFS Scenarios Portal (2024) *The future is uncertain: The NGFS climate scenarios provide a window into different plausible futures*, https://www.ngfs.net/ngfs-scenarios-portal/ (archived at https://perma.cc/3HQU-F6MN)

8 Copernicus (2024) *Copernicus: May 2024 is the 12th consecutive month with record-high temperatures. Copernicus report*, https://climate.copernicus.eu/copernicus-may-2024-12th-consecutive-month-record-high-temperatures (archived at https://perma.cc/7F8X-4ANU)

PART EIGHT
Different approaches

LEARNING OUTCOMES

Having studied this section readers will be able to:

- Describe risk management within the banking sector, including the provision of examples of key risks within the banking risk categories.
- Summarize the key features of the Basel Accord.
- Describe risk management within the insurance sector, including the provision of examples of key risks within the insurance risk categories.
- Summarize the key features of Solvency II.
- Describe the different types of insurance and the use of captive insurance companies.
- Summarize the key features of operational risk as practised in financial institutions such as banks and insurance companies.
- Describe the key sources of operational risk in financial institutions and provide examples of how these risks are managed.
- Describe projects, programmes and portfolios and differences between them and the risk management approach.
- Produce a brief description of the project lifecycle and the importance of risk management at each stage.

- Explain the key standards for project, programme and portfolio risk management.
- Produce example project, programme and portfolio risks.
- Describe the importance of the health and safety and the contribution of health and safety risk management to the success of an organization.
- Produce example health and safety risks.
- Explain the key standards for health and safety.
- Describe the importance of legal support and the contribution of legal risk management to the success of an organization.
- Produce example legal risks.
- Explain the key standards for legal risk management.
- Describe the importance of the supply chain and the contribution of supply chain risk management to the success of an organization.
- Produce example supply chain risks.
- Explain the key standards for supply chain risk management.
- Describe the importance of IT and the contribution of supply chain risk management to the success of an organization.
- Produce example IT risks.
- Explain the key standards for IT risk management.
- Explain the interconnectedness of risk and how ERM can act as a translation and escalation tool to integrate it into all organizational activities.

Different approaches to risk management

35

This section reviews some of the traditional specialist approaches to risk management. All organizational activities manage risks as part of good management, just as individuals do on a daily basis, without realizing that they are practising risk management. As noted in Chapter 2, formal risk management had its origins in the insurance industry, but specialist approaches to risk management exist across organizations in all industries.

For example, clinical risk management has been developing for some time. This area of risk management is primarily concerned with patient care, especially during surgical operations. The cost of medical malpractice claims has increased because the medical profession has increased the number of diseases they can improve combined with an increase in life expectancy. This means that not only can medicine improve more people's lives but its application to more ailments will inevitably result in some injury. Any subsequent payout for negligence will be multiplied by the 15 to 20 years' increase in life expectancy that medicine has enabled since the 1950s. This means that claim payments have increased disproportionately, resulting in risk management systems being introduced.

The energy sector has been applying risk management for many years. Techniques around the processing of volatile material were, of course, developed in the energy sector and the DuPont corporation introduced clear health and safety techniques in the 1990s that were demonstrably superior to their peers. Now risk management has extended to sustainability of energy production, the future price of energy and exploration risk.

Other specialist areas of risk management have developed over the past decades in relation to different activities, sectors and industries, including:

- medical
- energy
- sustainability
- reputation
- human resources

- compliance
- gaming/gambling
- logistics

All of the above specialist areas of risk management have contributed considerably to the development and application of risk management tools and techniques. Further specialisms that will be explored in more detail in following chapters include:

- banking
- insurance
- operational risk management
- projects, programmes and portfolios
- health and safety
- legal
- IT

Project risk management is an area where the application of risk management tools and techniques is particularly well established.

Information technology (IT) and information security risk management is another well-developed branch. The increasing importance of information to organizations, in terms of the management of and security of data, has resulted in the development of specific standards applicable to IT risk management

Risk management in the legal and supply chain industries has become increasingly important due the complex relationships in organizational value chains. This area has been highlighted further by the focus on risks in relation to the environment, social and governance arena, and the requirements in many countries for an understanding of organizations' carbon footprints and the use of renewable and non-renewable resources.

Risk management techniques have been applied in the finance sector, focusing on operational risks, as well as market, credit and other types of financial risks. Finance and insurance are highly regulated business sectors, governed by international standards such as Basel III and Solvency II. It is in the finance sector that the title of chief risk officer was first developed.

Operational risk management covers a variety of risk types, which include cyber, IT and change management, the individual specifics of which are beyond the scope of this book. Additionally, specialist areas such as credit risk management are beyond the scope of this book.

Further details on the specialist approaches to risk management are included in Chapters 36 and 37.

Banking, insurance and operational approaches to risk management

The banking industry

The banking industry is of systemic importance to any economy. All industries depend on access to money, transmission of money and the management of money. The vast majority of this industry is dominated by licensed banks although there is growing competition from the crypto, fintech and crowd funding challengers, many of whom are not subject to the extensive regulation that licensed banks are.

Key banking risks

To properly understand the risks associated with banking it is useful to examine, at a macro level, the key attributes of a bank and therefore its key risks, which are related to those that have money and those that do not. For example, for those who have money (the depositors), banks will have risks relating to the interest rates on deposits and market risks around fund management. For those who do not have money (the borrowers), banks will have risks relating to credit on loans and fraud on credit cards. In addition, there are risks that cover both depositors and borrowers. Like any organization, a bank is exposed to the full spectrum of risks associated with the achievement of their objectives. Banks typically consider risks using a taxonomy formulated by their regulators. Table 36.1 explains these categories of risk in more detail:

Table 36.1   Banking risk categories

Type	Description
Strategic	Uncertainties that may affect or may be created by an organization's business strategy and strategic objectives.
Credit	The risk of loss due to counterparty default. It is restricted to default or situations where the counterparty can, but refuses to, make payment when due.
Market	The risk of loss due to adverse economic changes in market conditions, rates or prices or fluctuations including price, volatility, interest rate and foreign exchange risk, among others.
Liquidity	The risk of not having adequate funds available to meet financial commitments as they fall due. This may be caused by local or foreign economic conditions, a reduction in credit rating or situations where the firm is interested in trading an asset but cannot do so because no one in the market wants to trade that asset.
Operational	The risk of loss, direct or indirect, resulting from inadequate or failed internal processes, people and systems or from external events. More on operational risk is included in this chapter.
Know your customer (KYC)	Guidelines used in the financial sector but used by other organizations to verify the identity and suitability of customers and know their risk and financial profiles. This should identify suspicious behaviour, such as fraud, money laundering or financial terrorism.
Conduct	The potential for an organization's actions, inactions and behaviours to cause harm to its customers, stakeholders or the integrity of the broader market. Banking regulators, particularly the FCA in the UK, have set stringent conduct risk standards for banks, their managers and employees. Much of this evolved from scandals such as Libor fixing and mis-selling of products to customers.
Financial crime	Illegal acts committed by an individual or group to obtain a financial or professional advantage, including dishonesty, misuse of information, handling the proceeds of crime and financing terrorism.
Fraud	The risk of individual, group or organizational intentional deception, such as false misrepresentation or abuse of position, to gain unlawful or unfair financial or professional advantage, such as intellectual property theft and misappropriation of funds or other resources.

Banking regulation and supervision

Unlike most other industries, banks and insurers (considered later in this chapter) are required to create a financial reserve to cover the risks they identify and analyse, as set out in the regulatory Basel Accord.

Table 36.2   Evolution of the Basel framework

Basel I (1988)	This was considered a landmark in international banking regulation, arising from the 1970s to 1980s banking crises. It aimed to ensure banks maintained minimum capital to absorb losses, focusing mainly on credit risk.
Basel II (2004)	The Asian financial crisis and some notable corporate collapses such as World Com and Enron prompted an upgrade to Basel II in 2004. Basel II provided a more comprehensive risk management framework to enhance the banking industry globally. It introduced a three-pillar approach illustrated in Figure 36.1.
Basel III (2010)	This framework is still in its implementation phase in many countries including the EU, US and the UK. It emerged as a response (lessons learnt) to the 2008 financial crisis, and was conceived to enhance the resilience of the global banking system and reduce the risk of future financial crises. The main new features of Basel III include: • requirement to hold higher level of reserves (risk capital) • need to hold high-quality liquid assets to meet short-term liquidity needs (e.g. withdrawal of monies by depositors) • limits set on concentration risk around lending, and • buffers to be built up during periods of economic growth and released during downturns to curb pro-cyclicality. Collectively these measures have contributed to the development of more robust risk management practices within banks, with a much greater focus now on stress testing and scenario analysis.
Basel III.I (or Basel IV) (2023)	This separate phase revises the standardized approaches for calculating credit risk, market risk, credit valuation adjustment and operational risk to give greater risk sensitivity and comparability. It also aims to reduce unwarranted variability in banks' calculations of risk-weighted assets through constraints on using internal models, and has introduced higher leverage ratio requirements on global systemically important banks, or G-SIBs.

Basel Accord

The Basel Accord is a framework comprising a full set of standards for the international banking system. It was established by the Basel Committee on Banking Supervision (BCBS), which comprises the world's top banking regulators. The framework's aim is to preserve the integrity of the banking system. At the heart of it lies the requirement for banks to maintain enough capital reserves to meet their obligations and absorb unexpected losses. A key enabler is a solid ERM framework.

Evolution of the Basel framework

Banking regulation continues to evolve, very often responding to significant failures in the industry. The evolution from Basel I to Basel IV framework is outlined in Table 36.2.

Basel's three-pillar approach aims to promote and market discipline through mandatory disclosure of relevant market information.

The Basel three pillars are:

1 *Pillar 1 sets out the minimum capital requirements* (risk reserve) – contains rules for calculating more refined risk weights for different kinds of loans. In addition, it outlines that capital should be held against operational risk.

- In simple terms the calculation is:

   Amount of risk × risk capital ratio = Risk capital to be reserved

- The amount of risk is generally referred to as risk-weighted assets. There are usually two options available to banks to carry out this calculation: a standardized approach or an internal models approach. In the case of the latter,

Figure 36.1   The Basel three-pillar approach

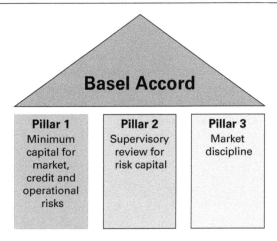

a supervisor (who oversees daily operations to ensure adherence to regulations and policies) will only allow this approach if it is satisfied with the robustness of a bank's internal models.

2 *Pillar 2 sets out the requirement for supervisory review of the adequacy of the risk capital* – supervisors are required to evaluate how well banks assess their capital needs relative to their risk. Enterprise risk management best practice is at the core of pillar 2. Banks must undertake an internal capital adequacy assessment process (ICAAP), which supervisors consider when they evaluate a bank. The methodology they regularly use is often referred to as a risk and control self-assessment (RCSA), considered in Chapter 29.

3 *Pillar 3 sets out the market discipline requirement* – to ensure transparency to stakeholders in a bank and the industry generally, and to provide market confidence. This requires a bank to make disclosures, including its exposure to credit, market and operational risks and its calculation of the risk-weighted assets specifying whether by way of the standardized or internal models approach.

These pillars focus on helping banks adopt a more risk-sensitive approach to capital allocation, better assess their risks, and strengthen their risk management practices.

The Basel framework and standards are non-binding. They are put forward as best practice, but it is up to the regulator in each country to implement and enforce under their own powers and laws. In many countries, supervisory bodies are provided through central or reserve banks, such as the Central Banks of Egypt, Brazil or Kenya, and the Reserve Banks of Australia or Malawi. In other countries, along with central banks, separate institutions have been established, such as the Financial Conduct Authority (FCA) in the UK, the Federal Reserve System in the US, or the Financial Services Agency in Japan.

The insurance industry

The insurance industry is no stranger to risk management. It is one of the oldest industries in the world and works on the basic premise that an insurer buys risk professionally in exchange for the receipt of a premium paid by the insured. Chapter 18 considered insurance as one of the control options for managing threats through risk transfer (involving others), which an organization can put in place normally through a regulated insurer.

Key insurance risks

To properly understand the risks associated with insurance, risk management is viewed below through the lens of the insurer. There are three core aspects of insurance: risk purchase (or underwriting of risk), the investment of funds received and the claims made against the insurance. For example, through risk purchase, insurers will take on a customer's risk, at a price, which will need to be evaluated by underwriters. Premiums are paid by customers upfront and claims are usually paid out at a much later date. Insurance is based on investing those premiums wisely until the claims are paid out. As such, the key risk around fund investment is the volatility of the market, and in relation to claims, the key risks relate to fraud or bogus claims, and the size of a claim.

Similar to the risk categories of the banking industry, insurers also face risks in relation to credit, market, liquidity and operational, as well as those from a financial crime perspective. The additional category in the insurance industry is the underwriter risk, as noted previously. This is the risk of loss if there has been an inaccurate assessment of the risks being covered, if there are sudden market changes, or if there is a change in the rate of incidents.

Typical insurance cover

Generally speaking, the three reasons why an organization will wish to purchase insurance cover are met through the broad areas in which insurance operates, being risk purchase, fund investment and claims made, as noted earlier. These are:

- balance sheet/profit and loss protection (first-party protection);
- mandatory legal and contractual obligations (third-party protection);
- protection of employee assets (benefits insurance).

Common types of insurance cover that may be required by an organization are set out in Table 36.3, which also notes the circumstances in which insurance should be purchased. These insurance types are based on a UK perspective, but many countries will have similar insurance offerings and requirements. In most cases, the purchase of insurance is not mandatory. However, most countries make the purchase of insurance compulsory for some liability classes, such as insurance cover to compensate injured employees and for the parties involved in road accidents. Professions often require their members to purchase professional indemnity insurance in order to carry on trading.

Apart from the compulsory classes, organizations can decide whether to purchase other classes of insurance. This decision will be based on the assessment of the risk and whether the nature and level of risk is within the threat tolerance of an organization. The cost of insurance (premium) and the extent of insurance coverage are also important considerations when deciding whether to buy insurance. Typically, insurance is purchased for low-likelihood/high-impact risks, such as flooding, hurricane damage and major fires.

Table 36.3   Different types of insurance

Mandatory, legal and contractual obligations
Employers' liability – compensation to employees injured at work
Public liability – compensation to public or customers
Motor third party – compensation following motor accident
Product liability – compensation for damage or injury
Professional indemnity – compensation to client for negligent advice

Balance sheet/profit and loss protection
Business premises – damage to premises by adverse events
Business interruption – loss of profit and increased cost of working
Asset protection – losses, such as loss of cash, goods in transit, credit risk and
fidelity guarantee (staff dishonesty)
Motor accidental damage – repair of own vehicles
Terrorism – compensation for damage caused by terrorism
Loss of a key person – compensation on loss of key staff member

Employee benefit/protection of employee assets
Life and health – benefits to employees that can include life cover, critical illness
cover, income protection, private medical costs, permanent health cover, personal
accident and travel injury/losses
Directors' and officers' liability – legal and compensation costs

---

Typical insurer types

There are three significant insurer types:

1   General insurers – those who offer various insurance products to individuals and businesses. Some are niche players, for example, BUPA (specializing in medical), while others are full-service.

2   Re-insurers – those who buy risks from other insurers and manage them, typically in a larger or specialist portfolio.

3   Captive insurers – generally an in-house company in a multinational group who collect all the insurance risks across their group and manage those risks centrally.

All of the above are generally subject to insurance regulation and supervision.

Insurer regulation and supervision

Similar to the banking industry most insurers are regulated, and those regulators re-quire insurers to hold risk capital reserves against their risks. The methodology is similar to banks. The international influencers are the International Association of Insurance Supervisors (IAIS) and in the EU through the Solvency II directive. However, similar to a bank, it is the national regulator that licences and supervises the insurer.

IAIS

The International Association of Insurance Supervisors (IAIS), established in 1994, is a global standard-setting body for the supervision of the insurance sector. The mission of the IAIS is to promote effective and globally consistent supervision of the insurance industry to develop and maintain fair, safe and stable insurance markets for the benefit and protection of policyholders, and to contribute to global financial stability. One of the key ways in which the IAIS achieves its mission is by the development of the Insurance Core Principles (ICPs) which cover:

1 Support the effective supervision and regulation of the insurance industry by providing guidance on the objectives, powers and responsibilities for insurance supervisors, stressing the importance of the independence of the insurance supervisor and requiring the confidential and timely sharing of information with and between supervisory authorities.

2 Set expectations for sound governance and risk management by requiring insurers to establish and implement a corporate governance framework which supports the sound and prudent management and oversight of the insurer's business. The framework is also expected to establish effective systems of risk management and internal controls including effective functions for risk management, compliance, actuarial matters and internal audit.

3 Provide prudential regulation and financial stability safeguards by, among other things, defining solvency standards and capital requirements, establishing guidelines for the valuation of assets held by insurers, and requiring the monitoring of the quality and liquidity of the investment portfolios of insurers.

4 Address consumer protection and market conduct by, among other things, setting expectations for the fair treatment of policyholders, the regulation of sales and distribution practices, the disclosure of significant information about insurance products as well as the management of complaints and the handling of disputes.

Solvency II

Solvency II has primary jurisdiction in the EU but is regarded as an international standard used by many non-EU countries. Like Basel, and developed in 2006, it has a three-pillar approach which insurance regulators use, as illustrated in Figure 36.2.

1 *Pillar 1 sets out quantitative requirements* including the level of risk capital that an insurer is expected to hold (Solvency Capital Requirement – SCR) and the absolute minimum floor level of capital, below which a regulator will intervene (Minimum Capital Requirement – MCR).

Figure 36.2   The Solvency II three-pillar approach

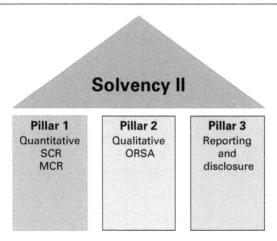

SOURCE Expert Partners (2020). Used with permission

2 *Pillar 2 sets out qualitative requirements* including governance, supervisory review and Own Risk and Solvency Assessment (ORSA). ORSA (similar to RCSA) enables insurers to assess the risks that they face, and manage these risks, as well as assisting in identifying the risk capital needed to run the business.

3 *Pillar 3 sets out the supervisory reporting and disclosure requirements* including reporting to the regulator through the solvency and financial condition report (publicly available) and the report to supervisors (to the regulators).

Operational risk management

The importance of managing operational risk is well established. Operational risk may be considered to be the type of risk that will disrupt normal everyday activities and that is inbuilt into the activities, processes and controls that deliver the main activities of an organization. The main goal of good operational risk management is to build operational resiliency and process reliability.

The Basel Committee on Banking Supervision in their *Principles for the Sound Management of Operational Risk* states:

> The Principles in this document for banks cover governance; the risk management environment; information and communication technology; business continuity planning; and the role of disclosure. These elements should not be viewed in isolation; rather, they are integrated components of the operational risk management framework (ORMF) and the overall risk management framework (including operational resilience) of the group.[1]

Definition of operational risk

Operational risks faced by banks and other financial institutions represent essentially the same types of disruptive threats that are faced by other organizations, although the definition may be broader and the terminology slightly different. The specific point in the case of operational risk for financial institutions is that the level of operational risk needs to be quantified, because the level of risk has to be covered by available capital within the institution. This leads to an imperative for the bank to reduce the level of operational risk to the lowest level that is cost-effective.

The Basel definition of operational risk includes legal risk but excludes strategic and reputational risk. The types of risks associated with the Basel definition include the following:

- internal fraud, for example misappropriation of assets, tax evasion and bribery;
- external fraud, for example theft, hacking and forgery;
- employment practices and workplace safety, for example fines resulting from harassment, discrimination or constructive dismissal;
- clients, projects and business practices, for example a fine for a breach of data protection rules;
- damage to physical assets, for example cost of repairing a building;
- business interruption and systems failures, for example an IT failure;
- execution, delivery and process management, for example a service complaint.

The losses associated with the failure to manage operational risk can be substantial. Losses suffered by so-called rogue traders are sometimes attributed to market risk. The argument is that the losses occurred because market conditions changed in an unexpected way and significant losses materialized. From an operational risk perspective, this analysis is incorrect. However, it is more correct to say that the losses occurred because of a failure to control the activities of traders. If the operations had been controlled by adequate operational risk controls, the traders would not have been in a position to have put substantial assets of the bank at risk. Blaming the losses on the market risk when such substantial assets of the bank should not have been in the market at all, is incorrect.

The Basel (2021) *Principles for the Sound Management of Operational Risk*, reflect the natural relationship between operational resilience, operational risk and Basel reforms. The 12 principles of 'sound practices' on operational risk encompass different aspects of the ERM framework, including roles and responsibilities and the reporting structure (architecture), leadership, risk appetite and risk culture (strategy) and aspects of the ERM process, including risk assessment, risk management, and monitoring, reviewing and reporting.

Measurement of operational risk

Operational risk has become a specific issue in financial institutions because of the requirement to measure/quantify the level of operational risk that they face. The measurement of operational risk can involve a number of methods, and these are

Table 36.4 Examples of operational risks faced by a bank or financial institution

Event category	Definition	Description	Examples
Internal fraud	Losses due to fraud, misappropriation or circumvention of regulations by internal party	Unauthorized activity, theft and fraud	Unreported transactions Unauthorized transactions Theft and fraud Tax non-compliance Insider trading
External fraud	Losses due to fraud, misappropriation or circumvention of the regulations by third party	Systems security, theft and fraud	Theft/robbery Forgery Hacking/theft of information
Employees	Losses arising from injury or non-compliance with the employment legislation	In a safe environment, damaged employee relations and discrimination	Compensation claim Discrimination allegation
Clients	Losses arising from failure to meet professional obligations to clients	Disclosure and fiduciary	Fiduciary breaches Disclosure violations Misuse of confidential information
Physical assets	Losses arising from loss or damage to physical assets	Disasters and other events	Natural disaster losses Terrorism/vandalism
Systems	Losses arising from disruption of business or system failures	Systems	Hardware or software failure Telecommunications Utility disruption
Processes	Losses from failed transaction processing or process management	Transaction capture, execution, documentation and maintenance	Data entry or loading error Missed deadline or responsibility Failed reporting obligation Incorrect records

normally based on historical information, simulated information or a combination of both. Table 36.4 sets out examples of operational risks faced by a bank or financial institution.

Basel III now provides a standardized approach to measuring operational risk for regulatory capital purposes, which is a function of a bank's income (captured through a Business Indicator) and historical losses (captured through the Internal Loss Multiplier).

In order to measure operational risk, the financial institution needs to adopt a structured approach. Even after the identification of the risks, quantification is only possible if the amount of damage and risk probabilities are determined. Operational risks are hard to quantify but attempts have been made using third-party databases maintained by consortium data; for example, the operational risk exchange.

Developments in operational risk

Before considering developments in operational risk, it is worth noting that concerns about operational risks are universal in all organizations. Although the banks and other financial institutions may have a specific approach to operational risk, the issues that are being considered are the same issues that affect all other types of organizations in the public, private and third sectors.

In a non-financial institution, the questions related to operational risk may well be: 'What is the value of my assets, how do I protect them and to what extent and value (or limit of indemnity) do I need to purchase insurance?' In the financial sector, the questions are more likely to be: 'What are the capital requirements attached to my assets?' and 'Can I afford to keep that amount of (non-productive) capital in reserve or do I need to purchase insurance, and to what value or limit of indemnity?'

It is generally accepted that operational risk concerns need to be integral to the management of a financial institution. It is often the case that management trainees within financial institutions spend some time in the risk management function as they progress with their career in the general management side of the business. It is the intention that this involvement with risk management will create greater awareness before the individual progresses into other roles.

The measurement of operational risk in financial institutions is still proving to be a challenge, and the global financial crisis showed that the extent of operational risk exposure was greater than most banks believed. Certain financial institutions are seeking to adopt risk management standards, such as ISO 31000, and the COSO 2017 framework.

The responsibility for the management of risk and the implementation of controls usually rests with line managers. If this responsibility is not accepted, there is a danger that operational risk management will not be fully integrated into management of the financial institution, with disastrous consequences, and this is emphasized by the Sound Principles guidance from the Basel Committee.

Note

1 Basel Committee on Banking Supervision (2021) *Revisions to the Principles for the Sound Management of Operational Risk*, https://www.bis.org/bcbs/publ/d515.pdf (archived at https://perma.cc/PG6K-8H9Z)

Project, health and safety, legal, supply chain and IT approaches to risk management

Projects, programmes and portfolios

Projects will be undertaken by organizations for a number of reasons, but mainly to bring in some form of change. When alterations to strategy are being planned, a project or series of projects will often be necessary in order to implement the revised strategy. In addition, improvements to operational core processes will require changes that will need to be implemented by undertaking a project. The selection of projects defines the tactics of an organization for the implementation of strategy. As noted, some organizations undertake more than one project at a time and may do so often. In larger organizations, projects may be grouped in programmes, and perhaps even as a portfolio of projects.

Projects

Projects are defined by the Project Management Institute (PMI) (2019)[1] as 'temporary endeavours undertaken to create a unique product, service or result'. The main requirements for any project are that it is delivered on time, within budget and to specification or performance, which has been described as the 'project iron triangle'. Projects are innately uncertain due to their underlying characteristics, summarized by Maylor and Turner (2022)[2] and highlighted in Table 37.1.

Projects can range in size, but, however large or small the project, a number of specific stages will always be present. Figure 37.1 illustrates the key stages in a 'definable work' project lifecycle. These are project inception, project planning, project execution and project closure. The activities within each of these four stages are

Table 37.1   Project characteristics

Project characteristic	Detail
Mission focused	Delivers benefits
Aspects of uniqueness	Exact project not undertaken before
	Aspects of the project have been undertaken before
Change	Impacts on individuals delivering
	Impacts individuals and organizations being delivered to
Temporary	Team disbanded when the project finishes
	Funding is aligned with the project
Integrating	Requires interlinking activities
	Requires knowledge and resources to be integrated
Social construction	Does not behave like a machine
	Involves people and organizations
	Dependency on third parties
Based on assumptions	Detailed requirements may not be known in advance

listed in the figure. It is important to understand the stages in the project lifecycle, so that the risk management inputs into each stage can be planned and executed, and the required benefits obtained.

Due to the increasingly volatile context within which projects exist, affected by both internal and external factors, the project lifecycle illustrated in Figure 37.1 may

Figure 37.1   Project lifecycle

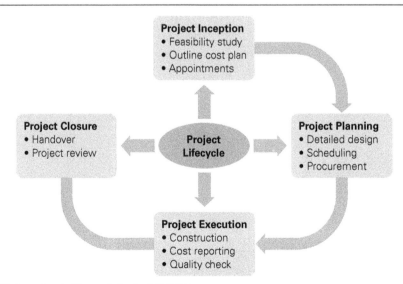

SOURCE Reproduced with permission from Feasible

not be an appropriate approach to managing projects that are considered high-uncertainty work projects. These projects are considered to have high rates of change, complexity and risk, and are managed better using an agile approach.

Agile project management involves short cycles of delivery both iteratively and incrementally, which releases benefits through the process rather than having to wait until the end of a project. This iterative approach would not be appropriate for the majority of construction projects, say, but is frequently used in IT or software development projects that do not necessarily follow a clear linear path.

A key focus on agile projects is around people, through the closer engagement and relationships with clients to understand requirements, and the building of stronger teams with motivated individuals working together to achieve objectives.

Programmes

Programmes (or programs) are defined by the PMI (2019) as 'related projects, subsidiary programs, and program activities managed in a coordinated manner to obtain benefits not available by managing program components individually'. Programmes include more than two projects and can manage up to 20 projects, depending on their nature, location, size and complexity.

Programmes, therefore, manage a collection of projects providing a layer of coordination between them to ensure benefits across them all, in an integrated manner. This approach also capitalizes on the commonality between projects and the resources available, and allows a better understanding and management of the complexities involved.

Portfolios

Portfolios are defined by the PMI (2019) as 'projects, programs, subsidiary portfolios, and operation managed as a group to achieve strategic objectives'. Portfolios include more than two projects or programmes of projects. As noted in the definition, the difference is that portfolios group projects or programmes around strategic objectives. As such, projects and programmes are focused on execution and delivery, that is, doing projects right, whereas portfolio management is about doing the right projects at the right time.

Most organizations would not be involved in sufficient projects to consider programme management or indeed portfolio management. However, in considering which projects to undertake and when, especially where resources are scarce, all organizations should perhaps take a portfolio view. Due to the ever-changing context within which organizations operate, many find that their employees suffer from 'new initiatives' fatigue. Change is considered further in Chapter 39.

Knowing which projects are being executed, where there are gaps and overlaps and where resources are being allocated, is important for all organizations. This knowledge will ensure a plan across any projects being undertaken, increasing the successful delivery of more projects and reducing frustration in organizations.

PMOs

Where organizations undertake projects regularly, usually medium- to large-scale ones, they may establish project management offices (PMOs) to assist in all aspects of the project activities. This 'office' is usually considered as a function within organizations recognizing the importance of projects and of project management professionals.

The role that a PMO covers depends on an organization, the work it undertakes, the industry and sector it works within, its organizational structure, and so on. It also changes as the organizational strategy changes and the project management capability of the organization matures.

A PMO can provide support in many different areas including planning, estimating in both cost and time, contracting, procurement, documentation, resource allocation, control management, monitoring and reporting. PMOs can be expensive to set up and run, but organizations usually recognize that this is compensated for by increased project success. Where organizations do not have the capability to establish PMOs they often outsource this work to external project management consultants.

Project risk management

As noted earlier, projects are inherently uncertain, and project risk management is concerned about the risks embedded within delivery of the project. Project risk management has become one of the best-developed and respected branches of risk management. This is not surprising, given the dynamic and pressured environment in which many projects are undertaken.

It is important to draw a distinction between project and programme risk management, which is about delivering the project on time, within budget and to quality, and portfolio risk management, which is about the reason why the project was undertaken.

Risk is often defined in terms of the deviation from the expected/required outcomes, and within project management, variability of outcomes is very undesirable. Therefore, the focus of risk management in projects is often on controlling the variability of outcomes and the management of both threats and opportunities. Due to the nature of projects, historical data will not usually be available. Accordingly, project risk management needs to be forward-looking in order to anticipate problems before they arise. One option to manage this variability is to include contingency for a project, defined in the active threat and opportunity management (ATOM) methodology[3] as the 'amount of time or money set aside against accepted risks, or to make allowance for unforeseen risks, to be used to compensate for the negative consequences of threats that occur, or to be used to take advantage of positive consequences of opportunities that occur'. This is similar to but not the same as the capital reserve held by financial institutions.

Contingency is usually calculated by taking account of the likelihood of risks occurring and the reasonable extreme of the cost in money and or time should the risks occur. This quantitative assessment commonly uses the Monte Carlo analysis, which considers the interconnectivity of risks in projects and the recognition that risks might overlap or there may be interdependency between them.

Key project risks

Projects and enhancements are fundamentally important to organizations. Most projects are undertaken either to keep ahead of competitors or to catch up with them. Some projects will implement remediations and/or manage risk as well.

As noted earlier, the key requirement for all projects is that they are delivered within the defined cost, time and quality parameters. There are, of course, other objectives for projects in relation to what they need to deliver, such as engagement with communities in which projects are executed, ensuring employees return home safely at the end of each working day, or ensuring regulatory compliance.

In order to identify risks in relation to those objectives, many projects use prompt lists or a risk breakdown structure, as detailed in the ATOM methodology, usually based around four key areas at level 1, and further detailed prompts at level 2, with some examples given in Table 37.2.

Each stage of the project lifecycle, highlighted in Figure 37.1, will have significant risk embedded within it. Figure 37.2 illustrates how uncertainty decreases during the various stages of a project.

Table 37.2 Example project prompt list

Level 1	Level 2
Technical	Scope, design technology, assumptions
Management	Organization, resources, communication, health and safety
Commercial	Contractual terms, procurement, suppliers and vendors, partnerships and joint ventures
External	Legislation, political, country, environmental, competition, site

Figure 37.2 Decreasing uncertainty during a project

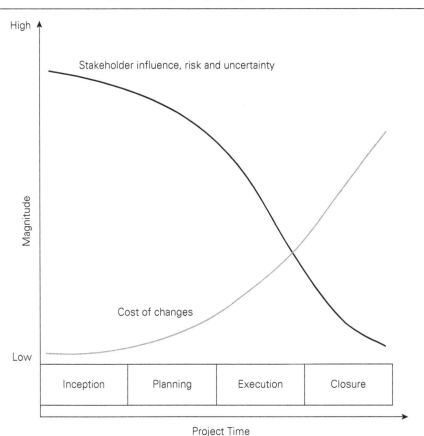

Influences on project risk management

All influences on project risk management contain similar guidance and tools and techniques to those employed in ERM, with best practice merging between the two. However, there are, as with other specialist approaches, specific project-related aspects that are evident in the different standards and frameworks for project risk management. The three approaches outlined here were established from different regional or sector foundations.

The UK's Association for Project Management (APM) developed the project risk analysis and management (PRAM) guide[4] in the mid-1990s. The PRAM approach represents a continuous set of activities that can be started at any stage in the lifecycle of a project. Although the PRAM guide uses a slightly different approach to project stages, benefit can be achieved from using the PRAM guide and be applied to the project stages indicated in Figure 37.1:

1 **Project inception:** At this stage the project is most flexible, enabling changes to be made that can reduce the risks at a relatively low cost.

2 **Project planning:** A clearer understanding of risks and their management is achieved, providing more clarity in decision making on whether to proceed.

3 **Project execution:** The likelihood of completing the project to cost and timescale will increase if all risks are identified and correctly managed.

4 **Project closure:** Outstanding risks are reassessed to ensure ongoing support or maintenance after the project has been handed over and gone live.

The Project Management Institute in the US has considered risk management in its project guidance for many years, and separately published the Standard of Risk Management in 2019. It provides guidance on the implementation of risk management across projects, programmes and portfolios. The PMI (2019) standard notes that:

> Risk management is an essential aspect of all organizational activities. This standard describes the application of risk management within an enterprise risk management (R+ERM) context that includes the portfolio, program, and project domains. Risk management shapes the decision-making processes across an organization and with each of the domains.

In 1989, the UK government formalized an approach to project management, originally for IT projects, called **PR**ojects **IN** Controlled Environments (PRINCE). After consultation with around 150 European organizations, PRINCE2 was developed in 1996 to be suitable for all projects.

To support the application of risk management in relation to PRINCE2, the Management of Risk (M_o_R) guidance was established. The purpose of M_o_R®4 (2022)[5] is described as:

> To provide a framework for decision-makers to understand how uncertainty, and risk arising from that uncertainty, might impact their objectives and to use that framework to make proportionate plans in order to create and protect value.

Health and safety

Health and safety is about preventing harm. It is also about keeping people safe and healthy, so that they do not get hurt in accidents or get illnesses or diseases. Basically, we all owe each other a duty of 'reasonable' care.

Within the context of organizations, the overall responsibility for health and safety rests with employers who must ensure employees, visitors, contractors or individuals who have premises or working areas, are protected by providing such thing as guidance, barriers, protecting equipment and so on. These employees, visitors, contractors and individuals also have a responsibility to follow that guidance, stay behind those barriers and use that protective equipment.

The focus has historically been on safety hazards, the impacts of which, if they cause an accident, are usually felt quite quickly. More attention is now being paid to the health aspect, including physical and mental health and the well-being of individuals. The impact of risks in these areas is often related to past exposures and issues, and not felt for months or years afterwards.

LONG-TERM HEALTH RISKS

The long-term effects of cigarette smoking are well understood, with smoking bans in work and public places in over 70 countries. Some countries are also hoping to create a smoke-free generation in the next 10 to 20 years.

This has led to an increase in the use of vapes as a way of giving up cigarettes or as an alternative. The long-term effect of vapes is not well understood, although it is thought that people who use e-cigarettes have a higher risk of respiratory disease than people who have never smoked, due to damage to the lungs and the promotion of cancer development.

As vapes typically lack warnings, are cheaper than cigarettes, and 'taste' nicer, these products are more likely to appeal to the younger generation. As such, increasing numbers of countries are introducing vaping bans in public areas, with the World Health Organization issuing publications on banning smoking and vaping in schools, including guidance and toolkits to support the creation of nicotine- and tobacco-free campuses.

Health and safety risk management

Health and safety has risk management at its core. All health and safety requirements start with an understanding of the hazards relating to a situation, being those things that could cause harm; for example, such things as chemicals, steps, exposed sharp edges, stressful work environments or travel to unsafe areas. Then, as part of risk assessment, consideration should be given to the risks in relation to those hazards, that is, the chance that the hazard will actually cause harm and the effective management of risks.

Most organizations will have a very low appetite for health and safety risks, with phrases such as 'zero tolerance' or 'zero risk' being used. However, it is impossible to completely eradicate health and safety risks, as even in an office environment, a broken ankle following a trip over a door threshold would, in the UK at least, need to be reported.

AS LOW AS REASONABLY PRACTICABLE (ALARP)

The requirement for risks to be ALARP is fundamental and in simple terms is a requirement to take all measures to reduce a risk, where doing so is reasonable. In most cases this is not done through an explicit comparison of costs and benefits, but rather by applying established relevant good practice and standards.

The development of relevant good practice and standards incorporates ALARP considerations, so in many cases meeting those standards is sufficient. In other cases, either where standards and relevant good practice are less evident, or not fully applicable, measures must be implemented to the point where the costs of any additional measures (in terms of money, time or trouble) would be grossly disproportionate to the further risk reduction (or safety benefit) that would be achieved.

At the same time, it is not prudent to manage health and safety risks at any cost. Most organizations follow a more practical approach, introduced in Chapter 15, which aims to manage risks to a reasonable level, commonly referred to as ALARP or 'as low as reasonably practicable'. In the UK, this approach is at the heart of health and safety regulation and practice. This does not stop some organizations from taking risk management too seriously.

TAKING HEALTH AND SAFETY TOO FAR?

There have been many stories in the past few years where organizations have taken health and safety rules too far, usually to protect themselves from possible claims – real or exaggerated.

For example, organizations not providing plasters or adhesive bandages in the office in case an employee was allergic to them. This ban went against reasonable health and safety practices.

A school in the UK banned three-legged races on sports days to prevent children from harming themselves and reduced the sporting activities for the same reason. This had an opposite effect with children becoming less active, and some finding other, more dangerous activities to occupy themselves.

Key health and safety risks

There are many health and safety risks faced by organizations, which will be different depending on the activities undertaken. The UK Health and Safety Executive[6] provides a list of around 18 common health and safety risks, including:

- Confined spaces
- Display screen equipment

- Electrical safety
- Fire safety
- Gas safety
- Manual handling
- Personal protective equipment
- Slips and trips
- Working at height

Influences on health and safety risk management

The ISO 45000 suite of international standards relates to health and safety. This suite covers different distinct topics as well as the general guidelines, including psychological risks, biorisk and infectious diseases. However, there are many more ISO standards covering specific health and safety issues, such as welding, hazardous substances, machinery and so on.

In the UK, the beginnings of health and safety came with factory inspectorates in the mid-1800s as a move to make people safer in the workplace and reduce the number of accidents and incidents.

Other industries followed suit in the following years, which culminated in the Health and Safety at Work Act in 1974, which is still in place more than 50 years on. More detailed laws and regulations have been developed since, including the Reporting of Incidents, Diseases and Dangerous Occurrences Regulations (RIDDOR) in 1986, the Control of Substances Hazardous to Health (COSHH) in 1989, the Control of Noise at Work Regulations in 2005 and so on.

All countries have their own laws and regulations in relation to health and safety. For example, in the US, the Occupational Safety and Health Administration is the regulatory body that ensures employees work in a safe and healthful environment. In France, health and safety requirements are embedded in the French Labour Code; in Brazil, the National Policy on Occupational Health and Safety includes nearly 40 regulatory standards; and in South Africa, the Occupational Health and Safety Act (Act 85) came into force in 1993.

Legal

The legal profession is a vocation based on the study, development and application of law. Although some occupations have expertise in law, such as the police service, this is not regarded as part of the legal profession. Legal professionals are those solicitors, barristers, lawyers, legal secretaries, arbitrators, mediators, judges and so on, who provide various services and perform different duties in respect of the law.

Legal risk management

Legal risk management is essentially the management of legal risks faced by organizations. It is essentially the same as ERM, with the same principles and process, although applied through a legal lens.

Key legal risks

Legal risks will be relevant to the industries, sectors and countries an organization operates within, but there are common categories that be relevant to many organizations, such as:

- Local and international laws
- Local, industry and international regulations
- Trade unions and employer organizations
- External service providers
- Acts or omissions of third parties
- Contracts and failure to fulfil obligations
- Litigation or legal action against an organization

LEGAL OR NOT

Betting organizations face a plethora of legal risks when operating around the world. Gambling is illegal in some countries, such as India, or one state in a country, such as Utah in the US. In some countries, such as the UK or states within a country, such as Nevada, gambling is legal, with regulations related to the activity. In some countries, gambling is legal, but there are no regulations attached to it, such as Bermuda, Malawi and Kosovo.

At the same time, regulations and laws surrounding gambling change constantly, which can change the legality of gambling itself. As such, an understanding of these changes can consume considerable time, money and effort, but are appropriate given the potential impacts, such as sanctions, fines, loss of licence or prosecution.

Influences on legal risk management

A key standard for legal risk management is ISO 31022 (2020),[7] which is based on ISO 31000, with a legal perspective. The standard notes that:

> Not only are organizations required to comply with the laws of all the countries within which they operate, legal and regulatory requirements can vary between different

countries, strengthening the need for organizations to understand and have confidence in their processes. Organizations need to keep pace with legal and regulatory environment changes and review their needs as new activities and operations are developed... The management of legal risk helps organizations to protect and increase value.

In addition to the principles and process, the standard includes templates in relation to risk identification, the risk register, risk criteria and key clauses when reviewing contracts.

The supply chain

The supply chain can be defined as the integrated journey from converting raw materials or component parts into finished products and services delivered to customers. This supply is both upstream in the sourcing of those raw materials to manufacturing of a product or service and the downstream distribution of the finished product or service.

Suppliers are often described as third parties. In the complex and global environments within which nearly all organizations operate, the number of parties in a supply chain can extend to thousands, leading to a lack of clarity in dependencies in that chain. Even small organizations that operate at a very local level can be dependent on suppliers from almost any country.

Supply chain risk management

Supply chain risk management is the process of finding and addressing potential vulnerabilities in an organization's supply chain. The process to identify and manage supply chain risks is similar to ERM, again with a different perspective.

As such, ERM tools and techniques can also be used; for example the Extended Enterprise, explored in Chapter 10, provides a simple value chain with identification of the upstream inputs and core processes and the downstream outputs. This tool and stakeholder mapping, considered in Chapter 11, can help identify key stakeholders or dependencies. Strategic tools, such as the value chain, noted in Chapter 30, can also identify upstream and downstream supply chains, and business continuity tools such as the business impact analysis can identify key suppliers and dependencies in an organization.

It is important to consider risks *of* the supply chain but also risks *in* the supply chain. Many organizations involve key suppliers in risk discussions and/or require suppliers to provide information on their risk management process and risks themselves in relation to the service they are providing

Key supply chain risks

Risks in the supply chain are similar to those found in ERM in general, but there are those that are particular to this topic. At the same time, the risks will have a different perspective depending on where an organization is in the supply chain. For example, an organization close to the start of the supply chain may have fewer risks relating to dependencies, so it matters at which point in the supply chain an organization becomes the customer.

Categories of supply chain risk include:

- Cyber-attacks and hacks
- Changes in the economy and inflation
- Shortages of resources and raw materials
- ESG
- Logistics and transportation
- Political unrest
- Climate change
- Demand volatility
- Supplier bankruptcies

GETTING STUCK IN THE SUPPLY CHAIN

There can be many threats in the supply chain in logistics and transportation, that is, getting things from A to B. For example, one of the largest container ships in the world, the Ever Given, ran aground in the Suez Canal in March 2021, blocking the busy shipping route for six days. The route, used by dozens of ships, carrying billions of dollars' worth of cargo every day, caused one of biggest and most expensive traffic jams, blocking 400 ships. The vessel, which was itself held, was not released until 106 days after the incident.

Not only was the cargo on the vessel delayed in transit, but also that carried by those stuck in the canal, and those that had to travel much longer routes. In addition, it was estimated that the blockage cost the world more than one billion USD. Lessons learnt from Covid, and particularly this incident, led many organizations to change their policy relating to the supply chain, moving away from the 'just in time' strategy of not storing supplies, but ordering them when needed, to a 'just in case' approach, where key supplies are stored ready for use when needed.

Influences on supply chain risk management

There is no single international standard or suite of standards related to supply chain risk management. The most commonly adopted standards that apply to the supply chain are ISO 9001, ISO 14001 and ISO 28001:

- ISO 9001:2015 Quality management.[8] This standard is a useful basis for organizations in the supply chain to demonstrate that they are managing their business to achieve good-quality products and services.
- ISO 14001:2015 Environmental management systems – Requirements with guidance for use.[9] This standard is a means for organizations to manage their environmental responsibilities to society, providing product transparency.
- ISO 28001:2007 Security management systems for the supply chain — Best practices for implementing supply chain security, assessments and plans — Requirements and guidance.[10] This standard is an option for organizations to establish and document reasonable levels of security within international supply chains and their components.

Information technology (IT)

The US National Institute of Standards and Technology or NIST,[11] defines IT as:

> Any equipment or interconnected system or subsystem of equipment that is used in the automatic acquisition, storage, manipulation, management, movement, control, display, switching, interchange, transmission or reception of data or information.

IT, therefore, includes computers, software, firmware, infrastructure, networking, support services and monitoring.

IT is fundamental to everyone, not just organizations, to function in day-to-day activities. It also provides connectivity and the transfer of information, literally at the touch of a button. However, this innate dependency has its advantages, improving the speed and efficiency of working for all organizations, but there are disadvantages too. For example, in 2023,[12] research found that 48 per cent of people in the world are addicted to their smartphones, with 38 per cent of adults in the age range or 18 to 24, and 27 per cent of adults in the age range of 25 to 34 admitting being addicted or reporting symptoms of addiction. Further research noted that 55 per cent of employers believe that smartphones are the biggest productivity killers in the workplace.

IT risk management

IT risk management, often known as information security risk management, is very similar to ERM in the steps taken to manage risks. Just as project management has three core objectives of cost, time and quality, IT risk management is focused on those risks that could impact on:

- Confidentiality – ensuring appropriate controls are in place relating to appropriate and authorized access to systems and information.
- Integrity – ensuring data is kept up to date, with the permission of the data owner.
- Availability – ensuring systems, software and networks operate as expected within the timelines expected, that is, they are not out of service outside of agreed parameters.

Key IT risks

Risks increase year on year in line with advances in the IT sector. In fact, it can be difficult at times to scan the horizon and be forward-looking with IT risks as the pace of change is so fast.

Some key IT risk themes include:

- Cybersecurity, including attack from internal and external bad actors
- Identify and access management
- Data management, quality and protection
- Use of cloud solutions
- Technology resilience, including business continuity
- AI in data analysis and performing tasks and generative AI, which can create new content, such as that created by ChatGPT
- Increased automation
- IT transformation and agility, often based on out-of-date infrastructure or applications resulting in technical debt (shortcuts in code writing leading to harder to maintain code)
- Cryptocurrency which is not maintained by a centralized authority, such as a government or bank
- Lack of end-to-end understanding and management.

Influences on IT risk management

There are a number of international standards relating to information technology, the main one being ISO 27001. In addition, the international professional association on IT governance, ISACA, produced the COBIT framework.

- ISO/IEC 27001:2022 – Information security, cybersecurity and privacy protection — Information security management systems — Requirements.[13] This standard was established to provide requirements for establishing, implementing, maintaining and continually improving an information security management system. It states that this system preserves the confidentiality, integrity and availability of information by applying a risk management process and gives confidence to interested parties that risks are adequately managed.

- COBIT® 2019 – Control Objectives for Information Technologies.[14] This framework was first developed in 1996 and has evolved to provide knowledge, tools and best practices to maximize the value of IT for organizations. It is based on six principles essential to the effective management and governance of IT across an organization, comprising:

  ○ Provide stakeholder value

  ○ Holistic approach

  ○ Dynamic governance system

  ○ Governance distinct from management

  ○ Tailored to enterprise needs

  ○ End-to-end governance system

Notes

1 Project Management Institute (2019) *The Standard for Risk Management in Portfolios, Programs and Projects*, Project Management Institute Inc., Pennsylvania

2 Maylor, H and Turner, N. (2022) *Project Management*, 5th Ed., Pearson Education Limited, Harlow, UK.

3 Hillson, D and Simon, P (2020) *Practical Project Risk Management – the ATOM Methodology*, Berett-Koehler Publishers, Inc., Oakland

4 APM (2004) *Project Risk Analysis and Management Guide*, APM Publishing Limited, High Wycombe

5 Axelos Ltd (2022) M_o_R®4

6 UK Health and Safety Executive (n.d.) *Managing risks and risk assessment at work – Common workplace risks*, https://www.hse.gov.uk/simple-health-safety/risk/common-workplace-risks.htm (archived at https://perma.cc/DE84-YGS2)

7 ISO (2020) *ISO 31022: Risk management – Guidelines for the management of legal risk*, https://www.iso.org/obp/ui/en/#iso:std:iso:31022:ed-1:v1:en (archived at https://perma.cc/LD5S-5CJ4)

8 ISO (2016) *ISO 9001: What does it mean in the supply chain?* https://www.iso.org/files/live/sites/isoorg/files/store/en/PUB100304.pdf (archived at https://perma.cc/H4CP-AEDN)

9 ISO (2015) *ISO 14001: Environmental management systems – Requirements with guidance for use* https://www.iso.org/obp/ui/en/#iso:std:iso:14001:ed-3:v1:en (archived at https://perma.cc/YG2C-Y2SU)

10   ISO (2007) *ISO 28001 Security management systems for the supply chain – Best practices for implementing supply chain security, assessments and plans – Requirements and guidance* https://www.iso.org/obp/ui/en/#iso:std:iso:28001:ed-1:v1:en (archived at https://perma.cc/RQT6-X2HX)

11   NIST (n.d.) *Computer Security Resource Center – Glossary,* https://csrc.nist.gov/glossary/term/information_technology (archived at https://perma.cc/5NLZ-GB9V)

12   Urban Recover (2023) *70 addiction to cell phone statistics, facts and demographics,* https://www.urbanrecovery.com/blog/addiction-to-cell-phone-statistics#:~:text=According%20to%20a%20recent%20report,48%25%20of%20the%20world's%20population (archived at https://perma.cc/HKP4-AAFB)

13   ISO (2022) *ISO 27001: Information security, cybersecurity and privacy protection – Information security management systems – Requirements,* https://www.iso.org/obp/ui#iso:std:iso-iec:27001:ed-3:v1:en (archived at https://perma.cc/KUC6-52G9)

14   ISACA (2019) *COBIT®2019,* https://www.isaca.org/resources/cobit (archived at https://perma.cc/4WLD-VUX5)

ERM as a translation tool 38

Many chapters in this book, particularly Chapters 30 to 37, have shown that there are different approaches to risk management, developed in relation to different perspectives and focuses, but all using very similar processes, tools and techniques.

However, it can be difficult in organizations, large or small, to understand the risks across the various specialisms in risk management. This chapter will explore how ERM can provide a connection across these diverse perspectives, supporting integration, collaboration, escalation and oversight.

Network and causal analysis

Risks and their controls are not mutually exclusive from each other and should be considered across an organization to understand the risk profile and the true exposure to both opportunities and threats.

As noted in Chapter 37, there are overlaps and dependencies between risks relating to activities, project, functions or departments; for example, where one risk could not occur if another does, or does not. Also, one risk may be more or less likely to happen if another occurs, or one control may affect more than one risk.

This interconnectedness between risks can be collated in risk management systems. For example, where causal analysis is being utilized, software is able to look deeper at the information gathered to find statistical links between cause-and-effect relationships. Network analysis works in a similar way to understand relationships between the network of risks and controls.

Figure 38.1 provides an example risk network, highlighting the sustainability relationship between mining and climate change requirements. Depending on the context of an organization's risks, their controls may sit in different nodes on this network.

Understanding these networks and linkages also provides information on how changes in context, risks and controls in one area can affect other risks and areas of an organization and an understanding of those cross-cutting, interrelated risks.

Figure 38.1 Example of a risk network

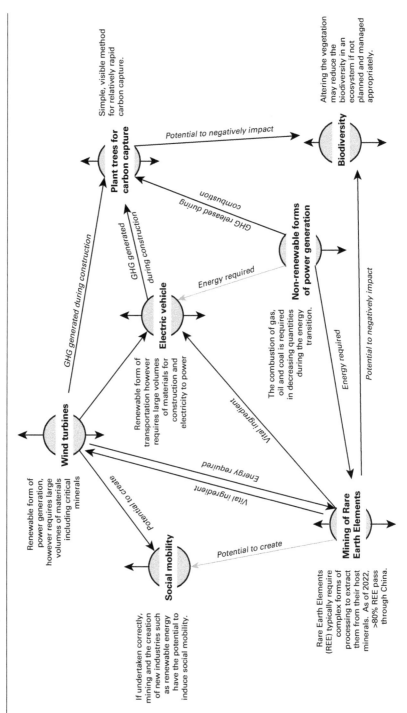

SOURCE SATARLA (2022).[1] Used with permission

For many organizations, these software systems may not be available, meaning that understanding of relationships in risk information would need to be identified and captured manually within the risk information system employed, whether, say, an Excel spreadsheet or a risk database.

This manual intervention requires a central risk management function that can look across an organization at the risk profile and has access to interrogate the risk information and use the findings. This may result in risk themes, escalation and/or amalgamation of risks and the sharing of controls across risks, in discussion with risk and control owners. Even where good-quality risk information has been collated and is updated regularly a central risk management function is still important to help identify emerging risks and recognize themes going forward.

The World Economic Forum Global Risk Reports[2] have included interconnections maps showing the relationships of different risks and different categories of risk. For example, in the 2024 report, the risk of disruptions to critical infrastructure in the economic category is linked to cybersecurity (technological), extreme weather events (environmental), insufficient infrastructure and services (societal) and interstate violence (geopolitical).

Integrated ERM

Tools and techniques are useful in understanding these relationships between risks and controls, but the ERM framework itself can support an integrated approach across an organization, as explored in Chapter 5.

As noted in other chapters, risk management should be applied to both the design and execution of an organization's strategy. Utilizing the knowledge and insight and foresight of the risk team will support effective decision making in the strategic direction and in ensuring the successful achievement of organizational goals.

ERM can also be used as a translation tool in understanding the different perspectives of other risk management activities being carried out and how risk cuts across activities, project, functions, departments and so on. For example, the inability to attract and retain talent may be felt in many different areas of an organization with separate controls but could be managed in a more co-ordinated manner. Figure 38.2 illustrates the overlay of integrated ERM across different specialisms in risk management.

As noted in Chapter 4, each specialist risk management function can continue to implement risk management in the manner and language required of regulators or the industry they are related to, such as health and safety, with ERM drawing together the different approaches. Or, as noted in ISO 31000, it allows risk management to be integrated into all organizational activities.

Figure 38.2 Integrated enterprise risk management

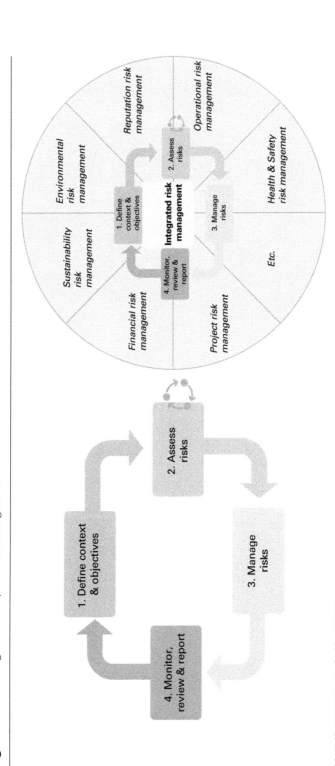

It should be recognized that, although the linkage of risks and controls across an organization is an important aspect of effective management of and assurance on those risks and their controls, an audit trail is required to trace these relationships. The use of unique identifiers for risk information is vital in ensuring the right information is held in the right place and acted upon by the right individuals and teams. Where the sharing, linking and amalgamation of risks and controls is required it should be traced back to its source to ensure a clear bottom-up and top-down understanding of actions being suggested, and support being requested.

The management of risks and controls should also involve those who set budgets within an organization. The management of risks and the establishment of a risk management framework can be expensive. An understanding of the risk profile across an organization will ensure the effective allocation of resources, balancing the needs of the different demands. This is similar to portfolio management, in ensuring the right risks are managed at the right time, and recognizing that risks should not be managed at any cost; that is, there should be a cost/benefit balance.

It is important that organizations recognize that risks do not exist in silos and that an understanding of the interconnectedness and interdependency of risks is key to providing assurance and the effective management of both threats and opportunities. As organizations increase their risk management maturity, understanding of these linkages should become easier, as long as they are mapped and managed consistently.

Notes

1 Gordon, S (2023) Environmental, societal and governance risk management. Hillson, D (ed.), *The Risk Management Handbook*, Kogan Page, London

2 World Economic Forum (2024) *The Global Risks Reports 2024*, 19th Ed., https://www3.weforum.org/docs/WEF_The_Global_Risks_Report_2024.pdf (archived at https://perma.cc/K7QR-Q8Q9)

PART NINE
Adding value

LEARNING OUTCOMES

Having studied this section readers will be able to:

- Describe the components of risk maturity of an organization (4Ns) and the influence on risk management activities (FOIL).

- Explain gap analysis and roadmaps to improvement.

- Summarize the importance of risk management information systems (RMIS).

- Describe change management and its role in risk management and continuous improvement.

- Describe barriers to the implementation of risk management and provide options for addressing those barriers.

- Explain how risk management adds value to an organization and produce examples of that value.

- Outline the technical skills required by a risk practitioner in relation to planning a risk management and architecture, measuring performance and learning lessons.

- Outline the people skills required by a risk practitioner summarized as communication, relationship, analytical and management (CRAM).

- Explain the importance of risk training and upskilling.

- Explain how a risk practitioner can become a trusted partner at all levels of an organization.

- Describe how a risk practitioner adds value, making an impact and a difference in a sustainable and resilient organization.

Maturity and continual improvement

The maturity of risk management has been considered in many chapters of this book, encompassing an organization's risk management principles, framework and process. The UK Corporate Governance Code (2024)[1] requires that the board establish and maintain an effective risk management and internal control framework, and monitor it with at least an annual review of its effectiveness.

Where any gaps are found and improvements are required, a planned approach should be developed to bring an organization's current level of risk management maturity to the desired level.

Critical success factors

A basis for understanding whether an organization has been successful in delivering on its ERM expectations is to look to its risk management policy, which has been considered in Chapter 6. This should provide an overview of a desired level of risk management maturity. For example, the policy should include the purpose of risk management, such as creating and adding value and informing decision making. The policy should also include principles stating what 'good' risk management looks like for an organization, for example, describing the PACED attributes: proportionate, aligned, comprehensive, embedded and dynamic.

As part of the planning element of PIML in implementing risk management, explored in Chapter 9, critical success factors should be developed. Hillson and Simon (2020)[2] consider four critical success factors and their associated attributes for effective risk management, highlighted in Table 39.1.

The initial, and perhaps most important step is ensuring that the risk management initiative is sponsored by a member of the board or a senior member of the executive committee. This support is likely only when it has been agreed and communicated that implanting an ERM approach will contribute to the success of an organization.

Table 39.1   Critical success factors

Supportive organization (culture)	Including clear objectives, adequate resources, risk-aware culture, buy-in from stakeholders
Simple, scalable process (process)	Including proportionate approach, with a clear framework, process and supporting
Competent people (experience)	Including common language and shared understanding, skilled and competent staff with appropriate attitudes and behaviour
Appropriate methods, tools and techniques (application)	Including training, infrastructure and software, integrated toolkit and factsheets on tools and techniques

As risk management changes and develops, the application of the process taken by different organizations will change. With the emergence of governance, risk and compliance (GRC), the risk management context has also changed. Risk management professionals need to be aware of these developments and ensure that their activities are always fully aligned with the other activities within an organization.

An understanding of these critical success factors supports the purpose of risk management for an organization, its effective application, metrics for measurement of success and highlights areas of improvement.

Risk maturity model

Increases in risk management effectiveness can be measured by the use of risk maturity models. The level of risk maturity in an organization is a measure of the quality of risk management activities and the extent to which they are embedded within an organization.

Risk maturity models can also be used to measure the current level of risk culture within an organization, instead of undertaking separate risk culture maturity models, which are considered in Chapter 24. The greater the level of risk maturity, the more embedded risk management activities will become within the routine operations undertaken by an organization.

The level of risk maturity within an organization is an indication of the way in which risk processes and capabilities are developed and applied. In an immature organization, informal risk management practices will take place. This may include a blame culture that leaps into action when things go wrong, potentially avoiding accountability for risk. Also, resources allocated to manage risks may be inappropriate for the level of risk involved.

When explicit risk management is in place, there should be attempts to keep the processes dynamic, relevant and useful. There is likely to be open dialogue and learning so that information is used to inform judgements and decisions about risks. There should be confidence that innovation and risk-taking can be managed, with support, when things go wrong.

When an organization or an industry sector becomes obsessed with risk, an over-dependence on process can emerge, and this may limit the ability to manage risk effectively. There may be over-reliance on information at the expense of good judgement, and dependence on process to define the rationale behind decisions. Individuals may become risk-averse for fear of criticism and procedures are followed only to comply with requirements, not because benefits are sought.

Table 39.2 sets out a model for determining the level of risk maturity within an organization with regard to risk management processes. This table sets out four levels of risk maturity, being the 4Ns of naïve, novice, normalized and natural.[3] These levels are based on the four critical success factors referenced earlier, which are culture, process, experience and application, as indicated in Table 39.1. In addition, each of the maturity levels has defined characteristics described in the table.

A fragmented (or siloed) approach to enterprise risk management is present when different risks are managed in different departments by specialists who do not necessarily work together. For example, an organization can have excellent health and safety, security and business continuity standards, but the benefits of working together may not have been established. The next stage is for these activities to become co-ordinated, so that the approach to enterprise risk management becomes more organized. All risks are then considered together, and the result is likely to be a comprehensive risk register.

However, there is more benefit to be gained from enterprise risk management. Organizations that establish ERM activities that are influential on decision making gain these additional benefits. Risk management (and the risk manager) influence decision making and ensure that risk-related issues are taken fully into account as strategy and tactics are developed. The final stage is for risk management to lead the development of strategy and tactics within an organization. This will require the risk manager to be part of a senior management team, so that the development of strategy and tactics is led by risk considerations, rather than the risk implications being considered after the strategy and tactics have been decided.

Clearly, it is better for an organization to seek a higher level of risk maturity. However, the approach to achieving risk maturity in an organization should be proportionate to the level of risk that an organization faces.

In many organizations, achieving an improved level of risk maturity may be one of the strategic aims for risk management within an organization. If that is the case, an established framework for measuring risk maturity is required. It is important that an organization uses a risk maturity model that aligns with its own ambitions in relation to risk management maturity and provides a practical approach that can be embedded within an organization.

Table 39.2　Four levels of risk maturity

Level	status (4Ns)	Characteristics (FOIL)
1	**Naïve** Level 1 organizations are unaware of the need for enterprise risk management and/or do not understand the benefits that will arise meaning there is little experience or application.	**Fragmented** Risk management activities are fragmented and focused on legal compliance activities, such as health and safety.
2	**Novice** Level 2 organizations are aware of the benefits of enterprise risk management, but have only just started to implement an ERM initiative, with limited experience and inconsistent application.	**Organized** Actions are planned to co-ordinate risk management activities across all types of risk, although plans may not have been fully implemented.
3	**Normalized** Level 3 organizations have embedded ERM into business processes, but management effort is still required to maintain adequate ERM activities with adequate experience and routine application.	**Influential** Embedded ERM processes are influencing processes and management behaviours, but this may not yet happen consistently or reliably.
4	**Natural** Level 4 organizations have a risk-aware culture with a proactive approach to ERM and risk is reliably considered at all stages to gain competitive advantage, with appropriate experience and widespread application.	**Leading** Consideration of risk is a substantial factor in making business decisions, and strategy decisions are led by ERM considerations.

Figure 39.1 provides an interpretation of the level of risk maturity of an organization, based on the 4Ns model. The figure suggests that there is a relationship between whether behaviour is embedded or automatic on the one hand, against competent or desirable on the other. A naïve organization will automatically accept incompetent or undesirable behaviours. A novice organization will become aware that the behaviours are incompetent or undesirable and will have started to make an effort to improve behaviour, but it will not yet have achieved change. However, as change is achieved, it will move towards improved normalized behaviours.

The normalized organization is successful in achieving competent or desirable behaviours, but these are not yet automatic. When an organization reaches the stage of being a natural in risk management, then the competent or desirable behaviours will become unconscious or automatic. The achievement at this point is to ensure

Figure 39.1   Risk maturity demonstrated on a matrix

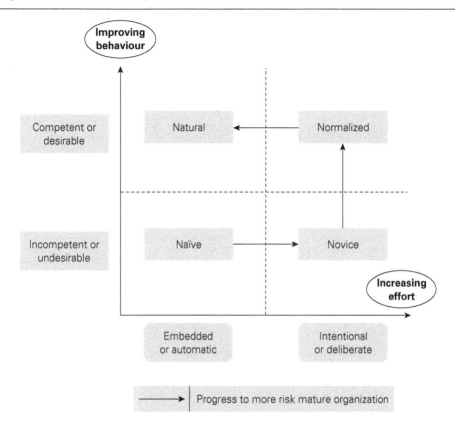

that behaviours are also consistent. One of the primary reasons for producing risk management policies and procedures is to ensure that appropriate behaviours are consistently achieved. Ensuring consistent desirable behaviours is one of the primary objectives of a risk management initiative.

This model provides a means of illustrating the four levels of risk maturity (4Ns) on a matrix and also indicates that the decline from natural behaviour back to naïve may be a short step for organizations that do not put sufficient effort into maintaining their level of risk maturity.

Gap analysis

Risk maturity modelling is typically carried out using surveys, questionnaires or interviews, depending on the requirement to understand the breadth and depth of an organization's maturity levels. The modelling should be based on the current level of maturity that exists rather than respondents providing aspirations of what is desired or what is desirable by an organization.

The measurement of risk maturity across an organization using the 4Ns model will indicate gaps in those contributors to maturity of culture, process, experience and application. It will also highlight differences and gaps in maturity in different parts of an organization. These gaps will be recognized as long as there is an understanding of the desired level of maturity. For example, it may be desirable for some parts of an organization to achieve a normalized maturity level in relation to process.

Continuous improvements

Any improvement plan is only a snapshot in time, and will, itself, need adjustments and updates, for example due to changes in contexts and lessons learnt through implementation. Continuous improvement is the ongoing process of analysing performance against target and making incremental changes to processes, products or services. This forms part of the cyclical planning, implementing, measuring and learning (PIML) methodology for applying risk management considered in Chapter 9, although the learning aspect is not well practised by many organizations.

Learning lessons and continuously improving risk management can streamline workflows, reduce costs, improve practices, and reduce wasted time and effort.

Some organizations recognize that the effective implementation of risk management can, in effect, be a change management programme where it is fundamental in influencing attitudes, behaviours and risk culture and transforming practices, procedures and policies.

Roadmaps to improvement

As noted above, improvements in the risk management performance of an organization will require a planned approach. The nature of the plan will depend on the size, complexity and nature of an organization. The drivers for undertaking risk management and the expected outputs and impacts will vary between organizations, but the purpose, principles and critical success factors will provide guidance on these matters.

There is no single correct approach; the gap analysis should form the basis of an improvement plan or 'roadmap'. Roadmaps allow organizations to plan improvement activities and the related timescales to achieve the appropriate level of maturity, as this takes time. At the least, not everything can be done at once. Activities for improvement are usually undertaken in stages, where resources need to be allocated appropriately, and the plan must be aligned with other initiatives being undertaken in an organization.

Figure 39.2 Improvement roadmap example

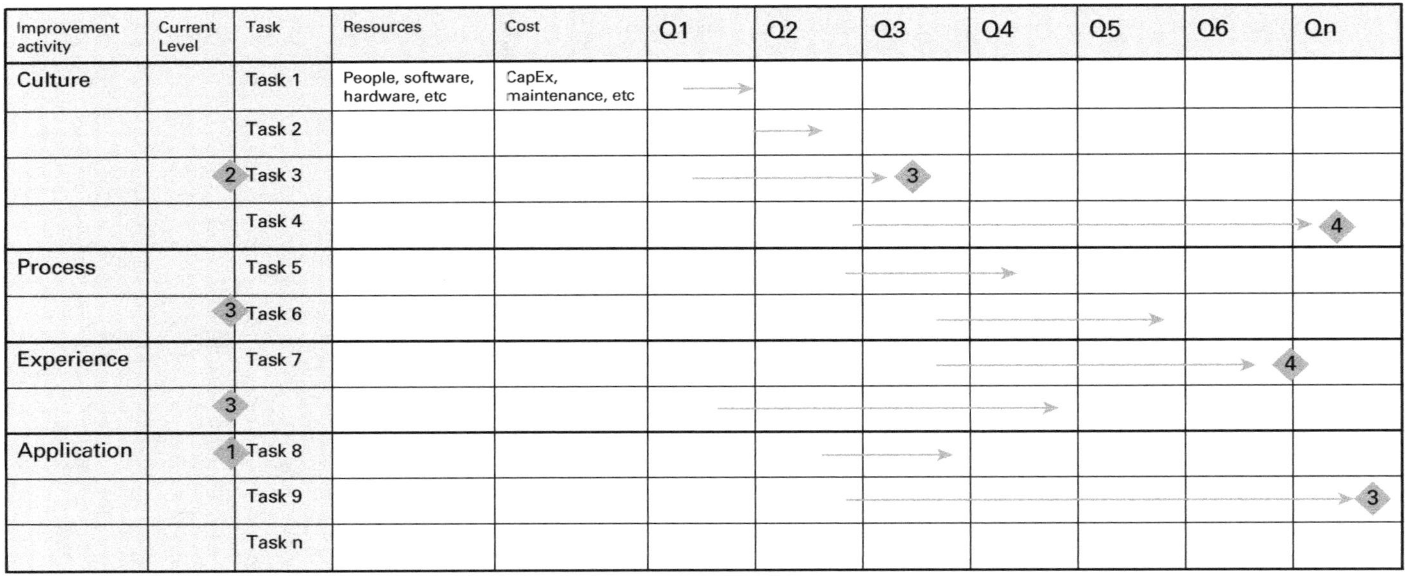

Improvement activity	Current Level	Task	Resources	Cost	Q1	Q2	Q3	Q4	Q5	Q6	Qn
Culture		Task 1	People, software, hardware, etc	CapEx, maintenance, etc							
		Task 2									
	2	Task 3					3				
		Task 4									4
Process		Task 5									
	3	Task 6									
Experience		Task 7								4	
	3										
Application	1	Task 8									
		Task 9									3
		Task n									

Figure 39.2 illustrates a simple road map based on the attributes of successful risk management indicating the actions needed to facilitate the improvement, the current and desired levels of maturity, the timescales involved, the order in which they should be undertaken, and the resources and costs required.

Some of the improvement activities highlighted in the roadmap indicate quick wins; those solutions that are easy and quick to implement at little cost, and which can be reversed. Quick wins have immediate benefits, which can boost confidence in the overall improvement plans. For example, improvements to risk articulation, encouragement to expose the 'unacknowledged' risks, introduction of target risk levels to consider the acceptable level of risk in relation to risk appetite, and so on.

Medium-term improvement plans tend to be more permanent solutions, such as revising and strengthening training programmes, updating the risk management framework, reviewing the impact scales, and so on. Longer-term plans are permanent solutions that usually require capital expenditure, such as the purchase of a risk management information system or the development of new policies and process. These long-term plans often build on the success of short- and medium-term plans.

Risk management information systems

Many organizations refer to their risk management information system (RMIS) as the risk register. An RMIS can collate and communicate a much wider range of risk information, as summarized in Table 39.3.

RMIS have been used for some time to record details of insurance claims. The use of an RMIS has become more sophisticated and is now likely to enable the recording of details of the risk exposure, risk control and risk action plans. In many cases, this is also linked to measures of the progress of activities being undertaken, which can inform reporting and any dashboard to measure risk across different time frames.

There are a number of software products that support a broad enterprise-wide approach. These include software packages that can undertake risk register reviews from lower divisional units to produce reports to the board level by categorizing and highlighting risks which are significant at that level. RMIS can also produce detailed risk analysis and dependency modelling reviews, although, as noted in Chapter 7, it may be easier and cheaper to undertake such analysis and modelling in separate, more sophisticated software.

RMIS are becoming more useful as more data becomes available and are themselves becoming more developed and sophisticated, offering a significant benefit to organizations that use them.

An analysis of the advantages and disadvantages of RMIS is set out in the next box. In general, an RMIS becomes more valuable when the risks are complex or the amount of data that needs to be recorded is substantial.

Table 39.3 Risk management information system

The following types of information may be handled, stored, managed, distributed and communicated using a risk management information system (RMIS):

Risk management policy and protocols
Risk profile data, values and information
Emergency contact arrangements and contact details
Insurance values and cost of risk data
Insurance claims handling and management protocols
Historical loss/claims experience/information
Insurance policy coverage and other information
Risk management action plans (risk register)
Risk improvement plans and implementation
Business continuity plans and responsibilities
Disaster recovery plans and responsibilities
Corporate governance arrangements and reports

ADVANTAGES AND DISADVANTAGES OF RMIS

There are many risk management information systems available commercially, although the market is consolidating as investment in new technologies is causing separate firms to combine forces. Initially, these systems required large amounts of separately held data to cross-reference activity in a company with loss activity or risk exposure. In addition, they were tailored to the individual companies concerned. The systems were often aimed at larger companies that had the resource and data to make the pursuit worthwhile.

Improvements in their ability to manage and analyse diverse datasets mean these systems are now becoming more competitive. Advanced technology enables risk managers to integrate techniques of modelling and scenario simulations to suit their individual context.

While the cost of developing systems is reducing, it must be shown that benefits will exceed whatever cost is involved. The costs are immediate and tangible; the benefit is difficult to estimate or demonstrate. It is a potential future benefit, not an assured, immediate expense reduction.

Whether the risk assessments from an RMIS are likely to lead to enough marginal benefits to offset the cost of data tracking and analysis depends on the risk profile of the company. Ultimately, an RMIS may pay for itself by enabling an organization to avoid or effectively finance that one catastrophic loss that would otherwise slash the financial results of the company.

> This has fuelled a debate on the use of the risk register in many organizations, considered in Chapter 7. Further technologies are being developed that integrate risk assessment, risk recording and risk action plans within the management information that is used for the day-to-day management of an organization.

Change management

Change management is defined by the Association for Project Management (APM)[4] as 'the overarching approach taken in an organization to move from the current to a future desirable state using a co-ordinated and structured approach in collaboration with stakeholders'. This is much the same as the approach taken through improvement roadmaps.

All organizations will be subject to change, although some may not recognize the need or be willing to facilitate any required changes. Change is often required to ensure the viability of an organization, financially or otherwise.

Change management is a link between strategy setting and its execution, implemented through modifications, alterations or transformations in operational activities to ensure the successful achievement of that strategy. Organizational change is usually driven by the external context, such as customer or market trends or technological advancement. However, it is reliant on alterations in the internal context especially through changes needed in attitudes, behaviours and culture within an organization.

The Change Management Institute[5] notes that change management focuses on people. To facilitate change, it is important to have a clear understanding of stakeholders who the change can affect, who are involved in it and who will be impacted by it. The APM suggests that early and regular engagement with stakeholders is needed to:

- Get individuals ready and prepare an organization for change
- Demonstrate the benefits of the change
- Encourage buy-in from all stakeholders, at all levels within an organization and those external to it
- Embed new expectations in attitude, behaviour and culture and capabilities required to deliver the change

The Change Management Institute has developed its Change Management Framework (2022) to support change managers and those involved in change with information on key activities, outputs and relevant knowledge in relation to change

Figure 39.3 Change practice framework

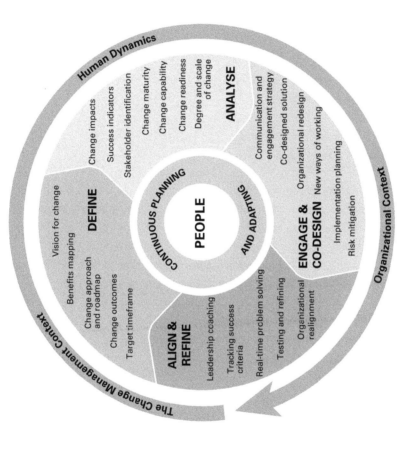

Human Dynamics

Organizational Context

The Change Management Context

DEFINE
Vision for change
Benefits mapping
Change approach and roadmap
Change outcomes
Target timeframe

ANALYSE
Change impacts
Success indicators
Stakeholder identification
Change maturity
Change capability
Change readiness
Degree and scale of change

CONTINUOUS PLANNING

PEOPLE

AND ADAPTING

ENGAGE & CO-DESIGN
Communication and engagement strategy
Co-designed solution
Organizational redesign
New ways of working
Implementation planning
Risk mitigation

ALIGN & REFINE
Leadership coaching
Tracking success criteria
Real-time problem solving
Testing and refining
Organizational realignment

SOURCE Change Management Institute (2022). Used with permission

initiatives, as illustrated in Figure 39.3. The framework is centred around people and the need for continuous planning and adapting, recognizing that change is a cyclical process, which must be agile and open to modification. This core focus is underpinned by three applied knowledge areas, which are the change management context, human dynamics and organizational context, and supported by four key activities or practices:

- Define, including the vision, benefits mapping and outcome
- Analyse, including success indicators, maturity, capability and degree and scale of change
- Engage and co-design, including communication and engagement, new ways of working, implementation planning and risk management
- Align and refine, including leadership coaching, real-time problem solving and organizational realignment.

A CHANGE TOO FAR?

A global organization producing gaming apps has recently undergone a number of organizational changes due to acquisitions of smaller, competitor organizations. The integration team led these acquisitions, developing initiatives to ensure the smooth incorporation of the acquired businesses and their employees.

The volume of change introduced to the business has led to 'initiative fatigue', resulting in lower morale across an organization, increased workload and stress, reduction in performance and the inability to retain staff, with the loss of key talent and corporate and specialist knowledge.

Unfortunately, the changes being introduced to an organization were task focused rather than people centric.

Notes

1 FRC (2024) *UK Corporate Governance Code*, https://media.frc.org.uk/documents/UK_Corporate_Governance_Code_2024_kRCm5ss.pdf (archived at https://perma.cc/6UMD-PX52)

2 Hillson, D and Simon, P (2020) *Practical Project Risk Management – the ATOM Methodology*, Berett-Koehler Publishers, Inc., Oakland

3 Hillson, D (2010) *Risk Doctor Briefing: How mature is your risk capability?* https://risk-doctor.com/wp-content/uploads/2020/06/58-How-mature-is-your-risk-capability.pdf (archived at https://perma.cc/6WU9-HZVR)

4 APM (n.d.) *What is change management and organisational change?* https://www.apm.org.uk/resources/what-is-project-management/what-is-change-management/ (archived at https://perma.cc/B4FN-CQ5G)

5 Change Management Institute (2024) *What is Change Management?* https://change-management-institute.com/what-is-change-management/ (archived at https://perma.cc/YN5N-ZJP3)

How risk management adds value

Across the chapters in this book, the benefits of risk management have been explored whether in relation to the ERM principles, framework, process, its relationship to strategy, tactical projects or operational activities, or as part of good governance.

The focus on and need for risk management increases year on year as individuals and organizations recognize its value in ensuring the successful achievement of objectives. When implementing or enhancing risk management practices there may be challenges from others to making the necessary changes or barriers to implementation.

Barriers to implementation

It can be helpful to identify the challenges (or barriers) others may set when implementing change. The arguments against change are often common and are set out in Table 40.1 together with actions to overcome these barriers. These include the fact that successful risk management requires the commitment of all parties, and that implementation will only be as good as the least committed member of a team. Analysis of these barriers within the context of a specific organization will lead to the identification of the best options to ensure that risk management delivers the optimum benefits.

There is no single action that will ensure adequate implementation and no single time frame by which implementation will be fully achieved, although experience indicates a two- and five-year time horizon is realistic.

Table 40.1   Implementation barriers and actions

Barrier	Action
Lack of understanding of value of risk management	Establish a shared understanding, common expectations and a consistent language of risk in an organization
Belief that risk management will suppress entrepreneurship	Encourage a positive approach as an enabler of business actions

(continued)

Table 40.1 (Continued)

Barrier	Action
Lack of support and commitment from senior management	Identify a sponsor on the main board of an organization and confirm shared and common priorities
Seen as just another initiative, so relevance and importance not accepted	Agree a strategy that sets out the anticipated outcomes and confirms the benchmarks for anticipated benefits
Benefits not perceived as being significant	Complete a realistic analysis of what can be achieved and the impact on the mission of an organization
Not seen as a core part of business activity and too time-consuming	Align effort with core processes and achievement of the mission of an organization
Approach too complicated and over-analytical (risk overkill)	Establish appropriate level of sophistication for risk management framework and undertaking risk assessments
Responsibilities unclear and any external expenditure agreed (including external consultants) resented	Establish agreed risk architecture with clear roles and accepted risk responsibilities
Risks separated from where they arose and should be managed	Include risk management in job descriptions to ensure that risks are managed within the context that gave rise to them and establish audit trails
Risk management seen as a static activity not appropriate for a dynamic organization	Align risk management effort with the mission of an organization and with the business decision-making activities
Risk management too expansive and seeking to take over all aspects of the company	Be realistic: do not claim that all the business activities within an organization are risk management by another name

What is the evidence of value?

Before discussing how risk management adds value in more detail, it is worth considering the evidence pointing to this conclusion. It is intuitively agreed that incorporating an ERM approach is of benefit; both regulators and credit agencies investigate and assess the ERM approach of individual companies. ISO, COSO and other bodies strongly support using a risk management approach that manages risk in an integrated fashion across the enterprise as a whole and not individual risks in isolation.

It is, however, an approach that is still considered to be in its infancy in some sectors and which some on the boards of companies may fear involves excessive expenditure for limited gain.

Conclusively showing that companies using an ERM approach generate better financial and business outcomes than those without is challenging. The evidence appears to show that an ERM approach is beneficial across sectors and regardless of the development status of the economy in which an organization operates. In other words, ERM works in developed, developing and emerging economies.

Studies usually rely upon financial data as a 'proof point', and while this does not directly apply to not-for-profit or governmental agencies, it might be argued that the beneficial effects in for-profit organizations reflect best practice management styles that can be transferred to other organizations and sectors. If ERM is beneficial in the commercial sector it is by helping those companies to achieve their objectives. These companies appear to have a competitive advantage when compared with peers who do not use an ERM approach. Non-commercial entities might well look to this as a way of helping them to achieve their objectives in a better fashion too.

The challenge in proving a positive link between ERM and improved performance in an organization has always been how to categorize those organizations that operate using ERM and those that do not. Conclusive proof remains elusive, but the direction of travel is positive.

The challenge is compounded in developed economies where information on the value added to organizations has a specific commercial value. Various consultants with risk management businesses such as Deloitte, McKinsey or Aon produce studies featuring examples of value added through the use of various techniques based on interview, survey or market data techniques. Each has merit and can be compelling, but it remains the case that such studies have an economic interest in the outcome.

Academic studies have been conducted in both developing economies (Brazil) and in emerging economies (Vietnam) which have the appeal of being less open to accusation of bias, however small it may be, in commercial studies from developed countries. Firstly, after performing a detailed search of 80 Brazilian listed companies' financial statements to assess those with a CRO or a well-structured governance, with a risk committee managed by the board of directors, Silva et al.[1] confirmed a positive association between firm value and the use of an ERM approach. They used quantitative techniques involving financial and market metrics that reflected the future expectation of shareholders. This was found after reviewing each firm on a total of 673 occasions and concluded in reports from 2013.

A second study, by Kommunuri,[2] reviewed the largest sample of companies in an emerging market economy using detailed statistical techniques. The findings from the research indicated that ERM adoption benefits a cross-section of industries. This study specifically noted that a 'key advantage is that ERM enables a highly significant increase in firm value'. The study also revealed that some firms did not experience improved profitability over the short term and implied that the costs of setting up systems may have been the reason for this.

Improved performance and key risk indicators

The justification for using an ERM approach as outlined above is an attempt to place a cash value on risk events being avoided, although it does also point towards an element of organizational improvement being responsible for the enhanced value generated.

Changes in business performance are often measured by key performance indicators (KPIs) such as an increase in sales in retail, or passenger numbers in the airline industry. If a risk management approach has been implemented in an organization this technique can be replicated into the use of key risk indicators (KRIs), as explored in Chapter 20. There are also ways in which KPIs such as financial, accounting or business management performance indicators may function as risk indicators. For example, a high level of business growth can put pressure on governance systems and internal controls, increasing the potential for fraud, human error, and so on. Indicators that relate to the performance of organizational systems, processes and human resources may also signal a change in operational risk.

Using these metrics will also provide an ongoing justification for the use of an ERM approach as a KRI acts as a proxy for risk exposure. A change in the value of the KRI will signal a change in probability and/or impact, as highlighted in Table 20.2 in Chapter 20.

The benefits of an ERM approach

It has been stated throughout this book that the perceived added value from an ERM approach is secure, compliant, legal and competitive operations that bring success to an organization, whatever the measures happen to be. At the same time, the cost of implementing an ERM approach should be less than the benefits obtained.

COSO (2017)[3] has stated that organizations that integrate ERM throughout their organization will realize many benefits, including:

- Increasing the range of opportunities: By considering all possibilities (both positive and negative aspects of risk), management can identify new opportunities and the challenges associated with current opportunities.
- Identifying and managing throughout the risk organization: Every organization faces risks and a risk can originate in one part of an organization but impact a different part. Management identifies and manages these organization-wide risks to sustain and improve performance.

- Increasing positive outcomes and advantage while reducing negative surprises: ERM allows organizations to improve their ability to identify risks and establish appropriate responses, reducing surprises and related costs or losses, while profiting from beneficial developments.

- Reducing performance variability: Performing beyond expectations may cause concern and ERM allows organizations to anticipate the risks that would affect performance.

These may perhaps be simplified into stating that an ERM approach encourages an organization to consciously consider the uncertainties it faces – in particular, to consider those uncertainties that might otherwise be overlooked, including.

In clarifying the risks, an organization will be better prepared, and in applying management techniques will be more resilient to changing circumstances. Using this approach should also provide an agreed framework for decision making and accountability, which should reduce the potential for internal disputes and allow the prioritization of resources, including investments.

Chapter 5 outlined some of the benefits of ERM, and Table 40.2 provides more detail for other key benefits.

Table 40.2   Benefits of ERM

	Benefits	Aspects of ERM that help realize them
1	Enhanced value and resilience of the business	Greater awareness of threats and opportunities to an organization's objectives, and the processes for dealing with them
2	Fewer unpleasant surprises and shocks for the company and its shareholders	Greater predictability of performance More confidence in the earnings guidance given to shareholders and the market
3	Greater shareholder confidence in the company	A structured and transparent risk management process, directly aligned to the company's objectives, that supports good governance (an aspect of benefit 1) An ability to demonstrate that shareholder capital is being protected and is being exposed to an appropriate level and type of risk
4	An improved organizational culture	A move away from a prescriptive 'rule-book' approach Clear allocation of accountability for material risks and for the assurance of critical controls A requirement for managers to act with foresight and hindsight

(continued)

Table 40.2 (Continued)

	Benefits	Aspects of ERM that help realize them
5	Improved business performance	Greater risk management effectiveness, through a structured approach that provides more confidence that important threats and opportunities have been identified and addressed appropriately (supporting benefit 1)
6	Better and faster decisions, and prudent risk taking	Better and more focused information about threats and opportunities, and greater confidence that decisions are being taken on a sound basis (a driver for benefit 5)
7	Better allocation of resources and capital	Agreed risk management standards and guidelines that are applied consistently across the business, thus allowing 'competing' risks and controls to be compared more readily (an aspect of benefit 6 that supports benefit 1)
8	Better responsiveness and adaptability in the face of changing circumstances	Identification, monitoring and review of emerging threats and opportunities and potential drivers of change (an aspect of benefits 5 and 6 that support benefit 1)
9	Reduced operational costs and management effort	A more structured and efficient risk management process, built on existing organizational practices, that reduces effort and allows managers to focus on the things that really matter (supporting benefits 5 and 6)
10	Improved organizational learning	Monitoring and review processes, including post-investment reviews and lessons learned activities, that support the capture and dissemination of knowledge about the drivers of successes and failures (supporting benefit 6)
11	Enhanced and more efficient control	Better priority setting that assists managers (and internal audit) to focus their assurance activities on the controls that are the most critical for the business
		Fewer redundant or inefficient controls, because controls are better related to the risks faced (supporting benefits 1, 3, 12 and 13)
12	Reduced losses and better incident management	Better identification, analysis and evaluation of what might cause loss of money or assets, or cause harm to people or the environment, leading to better and improved controls (supporting benefit 1)
13	Reduced insurance premiums	A transparent and demonstrable process for identifying and treating potential threats, with supporting control improvement and assurance processes (supporting benefit 9)
14	Satisfy legal, regulatory and internal compliance and reporting requirements	A codified and transparent process, with associated reporting on risk management status and improvements (supporting benefit 3)

SOURCE Reproduced with permission from Broadleaf Capital International http://broadleaf.com.au/resource-material/showing-that-effective-risk-management-adds-value/

Enterprise risk management is at the heart of effective decision making at all levels of an organization. Having a supported, simple approach, with appropriate tools and capable and competent individuals, will ensure an effective risk management framework is in place to help create, protect and maintain value for an organization.

Notes

1 Silva, J, da Silva, A and Chan, B (2018) Enterprise risk management and firm value: Evidence from Brazil, *Emerging Markets Finance and Trade*, 55 (3), pp 687–703

2 Kommunuri, J (2016) Firm performance and value effects of enterprise risk management, *New Zealand Journal of Applied Business Research*, 14 (2)

3 COSO (2017) *Enterprise Risk Management: Integrating with Strategy and Performance – Executive Summary,* https://www.coso.org/_files/ugd/3059fc_61ea5985b03c4293960642 fdce408eaa.pdf (archived at https://perma.cc/2MZ4-5UAR)

Risk practitioner competencies   41

As noted in Chapters 7 and 38, and other chapters within this book, there is a need for a central risk management function to ensure consistent application of effective risk management, and to provide and support the assurance of the four lines of sight: insight, foresight, hindsight and oversight.

A risk management function does not require a large department, even in the largest of organizations, but it does require sufficient individuals to be able to collate, interrogate, analyse and report on risks, and to support an organization in embedding ERM. Some organizations have central teams that go out to support an organization, whereas others have a smaller central team with risk champions in different functions, departments or entities.

Any approach to resourcing ERM must be proportionate to the size and complexity of an organization, the context within which it operates, its risk management maturity and what it is trying to achieve. It must also consider the competencies needed to effectively implement risk management.

Competency frameworks

Risk management has become a profession, rather than a set of activities. For any profession, it is essential that a set of competencies is established that defines the activities that practitioners within the profession will need to display. There are several styles and formats for competency frameworks, but most are based on the stages that are involved in the practice of the profession. Having identified the stages that are involved in the profession, the levels of competency required at different stages of seniority are then described. The IRM Professional Standards[1] provide these levels and competency requirements across four key components, being insights and context, strategy and performance, risk management process and organizational capability.

It is generally accepted that both technical or 'hard' skills and people or 'soft' skills are required to become a successful practitioner in the profession. The risk practitioner needs both these skills in order to successfully assist an organization with the design and implementation of a risk management framework.

Two areas of technical skills are required by a risk practitioner. Firstly, and most obviously, the practitioner needs to have competency across a range of risk management issues and activities. A range of business skills in order to understand the context (both external and internal) within which an organization operates is useful. An understanding of business and the development of appropriate business skills is essential if the risk management practitioner is to successfully develop an appropriate risk management process and supporting risk management framework.

In addition, people or interpersonal skills are required by practitioners, that may be taught or self-taught.

Technical skills

This book is not about the development of business skills, although some aspects are covered, such as strategy, resilience and sustainability. The greater focus of the book is placed on the risk management technical skills that will be required by the risk practitioner. Table 41.1 provides an overview of the risk management technical skills that will be required by a successful risk management practitioner.

Table 41.1   Risk management technical skills

Skills associated with planning risk management strategy	
Evaluate status	Evaluate an organizational context and objectives and map the external and internal risk context
Develop strategy	Develop risk strategy and risk management policy and develop the common language of risk
Skills associated with implementing a risk management architecture	
Design architecture	Design and implement risk management architecture, roles and responsibilities
Develop processes	Develop and implement the risk management processes, procedures and protocols
Build awareness	Build a culture of risk awareness aligned with other management activities
Skills associated with measuring risk management performance	
Facilitate assessments	Facilitate the identification, analysis and evaluation of risks, and design record-keeping procedures
Evaluate controls	Evaluate existing performance and evaluate efficiency and effectiveness of existing controls
Improve controls	Facilitate the design and implementation of necessary and cost-effective control improvements

(continued)

Table 41.1 (Continued)

Skills associated with learning from risk management experience	
Evaluate framework	Evaluate risk management strategy, policies and processes, and introduce improvements
Design reports	Develop understanding of reporting requirements, design reporting formats and produce appropriate reports

Interpersonal skills

Technical skills are usually considered to be associated with intellectual intelligence, whereas soft or people skills are associated with emotional intelligence. To be successful, the risk practitioner needs a combination of both types of intelligence and both sets of skills.

The importance of people skills has increased considerably as communication within and between organizations has changed, especially in the last few years with the mixture of face-to-face, online and hybrid working affecting the speed, style and delivery of communication so dramatically. Table 41.2 describes the range of people skills that are required in the business environment. These skills can be classified as communication, relationship, analytical and management (CRAM) skills.

Table 41.2 People skills for risk management practitioners

Key skill	Skill requirements
Communication	Excellent written and oral skills Presentation and public-speaking skills Committee and meeting participation skills
Relationship	Influencing skills to work with 'challenging' behaviour Negotiating skills to defuse conflict and identify solutions Networking skills across organizational silos
Analytical	Strategic thinking skills and creativity skills Data-handling skills to get to the heart of a problem Research skills to present arguments based on facts
Management	Time-management skills to manage teams and projects Leadership skills to motivate and develop staff Facilitation skills to assist with setting priorities

---

THE BENEFITS OF PEOPLE OR 'SOFT' SKILLS

While labelling them 'soft' may make them sound less important than technical skills, in fact, people skills are essential for all businesses, and can actually mean the difference between success and failure. Employing staff with good people skills will mean they are more effective when interacting with people. This is particularly important if your business is largely based on face-to-face contact with clients.

Just as technical skills can be learnt and developed, so too can people skills. In fact, people skills are continuously developed over the course of a lifetime, but there are ways that you can encourage this in your business. These include workshops, seminars and encouragement to staff to provide input, suggestions and advice in business discussions.

It is a greater challenge for risk practitioners to master the range of skills that are required in order to be successful. As such, the successful risk manager will also require the skills associated with self-management and self-development. Typically, these will be the skills expected of all technical professionals and will often be underpinned by adherence to a code of ethics or conduct together with a requirement to maintain knowledge through continuous professional development once certified. Self-development covers activities that enhance talents and potential, as well as increasing job satisfaction and future employability. Self-development also includes developing other people, and this may include activities such as teacher, mentor, training provider and/or professional coach.

Communication skills

A core soft skill for any risk practitioner is communication, as explored in Chapter 22 and noted above. Internal communication within an organization will be undertaken through the risk architecture, considered in Chapter 6. External risk communications will need to take place with external stakeholders, including the media, the general public and pressure groups.

The next box describes risk communication in relation to the global pandemic. It suggests that for the messages to resonate there needs to be an appeal to emotion as well as logic. The public perception of risk may not be aligned with the scientific evidence if the public is wary and afraid of any development. Information communicated by an organization needs to address these emotional concerns if it is to be heard.

DEVELOPMENT OF RISK COMMUNICATION

Perceptions of risk, and the behaviours that result, are a matter not only of the facts but also of our feelings, instincts and personal life circumstances. Communication that offers the facts but fails to account for the affective side of our risk perceptions is simply incomplete.

Risk communication is also commonly thought of as what to say under crisis circumstances, but this is inadequate. While it is certainly true that communication in times of crisis is important in managing the public response, countless examples have taught that a great deal of the effectiveness of risk communication during a crisis is based on what was done beforehand.

Covid-19 has highlighted the importance of communication, and in particular communication in relation to risk. The attempts by countries to manage the spread of the disease required a different approach when social interactions were restricted and non-verbal signals, such as eye contact and facial expressions, were literally 'masked'.

In addition, confusion around the facts of Covid-19, or what people believed to be the facts, led to inappropriate behaviours in preventing the disease from spreading across the globe. Also, the different responses to tackling the disease showed how views on the risk differed around the world.

For example, Italy and China instigated swift and strict lockdown protocols in relation to any outbreaks. In the UK, lockdown protocols were put in place and were relaxed and lifted as outbreaks moved around the country. In fact, the numbers of people testing positive for the disease were plotted on maps of the UK, allowing people to 'watch' the disease spread. Sweden, however, did not enforce strict lockdown measures, but relied instead on voluntary reduction measures.

The transmission of logical and evidence-based argument is becoming more important with the focus of ESG and the need to communicate with a wider range of external stakeholders to understand the double materiality of activities an organization undertakes. As noted in Chapter 33, double materiality requires important issues to viewed from the outside world in and the inside world out.

At the same time, this transmission of logical and evidence-based argument is made more problematic by the rise of the 'fake news' culture and disdain of 'experts' in favour of beliefs that appear attractive by appealing to the emotions of individuals who are vulnerable to these cries.

Communication skills are needed for both internal and external reporting, presentations, training and so on. The ability to communicate verbally, visually and through the written word is essential, having empathy with the audience and adopting the style of communication that fits within the culture of an organization. Report writing, for both internal and external distribution, is considered in Chapter 22.

When making any presentation, it is important for the risk practitioner to decide what the purpose of the presentation is and who will be receiving it. When communicating a message, it is useful to think about the '5Cs' of communication:

- Clear: Ensure that the recipient understands the purpose of the communication.

- Concise: It is more likely to be listened to.

- Coherent: It is logical and relevant to the main topic.

- Credible: There is substantiating evidence to address the audience's concerns and priorities.

- Complete: It provides the audience with everything they need in order to take necessary action.

A COMMON LANGUAGE OF RISK

The first reason an organization needs a risk language is to underpin its risk culture. Everyone in an organization has a role in an effective risk management process. Most organizations have many layers (for example, executives, line managers and employees) and 'silos' (for example, technology, treasury, operations, quality management and compliance). A common language is needed to cut through the layers and break down the silos. Without a common language, the risk management team will spend too much time resolving communication issues at the expense of their primary responsibilities.

Relationship and influencing skills

There is a range of relationship skills that are required, with perhaps the most important being the ability to influence. Influencing skills are vitally important in engaging with individuals and organizations to gain buy-in and embed risk management in guiding people in a particular direction or affecting change without coercion. Influencing requires a number of 'soft' skills, including:

- Leadership – to guide with authority, but without the need to be in charge.

- Empathy – to understand the feelings and perspectives of others.

- Observation – to notice what is going on and acquire information.

- Conflict resolution – to be patient, stay impartial, listen to both sides and collaborate.

- Negotiation – to seek compromise, recognizing the need to give and take.

- Active listening – to listen and observe, pay attention and provide feedback.

- Communication – to articulate and share ideas and opinions and to listen to views of others.

Listening skills are vitally important to influence a change of behaviour such as modifying risky activities. The point of view of an individual you are negotiating with or are seeking to influence must be clearly understood, and if possible, repeated back to them. Successful influencing is best achieved by individuals who have the ability to gain support, inspire others, create relationships and engage the imagination of other people. Generally speaking, influence is achieved by using positive energy and enthusiasm about the issues that need to be changed. Achieving improvements in risk management standards often requires continuous negotiation. The means of achieving successful negotiations are well established, and risk practitioners need to be aware of and embrace negotiating techniques.

In being a good influencer, the successful risk practitioner needs to understand the importance of 'political' skills. This usually means the need to understand the background or context of an individual who may be challenging and who displays inappropriate behaviours. The risk practitioner should be aware of the group dynamics and be able to negotiate so that those individuals can find some benefit from their stance, or as a minimum they do not 'lose face' in the discussion. It is important therefore to defuse conflict and negotiate solutions in a flexible way, including by being aware of cultural influences and differing stakeholder requirements.

In many ways, political skills are at their most important when the risk practitioner is chairing a meeting. All persons attending the meeting are entitled to voice their opinion in full, for as long as their message is clear, concise, coherent and credible. The role of a chairperson, especially when present in a non-executive role, is to stay neutral and remain unbiased while guiding the meeting to an appropriate consensus.

Analytical skills

Analytical skills range widely and require strategic and logical thinking. On occasions, when problem solving is involved, creative lateral thinking is also a key requirement of the risk practitioner. Analytical skills are not always mathematically based and well-developed problem-solving skills will be of considerable benefit to a typical risk practitioner.

In addition to analytical skills, research skills are often a requirement of many risk practitioners. The ability to locate and analyse information quickly and efficiently will be of considerable benefit to a risk practitioner.

Risk practitioners are often required to evaluate a great deal of information about a specific topic, find the common thread within that information and present the findings in a concise and logical manner. This is especially so when reviewing the network and interconnectedness of risks and recognizing themes and the need to amalgamate risks across an organization, as explored in Chapter 38.

An important aspect regarding information is the volume and type of data available. As noted in Chapter 20, organizations deal with and have access to far larger datasets than ever before. Key challenges with data are ensuring it is accurate and relevant, and that it is effectively stored and managed, so that it can be used easily and with confidence.

Analytical skill involves the ability to understand, challenge and articulate problems and concepts and thereby make decisions based on the available information. These skills include the ability to demonstrate and apply logical thinking to the gathering and analysis of information, as well as the designing and testing of solutions to problems. The output from analytical skills is the ability to formulate appropriate alternative solutions and challenge the alternatives so as to develop the most logical plan of action.

Management, leadership and facilitation skills

Some risk managers have a small number of people directly reporting to them; others may be in charge of large departments monitoring risks in all forms. Whichever situation they may be in, there is a need to understand management skills either to manage their team or understand the needs of other managers, in order to persuade those managers to take a different course of action.

Many of the people skills described in this section are also relevant as management skills. Firstly, the skill of self-management includes the ability to set appropriate priorities, meet necessary deadlines and maintain motivation. Time management, organizational and self-motivation skills will remain important for the risk practitioner throughout their working life.

Perhaps the most important of these people skills as a manager is that of being able to motivate others. Such motivational skills are important for risk practitioners where a change in behaviour or a development of risk-aware culture is required. The risk practitioner will need to motivate individuals, managers and directors to behave differently.

Perhaps it is worth reflecting on the fact that there is a difference between management and leadership. An individual may be able to manage a department by exercising tight control over the activities of individuals. This is not the same as a leader who has established a set of priorities and empowers members of the team to manage their own activities towards fulfilment of those priorities. Ideally, a leader will have ensured that the priorities have been developed in full consultation with the individuals responsible for delivering those priorities.

Finally, there are a number of basic skills that are required in running a successful workshop, but the starting point is to establish its structure and format. In general, the key will be to ensure that the discussion is well-structured and that all attendees have an opportunity to contribute on an equal basis.

The three stages to running an effective workshop are planning, running and following up. Although equally important, they do not take equal effort. It is suggested that the running time of a workshop is multiplied three times for planning for a workshop and four times when following up after a workshop:

- Planning – this requires an understanding of the purpose, the surrounding context and the expected outputs from the workshop. It should also include consideration of the appropriate attendees, the data needed, the logistics and equipment required and the relevant tools and techniques, in relation to the purpose and context.

- Running – this requires engagement from the facilitator and with the attendees. This will require the practice of directive, collaborative and supportive facilitation skills, depending on the workshop type and individuals involved. These skills may need to be adjusted when the dynamic in a workshop shifts, that is, the facilitator needs to be flexible and agile. Workshops should be fun, involving and empowering attendees and providing value to them, resulting in clear decisions and actions, and understanding of the next steps.

- Follow-up – this requires positive action to implement the next steps and ensure the information gained and decisions made are used to progress the assessment and management of risks.

The skills of the risk manager in facilitating workshops and training sessions will be needed to embrace online and face-to-face working methods accordingly.

Training

One of the main reasons for communicating risk information and providing risk training is to ensure that a consistent response to similar risk events is achieved. This can only be ensured by sharing information and experience.

Running training courses requires a different set of skills to facilitation, although the overriding requirement to plan effectively and engage all attendees remains a top priority.

Training in risk management should be related to the competency frameworks, not just for risk practitioners, but for an organization as a whole. Again, planning is required before training is delivered, including:

- developing training needs assessments;
- understanding and communicating the purpose and learning objectives;
- developing relevant content.

Table 41.3 Risk management training

Examples of when to undertake risk training
When a manager is newly appointed or has been given new or additional responsibilities.
When an individual member of staff has been given a new role and/or procedures have been updated.
Following a recent incident or loss at an organization or at a competitor's premises or location.
On a refresher basis – and this may be a legal requirement in certain circumstances.

Risk training is a key part of learning and communication, and it is essential for manager, staff and other stakeholder engagement. It should cover a wide range of topics and achieve a greater understanding of all the risk-related issues, as well as providing information on the control measures that are in place and the vital role played by staff in the successful implementation of these controls. Risk management training is required on a continuing basis, but Table 41.3 provides some examples of when risk management training might be particularly relevant and/or necessary.

The delivery of training is equally important, in that trainers should demonstrate active listening, be able to share experience and knowledge, provide opportunities to practise theories and new skills, and encourage and provide regular feedback. As with workshops, training should be fun, engaging and value adding.

Upskilling

It is clear that effective risk practitioners require a great many technical and soft skills. There are very few individuals who inherently possess all of these skills, as some of them need to be taught and some will be gained and/or enhanced through experience.

The competency framework can be used to understand where there may be gaps in capability, knowledge or experience and where upskilling may be required. The IRM (2019)[2] paper on how to hire a great CRO provides a list of core competencies for a chief risk officer (CRO). It also provides a sample list of questions related to behavioural and technical competencies that could be used to help risk practitioners recognize their strengths and weaknesses, in addition to when they may need help in improving their skills.

At the same time, risk practitioners should know when they may need support from others within their teams or perhaps external to an organization, playing off the strengths of others. Knowing when to ask for help is another core skill of the risk practitioner.

Notes

1 IRM (n.d.) *Professional Standards in Risk Management*, https://www.theirm.org/media/5909/irm-psrm-brochure_web.pdf (archived at https://perma.cc/W845-DJJQ)
2 IRM (2019) *How to hire a great Chief Risk Officer*, https://www.theirm.org/media/8461/how-to-hire-a-great-cro.pdf (archived at https://perma.cc/3UK9-GDGK)

How risk practitioners add value

Similar to Chapter 40, across the chapters in this book, the value of the risk practitioner and risk team has been explored in supporting the effective implementation of risk management and the management of risks.

The role of the risk manager was explored in Chapter 7, in establishing and maintaining risk documentation, facilitating a risk-aware culture, co-ordinating risk management activities and providing assurance to senior management and the board. As seen in Chapter 41, the responsibilities and skills of risk practitioners go far wider that those tasks, as does the value that a risk practitioner can bring to an organization.

Making an impact

Risk practitioners can make a positive impact on an organization, through tailoring and championing the risk management principles, framework and process. Risk practitioners are key to the successful buy-in to risk management. However, rather than being an enabler, some practitioners prefer to be the sole 'owner' of ERM, believing they are the only ones who can implement the process, use the software, and present on risk management activities.

Real impact is provided in the ability to see and enable others to understand the full profile of risk across an organization, and where there may be gaps in risks or controls, as part of risk management and risk assurance. This is supported through the communication, relationship, analytical and management skills of the risk practitioner.

Other risk practitioners believe that the more complex the process and systems in place, the more useful it will be, but this often alienates those involved and leads to compliance and box-ticking. As noted in Chapter 40, the critical success factors include being able to customize risk management for an organization and within an organization, so that it is simple and scalable, agile and effective.

Making a difference

The IRM paper on how to hire a great CRO[1] notes that a risk practitioner should be able to help bring about change in an organization, supporting and enabling, and influencing and leading where appropriate.

An article by McKinsey (2020)[2] notes that 'CROs are engaged in the most difficult decisions, providing management with perspectives and guidance on strategic business risks'. The article goes on to note that CROs contribute to sustainable business growth, by helping to maximize an organization's existing capabilities. In addition, their role in horizon scanning and resilience provides insight and foresight, influencing strategy decision making and strategic direction.

Risk practitioners can also make a difference to risk culture, behaviours and attitudes, using their skills as influencers, leaders, negotiators, observers, listeners and communicators. In addition, through mentoring and coaching, risk practitioners can help develop knowledge, learning and experience across an organization, whether that is other risk practitioners or other relevant members of an organization.

Coaching aims to support the development of an individual, in improving their specific skills and goals, and therefore, performance. Mentoring describes a relationship between two individuals, where the one with greater experience shares their knowledge with their more inexperienced colleague. Mentoring can take place within an organization where individuals work with each other from different levels, or within a profession where senior risk managers may help juniors in other organizations.

The willingness to share and support the development of others not only improves capability within an organization, but also makes an organizational and personal difference.

The trusted partner

In making an impact and making a difference, risk practitioners will use their skills to become a trusted adviser or trusted partner within an organization. The IRM CRO paper states that:

> The risk team, under the direction of the CRO, must create strong relationships and collaborate proactively and ethically with functions ranging from compliance, operations, customer service, finance, and human resources through to sales and technology.

As a trusted partner, individuals and teams will be more willing to engage with risk management and share information on risks, which will enable the risk practitioner to understand a far clearer and more transparent story on risk within an organization.

As with making an impact and a difference, gaining the trust of those inside and outside an organization will require the risk practitioner to continually develop their technical and behavioural skills for this dynamic role.

On the flip side, organizations should trust and value the risk practitioner's information and opinions. Support to raise those elephants in the room and hold those to account for managing or accepting risks is fundamental. Where this support is not provided, the value of the risk practitioner is eroded and, at times, can be valueless if the board refuses to listen.

The risk practitioner is a key role in any organization in supporting the creation, protection and maintenance of value, but it is a role that requires work to make an impact and make a difference.

Notes

1 IRM (2019) How to hire a great CRO, https://www.theirm.org/media/8461/how-to-hire-a-great-cro.pdf (archived at https://perma.cc/Q8JM-XPCT)

2 McKinsey & Company (2020) *A unique time for chief risk officers in insurance*, https://www.mckinsey.com/capabilities/risk-and-resilience/our-insights/a-unique-time-for-chief-risk-officers-in-insurance (archived at https://perma.cc/5LT9-3BVN)

APPENDIX A
Abbreviations and acronyms

The table below lists the 82 abbreviations and/or acronyms that are used in the book. This appendix should also be cross-referenced with the definitions set out in Appendix B. However, not all of the abbreviations and acronyms have corresponding entries in Appendix B, because some of the entries in this appendix relate to concepts and ideas, rather than a topic that can be summarized by way of a short definition.

The reference provided in the right-hand column is to a specific figure or table, where one is provided. If there is no specific figure or table, a general reference to the chapter that discusses the abbreviation or acronym is provided.

Abbreviation	Term in full	Reference
4Ns	naïve, novice, normalized and natural	Table 39.2
5Cs	clear, concise, coherent, credible and complete	Chapter 41
ABC	attitude, behaviour and culture	Chapter 24
ALARP	as low as reasonably practicable	Chapter 37
AML	anti-money laundering	Chapter 36
APM	Association for Project Management	Chapter 27
BCM	business continuity management	Chapter 32
BCP	business continuity plan/planning	Chapter 32
BIA	business impact analysis	Chapter 32
BPR	business process re-engineering	Chapter 11
CDP	not-for-profit charity helping organizations with disclosures on environment impacts	Table 34.2
CDSB	Climate Disclosure Standards Board	Table 34.2
CEO	chief executive officer	Chapter 7
CFC	chlorofluorocarbons	Chapter 33
COP	Conference of Parties	Table 34.2
CORR	customer, offering, resources and resilience	Chapter 30
COSO	Committee of Sponsoring Organizations of the Treadway Commission	Figures 3.2 and 3.3

(continued)

(Continued)

Abbreviation	Term in full	Reference
CRAM	communication, relationship, analytical and relationship	Table 41.2
CRO	chief risk officer	Chapter 7
CSR	corporate social responsibility	Table 33.1
CSRD	Corporate Sustainability Reporting Directive	Chapter 33
ERM	enterprise risk management	Chapter 4
ESG	environmental, social and governance	Table 33.1
ESRS	European Sustainability Reporting Standards	Chapter 33
FCA	Financial Conduct Authority	Chapter 36
FRC	Financial Reporting Council	Chapter 27
FIRM	finance, infrastructure, reputation and marketplace	Table 14.2
FOIL	fragmented, organized, influential and leading	Table 39.2
FMEA	failure modes effects analysis	Chapter 13
GHG	greenhouse gas	Chapter 33
GRC	governance, risk and compliance	Chapter 27
GRI	global reporting initiative	Chapter 33
HAZOP	hazard and operability	Chapter 13
HILP	high impact, low probability	Chapter 13
IAIS	International Association of Insurance Supervisors	Chapter 36
IFRS	International Financial Reporting Standards	Table 34.2
IIRC	International Integrated Reporting Council (now retired)	Table 34.2
iNED	independent non-executive director	Chapter 27
ISSB	International Sustainability Standards Board	Table 34.2
IIA	Institute of Internal Auditors	Chapter 32
IRM	Institute of Risk Management	Table 1.1
ISO	International Organization for Standardization	Chapter 2
KCI	key control indicator	Chapter 21
KPI	key performance indicator	Chapter 10
KRI	key risk indicator	Chapter 20
KYC	know your customer	Chapter 36

(*continued*)

(Continued)

Abbreviation	Term in full	Reference
LILAC	leadership, involvement, learning, accountability and communication	Table 24.1
MADE2	mandatory, assurance, decision making, effective and efficient core processes	Table 5.2
NED	non-executive director	Chapter 27
NFRD	non-financial reporting directive	Chapter 33
NGFS	Network for Greening the Financial System	Table 34.2
NIST	National Institute of Standards and Technology	Chapter 37
OECD	Organization for Economic Co-operation and Development	Chapter 27
ORM	operational risk management	Chapter 36
PACED	proportionate, aligned, comprehensive, embedded and dynamic	Table 5.1
PCDD	preventive, corrective, directive and detective	Table 19.3
PESTLE	political, economic, sociological, technological, legal and environmental	Table 14.3
PESTLIED	political, economic, sociological, technological, legal, international, environmental demographics	Chapter 14
PIML	plan, implement, measure and learn	Chapter 9
PMI	Project Management Institute	Chapter 37
PMO	project management office	Chapter 37
PRAM	project risk analysis and management	Table 31.4
PRINCE2	**PR**ojects **IN C**ontrolled **E**nvironments	Chapter 37
RAMP	risk analysis and management for projects	Chapter 2
RASP	risk architecture, strategy and protocols	Chapter 6
RCSA	risk and control self-assessment	Chapter 29
RMC	risk management committee	Table 7.3
RMIS	risk management information system	Table 39.3
SASB	Sustainability Accounting Standards Board	Table 34.2
SDG	sustainability development goals	Chapter 33
SMART	specific, measurable, achievable, relevant and time limited	Chapter 12
SOX	Sarbanes–Oxley Act of 2002	Chapter 27

(continued)

(Continued)

Abbreviation	Term in full	Reference
STEEPLE	sociological, technological, economic, environmental, political, legal and ethical	Chapter 14
STOC	strategy, tactics, operations and compliance	Chapter 1
SWOT	strengths, weaknesses, opportunities and threats	Chapter 13
TCFD	Task Force on Climate-Related Financial Disclosures	Table 34.2
TIFD	Task Force on Inequality Related Disclosures	Table 34.2
TNFD	Task Force on Nature-related Financial Disclosures	Table 34.2
TPT	Transition Plan Taskforce	Table 34.2
UNFCCC	United Nations Convention on Climate Change	Table 34.2
VRF	Value Reporting Foundation	Table 34.2

APPENDIX B
Glossary of terms

The table below sets definitions and (as necessary) cross-references for a total of 100 risk management terms used in this book. Appendix A provides a list of the abbreviations and acronyms that are used in the book.

The reference column provides information on the location within the book where further information is provided, including reference to a relevant figure or table when appropriate.

There is an international standard related to risk management vocabulary and definitions. This is ISO 31073:2022 Risk Management – Vocabulary. Where appropriate and to the extent that is possible, the definitions used in ISO 31073 are referenced in this book.

However, it is not possible to use a unified terminology because risk managers in different disciplines and business sectors use their own words and definitions. Indeed, the various risk management standards produced around the world use different terminology and definitions. ISO 31073 attempts to provide a unified language of risk, but it may take some time for these definitions to be universally adopted.

Term	Definition	Reference
accept	To accept the risk at its current level as further action is not necessary or desirable. Previously termed tolerate for threats only	Table 19.1
assess risk	Second step in the simple risk management process to identify, analyse and evaluate risks	Chapters 13, 15 and 17
assurance	An objective examination of evidence for the purpose of providing an independent assessment	Chapter 29
black swan	Random events with a large impact that are impossible to predict, but which people try to rationalize or find simple explanations for after the event occurs	Chapter 13
business continuity plan (BCP)	Plan to ensure continuity of business operations in the event of a serious incident that impacts an organization	Chapter 19

(continued)

(Continued)

Term	Definition	Reference
business impact analysis (BIA)	Analysis to assess the potential damage, loss or disruption that would be caused by the failure of critical business processes	Chapter 19
business model	Customer offering that utilizes resources, underpinned by resilience (CORR)	Chapter 20
cause	Anything that has the intrinsic potential to lead to a risk occurring, either directly or indirectly, and alone or in conjunction with one another	Chapter 13
change the size	To manage the causes and reduce or increase the chance of a risk occurring, or to manage the effects and reduce or increase the impact of the risk should it occur. Previously termed treat for threats only	Table 19.1
chief risk officer (CRO)	Job title for senior risk manager appointed to board or executive of an organization	Chapter 24
climate change	Long-term shifts in temperatures and weather patterns that may be natural or caused by human activities	Chapter 34
control	measure that maintains or modifies risk	Chapter 18
controllability / manageability	The degree to which an organization is able to control a risk's outcome	Chapter 16
control environment	Attitude, awareness and culture of an organization regarding risk management and/or internal control, referred to in COSO ERM as the 'internal environment'	Chapter 28
core process	Set of co-ordinated business activities to deliver a stakeholder expectation that may be strategic, tactical, operational or compliance (STOC)	Figure 11.2
corporate governance	Set of activities and policies that control the way in which an organization is directed, administered and/ or controlled	Chapter 27
corporate social responsibility (CSR)	Self-regulating business model built on the belief that businesses should act in a way that benefits the well-being of society and the environment	Table 33.1
current risk rating	The level of risk after the application of existing controls, taking into account the current effectiveness of those existing controls, sometimes referred to as 'net level' or 'residual level' of the risk	Table 15.2

(continued)

(Continued)

Term	Definition	Reference
define context and objectives	First step in the simple risk management process to understand the internal and external context within which an organization operates and what it is trying to achieve	Chapters 10 and 12
disruptor	Occurrence or change that interrupts planned activities, operations or functions, whether anticipated or unanticipated	Chapter 31
double materiality	Sustainability consideration, where the importance of an issue or risk to a business versus its importance to external stakeholders, or perspective of the financial impact versus impacts on the broader community of economy, environment and society	Chapter 33
effect	Anything that would reasonably impact an organization, positively or negatively, as the result of a risk occurring. See also 'impact'	Chapter 13
eliminate uncertainty	Controls put in place to prevent a threat from occurring (zero per cent chance) or ensure an opportunity occurs (100 per cent chance). Previously termed terminate for threats only.	Table 19.1
emerging risk	A risk that is new, or a familiar risk in a new or unfamiliar context or under new context conditions (re-emerging). Emerging risks are perceived to be potentially significant but which may not be fully understood and assessed, thus not allowing risk management options to be developed with confidence	Chapter 13
environmental, social and governance (ESG)	Environmental, social and governance and refers to a set of standards used to measure an organization's environmental and social impact	Table 33.1
enterprise risk management (ERM)	Integrated and co-ordinated approach to all the risks faced by an organization	Table 1.3
extended enterprise	Tool that produces a simple value chain of an area under consideration, exploring the inputs, core activities, outputs and external influences	Chapter 10
frequency	Term used to describe the potential for a risk to occur to more than once. See also 'likelihood' and 'probability'	Chapter 15

(continued)

(Continued)

Term	Definition	Reference
greenwashing	Making misleading claims about the environmental [and/or social] impacts or benefits of products and services to create a false sense of sustainability	Table 33.1
governance	Human-based system by which an organization is directed, overseen and held accountable for achieving its defined purpose	Chapter 27
governance, risk and compliance (GRC)	Integrated approach to risk management and risk assurance based on the three lines model	Chapter 29
horizon scanning	Tool to understand future risks across different time horizons	Chapter 10
impact	The outcome of an event affecting objectives. See also 'effect'	Chapter 15
inherent risk rating	The level of risk before controls are applied, or if all controls failed, sometimes referred to as the 'total level', 'gross level' or 'raw level' of the risk	Table 15.2
insurance	Well-established mechanism for transferring the financial impact of losses arising from threats	Chapter 18
internal audit	Internal or outsourced, yet independent group of people, or set of activities, monitoring the effectiveness and efficiency of control activities	Chapter 29
internal control	See Table 21.2 for a range of definitions	Table 21.2
involve others	To transfer (threat) or share (opportunity) the management of risk with a third party, or to transfer the liability of a threat should it occur, usually through financial mechanisms, such as insurance. Previously termed transfer for threats only	Table 19.1
key control indicator	Metrics that provide information on the extent to which a given control is meeting its intended objectives	Chapter 21
key risk indicator	Metrics used by organizations to provide an early signal of increasing risk exposures	Chapter 20
level of risk	Magnitude of a risk or amalgamation of risks, expressed in terms of the combination of their effects [impacts] and their likelihood	Chapter 15
liability risks	Those risks related to the legal impacts of adapting to climate change	Table 34.1

(continued)

(Continued)

Term	Definition	Reference
likelihood	Term used to describe the chance of something happening. See also 'probability' and 'frequency'	Chapter 15
loss control	Range of activities to reduce the potential impact of hazard risks on an organization, including loss prevention, damage limitation and cost containment	Chapter 19
magnitude	See 'level of risk'	Chapter 15
manage	Process to modify risk, by selecting and implementing options for controlling risk	Chapter 18
manage risk	Third step in the simple risk management process to select and implement controls and actions to take charge of and change or maintain and modify risks to an acceptable level, whether minimizing threats or capitalizing on opportunities.	Chapters 18 and 19
material controls	A control that, if found deficient, could impact the interests of an organization and its stakeholders	Chapter 29
materiality	Information is material if omitting, misstating or obscuring it could reasonably be expected to influence the decisions that the primary users of general-purpose financial statements make on the basis of those financial statements	Chapter 22
monitor, review and report	Fourth step in the simple risk management process to monitor for changes in risks, controls and context, to review the effectiveness of new and existing controls and to communicate critical risk information and support decision making	Chapters 21, 22 and 23
monitor	Continual checking, supervising, critically observing or determining the status in order to identify change from the performance level required or expected	Chapter 20
operational risk	Defined in Basel II as 'risk of loss or gain, resulting from inadequate or failed internal processes, people and systems or from external events' and capable of impacting the operations of an organization	Chapter 36
operational risk management (ORM)	Approach to risk management associated, in particular, with banks, insurance companies and other financial institutions, where the measurement of the level of 'operational risk' is required by Basel II, Solvency II or similar requirement	Chapter 36

(continued)

(Continued)

Term	Definition	Reference
opportunity	The 'effect of uncertainty on objectives'. Note that an effect is a deviation from the expected. It can be **positive**, negative or both, and can address, create or result in **opportunities** and threats – see Table 1.1 for a range of definitions	Chapter 1
physical risks	Those risks related to the physical impacts of climate change	Table 34.1
principles of risk management	Set of attributes defining the features of successful (enterprise) risk management, summarized as proportionate, aligned, comprehensive, embedded and dynamic (PACED)	Table 5.1
principal risk	Should include, but are not necessarily limited to, those [risks] that could result in events or circumstances that might threaten the company's business model, future performance, solvency or liquidity and reputation. In deciding which risks are principal risks companies should consider the potential impact and probability of the related events or circumstances, and the timescale over which they may occur.	Chapter 22
probability	Term used to describe the potential for a risk to occur to once, usually expressed mathematically or statistically. See also 'likelihood' and 'frequency'	Chapter 15
proximity	The nearness in time at which a risk is expected or predicted to occur	Chapter 16
report	Form of communication intended to inform particular internal or external interested parties by providing information regarding the current state of risk and its management	Chapter 22
resilience	The ability of an organization to absorb and adapt in a changing environment to enable it to deliver its objectives and to survive and prosper	Chapter 31
review	Activity undertaken to determine the suitability, adequacy and effectiveness of the subject matter to achieve established objectives	Chapter 21
risk	The 'effect of uncertainty on objectives' – see Table 1.1 for a range of definitions	Table 1.1

(continued)

(Continued)

Term	Definition	Reference
risk analysis	To comprehend the nature of risk and its characteristics, including, where appropriate, the level of risk	Chapter 15
risk and control self-assessment (RCSA)	Self-audit exercise completed by a manager or director to report on current status of controls and control activities	Chapter 29
risk appetite	Amount of risk that an organization is willing to seek or accept in pursuit of its long-term objectives	Table 25.1
risk appetite statement	Guidance from leadership to internal and external stakeholders providing direction regarding the amount of risk an organization is willing to take or accept in pursuit of its objectives	Chapter 26
risk attitude	The chosen position adopted by an individual or group towards risk, influenced by risk perception and predisposition	Chapter 1
risk bias	Mental shortcuts individuals use to make decisions on situations, usually when there is little information about a situation, or when a situation is first encountered	Chapter 23
risk capacity	Measure of how much risk an organization should take or can afford to take	Chapter 25
risk clockspeed	The rate at which information necessary to understand and manage a risk becomes available	Chapter 16
risk criteria	Basis for ranking or analysing of the significance of a risk – will define the risk impact scales and risk appetite of an organization	Chapter 10
risk culture	Values, beliefs, knowledge and understanding about risk shared by a group of people with a common purpose	Chapter 23
risk dashboard	Risk information provided on one page to inform decision making and accountability	Figure 22.1
risk identification	Identifying, recognizing and acknowledging risks in relation to the context and objectives set (both opportunities and threats)	Chapter 13
risk management	Management activities to deliver the most favourable outcome and reduce the volatility or variability of that outcome – see Table 3.1 for range of definitions	Table 1.3

(continued)

(Continued)

Term	Definition	Reference
risk management framework	Set of activities that support the risk management process, referred to as the risk architecture, strategy and protocols (RASP)	Chapter 6
risk management manual	Documentation that includes all risk management policies, procedures, protocols and guidelines	Chapter 7
risk management policy	Statement of overall intentions and direction of an organization related to risk management	Chapter 6
risk management process	Activities that deliver management and control of risks	Figure 8.1
risk matrix	Presentation of risk information on a grid or graph, also referred to as a risk map or heat map and often used to illustrate information from the risk register	Figure 15.1
risk maturity model	Structure for determining the level to which risk management is embedded within an organization (4Ns)	Table 39.2
risk perception	Subjective judgements that individuals make about the characteristics and size of risks and their response to risks	Chapter 23
risk predisposition	Level to which people are sensitive to risk in relation to their resilience, cautiousness, pessimism or optimism and ranges from risk averse to risk seeking	Chapter 23
risk register	Repository of risk information	Chapter 7
risk status	Lifecycle stages or status values of risks, such as draft, active, ongoing, closed (managed) and closed (occurred)	Table 20.1
risk tolerance	Boundaries of risk taking outside of which an organization is not prepared to venture in the pursuit of its long-term objectives. It relates to those risks which, 'if push came to shove', organizations might put up with for a certain amount of time but will be working actively to bring them to an acceptable level or within risk appetite	Chapter 25
risk universe	The full range of risks which could impact, either positively or negatively, on the ability of an organization to achieve its long-term objectives	Chapter 25

(continued)

(Continued)

Term	Definition	Reference
Sarbanes–Oxley Act of 2002	US legislation that encourages use of the COSO internal control cube (2013) to ensure that the information disclosed by companies listed by the SEC is accurate	Chapter 27
scenario analysis / planning	Range of techniques used to consider how the future might turn out, by building imaginary but credible future situations	Chapter 31
stakeholder	Person or organization that can affect, be affected by, or perceives itself to be affected by a decision or activity	Chapter 11
strategy	The intelligent allocation of resources through a unique system of activities to achieve a goal	Table 30.1
sustainability	Sustainability integrates natural systems with human patterns and celebrates continuity, uniqueness and placemaking	Table 33.1
sustainable development	Development that meets the needs of the present without compromising the ability of future generations to meet their own needs	Table 33.1
target risk rating	The desired level of risk after the application of planned controls that bring the risk to an acceptable level	Table 15.2
threat	Defined in ISO 31073 as 'effect of uncertainty on objectives'. Note that an effect is a deviation from the expected. It can be positive, **negative** or both, and can address, create or result in opportunities and **threats** – see Table 1.1 for a range of definitions	Chapter 1
transition risks	Those risks related to the changing social and economic environment	Table 34.1
triple bottom line	People, plant and prosperity – the idea that companies should focus on social and environmental concerns as much as they do on profit	Table 33.1
velocity	How quickly the risk would have an impact on objectives should it occur	Chapter 16

INDEX

Numbers within main headings are filed as spelt out, excepting Basel Accords, ISO standards and SOX sections, which are filed chronologically. Acronyms are filed as presented. Page numbers in *italic* denote information contained within a figure or table.

Looking for another book?

Explore our award-winning
books from global business
experts in Risk and
Compliance

Scan the code to browse

www.koganpage.com/risk-compliance

More books from Kogan Page

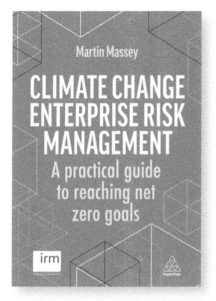
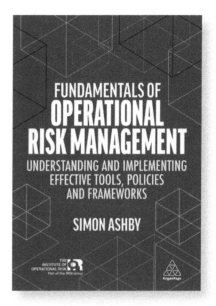